FREEDOM OF INFORMATION
IN SCOTLAND IN PRACTICE

FREEDOM OF INFORMATION IN SCOTLAND IN PRACTICE

Kevin Dunion
OBE, MA, MSc, FRSA

*Scottish Information Commissioner and
Co-Director of the Centre for Freedom of Information,
The School of Law, University of Dundee*

DUNDEE UNIVERSITY PRESS
2011

Published in Great Britain in 2011 by
Dundee University Press
University of Dundee
Dundee DD1 4HN

www.dundee.ac.uk/dup

ISBN 978-1-84586-122-3

No natural forests were destroyed to make this product;
only farmed timber was used and replanted

British Library Cataloguing-in-Publication data
A catalogue for this book is available on request from the British Library.

Typeset by Waverley Typesetters, Warham
Printed by Bell & Bain Ltd, Glasgow

CONTENTS

FOREWORD

One of the documents which regularly comes into my Advocate General's box is the legal update prepared by the Solicitors' Legal Information Centre. What particularly strikes me about the brief digest of cases and news is the number of reported decisions of the Scottish Information Commissioner. Covering a range of issues, involving a variety of local and public authorities, the Commissioner has a prodigious output, suggesting that Scottish Freedom of Information legislation is alive and kicking.

It is therefore welcome, as he approaches the end of his term of office, that Kevin Dunion should have compiled this impressive guide to the Freedom of Information (Scotland) Act 2002 (FOISA). He brings together many of the judicial cases and his own decisions, as well as giving us an important insight into his thinking, when interpreting sections of the Act. There is also an illuminating guide to the work of his office and how individual cases are handled.

Of particular interest and value are the reflections on a number of key issues which have arisen, including a pointed reminder to Ministers (past, present and future) of the crucial difference between class-based and content based exemptions.

One recurring feature of recent Commissioner's decisions has been the finding that the application should have been dealt with under the parallel but different Environmental Information Regulations (EIRs) rather than FOISA. The book contains a very useful analysis of the wide-ranging circumstances where an EIR approach is the correct one, and the material differences in the two systems. For practitioners, this provides timely and helpful advice.

Kevin Dunion quotes a passage from the lecture which I gave at the opening of the Centre for Freedom of Information at the University of Dundee in January 2009, when I observed from reading Commissioner's decisions and court judgments "just how technical and legalistic much of this has become".

But, at the same event, we heard a father of a pupil at a rural school, threatened with closure, describe how FOISA had enabled him and other parents successfully to challenge spurious claims made by the local authority. It was an encouraging example of how FOISA was intended to work for the citizen. The Commissioner cites other examples in the book; and while he explains the need for his decisions to be couched in somewhat formal language, the book itself presents technical issues in a highly readable manner.

However, crucially, Mr Dunion recognises that legislation only takes us so far. When piloting the Bill through the Scottish Parliament, I never had any doubt that the law, however radical, would be only half the story. For a truly open society, the default setting for official minds and processes had to switch from a culture of secrecy to one of transparency.

Kevin Dunion's period in office has done much to promote that much-needed cultural change. Not only have his decisions sought to reflect the spirit of the legislation, but he has been proactive in commending good practice by public authorities, while being constructively critical of poor practice. He has encouraged the development of publication schemes which can ensure greater public access to information, without resort to the procedures of FOISA. The Model Publication Scheme 2011, which all public authorities are being recommended to adopt, is set out in this book.

But there is still some way to go in the quest for culture change. The "Afterword" recognises the many strengths of the 2002 Act, but jolts us out of any creeping Caledonian complacency. I share his disappointment that the Scottish Government has rowed back from designating new bodies to be subject to FOISA under s 5 of the Act. That the extension was not favoured by the majority of the bodies proposed for coverage is possibly as predictable as it is concerning. Clearly, for many bodies, the openness which FOISA seeks to promote is still viewed in a negative light.

Nevertheless, the Commissioner still concludes that information is now being disclosed to ordinary citizens, which might otherwise have been routinely kept from them.

That is a positive reflection on the legislation and in no small way on Kevin Dunion's tenure of office as Scotland's first Information Commissioner. His book should not only be on the shelves of all who have an interest or practice in the field of Freedom of Information – it should be well thumbed too.

LORD WALLACE OF TANKERNESS
September 2011

PREFACE

On being appointed as the first Scottish Information Commissioner, and faced with the challenge of implementing and interpreting our freedom of information laws, I looked internationally, to the experience of other Commissioners. I could find some who published the text of their decisions on appeals; others with solid data in their annual reports about how their office functioned; and some who had copies of their articles and speeches on their websites, giving their views on aspects of FOI performance in their country. However none, then or since, brought their knowledge together in a single publication. As I come to the end of my term as Commissioner, many practitioners have suggested it would be useful if I were to do so.

In any case, the need for a book setting out an interpretation of Scottish law and practice is surely apparent. Several academic and legal commentators have published guides to UK law and some of these are recent enough to reflect on decisions of the UK Information Commissioners and Tribunals. However, with the exception of the estimable *Current Law Statutes*, which was published prior to the Freedom of Information Scotland Act coming into effect, there is no title which is focused upon the Scottish law, decisions and guidance.

Freedom of Information in Scotland in Practice is my attempt to distil current thinking and practice. However, it needs to be acknowledged from the outset that it could not have been done without the considerable support of all my colleagues who have over the years investigated cases on my behalf, and kept abreast of developments in law. In helping me to bring this book to fruition I want to thank in particular Margaret Keyse, Head of Enforcement, who has not only reviewed drafts but also contributed to the text; and Sarah Hutchison, Head of Policy and Information, who managed the project internally and, with Susan Gray and Paul Mutch, sourced relevant material. Euan McCulloch has reviewed the text and helpfully suggested changes and corrections. My indispensable PA, Kim Berry, managed version control as the various drafts were exchanged and commented upon, as well as juggling my diary commitments to allow me time to work on the book.

Over the years I have also been fortunate to have received external legal advice on thorny matters from Fiona Killen and Robert Carr at Anderson Strathern, LLP and Christine O'Neill and Charles Livingstone at Brodies, LLP, as well as wise counsel from David Johnston, QC, Heriot Currie, QC and Paul Cullen, QC (now Lord Pentland), as well as from Morag Ross and Jane Munro. Any deficiencies in this book are entirely down to my failing properly to act on their advice.

One of the great pleasures of being one of a relatively small international band of Commissioners is the collegiate exchange and support. I am particularly grateful to the UK Information Commissioner, Christopher Graham (and his predecessor, Richard Thomas) as well as to his Deputy Commissioner, Graham Smith, and Head of Policy Delivery, Steve Wood; to the Irish Information Commissioner, Emily O'Reilly, and her Director-General, Pat Whelan; to the Slovenian Commissioner, Natasa Pirc Musar; and to former Mexican Commissioner, Juan Pablo Guerrero, for their advice and assistance.

More broadly, my thinking on FOI has been enriched and challenged by the research and experience of many people I have had the privilege to get to know, especially Professor Alasdair Roberts, Suffolk University Law School; Professor Janet McLean, University of Auckland; Professor Cheng Jie, Tsingshua University, Beijing; Professor Richard Calland, University of Capetown; Professor Maeve McDonagh and Dr Áine Ryall, University College Cork; Professor Alan Page, University of Dundee; Professor Hector MacQueen, University of Edinburgh; Dr Will Dinan, University of Strathclyde; Dr Eleanor Burt, University of St Andrews; Professor Robert Hazel and Dr Ben Worthy of The Constitution Unit, UCL; Sarah Holsen, Research Associate, Swiss Graduate School of Public Administration; Dr Patricia Jonason, Södertörn University; Professor Dan Metcalfe, Washington College of Law; Professor Rick Snell, University of Tasmania; Laura Neuman, The Carter Center, Atlanta; Carole Excell, World Resources Institute, Washington; Mukelani Dimba, Open Democracy Advice Centre, Capetown; David Banisar, Privacy International; Rosalind MacInnes, Principal Solicitor, BBC Scotland; and David Goldberg.

Carole Dalgleish, Director, Dundee University Press, has enthusiastically supported the purpose of this book since its proposal and Karen Howatson, Managing Editor (Law), has expertly brought it to publication.

Special mention needs to be made of Maurice Frankel and Lord Wallace. Maurice has been the driving force behind the Campaign for Freedom of Information since 1984 and without his indefatigable efforts we would not have the legislation that exists today, north or south of the Border. His advocacy of measures to improve transparency remains invaluable. As Minister for Justice, Jim Wallace shaped the progressive Freedom of Information (Scotland) Bill and skilfully steered it through the Scottish Parliament. I regard it as an honour that he has provided a foreword to this book, now as the Rt Hon Lord Wallace of Tankerness and Advocate General for Scotland

Finally, can I thank my wife Linda – this is not the first time she has coped with evenings, weekends and holidays being swallowed up by the demands of getting a manuscript to the publishers. As ever, she has been wholly supportive, although I may be pushing my luck if I suggest another book in the near future.

KEVIN DUNION
St Andrews
October 2011

AUTHOR'S INTRODUCTORY NOTE

Throughout this book I have quoted from my decisions etc as Scottish Information Commissioner in the third person. There are three reasons for this. First, after initially writing my decisions in the first person, for some time now they have been couched in the third person, reflecting the fact that many are now signed by the Head of Enforcement under delegated authority. Second, should a second edition of this book be published, a distinction need not be made between decisions of the Commissioner issued while I held the post and those of my successor. Finally, given the frequency with which material is quoted from my decisions etc, expressing these as "the Commissioner said" rather than "I said" avoids a profusion of the "perpendicular pronoun" as Yes Minister's Sir Humphrey Appleby referred to it.

However, the Afterword is written in the first person, reflecting the personal nature of the opinions expressed.

Throughout this book reference is made to the "Scottish Administration", the "Scottish Executive", the "Scottish Government" and the "Scottish Ministers". By way of explanation, the Scotland Act 1998 provided for "the establishment of a Scottish Parliament and Administration". The Administration is headed by a Scottish Executive, the members of which are collectively known as the "Scottish Ministers". In 2007 the Scottish Executive was re-branded as the "Scottish Government", although this did not alter any statutory references. The obligation to comply with FOISA falls upon the Scottish Ministers.

TABLE OF DECISIONS

SCOTTISH INFORMATION COMMISSIONER

Arranged in order of decision number

Arranged in alphabetical order by public authority

TABLE OF CASES

Upper Tribunal

TABLE OF LEGISLATION

Note: **Bold** references denote paragraphs where the relevant legislation is reproduced.

United Kingdom, including measures of the Scottish Parliament

Statutory Instruments

Other jurisdictions

Australia

Part I

THE LAW IN PRACTICE

Chapter 1

THE FREEDOM OF INFORMATION (SCOTLAND) ACT 2002

The Freedom of Information (Scotland) Act 2002 is hereby reproduced **1.01**
in bold text under the terms of Crown Copyright Policy Guidance
issued by HMSO. The author's annotations appear in plain text and
text boxes.

The Bill for this Act of the Scottish Parliament was passed by the
Parliament on 24 April 2002 and received Royal Assent on 28 May 2002.

An Act of the Scottish Parliament to make provision for the disclosure
of information held by Scottish public authorities or by persons
providing services for them; and for connected purposes.

THE FREEDOM OF INFORMATION (SCOTLAND) ACT 2002

(asp 13)

CONTENTS

Part 1

ACCESS TO INFORMATION HELD BY SCOTTISH PUBLIC AUTHORITIES

Right to Information

Part 7

MISCELLANEOUS AND SUPPLEMENTAL

Part 1

ACCESS TO INFORMATION HELD BY SCOTTISH PUBLIC AUTHORITIES

Right to information

1 General entitlement

(1) **A person who requests information from a Scottish public authority which holds it is entitled to be given it by the authority.**

By this plain yet profound statement of entitlement the Freedom of Information (Scotland) Act 2002 (hereafter referred to as "FOISA") confers wide rights to information held by Scottish public authorities on anyone, anywhere in the world. The entitlement is not confined to individuals but can also be exercised by companies and by public authorities, for example. Nor is there a restriction by age. (It is often not appreciated that children have the same rights under FOISA as anyone else, although if the child is under 12 years of age the authority may enquire as to whether the child understands what they are doing when making a request. See s 69.)

1.02

This wide entitlement goes further than some other regimes, as there is no restriction by nationality, citizenship or place of residence. (The New Zealand Official Information Act 1982 limits rights by citizenship, and residence;[1] in Australia the federal law required, until recently, a specific "address in Australia at which notices … may be sent to the applicant".[2]) FOISA is fully retrospective, applying to information of any age, unlike in Ireland, for instance, where the right

1.03

---

1 Official Information Act 1982, s 12: "Any person, being – (a) a New Zealand citizen; or (b) a permanent resident of New Zealand; or (c) a person who is in New Zealand; or (d) a body corporate which is incorporated in New Zealand; or (e) a body corporate which is incorporated outside New Zealand but which has a place of business in New Zealand, – may request a department or Minister of the Crown or organisation to make available to him or it any specified official information."

2 Federal Freedom of Information Act 1982, s 15(2)(c).

applies only to information which originates after the commencement of that country's equivalent legislation.[3]

1.04   "Information" means information recorded in any form and therefore includes information contained in printed publications, e-mails, photographs, maps, plans or spreadsheets (see s 73). It could be held in an authority's structured filing system or in an individual's desk drawer. It could be held electronically, in a central server, on a hard drive or on a memory stick. However, FOISA does not give a right to receive facsimile copies of such documents; only for the recipient to be provided with the information contained within them. This was confirmed by the Court of Session which said:

> "it is implicit in the definition that a distinction is drawn between the record itself and the information which is recorded in it ... What a person can request, in terms of section 1(1), is the information which has been recorded, rather than the record itself. The right conferred by section 1, where it applies, is therefore to be given the information, rather than a particular record (or a copy of the record) that contains it. Put shortly, the Act provides a right of access to information, not documentation."

However, as the court observed, and is the case in practice, it is usually found that the most practicable way to provide the information is to provide a copy of the relevant document.[4]

1.05   The right does not extend to unrecorded information which may be known to the authority, for example information which was verbally imparted to officials but not documented, or the recollections of officials regarding information once contained in documents which have since been destroyed or deleted. By contrast, in New Zealand the law does not specify that information should be recorded. (The New Zealand courts have ruled that "the right is not confined to the written word but embraces knowledge, however gained or held, by the named bodies in their official capacities".[5])

General entitlement – s 1(2)

(2) **The person who makes such a request is in this Part and in Parts 2 and 7 referred to as the "applicant".**

1.06   The term "applicant" is used under FOISA to refer both to a person making a request for information and to a person making an application

---

3 Freedom of Information Act 1997, s 6(4).
4 *Glasgow City Council and Dundee City Council v SIC* [2009] CSIH 73, para 43.
5 *Commissioner of Police v Ombudsman* [1985] 1 NZLR 578, [1988] 1 NZLR 385, per Jeffries J.

for decision by the Commissioner. In the equivalent UK legislation, the Freedom of Information Act 2000 (hereafter "FOIA"), an "applicant" is the term used for a person making a request for information but the term "complainant" is used for the person applying to the Commissioner for a decision.

General entitlement – s 1(3)

(3) If the authority –
  (a) requires further information in order to identify and locate the requested information; and
  (b) has told the applicant so (specifying what the requirement for further information is),

then, provided that the requirement is reasonable, the authority is not obliged to give the requested information until it has the further information.

Sometimes it is not clear what the applicant is looking for, and in order to identify and locate the information the authority may require further information. In doing so the authority may think it useful to know the purpose to which the information may be put (which may narrow down the search). However, it should be recognised that an important feature of the legislation is that applicants do not have to give a reason as to why they wish information. In that respect the legislation, both in Scotland and in the rest of the UK, is often said to be "purpose blind". (For example, the UK Information Tribunal has said: "FOIA is, however, applicant and motive blind."[6])   1.07

Only rarely should the reasons as to why the information was being requested be required for the purposes of locating information. In most circumstances authorities cannot base their decisions on whether to disclose information on the lack of reasons given for the request, or what they suppose are the reasons for the request, for example by assuming that the information will be used to criticise the authority publicly.   1.08

However, this stricture against enquiring into the reasons for the requests means that authorities sometimes assume that they are forbidden from asking an applicant for any information about the application. Section 1(3) shows that is not the case. Authorities are entitled to ask for more information if it is needed – either to be   1.09

---

6 S v Information Commissioner and the General Register Office (EA/2006/0030).

clear about what is being requested or to help locate it. (In response, the applicant may choose to provide the reason for their request.)

1.10   Where information is needed (not merely where it would be helpful for an authority to know), this does not render the request invalid. Rather, the 20-working-day time limit within which the authority must respond to the applicant's request starts on receipt of the information required. If an authority informs an applicant that it requires further information in order to deal with the request, this is not to be regarded as a refusal notice under s 16 of FOISA.

1.11   However, authorities should not use this provision as a matter of course to delay or impede the provision of information. Applicants can ask the Commissioner to decide whether a public authority has acted reasonably in requiring them to provide additional information.[7]

Clarifying requests

It is not unusual for authorities to require further information from applicants to locate and identify the requested information. On occasion, however, such a requirement does not appear to be reasonable. A journalist complained to the Commissioner that his requests to a police force were being met with a policy of "requiring clarification of very obvious English words". One of his requests was "for all documentation held by your force on the subject of Scotland's High Court judges. I seek all memos, e-mails, policy papers, briefings, correspondence, notes, advice to officers, feedback reports, sentencing records, assessments of likely views, and views on policy of judges towards evidence and offences".

In response the authority said that to progress the request it required further information and in particular asked whether the journalist could "clarify what you mean by the following:- Policy papers, Briefings; Correspondence . . ." etc. The journalist described this as an authority "trying to be intentionally stupid as a delaying tactic".

General entitlement – s 1(4)

(4)   **The information to be given by the authority is that held by it at the time the request is received, except that, subject to subsection (5), any amendment or deletion which would**

---

7   Decision 103/2010: Jane Saren and the City of Edinburgh Council.

have been made, regardless of the receipt of the request, between that time and the time it gives the information may be made before the information is given.

What matters is whether the information is held, not whether it was created by or owned by the authority (except in certain specific circumstances when the authority holds it on behalf of another – see s 3(2) below). If an applicant applies to the Commissioner for a decision, the Commissioner will have regard only to that information which is held by the authority at the time of the request – and not relevant information which may have been acquired or created by the authority between the date of that request and the application, even though that may be the information which the applicant is seeking. In such circumstances the applicant would have to make a new request for information.

1.12

For example, a request to Central Scotland Fire Board about the authorisation for the negotiation of pay and conditions for fire and rescue services in Scotland following devolution formed the basis of an application to the Commissioner. During the course of the Commissioner's investigation the authority volunteered information to the applicant that it had since acquired on the matter. However, as this was not held at the time of the request, it could not be taken into account in the Commissioner's decision.[8]

1.13

Crucially, given this focus on information held at the time of a request, an authority must not frustrate the request by permitting that information to be amended or deleted once that request has been made. Section 1(4) does, however, provide for an authority making changes to the information which would otherwise have been made. In practice this has rarely been an issue, but circumstances in which it could occur can be imagined, for example changes to monitoring data which is automatically generated and updated or to CCTV footage which has been overwritten. (See *Decision 150/2011: Mr Z and the Scottish Prison Service*.)

1.14

Sometimes authorities, in good faith, wish to make amendments to the information requested prior to release in order to correct obvious errors or to provide more up-to-date information. This does not, however, justify making changes or deletions to the information held at the time of the request. Instead, there is nothing to prevent an authority providing *additional* information or explanation which it regards as more useful.

1.15

---

8   Decision 046/2006: Mr James Bell and Central Scotland Fire Board.

1.16   Plainly, however, authorities are not obliged to acquire or create new information in order to satisfy the request. Yet even that clear understanding is not without its complications, as authorities sometimes fail to appreciate that they may have to compile or re-order *existing* information so as to satisfy a request. This is not regarded, for the purpose of FOISA, as creating new information. So, for example, an authority may hold certain statistical health data which it has not felt the need to compile or has used for only limited analysis. If an applicant asks for the information in total, or tabulated in a manner differently from that drawn up by the authority, then the authority cannot claim that it does not hold that information, even though it is not held in the form in which the applicant wants to receive it.

Producing statistics – creating or compiling information?

When a journalist asked the Common Services Agency for the Scottish Health Service ("CSA") to provide him with a complete list of clinical outcomes (mortality rates) for all surgeons,the CSA refused. It maintained that although it could produce such a list, it was not obliged to provide it. It argued that the information requested should not be regarded as being held by the CSA because, as it did not routinely analyse the available data to provide such information, it could not be required to generate such information in response to a request under FOISA.

The Commissioner disagreed, saying: "It seems to me that if an authority gathers data and chooses to use it for its preferred purpose, such as to produce tables of statistics for a particular location or time series, and is then asked to compile the existing data to produce information for a different geographical base or time series, then this is information retrieval, compiled in a stated form, rather than being new information. Under FOISA, an applicant cannot require an authority to go out and acquire new information, but in this case what is being asked is for the existing data to be presented in a particular digest (as provided for by s 11(2)(b) of FOISA), which it is demonstrably practicable for the CSA to do."[9]

This does not, however, mean that an authority has to carry out research and analysis of any data sets which it holds. A Scottish local

---

9   Decision 066/2005: Mr Peter MacMahon of *The Scotsman* and the Common Services Agency for the Scottish Health Service, para 32.

council was asked for the number of its employees in arrears with council tax.[10] The council held information about residents in council tax arrears and it held a database of information about its employees. However, providing the information requested would necessitate going far beyond simply compiling information from two sources. The council would have to validate matched information to ensure that an employee with the same name and address as a person in arrears was in fact the council tax payer (and not, for example, the son or daughter of the person actually liable).

Furthermore, this process of matching personal data from two unrelated databases is likely to be neither fair nor lawful (in terms of the Data Protection Act 1998). The Commissioner concluded that the complexities of cross-referencing the databases, of validating the information and consulting the staff to allow data matching involved the council in creating new information in response to the request, and that therefore it did not "hold" the information.

Disclosing information under FOISA will not in itself breach copyright. **1.17** Section 50 of the Copyright, Designs and Patents Act 1988 states: "Where the doing of a particular act is specifically authorised by an Act of Parliament ... the doing of that act does not infringe copyright." An amendment to s 80 of the Freedom of Information Act 2000 by the Freedom of Information (Scotland) Act 2002 (Consequential Modifications) Order 2004 makes it clear that disclosing information in response to an information request is an "act" which, in terms of s 50 of the 1988 Act, will not infringe copyright. Copyright restrictions will apply to the subsequent use of the information by the applicant, although in many cases the "fair dealing" provisions in the 1988 Act will cover any subsequent use.

General entitlement – s 1(5)

(5) The requested information is not, by virtue of subsection (4), to be destroyed before it can be given (unless the circumstances are such that it is not reasonably practicable to prevent such destruction from occurring).

---

10 Decision 036/2005: Mr George Munro and Inverclyde Council – number of council employees in arrears with council tax.

1.18   The authority should be vigilant not to destroy information, following receipt of a request, which is the subject of that request. Very occasionally, the Commissioner has discovered that this has happened in error, and has called upon the authority to review its procedures.[11] If destruction or amendment is done deliberately with the intent to prevent disclosure then that is a criminal offence (see s 65).

1.19   Circumstances in which it has not been reasonably practicable to avoid destruction have not so far emerged. However, s 1(5) could cover situations where, for example, information which is the subject of a request may be found within documents already held in waste sacks in the course of collection for off-site disposal. In such circumstances, the information is technically "held" but it is not reasonably practicable to prevent its destruction.

1.20   Sometimes information is "held" even where the authority believes that it has been deleted or destroyed. When the Scottish Qualifications Authority moved premises, all documents were reviewed and either retained, scanned to an electronic file or destroyed.[12] So, when a search for certain meeting notes returned no records it was assumed that the information had been routinely destroyed and was no longer held. The authority was unaware that an individual employee had retained notes from nine meetings, which only came to light during the Commissioner's investigation.

1.21   Searches for information may initially identify no material relevant to requests, only for the authority subsequently to find information readily recoverable from a computer desktop "deleted items" folder which had not been emptied.

1.22   In such circumstances the fact remains that the information was "held" at the time of the request and the prior intention to destroy it would not justify attempts at more effective disposal, subsequent to the request being received.

General entitlement – s 1(6)

(6)   This section is subject to sections 2, 9, 12 and 14.

1.23   The right of access to information is far from unlimited. An authority may be entitled (not necessarily obliged) to refuse a request or to impose certain conditions, including costs, on answering it. The ability to do so is provided by:

- s 2: which provides that certain information is exempt;

---

11   Decision 080/2008: Mr Frank French and the Scottish Public Services Ombudsman.
12   Decision 060/2009: Mr F and the Scottish Qualifications Authority.

- s 9: which permits a fee to be charged;
- s 12: which allows information to be withheld (even if not exempt) if the estimated cost of complying with a request is excessive;
- s 14: which does not oblige an authority to comply with a request which is vexatious or repeated.

2 Effect of exemptions

(1) To information which is exempt information by virtue of any provision of Part 2, section 1 applies only to the extent that –

    (a) the provision does not confer absolute exemption; and

    (b) in all the circumstances of the case, the public interest in disclosing the information is not outweighed by that in maintaining the exemption.

(2) For the purposes of paragraph (a) of subsection (1), the following provisions of Part 2 (and no others) are to be regarded as conferring absolute exemption –

    (a) section 25;

    (b) section 26;

    (c) section 36(2);

    (d) section 37; and

    (e) in subsection (1) of section 38 –

        (i) paragraphs (a), (c) and (d); and

        (ii) paragraph (b) where the first condition referred to in that paragraph is satisfied by virtue of subsection (2)(a)(i) or (b) of that section.

The effect of s 1 of FOISA is to create a general entitlement to infor-   **1.24**
mation. However, as s 2 makes clear, this is tempered by a series of exemptions which fall into two types – *absolute* and those which are often called *qualified*.

Absolute exemptions

Absolute exemptions apply to certain classes of information where: **1.25**

    (a) the information is otherwise accessible (s 25);

    (b) there is a prohibition on disclosure (s 26);

    (c) disclosure would constitute an actionable breach of confidence (s 36(2));

(d) the information is contained in court records (s 37);

(e) it is personal information (except in very limited circumstances) (s 38).

1.26   It needs only to be determined that the information requested falls within those categories or classes for the exemption to apply. Consideration of whether it would be in the public interest to release the information under FOISA is unnecessary.

1.27   So if it is established, for example, that the information is contained in court records then that is sufficient to allow the request to be refused. Nothing more need be demonstrated, although an authority withholding information under an absolute exemption must still tell the applicant which exemption(s) it is applying and why (as required by s 16).

Qualified exemptions and the "public interest" test

1.28   The approach to be taken is quite different when considering other exemptions which are often termed "qualified" exemptions. The determining factor as to whether the request should be refused is not just whether the information requested falls into a "class" of information covered by the exemption but rather whether "in all the circumstances of the case" the public interest favours disclosure.

1.29   This is a highly significant provision, as it effectively creates a general public interest in disclosure, as the courts have acknowledged:

> "That the statute creates or at least acknowledges a public interest in the disclosure of requested information is confirmed by the terms of section 2(1) which requires, in the case of non-absolute exemptions, the weighing of 'the public interest in disclosing information' against the public interest in maintaining the exemption."[13]

1.30   Furthermore where the public interest arguments are evenly balanced, then the wording of s 2(1)(b) creates a presumption in favour of disclosure, as the information can be withheld only if the public interest in maintaining the exemption *outweighs* the public interest in disclosing it. It is important that the way in which this public interest balancing test is conducted reflects the provisions of this section.

---

13   *Scottish Ministers v Scottish Information Commissioner (William Alexander's Application)* [2006] CSIH 8 at para 11.

The temptation is to assume that if the information is covered by a qualified exemption, then the issue is whether the public interest in disclosure outweighs the maintenance of that exemption. That is not the correct test.

For example, an authority might readily establish that information   1.31
which has been requested relates to ministerial communications. If so, no matter the content of those communications, the exemption applies (see s 29(1)(b)). However, the authority would have to then take account of the circumstances of the case in determining whether the public interest in disclosing the information was outweighed by that in maintaining the exemption.

In one specific case[14] the Commissioner agreed that information   1.32
regarding the decision as to where to locate the permanent head-quarters of the National Theatre of Scotland was exempt by virtue of being ministerial communications. However, he determined that disclosure of the information on what was a disputed decision was in the public interest. Set against that, the sensitivity of the information was regarded as low. Consequently, there were insufficient public interest reasons for maintaining the exemption and the information was ordered to be disclosed.

For several of the qualified exemptions the "balance of the public   1.33
interest" test is considered only after it is established that disclosure of the information would be sufficiently harmful to warrant exemption. The test is usually whether disclosure of the information "would or would be likely to *prejudice substantially*" the interest of that particular exemption. (The exceptions to this wording are at s 30(b), where the "harm" test is one of "would, or would be likely, to *inhibit substantially* ...", and s 39(1), where the test is "*would, or would be likely to, endanger* ...".) If disclosure would not cause sufficient harm, then the exemption does not apply and the matter of the public interest does not even have to be considered.

The "harm" test is therefore a significant hurdle to be overcome   1.34
before the exemption can apply. As Chapter 4 (Key Issue 2: Where is the Harm?) makes clear, generalised assertions, hypothetical but unlikely scenarios, and indiscriminate claims to harm (with little distinction between relatively innocuous and sensitive content of information) make for unconvincing arguments in the event of an application to the Commissioner. However, where a convincing submission has been made and it has been accepted that disclosure would result in substantial prejudice, then in most cases the Commissioner has

---

14   Decision 039/2007: Mr Michael Matheson, MSP and the Scottish Executive.

determined that the public interest in disclosure is outweighed by the public interest in maintaining the exemption.

1.35   So far as environmental information is concerned, following a referral to the European Court of Justice by the Supreme Court in relation to a request made under the UK Environmental Information Regulations, the ECJ has considered how the "public interest" test should be carried out.[15] The ECJ took the view that, when a public authority applies more than one exception to the same information, a *two-stage* "public interest" test should be carried out by the authority. The first step is to consider whether, in relation to each exception cited (whereas FOISA refers to "exemptions", the EIRs refer to "exceptions"), the public interest in making the information available is outweighed by that in maintaining the exception. The second is cumulatively to weigh all the grounds for refusing to disclose the information against all of the public interests served by disclosure and to come to a conclusion as to whether the information should be disclosed. The manner and consequence of giving effect to this dual test are not yet obvious. However, the judgment of the ECJ does not affect the way in which the "public interest" test is carried out under FOISA.

The nature of public interest

1.36   As to what constitutes the "public interest", the term is not defined in FOISA. This is not unusual – a review of the "public interest" test in FOI legislation in the UK, Canada, New Zealand, Australia and Ireland found that none defined the concept of public interest and that this was intentional so that "determinations must be made with regard to the specifics of each request".[16]

1.37   In terms of general principle, the High Court of Australia has said: "the expression 'in the public interest', when used in a statute, classically imparts a discretionary value judgment to be made by reference to undefined factual matters, confined only in so far as the subject matter and the scope and the purpose of the statutory enactments may enable".[17] Generally it is often described as something that is of serious concern or benefit to the public, not merely of individual interest. It has also been stated that "public interest" does not mean "of interest to the public" but "in the interest of the public".

---

15   *Office of Communications v Information Commissioner* (C–71/10) [2011] EUECJ.
16   M Carter and A Bouris, *Freedom of Information – Balancing the Public Interest* (The Constitution Unit, UCL, May 2006), p 1.
17   *O'Sullivan v Farrer* (1989) 168 CLR 210 at 216, quoted in Carter and Bouris, n 16, p 5, para 2.9.

According to previous guidance issued by the Scottish Ministers,[18]   **1.38**
the factors which may inform a decision as whether the public
interest in maintaining an exemption outweighs the public interest in
disclosing the information include whether disclosure would:

- enhance scrutiny of decision-making processes and thereby improve accountability and participation;
- contribute to the administration of justice and enforcement of the law, including the prevention or detection of crime or the apprehension or prosecution of offenders;
- affect the economic interests of the whole or part of the United Kingdom;
- contribute to ensuring effective oversight of expenditure of public funds and that the public obtain value for money;
- keep the public adequately informed of any danger to public health or safety, or to the environment;
- impact adversely on safeguarding national security or international relations;
- contribute to ensuring that any public authority with regulatory responsibilities is adequately discharging its functions;
- ensure fairness in relation to applications or complaints, reveal malpractice or enable the correction of misleading claims;
- contribute to a debate on a matter of public interest;
- prejudice the protection of an individual's right to privacy.

The Ministers added that "in deciding whether a disclosure is in the   **1.39**
public interest, authorities should not take into account:

- possible embarrassment of government or other public authority officials;
- the seniority of persons involved in the subject-matter;
- the risk of the applicant misinterpreting the information;
- possible loss of confidence in government or other public authority".

Consideration of public interest is directly referred to elsewhere in   **1.40**
FOISA. For example, in adopting or reviewing their publication scheme,
authorities must have regard to the public interest in:

---

18 *Scottish Ministers' Code of Practice on the Discharge of Functions by Public Authorities under the Freedom of Information (Scotland) Act 2002*, paras 74–75 (6 September 2004) (superseded).

"(a) allowing public access to information held by it and in particular to information which –
   (i) relates to the provision of services by it, the cost to it of providing them or the standards attained by services so provided; or
   (ii) consists of facts, or analyses, on the basis of which decisions of importance to the public have been made by it;
(b) the publication of reasons for decisions made by it."[19]

1.41   Even more specifically, the Scottish Administration "must have regard to the public interest in the disclosure of factual information which has been used, or is intended to be used, to provide an informed background to the taking of a decision " (s 29(3)) when determining the public interest in disclosure (under s 2(1)(b)) of information relating to the formulation or development of government policy (which is exempt information by virtue of s 29(1)(a)).

3 Scottish public authorities

(1) **In this Act, "Scottish public authority" means –**
   (a) **any body which, any other person who, or the holder of any office which –**
      (i) **is listed in schedule 1; or**
      (ii) **is designated by order under section 5(1); or**
   (b) **a publicly-owned company, as defined by section 6.**

1.42   The approach to determining which bodies fall within the scope of FOISA is primarily to list them in Sch 1, by name or type, and make provision in the law for that list to be added to. (By contrast, however, there is no list of publicly owned companies subject to FOISA.) In this manner an extensive range of bodies, encompassing the Scottish Parliament, through local authorities, the police and universities, down to individual GP practices, were brought within the scope of FOISA in a reasonably clear fashion. The strength of the list-based approach is that it reduces uncertainty – for authorities as well as the public – as to which bodies must comply with the legislation. The drawback is that the original list becomes overtaken by developments, as some bodies cease to exist and others, which should be covered by FOISA, are created. That is why provision has been made to list new public authorities (s 4) or to designate others as public authorities (s 5). However, as a result, Sch 1 to the originally published Act is outdated, and reference has to be made elsewhere for an up-to-date list. Legislation sites such

---

19   FOISA, s 23(3).

as legislation.gov.uk,[20] Westlaw and the Scots Law Database provide legislation updates. The Commissioner also maintains an updated Sch 1 list on his website.[21]

More fundamentally, by not describing the nature of the functions or types of bodies within the Act's scope, the list-based approach tends not to keep pace with the changes in delivery in public services. As a result, information rights can be lost if the responsibility for providing the public service is no longer delivered by an authority specifically listed in Sch 1 but by another external or arm's-length body which the Government fails to designate.   1.43

This has occurred with the transfer of social housing from local councils to housing associations and, similarly, by transferring undertakings to charitable trusts to run local authority recreation and leisure services.   1.44

Scottish public authorities – s 3(2)

(2) For the purposes of this Act but subject to subsection (4), information is held by an authority if it is held –
   (a) by the authority otherwise than –
      (i) on behalf of another person; or
      (ii) in confidence, having been supplied by a Minister of the Crown or by a department of the Government of the United Kingdom; or
   (b) by a person other than the authority, on behalf of the authority.

Even where there is little doubt as to whether information is "held" by an authority – given that it is to be found on its premises or within its electronic information systems – there may still be doubt as to whether it is held "for the purposes of FOISA". If it can be established that it is held on behalf of another person, then it is not "held".   1.45

So, any authority which is storing information – physically or electronically – on behalf of another authority need not concern itself with what is contained in such files when dealing with a request for information in its own right, as that information is held on behalf of another person. (Authorities need to be aware that there are no equivalent provisions in the EIRs and so even where environmental information is held on behalf of another person, it is held by the authority receiving the request under the terms of the EIRs.[22])   1.46

20 For example, www.legislation.gov.uk/asp/2002/13/contents.
21 http://www.itspublicknowledge.info/YourRights/Whoiscovered.asp.
22 EIRs, reg 2(2)(a) provides simply that information is held by a Scottish public authority if it is in its possession and it has been produced or received by that authority.

1.47   The corollary of this, however, as shown by subs (2)(b), is that information need not be physically within the possession of the authority in order to be held; if an authority has arranged for its records to be stored in the premises of another public body or in a commercial storage facility, then it is still "held" by it. It is important then for the authority to know what information is stored in such a manner and to have a means of retrieving it (within the timescales set down by the Act) in response to a request under FOISA.

1.48   Information is not held by the authority if it is held in confidence, having been supplied by a Minister of the Crown or by a Department of the UK Government. There is no equivalent of this provision in the UK Act. Briefly, its provenance arises from a somewhat belated recognition that the Scotland Act 1998 did not reserve to Westminster the right to legislate on freedom of information, so that in effect the Scottish Parliament could pass laws affecting UK bodies. To avoid this, secondary legislation[23] was passed which reserved the right to legislate on public access to information to Westminster except for information held by the Scottish Parliament, any part of the Scottish Administration, the Scottish Parliamentary Corporate Body or any public authority with mixed or no reserved functions "unless supplied by a Minister of the Crown or government department and held in confidence".

1.49   Security markings such as "Secret", "Restricted" or "Confidential" may indicate that information is – or at least once was – regarded as being held in confidence. Even in the absence of such markings it may be possible to argue that the material has the necessary quality of confidence.[24] Markings, however, are not conclusive. It is not enough for the information to have been held in confidence at the time it was supplied, as the confidential quality may be lost over the passage of time. Thus, an authority must be able to demonstrate that the information remained confidential at the time of the request.

Information held on behalf of MSPs and councillors

A question has arisen as to whether information held by elected representatives – Members of the Scottish Parliament or councillors – is held for the purposes of FOISA. The parliamentary authorities provide offices and storage capacity for all MSPs and their staff,

---

23   Scotland Act 1998 (Modifications of Schedules 4 and 5) Order 1999 (SI 1999/1749).
24   See, for example, Decision 036/2009: Mr Rob Edwards and the Scottish Ministers.

who also have access to electronic information systems provided and maintained by the Parliamentary Corporate Body. Mail can simply be addressed to the relevant MSP at the Parliament's generic postal address. Similar arrangements exist for councillors with local authorities.

The Commissioner has concluded that although such information is received and retained on premises and systems of public authorities covered by FOISA, it is held on behalf of another person, ie the elected representatives.[25] This is founded on the view that MSPs and councillors have an identity distinct from the bodies to which they have been elected. In so far as they are carrying out their role as constituency representatives, requests made directly to them for information are not to be regarded as requests under FOISA and where their information is held by the Parliament or Council, it is held on their behalf.

In coming to this view, account was taken of the Information Commissioner's guidance on the implications of the Data Protection Act 1998 for councillors.[26] This guidance suggests that only when the councillor is acting as a member of the Council (ie in pursuance of its corporate functions) are they part of the Council.[27]

In effect, a distinction has been drawn between the individual representative role of the MSP or councillor and any role which they hold as part of the Parliament, Government or Council. So, for example, information received by an MSP in their individual mailbox is held on their behalf by the SPCB which provides the mail facilities. However, information addressed to an MSP in their capacity as, say, a Minister, or Presiding Officer, or to a councillor as Provost or Convener is likely to be held by the relevant authority for the purposes of FOISA.

This is a distinction which may not be without its drawbacks. When Scottish Government officials were asked about searches for information relevant to a FOISA request they indicated that an exhaustive search had been conducted of a Minister's mailbox. They could not, however, guarantee that information relevant to the request had not been communicated directly to the Minister in his capacity as an individual MSP.[28]

25   Decision 008/2005: Duncan Shields and the SPCB.
26   Information Commissioner's Office, "Data Protection Good Practice Note: Advice for the elected and prospective members of local authorities", issued 23 April 2007.
27   Decision 132/2006: John Egan and West Dunbartonshire Council.
28   Decision 016/2010: Mr Tony Cameron and the Scottish Ministers.

Scottish public authorities – s 3(3)

(3) Subsection (1)(a)(i) is subject to any qualification set out in schedule 1.

1.50 Ministers may wish to apply the provisions of FOISA only to certain functions carried out by a public body. They can do so by qualifying the designation. For example, general practitioners are listed in Sch 1 – but only to the extent of services provided under Pt II of the National Health Service (Scotland) Act 1978. The right to information, then, is restricted to that which relates to the provision of those services.

1.51 A Scottish GP successfully argued to the Commissioner that a request for information held by his medical practice on human clinical trials being conducted by a pharmaceutical company was not valid. This was because any activity of the GP (which would be confined to signing a letter of "no objection" regarding patients who had volunteered for such trials) was not a general medical service provided under the relevant statute and regulations.

Scottish public authorities – s 3(4)

(4) Information is not held by the Keeper of the Records of Scotland if it is contained in a record transferred to the Keeper by a public authority within the meaning of the Freedom of Information Act 2000 (c.36) unless it is information –
    (a) to which subsections (2) to (5) of section 22 apply by virtue of subsection (6) of that section; or
    (b) designated by that authority as open information for the purposes of this subsection.

1.52 The Keeper of the Records of Scotland is head of the National Archives of Scotland. Before 1999 the National Archives of Scotland was known as the Scottish Record Office.

1.53 If a UK public authority (as listed under Sch 1 to FOIA, or designated by an Order under that Act), such as a Government Department, transfers a record to the Keeper of the Records, that information is not "held" by the Keeper for the purposes of FOISA.

1.54 There are two exceptions. First, if the UK authority has designated the information as being "open" then it is "held". This is a sensible provision, as it means that an applicant does not have to make a subsequent, duplicate, request for information to a UK public authority when it has already been determined that the information can be made publicly available. Second, if the information was transferred by the Secretary of State for Scotland before 1 July 1999, then it is regarded as being held by the Keeper. This makes clear that records transferred after that date from the Secretary of State for Scotland come from a UK public authority. For records transferred prior to that date, Scottish Ministers have the power to designate the information contained in the record as being open or to come to a decision, for example as to whether the information requested is exempt (as confirmed by subs (5) below).

Scottish public authorities – s 3(5)

(5) **Where the public authority mentioned in subsection (4) is the Secretary of State for Scotland and the information is contained in a record transferred as is mentioned in subsection (6) of section 22 the reference in subsection (4)(b) to "that authority" is to be construed as a reference to the Scottish Ministers.**

4 Amendment of schedule 1

(1) The Scottish Ministers may by order amend schedule 1 by –
    (a) adding to that schedule a reference to –
        (i) any body which; or
        (ii) the holder of any office which,
        is not for the time being listed there and is either a part of the Scottish Administration or a Scottish public authority with mixed functions or no reserved functions; or
    (b) removing from that schedule an entry for the time being listed there.

Since FOISA was passed there have been 73 changes to Sch 1 as public authorities have been created or abolished, or have simply changed their names. Thirty-four authorities have been removed, such as the Ancient Monuments Board for Scotland, area tourist boards and the Scottish Health Advisory Board, and 29 additions have been made, such as Quality Meat Scotland, VisitScotland and the Scottish Police Services Authority.   1.55

Additions to Sch 1 may be made by a provision in the primary legislation which brings new authorities into being, as was the case   1.56

for the Scottish Commission for Human Rights.[29] However, bodies which perhaps should have been included at the time of the passage of their legislation can still be added at a later date, as happened with the Commissioner for Children and Young People in Scotland, who was added to Sch 1 by virtue of a s 4 Order.[30]

Amendment of schedule 1 – s 4(2)

(2) **The reference in paragraph (a) of subsection (1) to an authority with mixed functions or no reserved functions is to be construed in accordance with paragraphs 1(4) and 2 of Part III of Schedule 5 to the Scotland Act 1998 (c.46).**

1.57   The Scotland Act does not reserve any Scottish public authority if *some* of its functions relate to reserved matters and some do not (unless it is specified as a cross-border authority) or all its functions relate to devolved matters.

1.58   For instance, local government is not a matter reserved to Westminster, and the Scottish Government can confer or remove any functions "specifically exercisable in relation to the authority"[31] *except* if that function related to reserved matters.[32] Scottish local authorities do have certain powers and obligations in respect of reserved matters such as health and safety legislation. The Health and Safety Executive, a UK non-departmental public body, issues guidance to local authorities, as enforcing authorities, which they must follow. Under the terms of the Scotland Act 1998, local authorities therefore have mixed functions, but, whether in respect of reserved functions or not, all information requests made to Scottish local authorities are to be dealt with under the terms of FOISA.

1.59   A "cross-border public authority" means any body, Government Department, office or office-holder specified in an Order in Council.[33] The general provisions in the Scotland Act for transferring functions to the Scottish Parliament and Scottish Ministers do not apply to cross-border public authorities. (However, for all cross-border public authorities, UK Ministers must consult Scottish Ministers before making appointments or exercising any function in relation

---

29   Scottish Commission for Human Rights Act 2006, s 17 and Sch 1.
30   FOISA Amendment Order (SSI 2008/297).
31   Scotland Act 1998,Sch 5, Pt III, para 1(2)(b).
32   *Ibid*, para 1(3).
33   As specified by the Scotland Act 1998 (Cross-Border Public Authorities) (Specification) Order 1999 (SI 1999/1319).

to the authority which might affect Scotland other than in relation to reserved matters. Any reports relating to cross-border public authorities that must be laid before the UK Parliament must also be laid before the Scottish Parliament.)

Cross-border authorities include, variously, the British Wool   1.60
Marketing Board, the Criminal Injuries Compensation Authority, the Office of Surveillance Commissioners, and the Sea Fish Industry Authority.

Amendment of schedule 1 – s 4(3)

(3) An order under subsection (1) may relate to a specified person or office or to persons or offices falling within a specified description.

5 Further power to designate Scottish public authorities

(1) The Scottish Ministers may by order designate as a Scottish public authority for the purposes of this Act any person mentioned in subsection (2) who –
  (a) is neither for the time being listed in schedule 1 nor capable of being added to that schedule by order under section 4(1); and
  (b) is neither a public body nor the holder of any public office.

(2) The persons are those who either –
  (a) appear to the Scottish Ministers to exercise functions of a public nature; or
  (b) are providing, under a contract made with a Scottish public authority, any service whose provision is a function of that authority.

(3) An order under subsection (1) may designate a specified person or persons falling within a specified description.

(4) An order under subsection (1) made by virtue of –
  (a) subsection (2)(a) must specify the functions of a public nature which appear to be exercised;
  (b) subsection (2)(b) must specify the service being provided.

(5) Before making an order under subsection (1), the Scottish Ministers must consult –
  (a) every person to whom the order relates; or
  (b) persons appearing to them to represent such persons.

1.61 In recognition that public functions may be carried out other than by the public bodies listed in Sch 1, provision has been made to designate as public authorities persons or organisations exercising, or providing under contract, functions of a public nature. This could include private companies or charitable bodies.

1.62 There was a clear expectation that this power would be used regularly so that the right to information kept pace with changes in the delivery of public services.[34]

1.63 In practice this has not happened, and no bodies have been designated under s 5 since FOISA came into force.[35]

6 Publicly-owned companies

(1) A company is a "publicly-owned company" for the purposes of section 3(1)(b) if it is wholly owned –
(a) by the Scottish Ministers; or
(b) by any other Scottish public authority listed in schedule 1, other than an authority so listed only in relation to information of a specified description.

(2) For the purposes of subsection (1), a company is wholly owned –
(a) by the Scottish Ministers if it has no members except –
(i) the Scottish Ministers or companies wholly owned by the Scottish Ministers; or
(ii) persons acting on behalf of the Scottish Ministers or of such companies; and
(b) by any other Scottish public authority if it has no members except –
(i) the authority or companies wholly owned by the authority; or
(ii) persons acting on behalf of the authority or of such companies.

---

34 While s 5 was being debated in the Scottish Parliament, Jim Wallace, the Justice Minister, said: "Provisions allow providers of services to the public to be added to the Bill case by case, and I reassure the Parliament that that power will be exercised." (*Scottish Parliament Official Report*, 24 April 2002, col 111.)

35 In July 2010, Scottish Ministers did publish a formal consultation, in line with s 5(5), indicating that they were minded to extend the coverage of FOISA to a range of bodies (such as PFI/PPP contractors, Glasgow Housing Association and local authority leisure, sport and cultural trusts). However, in January 2011, the Government announced that none would, after all, be designated.

(3) In subsections (1) and (2), "company" includes any body corporate.

FOISA does not provide a list of publicly owned companies. Indeed, it does not appear that a comprehensive list of such bodies exists for any purpose. The Commissioner has identified some 300 publicly owned companies, which include The Andrew Carnegie Business School Ltd and NorthLink Ferries Ltd.   1.64

The basis of identification that a company is wholly owned by a Scottish public authority is: 1.65

- if it has no members other than those specified in s 6(2)(a) and (b). In other words, the concept of "wholly owned" is defined by reference only to the existence and identity of the members;

- where it is wholly owned by one or more public authorities. "Authority" is taken to include the plural "authorities" by virtue of s 6 of the Interpretation Act 1978. (A different conclusion has been arrived at by the UK Information Commissioner, who does not regard companies owned by more than one public authority as "wholly owned".[36]) On this basis, decisions have been issued in respect of Investors in People Scotland (jointly owned by Scottish Enterprise and Highlands and Islands Enterprise) and the Scottish Further Education Unit (jointly owned by all of Scotland's further education colleges).

During the passage of the legislation, some concern was expressed that companies might be established which were very substantially publicly owned but, by virtue of having external members or minority ownership, would be excluded from FOISA. This has come to pass, given the construct of many arm's-length companies delivering public services, such as local authority leisure and recreation trusts. It is open to Ministers to designate such bodies under s 5.   1.66

Wholly owned companies – East/West divide

Over the past decade and more, local authorities have established companies to provide the facilities and services for which they are

---

36 However, the Protection of Freedoms Bill (cl 93), if brought into force, would make it clear that a company wholly owned by more than one public authority will be covered by FOIA.

responsible, such as leisure and recreation. While these companies may look similar, some come within the scope of FOISA and others do not.

Edinburgh Leisure was established by the City of Edinburgh Council in 1998, to provide leisure and recreation services on behalf of the council. A not-for-profit company, it received £8 million of its £25 million income from the Council. Its Board of Directors includes five city councillors; however, the membership of the company is made up of all 15 Directors, including external nominees, so it is not wholly publicly owned for the purposes of FOISA.

Culture and Sport Glasgow was established in 2007 to provide a wide range of museum, library, sports and music services on behalf of Glasgow City Council. It has a turnover of over £100 million, of which 70 per cent comes by way of a service fee paid by the Council. It too has a Board with what are described as "independent members", but the membership of the company is vested only in Glasgow City Council. It is therefore a wholly publicly owned company for the purposes of FOISA.

7 Public authorities to which Act has limited application

(1) An order under section 4(1)(a) may, in adding an entry to schedule 1, list the authority only in relation to information of a specified description; and where an authority is so listed nothing in this Act applies to any other information held by the authority.

(2) The Scottish Ministers may by order amend that schedule –

(a) by limiting the entry relating to an authority to information of a specified description; or

(b) by removing or amending any such limitation for the time being contained in an entry so relating.

1.67   Most authorities listed in Sch 1 or wholly owned companies are covered by FOISA in their entirety. However, for some, such as general practitioners, FOISA has limited application. The specific provision in Sch 1 applies to "a person providing primary medical services under a general medical services contract (within the meaning of the National Health Service (Scotland) Act 1978), or general dental services, general ophthalmic services or pharmaceutical services under Part II of that

Act, but only in respect of information relating to the provision of those services".[37]

A similar limitation applies to persons providing primary medical services or personal dental services, who are covered only in respect of information relating to services under s 17C of the 1978 Act.   **1.68**

Public authorities to which Act has limited application – s 7(3)

(3) Nothing in this Act applies to information held by a person designated as a Scottish public authority by order under subsection (1) of section 5 if the order is made by virtue of –
  (a) subsection (2)(a) of that section and the information does not relate to the functions; or
  (b) subsection (2)(b) of that section and the information does not relate to the service,
specified in the order.

A decision to designate, say, a contractor providing a service which is the function of a public authority, would have the unintended effect of giving an entitlement to any information held by that contractor unrelated to that service (for example, entirely commercial contracts with private clients), unless some limitation was put upon that entitlement. Section 7(3) makes it clear that the information which can be requested under the terms of FOISA is only that which relates to the functions or service for which the body was designated.   **1.69**

Public authorities to which Act has limited application – s 7(4)

(4) Nothing in this Act applies in relation to information –
  (a) held by a publicly-owned company; and
  (b) of a description specified in relation to that company in an order made for the purposes of this subsection by the Scottish Ministers.

This makes provision, for reasons which are not at all clear, for Ministers to make an order to exempt information held by a publicly owned company. A similar provision exists, however, in the equivalent UK legislation.[38]   **1.70**

---

37 FOISA, Sch 1, as amended by the Primary Medical Services (Scotland) Act 2004, Sch 5.
38 FOIA, s 7(7) and (8).

8 Requesting information

(1) Any reference in this Act to "requesting" information is a reference to making a request which –

(a) is in writing or in another form which, by reason of its having some permanency, is capable of being used for subsequent reference (as, for example, a recording made on audio or video tape);

(b) states the name of the applicant and an address for correspondence; and

(c) describes the information requested.

1.71   It was intended that there should be an absence of formality to making a freedom of information request. If any person writes to an authority, reasonably clearly describing the information they want, and provides their name and an address for a response, then the requirements of s 8(1) have essentially been met.

1.72   There is no requirement to invoke or cite FOISA to alert an authority that a formal request is being made. (In other countries, the applicant may have to invoke or cite the statute. In Ireland, for example, "the request must be expressed to be made under the Act".[39]) Sometimes applicants do indicate that they are "making a freedom of information request". However, the onus is on the authority to recognise that a request has been received and to establish which statutory regime applies. It is quite possible to find that the component parts of a single request can constitute a request under FOISA, a request for environmental information under the EIRs and a subject access request under the Data Protection Act 1998.

1.73   There is no need to fill out a special form. (By contrast, in South Africa applicants have to make the request "in the prescribed form" to the information officer of the public body concerned.[40]) Some authorities have attempted to assist applicants by providing online forms on which a request can be made and a specific address to which it can be submitted.

1.74   However, it is clear that there is no requirement to use such a procedure and a request does not have to be made to a specific person within the authority. Furthermore, unless the applicant has the capacity to save or print off such forms, they may find it difficult to show whether or when a request was made.

---

39   M McDonagh, *Freedom of Information Law in Ireland* (1998), p 95.
40   Promotion of Access to Information Act, Act 2 of 2000, s 18(1).

What constitutes a valid request under s 8 is a contested area. **1.75** Questions have been raised over:

- what constitutes a name or address;
- who the "true' applicant is;
- whether a request can be made by reference to documents;
- when it can be said that an e-mail request has actually been received.

Name and address

The request must state the name of the applicant. The view has **1.76** been taken in Scotland that it is not sufficient simply to provide a first name. Nor is it felt sufficient to provide an e-mail address which apparently incorporates a name, for example "davedee@zmail.com". Beyond that, however, if the request states the name and an address for correspondence (which could be a postal or electronic address),the request is in that respect treated as valid.

This would apply, for example, where the applicant has not stated **1.77** her full name, but describes herself, for example, as "Ms MacDonald". The courts have made it clear that the Commissioner has no obligation to make general enquiries as to the identity of an applicant and authorities should not do so either.[41] (However, there may be a need to do so in particular circumstances. If the request from an "M Johnston" involves the personal information of, say, a Mrs Margaret Johnston of the same address, the authority may need to establish whether this is the identity of the applicant so as to apply the exemption at s 38 appropriately.)

"True applicant"

Identifying who the applicant is matters where it is not clear whether a **1.78** request has been made by the named person or on behalf of another. In the case *Glasgow City Council and Dundee City Council v Scottish Information Commissioner*[42] an application by a firm of solicitors acting on behalf of an unnamed client was found by the Court of Session to be invalid, on the ground that the agents were not the "true applicant" (see Box) and therefore the request had not stated the name of the applicant.

41　*Glasgow City Council and Dundee City Council v Scottish Information Commissioner* [2009] CSIH 73.
42　*Ibid.*

Undisclosed client is true applicant

In the case of *Glasgow City Council* v *Scottish Information Commissioner* the Court of Session found that an information request made by MacRoberts Solicitors on behalf of an unnamed client (later established to be a company called Millar and Bryce Ltd) was invalid in terms of s 8(1) of FOISA. The court held that Millar and Bryce was the "true applicant" and should have been identified as such at the time of application.

The court rejected the notion that an agent making a request, on behalf of a client, satisfies the provision in s 1(2) which defines an applicant as "the person making a request". The question was which of them – the agent or the client – should be regarded as making the request for the purposes of FOISA. The court had regard to other sections of FOISA which depend upon the identity of the applicant, such as: considering whether an application is vexatious (s 14(1)); whether the information is otherwise accessible to the applicant (s 25(1)); or whether the information requested is "personal data of which the applicant is the data subject" (s 38(1)(a)).

It concluded that "several of the provisions of the Act can only operate sensibly and effectively, and as the Scottish Parliament must therefore be taken to have intended, if the applicant in a case where the request is made by an agent acting on another person's behalf is taken to be the person on whose behalf it is made".

As a consequence of failing to name the client in the Glasgow case, no valid application had been made.

1.79   Therefore, if a request is made on behalf of another person, then it is that other person who is to be regarded as the applicant. Requests on behalf of another person may come not only from solicitors on behalf of clients but also from, say, MPs, MSPs or councillors on behalf of constituents. If it is apparent to an authority that the request is being made on behalf of another person who is not named, the request is invalid. However, the request cannot be ignored or simply rejected. There is an obligation on the authority (under s 15) to explain why and what needs to be done to make the request valid (usually, to make a new request naming the client). There is no need for the true applicant's address to be provided for this purpose, as the address of the agent satisfies the requirement for an address for correspondence under s 8(1)(b).

(The issue of the true applicant is dealt with in more detail in   **1.80**
Chapter 7 (Key Issue 5: Who Wants to Know?).)

Describing the information

The same Court of Session opinion also concluded that when des-   **1.81**
cribing the information, it should be clear that the request was for
information and not specific *documents*, saying: "it is implicit in the
definition that a distinction is drawn between the record itself and
the information which is recorded in it. What a person can request, in
terms of s 1(1), is the information which has been recorded, rather than
the record itself. The right conferred by s 1, where it applies, is therefore
to be given the information, rather than a particular record (or a copy
of the record) that contains it. Put shortly, the Act provides a right of
access to information, not documentation".[43]

However, a request for a document does not automatically   **1.82**
invalidate an application. A reference to a specific document is a
commonplace way of describing the information sought and can be of
assistance to an authority in identifying and locating the information.
Such a reference can also benefit the authority by limiting the scope of
the information request, for example to that contained in a minute of
a certain date. If a request is for "a copy of correspondence" between
two individuals, it is reasonably clear that what is being asked for is
the information contained within that correspondence.[44] In any case,
as the court observed and as happens in practice, authorities may find
that the most practicable way to provide the information is to provide
a copy of the relevant document.

(An important question is whether the *Glasgow City Council* case   **1.83**
has any effect on the way in which public authorities should deal
with requests for environmental information under the EIRs. It
would appear not: the case was not concerned with the EIRs and the
court did not discuss them. The Aarhus Convention (Art 4(3)) obliges
public authorities to make environmental information available when
requested, including "copies of the actual documentation containing
or comprising such information". Consequently, there would appear to
be nothing wrong with making a request under the EIRs formulated in
terms of "documents" rather than "information".[45])

---

43   *Glasgow City Council and Dundee City Council v SIC* [2009] CSIH 73, para 43.
44   *Ibid*, para 45.
45   See Chapter 2.

Valid request by reference to documents

The City of Edinburgh Council was asked for a "copy of all invoices received from Common Purpose" (a not-for-profit organisation that runs leadership development courses) and "copies of all e-mail traffic and attachments" between a named person and Common Purpose from specific months in 2009.

The Council, by reference to the Court of Session ruling in the case of *Glasgow City Council* v *Scottish Information Commissioner*, stated in its response that the parts of the information request seeking invoices and e-mails did not describe the information as required by s 8(1)(c) of FOISA. The Council invited the applicant to re-submit his request, clarifying exactly what information he was seeking.

The Commissioner's decision noted that the statutory requirement, under s 8(1)(c) of FOISA, is confined to a description of the information requested. The purpose of the description is to allow the public authority to identify and locate the information and the purpose of the reference in FOISA to "information" is to relieve the applicant from specifying particular documents, since he or she cannot be expected to know in what form information is held.

Notwithstanding the expression in terms of requests for copies of particular documents (e-mails and attachments and invoices), the Commissioner considered it to be clear that the request sought all information that was *contained in* the documents requested. The descriptions of the information (for example, by type, between two parties, and by date) were "sufficiently clear to enable the identification and location of that information, which must be the primary consideration in determining whether a request is valid".

Decision 188/2010: Mr Roger Hayes and City of Edinburgh Council

Requesting information – s 8(2)

(2) For the purposes of paragraph (a) of subsection (1) (and without prejudice to the generality of that paragraph), a request is to be treated as made in writing where the text of the request is –

(a) transmitted by electronic means;

(b) received in legible form; and

(c) capable of being used for subsequent reference.

Receipt of electronic requests

A request may be made by e-mail or fax so long as it is received in   **1.84**
legible form. Illegibility may occur if the request cannot be read by the
authority because it has been created using a software program which
is not recognised by the authority's systems. A fax may be illegible
if the original image is of insufficient quality to be transmitted and
understood by the recipient authority. This should be matter of fact.

When can it be said that an electronic request has been "*received*"?   **1.85**
One local authority found that 106 requests had been inappropriately
quarantined by its e-mail gateway, and so had not been viewed.
It argued that the requests could not be said to be received until
the authority was aware of them.[46] However, s 74(2)(b) of FOISA
provides that a thing "transmitted by electronic means is presumed
to be received on the day of transmission". As this is a rebuttable
presumption, the onus lay with the Council to demonstrate that
an e-mail was not received on the day of transmission, which it was
unable to do.

9 Fees

(1) **A Scottish public authority receiving a request which
requires it to comply with section 1(1) may, within the time
allowed by section 10 for so complying, give the applicant a
notice in writing (in this Act referred to as a "fees notice")
stating that a fee of an amount specified in the notice is to
be charged by the authority for so complying.**

No fee is payable for making a request for information (unlike, say,   **1.86**
in Ireland and in parts of Canada). However, authorities can make a
charge for complying with a request. The applicant has to be notified
of this charge and how it has been calculated, by way of a fees notice.
This must be issued within 20 working days of the request being
received.

Fees – s 9(2)

(2) **Subsection (1) is subject to section 19.**

The fees notice must contain particulars of the procedure provided   **1.87**
by the authority for dealing with complaints about its handling of
requests for information and about the rights of application to the

---

46   Decision 112/2007: MacRoberts Solicitors and Glasgow City Council.

authority for a review of its actions and decisions and, subsequently, of the right of application to the Commissioner for a decision, where applicants are dissatisfied with the way in which the authority has dealt with the request for information.

Fees – s 9(3)

(3)   **If a fees notice is given to the applicant, the authority is not obliged to give the requested information unless the fee is duly paid; and for the purposes of this subsection and section 10(2) due payment is payment within the period of three months beginning with the day on which the notice is given.**

1.88   The fees notice is essentially a quote, based upon projected costs of complying with a request. In this way the authority gives notice to the applicant how much they will have to pay to receive the information. The applicant can indicate that they do not want to proceed with the request, in which case the authority has not incurred the costs associated with complying with a request for which the applicant has declined to pay.

1.89   The applicant may wish to establish what information can be provided free of charge or for a lesser cost. Under s 15, the authority is expected to provide such advice as to how costs can be reduced or avoided, for example by limiting the scope of a request.

Fees – s 9(4)

(4)   **Subject to subsection (7), a fee charged under subsection (1) is to be determined by the authority in accordance with regulations made by the Scottish Ministers.**

1.90   Authorities are not entirely free to determine what components of the process involved in responding to information requests can be charged for or how much can be charged. Ministers have made Fees Regulations (the Freedom of Information (Fees for Required Disclosure) (Scotland) Regulations 2004 (SSI 2004/467)) which circumscribe matters such as the amount to be charged for staff time and the extent to which information should be provided free of charge.

Fees – s 9(5)

(5)   **Without prejudice to the generality of subsection (4), the regulations may in particular provide that –**

    (a) a fee is not to exceed such amount as may be specified in, or determined in accordance with, the regulations;

    (b) a fee is to be calculated in such manner as may be so specified; and

    (c) no fee is payable in a case so specified.

The Fees Regulations have not been changed since their introduction in 2004. The key elements of these are: **1.91**

- The first £100 of costs are provided free of charge – in other words, the authority cannot issue a fees notice where it would cost £100 or less to comply with the request.
- For projected costs above £100, authorities may make a charge of up to 10 per cent of these costs. (So, if the authority estimates that it would cost £450 in total to comply with the request, it must disregard the first £100 and may issue a fees notice for up to 10 per cent of the remainder, which amounts to a maximum of £35.)
- When calculating these costs an authority can charge for the direct and/or indirect costs incurred in locating, retrieving and providing the information in accordance with FOISA.
- However, in so doing it must not charge more than £15 per hour for staff time (no matter the seniority of the official involved). It must charge less if the actual staff costs are less than £15 per hour (calculated on the basis of normal salary, rather than, for example, overtime).[47]
- Costs cannot be charged for determining whether an authority actually holds the information. Nor can a charge be made for costs incurred by the authority deliberating about whether or not to provide the information, such as determining whether or not to apply exemptions.
- The most practicable means of providing information may be to extract it from a document or to redact information contained within that document which is exempt or outwith the scope of the request. Some of the costs of carrying out this procedure may be eligible to be charged under the Fees Regulations.
- A High Court decision in England has held, on the basis of the differently worded UK Fees Regulations,[48] that an

---

47 Decision 012/2008: Councillor Paul Welsh and North Lanarkshire Council.

48 Freedom of Information and Data Protection (Appropriate Limit and Fees) Regulations 2004 (SI 2004/3224).

authority cannot charge for the process of physically redacting information which it believes is exempt.[49] However, in Scotland, the Commissioner considers that the charging for the costs of redaction (as opposed to determining whether to apply an exemption) is allowed under the Fees Regulations, as part of the costs of *providing* information.

- Charges can also be made for the cost of physically providing the information, for example photocopying and postage costs, or providing it in some other requested format, for example on a CD or DVD.

Fees – s 9(6) and (7)

(6) **Before making the regulations, the Scottish Ministers are to consult the Commissioner**

(7) **Subsection (4) does not apply where provision is made, by or under any enactment, as to the fee that may be charged by the authority for the disclosure of the information.**

1.92 The amount to be paid for certain information, and the manner in which such a fee is to be calculated, may be separately determined by enactment, in which case the Freedom of Information (Fees for Required Disclosure) (Scotland) Regulations 2004 (SSI 2004/467) would not apply.

1.93 As an example, the fee for purchasing a copy of the (edited) electoral register is set in accordance with the Representation of the People (Scotland) Regulations 2001.

1.94 Similarly, the basis for charging for information held in the Register of Sasines and the Land Register is established by s 25 of the Land Registers (Scotland) Act 1868, as amended by the Land Registration (Scotland) Act 1979. Fees may be required "in respect of the provision by the Keeper of searches, reports, certificates or other documents or copies of any document or of information from any such register; and the amount of the fees so fixed shall not be greater than is reasonably sufficient for defraying the expenses of the department of the Keeper, including the expenses of the improvement of the systems of such registration and recording". The actual amount of such fees is set out in a Schedule as required by the Fees in the Registers of Scotland Order 1995 (SI 1995/1945).

---

49 *Chief Constable of South Yorkshire Police v Information Commissioner* [2011] EWHC 44 (Admin).

It is important to note that the basis for charging under the EIRs   1.95
can be different. The significance of this is dealt with in Chapter 8
(Key Issue 6: Charging for Information).

10 Time for compliance

(1) Subject to subsections (2) and (3), a Scottish public
    authority receiving a request which requires it to
    comply with section 1(1) must comply promptly; and in
    any event by not later than the twentieth working day
    after –
    (a) in a case other than that mentioned in paragraph (b),
        the receipt by the authority of the request; or
    (b) in a case where section 1(3) applies, the receipt by it of
        the further information.

Authorities have up to 20 working days to comply with a request   1.96
(with the time starting on the day *after* the request has been received).
However, as s 10 makes clear, it is expected that they should not delay
the provision of information and must respond promptly. Often,
authorities work on the basis that they do not have to respond before
the 20th working day and therefore they will utilise the maximum
time. Of course, time may be required to deliberate on whether
disclosure is required under FOISA. However, where, for example,
the authority takes the maximum time allowed because it is further
considering the reputational consequences of disclosure or arranging
simultaneous public release, then the delay may not be regarded as
prompt compliance with the timescales. This procedure may not be
regarded as promptly complying with a request, and there are instances
where such an approach has caused authorities to exceed the statutory
deadline.

Ministerial clearance delaying responses to FOI requests

An assessment of one Government executive agency, Transport
Scotland, found that it failed to respond to 20 per cent of requests
within the statutory 20-working-day time limit. Delay in securing
clearance from Ministers was the single most common cause for
the failing. In a sample of 45 cases dealt with by Transport Scotland,
13 had been submitted to Ministers. Nearly half of these were not

> cleared in time and led to the response to the applicant exceeding the 20-working-day limit.
>
>   It is estimated that some 10 per cent of FOI requests to the Scottish Government are submitted to Ministers for clearance.[50]

1.97 Where authorities need additional information to locate or retrieve the information requested (as provided for by s 1(3)), then the 20 working days start the day after the public authority has received the further information. Authorities should not act unreasonably and delay complying with a request by asking for information which is not necessary.

1.98 (There is no equivalent in FOISA of the provision in s 10(3) of FOIA for extending the time taken to respond beyond 20 days to consider whether the public interest in maintaining an exemption outweighs that in disclosing the information.)

Time for compliance – s 10(2)

(2) If –

  (a) the authority is the Keeper of the Records of Scotland; and

  (b) the information is information to which section 22(2) to (5) applies,

  subsection (1) applies with the substitution, for the reference to the twentieth working day, of a reference to the thirtieth working day.

1.99 Where a request for information or requirement for review is made to the Keeper for information contained in a record transferred to the Keeper by a public authority, this section extends to 30 working days the time for complying with the request. This is because the Keeper is required by s 22 to send a copy of that request to the authority which transferred the information, to be instructed by it (for example, as to whether an exemption applies) and then to respond to the applicant accordingly.

Time for compliance – s 10(3)

(3) Where the authority gives a fees notice to the applicant and the fee is duly paid, the working days in the period –

---

50 Scottish Information Commissioner, *Practice Assessment of Transport Scotland*, 25 August 2010, paras 4.27–4.34.

(a) **beginning with the day on which that notice is given; and**

(b) **ending with the day on which the fee is received by the authority,**

are to be disregarded in calculating, for the purposes of subsection (1), the twentieth (or as the case may be the thirtieth) working day mentioned in that subsection.

When calculating the time within which an authority must comply   1.100
with a request, the "time-elapsed" clock stops while the authority
awaits payment in response to a fees notice and resumes once the fee
is paid. For the purposes of counting the 20 working days, no account is
taken of the day on which the fees notice is sent, the day the payment
is made or any day in between.

Time for compliance – s 10(4)

(4) **The Scottish Ministers may by regulations provide that subsections (1) and (3) are to have effect as if references to the twentieth (or as the case may be the thirtieth) working day were references to such other working day, not later than the sixtieth, after receipt by the authority of the request as is specified in, or determined in accordance with, the regulations.**

Scottish Ministers have not made any regulations extending the   1.101
time period for requests but UK Ministers have done so, using similar
provisions at s 10(4) of FOIA. Where an information request is received
by the governing body of a maintained school or a maintained nursery
school or by a school maintained by the Secretary of State for Defence,
the time which can be taken to respond is the 20th working day
following the date of receipt, disregarding any working day which is
not a school day, or the 60th working day following the date of receipt,
whichever occurs first. This is clearly meant to accommodate requests
arriving during school holidays.[51]

Time for compliance – s 10(5)

(5) **Regulations under subsection (4) may –**
    (a) **prescribe different days in relation to different cases; and**

---

51   Under reg 3 of the Freedom of Information (Time for Compliance with Request)
     Regulations 2004 (SI 2004/3364). Similar provision was made for certain schools in
     Northern Ireland by virtue of the Freedom of Information (Time for Compliance with
     Request) Regulations 2009 (SI 2009/1369).

(b) confer a discretion on the Scottish Information Commissioner, exercisable both at the request of the authority and where no such request has been made.

1.102 Again, no such regulations have been made in Scotland. Under the UK regime, regulations have been made which allow for an extension of time for complying with requests to be given at the discretion of the UK Commissioner. Where the request involves information held outside of the UK or requires information to be obtained from any individual "who is actively involved in an operation of the armed forces of the Crown, or in the preparations for such an operation and a response cannot be given by the twentieth working day then, in both these circumstances, the authority can apply to the UK Commissioner for an extension of time".[52]

11 Means of providing information

(1) Where, in requesting information from a Scottish public authority, the applicant expresses a preference for receiving it by any one or more of the means mentioned in subsection (2), the authority must, so far as is reasonably practicable, give effect to that preference

(2) The means are –

   (a) the provision to the applicant, in permanent form or in another form acceptable to the applicant, of a copy of the information;

   (b) such provision to the applicant of a digest or summary of the information; and

   (c) the provision to the applicant of a reasonable opportunity to inspect a record containing the information.

1.103 The applicant is entitled to a copy of the *information* (which is not the same as being provided with a copy of a *document* – see s 8). The entitlement is for the information in permanent form (for example, a paper copy). There may be occasions, however, where the applicant is satisfied with simply being provided with the information verbally.

1.104 A summary or digest may be sought. For example, the applicant may prefer to be given totals of figures rather than disaggregated data.

---

52 Freedom of Information (Time for Compliance with Request) Regulations 2004 (SI 2004/3364), reg 5(3).

The applicant may express a preference for inspecting the record   1.105
containing the information (perhaps because a cost would otherwise
be incurred). It is clear that this does not allow unfettered access:
the authority can still withhold information which it believes to be
exempt. In one case an applicant sought to have access to an original
voice recording, rather than only being provided with a copy of the
recording which, in her view, made it susceptible to tampering. She
would have been entitled to do so, save for the fact that an exemption
applied.[53]

Means of providing information – s 11(3)

(3) In determining, for the purposes of subsection (1), what
     is reasonably practicable, the authority may have regard
     to all the circumstances, including cost; and where it
     determines that it is not reasonably practicable to give
     effect to the preference it must notify the applicant of the
     reasons for that determination.

The authority may conclude that it is not reasonably practicable to give   1.106
effect to the preference expressed by the applicant and any conditions
attached to that, such as expecting to be allowed unsupervised access
to inspect files and without limit upon time taken.[54]

Technically possible but not reasonably practicable

Glasgow City Council told an applicant who wanted to receive a
digitised copy of information contained in the lair books for a specific
cemetery that it would have to buy specialist equipment to digitise
the records, and furthermore that it would take staff over 100 hours
to scan the 32 volumes, each containing 200 pages. As this would
clearly exceed the upper cost limit, the applicant proposed instead
that, through his own digital archiving company, he would scan the
material, at no cost to the authority. The Council declined the offer
and the Commissioner found that it was entitled to decide by whom
and by what means its information could be copied. In any case he
found that it was not reasonably practicable to give effect to this
preference, as the condition of the historical material meant that

---

53   Decision 101/2007: Ms Margaret Gokce and the Scottish Ambulance Service Board.
54   Decision 020/2010: Mr Michael Peterson and Shetland Islands Council.

> staff members from the Council would have to be in attendance throughout the process of copying.
>
> *Decision 048/2010: Mr Tom McPherson and Glasgow City Council*

Means of providing information – s 11(4)

(4) Subject to subsection (1), information given in compliance with section 1(1) may be given by any means which are reasonable in the circumstances.

1.107   So, for example, if the request is made by e-mail, the authority may regard it as reasonable in the circumstances to provide the information as an attachment to an e-mail in reply, unless the applicant expresses a preference to the contrary.

Means of providing information – s 11(5)

(5) Such tests of reasonable practicability as are imposed by this section are not to be construed as detracting from any duty which a person has under or by virtue of s 29 of the Equality Act 2010 (provision of services etc) (duty to make adjustments to practices, policies, procedures or physical features so that use of services by disabled persons is facilitated or made possible).[55]

1.108   An applicant complained to the Commissioner that she had not been provided with the information requested in Braille within the 20-working-day period. It was established that the authority had not previously translated documents and the time limit had been breached as it sought to find a suitable external translation service.[56] Given the obligations arising from the Equality Act 2010, it would be good practice for authorities to anticipate such requests and to make prior provision for translation so that applicants are not disadvantaged.

---

55 The original text of this section has been amended by the Equality Act 2010 (Consequential Amendments, Saving and Supplementary Provisions) Order 2010 (SI 2010/2279), Pt 2, para 102.

56 Decision 205/2007: Ms Suzi Eskandari and the Scottish Children's Reporter Administration.

12 Excessive cost of compliance

(1) Section 1(1) does not oblige a Scottish public authority
to comply with a request for information if the authority
estimates that the cost of complying with the request
would exceed such amount as may be prescribed in
regulations made by the Scottish Ministers; and different
amounts may be so prescribed in relation to different
cases.

Regulations have prescribed the maximum amount which may   1.109
be incurred in complying with a request at £600.[57] Put simply, if
the estimated cost of providing the information is more than
£600 then the authority does not have to comply with the request.
No other consideration applies. Not surprisingly, then, the basis
on which authorities have come to such an estimation has been
challenged.

Even where a public authority has not relied on cost grounds to   1.110
refuse to provide information, but it comes to the Commissioner's
attention during an investigation that the costs would exceed £600,
he cannot order the public authority to disclose the information.[58]

Excessive cost of compliance – s 12(2)

(2) The regulations may provide that, in such circumstances
as they may specify, where two or more requests for
information are made to the authority –
(a) by one person;
(b) by different persons who appear to it to be acting
in concert or whose requests appear to have been
instigated wholly or mainly for a purpose other than
the obtaining of the information itself; or
(c) by different persons in circumstances where the
authority considers it would be reasonable to make
the information available to the public at large and
elects to do so,
then if the authority estimates that the total cost of
complying with both (or all) of the requests exceeds the

---

57 Freedom of Information (Fees for Required Disclosure) (Scotland) Regulations 2004
(SSI 2004/467), reg 5.
58 This is considered in Decision 206/2006: Michael Carberry and the Chief Constable of
Strathclyde Police.

> amount prescribed, in relation to complying with either (or any) of those requests, under subsection (1), section 1(1) does not oblige the authority to comply with either (or any) of those requests.

1.111   Ministers have elected, after consultation with the Commissioner, not to make regulations bringing subss (2)(a) and (b) into effect. The intended effect of such provisions was to protect authorities from excessive and burdensome requests. However, the practical consequences may have been to unreasonably deny information to applicants. (This is addressed in more detail in Chapter 8 (Key Issue 6: Charging for Information).)

1.112   For instance:

- "Two or more requests from one person" could mean that an applicant who made a new request while an existing request on an entirely unrelated matter was still being considered by the authority on review could be denied information in respect of both requests where, in combination, the cost of complying with them exceeded £600.

- Combining requests from different persons appearing to act in concert would permit an authority to refuse to respond to any request for information on a matter of significant local or national concern which had prompted requests for information from many individuals. (If such requests were instigated for a purpose other than to receive the information, for example seeking to overwhelm the resources or systems of the authority, then the provisions of s 14 (Vexatious and repeated requests) are likely to provide an adequate safeguard.)

1.113   Ministers did bring into effect provisions regarding subs (2)(c) concerning requests made by different persons in circumstances where the authority considers it would be reasonable to make the information available to the public at large and elects to do so. However, these specify that the aggregation of costs should apply only where "the information sought in the requests covers the same subject matter or overlaps to a significant extent" and where the authority estimates that the total cost of complying with both or all of the requests would exceed the prescribed amount.[59]

---

59 Freedom of Information (Fees for Required Disclosure) (Scotland) Regulations 2004 (SSI 2004/467), reg 6(a) and (b).

Excessive cost of compliance – s 12(3)

(3) The regulations may, in respect of an election made as mentioned in subsection (2)(c), make provision as to the means by which and the time within which the information is to be made available to the public at large.

By regulation, an authority which so elects must put the information into the public domain within 20 working days of the receipt of the first request and notify each applicant that it has done so. The regulations do not specify the means by which the information is to be put into the public domain.[60]   1.114

Excessive cost of compliance – s 12(4)–(6)

(4) The regulations may make provision as to –
   (a) the costs to be estimated; and
   (b) the manner in which those costs are to be estimated.
(5) Before making the regulations, the Scottish Ministers are to consult the Commissioner
(6)[61] References in this section to the cost of complying with a request are not to be construed as including any reference to costs incurred in fulfilling any such duty under or by virtue of the Equality Act 2010 as is mentioned in section 11(5).

13 Fees for disclosure in certain circumstances

(1) A Scottish public authority may charge for the communication of any information –
   (a) which by virtue of section 12(1) or (2) it is not obliged to communicate; and
   (b) which it is not otherwise required by law to communicate,
   such fee as may be determined by it in accordance with regulations made by the Scottish Ministers.
(2) Without prejudice to the generality of subsection (1), the regulations may in particular provide that a fee –

---

60 Freedom of Information (Fees for Required Disclosure) (Scotland) Regulations 2004 (SSI 2004/467), reg 6(d) and (e).
61 The original text of s 12(6) was amended by the Equality Act 2010 (Consequential Amendments, Saving and Supplementary Provisions) Order 2010 (SI 2004/2279), Pt 2, para 104.

(a) is not to exceed such amount as may be specified in, or determined in accordance with, the regulations; and

(b) is to be calculated in such manner as may be so specified.

(3) Before making the regulations, the Scottish Ministers are to consult the Commissioner.

(4) Subsection (1) does not apply where provision is made, by or under any enactment, as to the fee that may be charged by the authority for the disclosure of the information.

1.115   Even if an authority is not obliged to provide information because the projected costs of doing so would exceed £600, it can choose to do so in full or part. Regulations provide that it can agree a charge for this information with the applicant but this shall not exceed the sum of £50 plus the amount by which the projected costs exceeds £600.[62]

14 Vexatious or repeated requests

(1) Section 1(1) does not oblige a Scottish public authority to comply with a request for information if the request is vexatious.

1.116   There is no definition of "vexatious" in FOISA and Ministers resisted attempts to clarify what was meant by it on the ground that "the term vexatious is well established in law and in administrative practice … Therefore, the Commissioner would be familiar with the term and its interpretation".[63]

1.117   Much the same reason appears to warrant not defining the term in specific legal provision such as the Vexatious Actions (Scotland) Act 1898. The sanction in that Act is to prevent any person who has "habitually and persistently instituted vexatious legal proceedings without any reasonable ground for instituting such proceedings" in court from raising further proceedings.

1.118   The courts have said that the "hallmark of a vexatious proceeding" is that "whatever the intention of the proceeding may be, its effect is to subject the defendant to inconvenience, harassment and expense out

---

62   Regulation 4 of the Freedom of Information (Fees for Disclosure under Section 13) (Scotland) Regulations 2004 (SSI 2004/376).

63   Dr Richard Simpson, MSP, Scottish Parliament Justice 1 Committee, Tuesday 12 February 2002, col 3209.

of all proportion to any gain likely to accrue to the claimant; and that it involves an abuse of the process of the court".[64]

This is helpful in considering what a vexatious request might be – in particular, it suggests that it can be the *effect* of the request on the authority which is vexatious, even if the applicant did not *intend* it to be so; and it indicates that even where rights exist they cannot be pursued for a purpose for which they are not intended. In the case of FOISA, as indicated earlier, this might be where an authority is inundated with information requests for the purpose of testing the authority's systems or disrupting its normal operations.   1.119

In interpreting this provision, the balance to be struck is between the right of applicants to make requests, and not permitting that right to be abused so as to overwhelm an authority's resources, or to harass its staff. It does not provide a basis for authorities avoiding their responsibilities because they dislike the applicant or the nature of their requests. The onus lies on the authority to show why it could not reasonably have been expected to comply with the request.   1.120

However, s 14 does not permit the authority or the Commissioner to determine that *an individual* is excluded from exercising their rights under s 1(1). The focus of this section in FOISA is the vexatious *request*, not the person.   1.121

A request (which may be the latest in a series of requests) may be said to be vexatious where it would impose a significant burden on the public authority *and*:   1.122

- it does not have a serious purpose or value; and/or
- it is designed to cause disruption or annoyance to the public authority; and/or
- it has the effect of harassing the public authority; and/or
- it would otherwise, in the opinion of a reasonable person, be considered to be manifestly unreasonable or disproportionate.

In coming to a view, it is not the identity of the applicant that determines whether a request is vexatious, but the nature and effect of the request. However, an applicant's identity, and the history of their dealings with a public authority, *may* be relevant. In that respect, determining whether a request is vexatious (or repeated) is not applicant or motive blind. However, a series of demanding requests,   1.123

---

64 Master of the Rolls, Lord Phillips of Worth Matravers in *Bhamjee v Forsdick* [2004] 1 WLR 88 at [7], quoted by Eugene P Creally in a speech, "What is Vexatious – The Legal Perspectives", delivered at the Centre for Freedom of Information, Dundee, 17 November 2011.

even on one issue, does not necessarily mean that a pattern of vexatious behaviour is evident. Academic research distinguishes between querulous behaviour which involves "the unusually persistent pursuit of a personal grievance" and "social reformers and campaigners who use litigation and complaint to advance agendas of potential public interest".[65]

1.124   Requests have been deemed vexatious by the Commissioner where:

- offensive or demeaning language has been used;[66]

- hundreds of related requests were submitted to an authority on the same day by solicitors on behalf of a client. This was held to be "manifestly unreasonable";[67]

- the request was the latest in voluminous and persistent requests on the same matter stretching back over 10 years.[68]

1.125   However, the Commissioner has not accepted claims that requests are vexatious where:

- the relationship with the applicant was acrimonious but otherwise the request was manifestly reasonable;[69]

- the applicant wanted information about the handling of a previous FOI request;[70]

- the authority held that the request was one of a series, the purpose of which was to secure information for a website critical of the authority, and the effect of which was claimed to be harassment;[71]

- a request was made for Board minutes by an applicant believed by the authority to be acting in concert with another whose requests had been deemed vexatious.[72]

Vexatious or repeated requests – s 14(2)

(2) Where a Scottish public authority has complied with a request from a person for information, it is not obliged to

---

65   P Mullen and G Lester, "Vexatious Litigants and Unusually Persistent Complainants and Petitioners: From Querulous paranoia to Querulous Behaviour", in (2006) 24 *Behavioural Sciences and the Law* 333–349 at 34.

66   Decision 080/2005: Mr David Emslie and the Scottish Executive.

67   Decision 062/2005: MacRoberts and the Scottish Executive.

68   Decision 012/2010: Mr M W Williams and the Scottish Ministers.

69   Decision 118/2009: Ms N and East Lothian Council.

70   Decision 105/2008: Mr Rob Edwards and the Scottish Ministers.

71   Decision 187/2010: Mr Peter Cherbi and Scottish Legal Complaints Commission.

72   Decision 046/2011: Calibre Recruitment and Scottish Water.

comply with a subsequent request from that person which is identical or substantially similar unless there has been a reasonable period of time between the making of the request complied with and the making of the subsequent request.

It may appear to be a relatively straightforward matter to establish whether a request is identical or substantially similar to a previous request. However, attention should be given as to whether the information requested, not the request, is identical or substantially similar, especially if the passage of time between requests means that additional or different information would come within its scope (see Box). 1.126

It is a question of judgement as to whether a reasonable period of time has elapsed between requests. It may well be that the previous information was incomplete or partial – in which case it may be judged that a reasonable period has elapsed if sufficient time has passed to allow the information to be altered or updated. 1.127

Section 14(2) is discretionary, not mandatory. Even if this section applies, it might still be reasonable to comply with the request; for instance, where the applicant has lost or failed to retain the information, but then realised that they still needed it. It would be reasonable for public authorities to give due weight to such representations where they are made. 1.128

Similar request; different information

In January 2007, North Ayrshire Council received a request for copies of all correspondence between Council officials and the Scottish Executive on the Council's Schools PPP Project. The Council refused the request, claiming that it repeated a previous one, made in June 2005, that was identical or substantially similar. However, the Commissioner found that in the 18 months which had elapsed since the first request, the Council had corresponded further with the Executive about the Schools PPP Project. Although the request was couched in somewhat similar terms, the information sought was not identical and the applicant had made clear that he was only seeking information not previously supplied in response to his earlier request.

Decision 159/2007: Mr Campbell Martin and North Ayrshire Council

15 Duty to provide advice and assistance

(1) **A Scottish public authority must, so far as it is reasonable to expect it to do so, provide advice and assistance to a person who proposes to make, or has made, a request for information to it.**

1.129   This is a particularly significant provision. It places a duty on an authority to provide advice and assistance to someone who proposes to make, or has made, an information request to it. It is expected that the authority will be helpful, not just dutifully compliant (far less deliberately unhelpful) when dealing with potential or current applicants. Many people will be unaware of their rights and how the law is being interpreted, so advantage should not be taken of shortcomings in their applications simply to refuse information. (The Court of Session has made it clear, for instance, that even if a request is invalid by virtue of not reasonably clearly describing the information being sought, then the onus is on the authority to offer advice and assistance to the applicant in framing a new request. The level of advice and assistance to be given will depend on the applicant.[73])

1.130   The Commissioner has found instances where authorities have been less than helpful, for instance:

- where it should have been clear to the authority what the applicant was looking for; reasonably straightforward for it to explain why it did not hold the requested document; and what other relevant information it did hold which may be of assistance to him.[74]
- even where the information requested would cost more than £600 to provide (and therefore there was no need to comply with the request) the authority should assist the applicant by advising what information could be made available free or for a fee if the terms of the request were narrowed.[75]

1.131   It should not be overlooked that the obligation to provide assistance also applies where a person *proposes* to make a request, so authorities should respond helpfully to telephone or personal enquiries, not just to written requests. The advice should be full and competent (for example, by helping the applicant to describe clearly the information

73 *Glasgow City Council and Dundee City Council v Scottish Information Commissioner* [2009] CSIH 73, para 78.
74 Decision 148/2009: Mr James Elder and East Lothian Council.
75 Decision 026/2006: Mr David Ewen of the *Evening Express* and Aberdeen City Council.

they want) such that a person acting upon it will be capable of submitting a request which is valid and to which the authority is in a position to respond.

Authorities can also assist and advise an applicant *after* a request has been received. As the Court of Session has made plain, authorities are expected to do so if the request does not describe the information wanted in a reasonably clear manner. Authorities may have been reticent about asking an applicant to describe more fully the information they wanted, particularly if it appeared that they were enquiring into the purpose to which the information would be put. Quite rightly, authorities have recognised that they cannot choose to withhold or disclose information, depending upon their view of the purpose, and in any case cannot oblige the applicant to give a reason for their request.

1.132

However, it may well be that the applicant is willing to explain why they want the information and in so doing this may help the authority to understand what specific information is being sought.

1.133

Duty to provide advice and assistance – s 15(2)

(2) **A Scottish public authority which, in relation to the pro-vision of advice or assistance in any case, conforms with the code of practice issued under section 60 is, as respects that case, to be taken to comply with the duty imposed by subsection (1).**

In dealing with information requests, public authorities must be aware of the requirements of what is often referred to as the "Section 60 Code". An updated version of the Code, incorporating guidance for dealing with requests under the EIRs, was published by the Ministers in December 2010 as the Scottish Ministers' Code of Practice on the Discharge of Functions by Scottish Public Authorities under the Freedom of Information (Scotland) Act 2002 and the Environmental Information (Scotland) Regulations 2004. It sets out recommended good practice on:

1.134

- providing advice and assistance and seeking clarification;
- transferring requests to other authorities;
- consulting with third parties;
- the disclosure of information relating to Contracts or Procurement Processes;
- handling reviews (complaints);

- collecting and recording statistics about handling information requests;
- proactively publishing information.

(See Appendix 3.)

Responses to request

16 Refusal of request

(1) **Subject to section 18, a Scottish public authority which, in relation to a request for information which it holds, to any extent claims that, by virtue of any provision of Part 2, the information is exempt information must, within the time allowed by or by virtue of section 10 for complying with the request, give the applicant a notice in writing (in this Act referred to as a "refusal notice") which –**
   (a) **discloses that it holds the information;**
   (b) **states that it so claims;**
   (c) **specifies the exemption in question; and**
   (d) **states (if not otherwise apparent) why the exemption applies.**

1.135 Where an authority is refusing to provide all or some of the information it holds, then it must give the applicant a refusal notice. This is not just a legal formality. It is an opportunity for the authority to explain to the applicant *why* they cannot be given the information requested. A well-written notice will often satisfy the applicant that their request has been properly considered and provide reasons for withholding the information which the applicant may find acceptable. A cursory refusal which fails to attempt to explain matters is simply likely to prompt a request for review or application to the Commissioner.

1.136 The notice must:

- inform the applicant that the authority holds the information requested;
- confirm that the authority is claiming that the information is exempt. (This may apply to only some of the information being requested, with other information being disclosed.)

1.137 It is not sufficient to claim simply that the information is exempt. The authority must specify which of the exemptions under Pt 2 applies. In so doing, the authority is expected to explain why the exemption applies. If, for example, s 25 applies because the information is otherwise reasonably accessible, then the authority would be expected to explain why it is accessible and where it can be found.

The refusal notice must be provided within 20 working days (or 30 days if it is a request to the Keeper of Records for information contained in records transferred to him from another authority). **1.138**

The only occasion when an authority need not provide a refusal notice in such terms is where, under s 18, the authority considers that to reveal whether the information exists or is so held would be contrary to the public interest. **1.139**

Refusal of request – s 16(2)

(2) Where the authority's claim is made only by virtue of a provision of Part 2 which does not confer absolute exemption, the notice must state the authority's reason for claiming that, in all the circumstances of the case, the public interest in maintaining the exemption outweighs that in disclosure of the information.

Where the exemption claimed is not absolute, ie other than where: **1.140**

- the information is otherwise accessible (s 25);
- there is a prohibition on disclosure (s 26);
- disclosure would constitute an actionable breach of confidence (s 36(2));
- the information is contained in court records (s 37); or
- it is personal information, except in very limited circumstances (s 38)

then the authority must explain why disclosure is not in the public interest.

Refusal of request – s 16(3)

(3) The authority is not obliged to make a statement under subsection (1)(d) in so far as the statement would disclose information which would itself be exempt information.

Clearly, the authority is not obliged to provide (and would wish to avoid providing) information by way of explanation which would reveal exempt information, for example revealing the identity of an individual whose personal information was being withheld. **1.141**

Refusal of request – s 16(4)

(4) A Scottish public authority which, in relation to a request for information, claims that section 12(1) applies must, within the time allowed by or by virtue of section 10 for complying with the request, give the applicant a notice which states that it so claims.

1.142   A refusal notice must also be given where the authority estimates that the cost of complying with the request is excessive under the provisions of s 12 (ie currently that it would exceed £600 as calculated by the Fees Regulations).

Refusal of request – s 16(5)

(5) A Scottish public authority which, in relation to such a request, claims that section 14 applies must, within that time, give the applicant a notice which states that it so claims; except that the notice need not be given if –
   (a) the authority has, in relation to a previous identical or substantially similar such request, given the applicant a notice under this subsection; and
   (b) it would in all the circumstances be unreasonable to expect it to serve a further such notice in relation to the current request.

1.143   Where the authority is refusing to comply with a request because it believes that it is vexatious or repeated then it must issue a refusal notice so claiming. It would be good practice to explain why the request is vexatious or repeated.

1.144   However, where the authority has previously issued a refusal notice in respect of an identical or substantially similar request, it need not issue another refusal notice if it believes that, in all the circumstances, it would be unreasonable to do so. (This is likely to apply relatively rarely, but it could be that the authority is subject to several repeat requests, the applicant having simply ignored previous refusal notices.)

Refusal of request – s 16(6)

(6) Subsections (1), (4) and (5) are subject to section 19.

1.145   Section 19 deals with the content of certain notices. It requires that a refusal notice give details of the authority's procedure for dealing with complaints about its handling of requests for information and also about the rights of application to the authority for review and to the Commissioner for a decision.

Responding to requests – getting it right first time

The key to making the legislation work in the best interests of applicants – and authorities – is making sure that proper responses are made to requests in the first instance. As a previous Lord Advocate has said: "Making the best possible decisions first time round will increase public confidence in the quality of decision making within Scotland's public authorities. A decision which has been properly made will also be better equipped to withstand scrutiny and challenge, whether by internal review or by external bodies."[76]

Getting it right first time is particularly important if the information requested is not going to be provided. The onus is on the authority to justify why it is not able to provide the information. This means that the various notices have to meet the requirements and expectations of the legislation. Yet, assessments carried out by the Commissioner have found that responses are often deficient in some respect.

The key elements of a refusal or other notice are:

- acknowledgement that a request has been made (often, an applicant will not be aware that their request comes within the ambit of the law);
- proper and full citation of any provision of the law which justifies not complying with the request (that means, for instance, identifying which subsection of an exemption is being applied);
- provision of an explanation as to why the exemption applies in the circumstances of that particular request;
- explanation of how the balance of the public interest favours withholding the information, where applicable. (The authority should indicate what factors it acknowledges favour disclosure and how these are outweighed by the public interest factors in maintaining an exemption);
- provision of the basis of calculation for any fees notice or notice of excessive cost (for example, including how many hours; for what purpose; at what rate; and/or the charge for copying per sheet); and

---

76 Rt Hon Eilish Angiolini, QC, Lord Advocate, *Right first time: A practical guide for public authorities in Scotland to decision-making and the law* (Scottish Government, February 2010) (http://www.scotland.gov.uk/Publications/2010/02/23134246/0).

> • letting the applicant know of their right of complaint, review or application to the Commissioner. (Assessments and investigations have shown that it is frequently the case that this final element is missing.)
>
> If this is done well, then the applicant is more likely to accept the outcome and the notice will meet the requirements of the law. As a result, fewer requests for review or application to the Commissioner will be made by aggrieved applicants (especially for technical deficiencies), reducing the burden on authorities.

17 Notice that information is not held

(1) Where –

    (a) a Scottish public authority receives a request which would require it either –

        (i) to comply with section 1(1); or

        (ii) to determine any question arising by virtue of paragraph (a) or (b) of section 2(1),

    if it held the information to which the request relates; but

    (b) the authority does not hold that information,

    it must, within the time allowed by or by virtue of section 10 for complying with the request, give the applicant notice in writing that it does not hold it.

(2) Subsection (1) is subject to section 19.

(3) Subsection (1) does not apply if, by virtue of section 18, the authority instead gives the applicant a refusal notice.

1.146 Where an authority does not hold the information requested it should not issue a refusal notice (except where it is applying the provisions of s 18 in the rare circumstances that to reveal whether or not the information is held would be contrary to the public interest).

1.147 Instead, it should issue a notice saying that it does not hold the information. This applies where the authority has never held or no longer holds the information. The notice has to provide details of the authority's procedure for dealing with complaints about its handling requests for information and also about the rights of application to the authority for review and to the Commissioner for a decision.

1.148 If the authority *does* know where the information is held it would be expected, under the s 15 duty to provide advice and assistance, to inform the applicant. (Under FOISA, there is no obligation on an authority to transfer the request to another which holds the information, but there is a requirement to do so under the EIRs or supply the name and address of the authority.)

18 Further provision as respects responses to request

(1) Where, if information existed and was held by a Scottish public authority, the authority could give a refusal notice under section 16(1) on the basis that the information was exempt information by virtue of any of sections 28 to 35, 39(1) or 41 but the authority considers that to reveal whether the information exists or is so held would be contrary to the public interest, it may (whether or not the information does exist and is held by it) give the applicant a refusal notice by virtue of this section.

This is sometimes referred to as the "neither confirm nor deny" provision. It applies where an authority believes that simply to confirm whether or not it holds the information requested would not be in the public interest.   1.149

Most cases dealt with by the Commissioner have concerned police authorities. Often, requests have been for details of surveillance activities or investigations which may or may not have been undertaken. The police have argued that to confirm or deny that such activities have been carried out would be contrary to the public interest. This is typified in submissions made to the Commissioner regarding a request for details of Special Branch files, in which the police contended that: 1.150

> "the existence of a file containing intelligence material relating to an individual or organisation is in itself information that could prove useful to that individual or organisation. The non-existence of such a file could also prove useful, as it would indicate the absence of police knowledge of (or activity relating to) the individual or organisation concerned. The Police consider that an approach of neither confirming nor denying whether such information exists or is held is, therefore, necessary and must be applied consistently if it is to be effective".[77]

However, it is not enough for the police or any other authority simply to state this case. It must also be demonstrated that one or more of   1.151

---

77 Decision 128/2006: Christine Grahame, MSP and the Chief Constables of Central Scotland Police, Dumfries and Galloway Constabulary, Grampian Police, Lothian and Borders Police, Northern Constabulary, Strathclyde Police and Tayside Police.

certain exemptions would apply to the information if it did exist. In the case of the police these are usually those exemptions relating to investigations by Scottish public authorities (s 34) or law enforcement (s 35).

1.152   The s 18 provision does not apply to personal information which would be exempt under s 38. (However, under the EIRs authorities can "neither confirm nor deny" whether they hold personal information[78] and the Scottish Ministers sought to do so in a case seeking information on representations made to Ministers by the Prince of Wales.[79])

Further provision as respects responses to request – s 18(2)

(2)   **Neither paragraph (a) of subsection (1) of section 16 nor subsection (2) of that section applies as respects a refusal notice given by virtue of this section.**

1.153   A public authority relying on s 18 must still issue to the applicant a refusal notice under s 16. However, because of the provisions of s 18, the refusal notice does not have to disclose whether it holds the information or specify why the public interest in maintaining the exemption listed in s 18(1) outweighs that in disclosure of the information. The public authority must explain why it would not be in the public interest for it to reveal whether the information exists or is held by it.

Content of certain notices

19 Content of certain notices

A notice under section 9(1) or 16(1), (4) or (5) (including a refusal notice given by virtue of section 18(1)) or 17(1) must contain particulars –

(a) of the procedure provided by the authority for dealing with complaints about the handling by it of requests for information; and

(b) about the rights of application to the authority and the Commissioner conferred by sections 20(1) and 47(1).

1.154   Where an authority issues a notice because it:

- intends to charge a fee;
- regards the cost of complying as excessive;

---

78   Regulation 11(6): Personal data.
79   Decision 039/2011: Mr Dominic Kennedy of *The Times* and the Scottish Ministers.

- claims that the information is exempt from disclosure;
- considers the request to be vexatious or repeated;
- does not hold the information; or
- wishes neither to confirm nor deny that it holds the information requested,

then the notice has to provide details of the authority's procedure   **1.155**
for dealing with complaints about the handling by it of requests for information and also about the rights of applicants to require the authority to review its decision and to apply to the Commissioner for a decision.

Review of refusal, etc.

20 Requirement for review of refusal etc.

(1) **An applicant who is dissatisfied with the way in which a Scottish public authority has dealt with a request for information made under this Part of this Act may require the authority to review its actions and decisions in relation to that request.**

Where an applicant is in *any* way dissatisfied with the way in which   **1.156**
their request for information has been dealt with, the legislation provides an internal appeal process which requires the authority to review its actions and decisions. Authorities should be aware that the dissatisfaction could be in respect of one or more of a number of issues, including:

- a failure to respond to the request;
- not responding in time;
- the basis on which exemptions have been applied to withhold information;
- the balance of public interest;
- a claim by the authority that the information is not held or, where information has been disclosed, that no other relevant information is held;
- the basis on which fees have been charged;
- the estimation that the cost of complying with the request would be excessive

Requirement for review of refusal etc. – s 20(2) and (3)

(2) **A requirement under subsection (1) is referred to in this Act as a "requirement for review".**

(3)   A requirement for review must –

   (a) be in writing or in another form which, by reason of its having some permanency, is capable of being used for subsequent reference (as, for example, a recording made on audio or video tape);

   (b) state the name of the applicant and an address for correspondence; and

   (c) specify –

      (i) the request for information to which the requirement for review relates; and

      (ii) the matter which gives rise to the applicant's dissatisfaction mentioned in subsection (1).

1.157   For a valid requirement for review to be made, the same provisions apply as for an original request. The applicant should identify for the authority the request for information about which they are concerned and the reasons for their dissatisfaction. There is no need to complete a special form or cite the legislation. The applicant cannot be required to submit the requirement for review to a named official.

1.158   The revised Code of Practice issued by Scottish Ministers states:

> "If, when notifying the applicant of their right to a review, the public authority has told them where they should direct a request for review, the public authority may reasonably expect those instructions to be followed. However, where an applicant fails to follow that procedure and sends the review request to the incorrect person and/or address, that does not invalidate the review request (provided the requirements of section 20(3) of FOISA are met)."[80]

1.159   Applicants do not have to use the term "requirement for review". If their dissatisfaction is plain in any correspondence relating to the request and the basis for that dissatisfaction is expressed then it can be said that a requirement for review has been made.

1.160   This is not always straightforward. Applicants may express dissatisfaction on a number of matters. At the same time, they may seek to modify their request in the light of the response by the authority (for example, by limiting the scope of the information sought to a more constrained time period). They may also express a wish for additional information prompted by the authority's response, which may constitute a new information request. However, authorities are

---

80 Scottish Ministers' Code of Practice on the Discharge of Functions by Scottish Public Authorities SG/2010/257, para 5.2.

expected to be alert to the fact that an expression of dissatisfaction is likely to constitute or contain a requirement for review.

Requirement for review of refusal etc. – s 20(4)

(4) For the purposes of paragraph (a) of subsection (3) (and without prejudice to the generality of that paragraph), a requirement for review is treated as made in writing where the text of the requirement is as mentioned in paragraphs (a) to (c) of section 8(2).

As with an original request, an applicant can submit a requirement for review electronically, for example by e-mail.   **1.161**

Requirement for review of refusal etc. – s 20(5)

(5) Subject to subsection (6), a requirement for review must be made by not later than the fortieth working day after –
   (a) the expiry of the time allowed by or by virtue of section 10 for complying with the request; or
   (b) in a case where the authority purports under this Act –
      (i) to comply with a request for information; or
      (ii) to give the applicant a fees notice, a refusal notice or a notice under section 17(1) that information is not held,
   but does so outwith that time, the receipt by the applicant of the information provided or, as the case may be, the notice.

Applicants have effectively 8 weeks (up to "the fortieth working day") to make a requirement for review. The time from which this period starts depends on the circumstances of the case.   **1.162**

Where the applicant receives a response from the authority which is said to comply with the request or receives a refusal notice etc, the 40-working-day period starts from the date of receipt of that response.   **1.163**

If no response is received, the period starts from the expiry of the 20th working day within which the authority should have complied with the original request.   **1.164**

However, if the applicant receives a response from the authority after the 20 working days, either giving information by which it claims to be complying with the request, or serving one of a number of notices, then the 40 working days for an applicant to make a request for review   **1.165** start from the receipt of the information or notice. (If, prior to receipt of this late information, the applicant has already submitted a request for review, then this section does not apply.)

Requirement for review of refusal etc. – s 20(6)

(6) A Scottish public authority may comply with a requirement for review made after the expiry of the time allowed by subsection (5) for making such a requirement if it considers it appropriate to do so.

1.166   The authority, at its own discretion, can accept and respond to a requirement for review made beyond the 40th working day. (This is not the case, however, under the EIRs, where reg 16(2) requires representations to be made by "no later than 40 working days" and does not confer any discretion on the authority.)

Requirement for review of refusal etc. – s 20(7)

(7) The Scottish Ministers may by regulations provide that subsections (5) and (6) are to have effect as if the reference in subsection (5) to the fortieth working day were a reference to such other working day as is specified in (or determined in accordance with) the regulations.

1.167   No provision has been made to alter the period, which remains at 40 working days.

Requirement for review of refusal etc. – s 20(8) and (9)

(8) Regulations under subsection (7) may –
     (a) prescribe different days in relation to different cases; and
     (b) confer a discretion on the Scottish Information Commissioner.
(9) In subsection (1), the reference to "actions" and "decisions" includes inaction and failure to reach a decision.

1.168   Where an authority simply fails to act on or respond to a request for information or review, this is sometimes called a "mute or deemed refusal". There is no onus on applicants to send a reminder to the authority if they have not received a proper response within the relevant time. They can make a requirement for review regarding this lack of action or failure to reach a decision (where, for example, the authority has been in touch about the request but has still failed to provide all of the information or serve a notice).

If, after receipt of this requirement for review, the authority sub-   1.169
sequently provides a substantive response to the original request (ie by providing the information or issuing a notice) it has forfeited the right to require the applicant to make a further requirement for review before referring the matter to the Commissioner. If the applicant is dissatisfied with the substantive response they are entitled to make an application directly to the Commissioner.

Late response to a request becomes *de facto* a response to a requirement for review

When, in late August 2009, an applicant had still not received a response from Strathclyde Police to a request, made over 2 months earlier, for information relating to a police investigation, she submitted a requirement for review. Almost by return, the police replied, providing a substantive response to her original request – which was a notice under s 18 neither confirming nor denying that the information was held. The applicant was invited to make a requirement for review if she was dissatisfied. Instead, the applicant applied to the Commissioner for a decision. The Commissioner accepted this as a valid application on the basis that Strathclyde Police's response, given after the applicant had required a review, complied with one of the possible outcomes of a review as set out in s 21(4) of FOISA, in that the authority had reached a decision where none had been made before. That being the case, the applicant was free to apply directly to the Commissioner.

Decision 017/2010: Ms Jessie Gilmour and Strathclyde Police

---

21 Review by Scottish public authority

(1) Subject to subsection (2), a Scottish public authority receiving a requirement for review must (unless that requirement is withdrawn or is as mentioned in subsection (8)) comply promptly; and in any event by not later than the twentieth working day after receipt by it of the requirement.

The same 20-working-day timescale applies to complying with require-   1.170
ments for reviews as for requests for information. The applicant may

withdraw the requirement for review, in which case the authority need not comply.

Review by Scottish public authority – s 21(2)

(2) If –
   (a) the authority is the Keeper of the Records of Scotland; and
   (b) a different authority is, by virtue of section 22(4), to review a decision to which the requirement relates,
   subsection (1) applies with the substitution, for the reference to the twentieth working day, of a reference to the thirtieth working day.

1.171   The Keeper has 30 working days to comply with a requirement for a review which relates to a request for information contained in records which have been transferred to him from another Scottish public authority. The extended timescale recognises that, as the decision on the original request for information will have been made by the authority, in turn the review of that decision will have to be made by it, the outcome of which has then to be communicated to the Keeper.

Review by Scottish public authority – s 21(3)

(3) A requirement for review may be withdrawn by the applicant who made it, by notice in writing to the authority, at any time before the authority makes its decision on the requirement.

1.172   The requirement for review may be withdrawn, for instance where the authority belatedly supplies the information originally requested, or where the authority takes some other action following receipt of the requirement for review.

Review by Scottish public authority – s 21(4)

(4) The authority may, as respects the request for information to which the requirement relates –
   (a) confirm a decision complained of, with or without such modifications as it considers appropriate;
   (b) substitute for any such decision a different decision; or
   (c) reach a decision, where the complaint is that no decision had been reached.

The purpose of a review is not simply to consider whether the   1.173
original decision was reasonable in its conclusions. The review is an
opportunity for the authority to consider its decision afresh. It can take
into account any change of circumstance since the original decision –
for example, where the passage of time (which could be several weeks)
has altered the basis on which information has been withheld. It can
reflect on whether the appropriate exemptions have been claimed – it
can abandon any or all of those originally claimed or apply others not
previously claimed. In that respect the review can come to the same
decision, or come to an entirely different conclusion in full or in part.

Review by authority

The opportunity for the authority to review its original decision is
an important feature of the FOI appeal process. Essentially, it allows
the authority to remedy or address failures in compliance and to
think again as to whether the application of exemptions, fees etc is
justified. The importance of this internal appeal step is clear when
it is appreciated that the applicant cannot make an application to
the Commissioner without first requiring the authority to conduct a
review. (More than a quarter of the cases closed by the Commissioner
without investigation are because the applicant had not made a
request for review.[81])

Yet authorities frequently fail to inform applicants of their right
of review when withholding information, or fail to conduct reviews
when required.

FOISA does not specify how a review is to be carried out but it is
good practice for it to be conducted by a person who did not take
the original decision which gave rise to the requirement for review.[82]
Usually the review is best conducted by an official or officials of
sufficient seniority to override the original decision, for example
permitting the release of information previously withheld. However
seniority is not sufficient – the reviewer(s) should be familiar with the
legislation and preferably be aware of precedent.

If the applicant subsequently appeals to the Commissioner, it is
the decision taken at review which the Commissioner will investigate.
It is important that the reasoning behind any review decision is
documented and retained by the authority.

---

81 *Scottish Information CommissionerAnnual Report 2009*, p 9.
82 Code of Practice (December 2010), para 5.4: "The review should, where practicable, be
    handled by staff who were not involved in the original decision."

Review by Scottish public authority – s 21(5)

(5) Within the time allowed by subsection (1) for complying with the requirement for review, the authority must give the applicant notice in writing of what it has done under subsection (4) and a statement of its reasons for so doing.

1.174   Within 20 working days the authority must tell the applicant of the outcome of the review and why it has come to its decision. It must also carry out any actions which are required by its decision, for example disclosure of information, within that timescale.

Review by Scottish public authority – s 21(6) and (7)

(6) The Scottish Ministers may by regulations provide that subsections (1) and (5) and section 47(4)(b) are to have effect as if the reference in subsection (1) to the twentieth (or as the case may be the thirtieth) working day were a reference to such other working day as is specified in (or determined in accordance with) the regulations.

(7) Regulations under subsection (6) may –
   (a) prescribe different days in relation to different cases; and
   (b) confer a discretion on the Scottish Information Commissioner.

1.175   To date, no regulations have been made under s 21(6) and so the 20-day timescale for responding to a requirement for review (or 30 days when the request for review is to the Keeper) remain in place.

Review by Scottish public authority – s 21(8)

(8) Subsection (1) does not oblige a Scottish public authority to comply with a requirement for review if –
   (a) the requirement is vexatious; or
   (b) the request for information to which the requirement for review relates was one with which, by virtue of section 14, the authority was not obliged to comply.

1.176   An authority does not have to carry out a review if it regards the requirement for that review as vexatious (even though the original request for information was not held to be vexatious).

1.177   Furthermore, the review need not be conducted if it relates to a request for information which was held to be vexatious or was identical or substantially similar to a previous request which had been complied with.

Review by Scottish public authority – s 21(9)

(9) **Where the authority considers that paragraph (a) or (b) of subsection (8) applies, it must give the applicant who made the requirement for review notice in writing, within the time allowed by subsection (1) for complying with that requirement, that it so claims.**

An authority which does not intend to comply with a requirement for review because it regards it as vexatious or it relates to a request for information which in itself was held to be vexatious or repeated cannot simply ignore the applicant. It must write to the applicant within 20 working days, saying that it is not obliged to comply.   1.178

Review by Scottish public authority – s 21(10)

(10) **A notice under subsection (5) or (9) must contain particulars about the rights of application to the Commissioner and of appeal conferred by sections 47(1) and 56.**

Whatever response the authority has given – whether to confirm the original decision, or substitute a fresh one or claim that it does not have to comply with the requirement for review at all – it must inform the applicant of their right to appeal to the Commissioner and of their subsequent right of appeal to the Court of Session on a point of law.   1.179

22 Special provisions relating to records transferred to Keeper

(1) **Subsections (2) to (5) apply to information which –**
     (a) **is contained in a record transferred to the Keeper of the Records of Scotland by a Scottish public authority; and**
     (b) **has not been designated by the authority as open information for the purposes of this section.**

These special provisions apply to records transferred to the Keeper by another Scottish public authority. They do not apply to records transferred or obtained from a UK authority or commercial body or private individual. A "record" here can be taken to mean information transferred for archival purposes.   1.180

Special provisions relating to records transferred to Keeper – s 22(2)

(2) The Keeper must, as soon as practicable after receiving a request for information to which this subsection applies, send a copy of that request to the authority which transferred the information; and it is for the authority, instead of the Keeper, to come to a decision as to whether the information is exempt information by virtue of any provision of Part 2 and to determine any question then arising by virtue of paragraph (a) or (b) of section 2(1) as respects the information.

1.181   If the Keeper receives a request for information which, in full or in part, relates to information contained within a record transferred by another Scottish public authority, the Keeper must transfer that request to the authority "as soon as practicable". It is for that authority to determine that the information is exempt under Pt 2, in which case, if the exemption is not absolute, it must determine whether the public interest in disclosing the information is outweighed by that in maintaining the exemption.

Special provisions relating to records transferred to Keeper – s 22(3)

(3) After receiving the copy, the authority must, within such time as will make it practicable for the Keeper to comply with section 10 as respects the request, inform the Keeper of the decision mentioned in subsection (2) and of any determination required by virtue of that decision.

1.182   Whatever view it takes, the authority does not communicate its decision to the applicant, but instead must inform the Keeper who in turn will inform the applicant. In all of this, both the Keeper and the authority have to act in a timely manner, mindful of the requirement for the Keeper to meet the timescales set down in the legislation. However, in recognition of the delays which may result from following these special provisions, the Keeper has 30 working days, not 20, to comply with the request.

Special provisions relating to records transferred to Keeper – s 22(4)

(4) The Keeper must, as soon as practicable after receiving a requirement for review in which the specification under

section 20(3)(c)(ii) relates to a decision made by the authority by virtue of subsection (2), send a copy of that requirement to the authority; and it is for the authority, instead of the Keeper, to review the decision and to do anything which is to be done under section 21(4).

The same procedure is to be followed if the Keeper receives a requirement for review, expressing dissatisfaction with a decision which was made by the transferring authority. In this case the timescale allowed is again extended to 30 working days.(If the dissatisfaction is to do with some other matter, for example the time taken to respond to the request, or a fees notice, then it is for the Keeper, not the authority, to comply with the requirement for review and to do so within the normal 20 working days.) **1.183**

Special provisions relating to records transferred to Keeper – s 22(5)

(5) After receiving the requirement, the authority must, within such time as will make it practicable for the Keeper to comply with subsection (5) of section 21 as respects the requirement, inform the Keeper of what it has done under subsection (4) of that section and provide a statement of its reasons for so doing; and it is that information and statement which the Keeper shall, in the notice in writing, give in so complying.

It is for the authority which has transferred the records to: **1.184**

- confirm a decision complained of (with or without modifications); or
- come to a different decision, in substitution for the original decision; or
- reach a decision where the complaint is that it had failed to do so.

Special provisions relating to records transferred to Keeper – s 22(6)

(6) Subsections (2) to (5) also apply to information which is contained in a record transferred to the Keeper, before 1st July 1999, by the Secretary of State for Scotland and is not designated by the Scottish Ministers as open information for the purposes of section 3(4); but for the purposes of that application references in subsections (2) to (5) to "the

authority" are to be construed as references to the Scottish
Ministers.

1.185   Although the Secretary of State for Scotland is now, as part of the UK
Government, subject to FOIA and not FOISA, a request for information
in records transferred by the Secretary of State to the Keeper *prior* to
devolution falls within the scope of these special provisions. In this
case the Keeper shall send a copy of the request not to the current
Secretary of State, but to the Scottish Ministers who must come to a
decision on whether the information is exempt. Similarly, the Scottish
Minsters would be asked by the Keeper to confirm that decision or come
to some other if a subsequent requirement for review was received.[83]

Do requests to the Keeper which are vexatious or with which it would be excessively costly to comply have to be transferred?

The decision as to whether information transferred to the Keeper by a public authority (which is not designated as open) is exempt and where the public interest lies is a matter for the public authority.

However, the only issue for the transferring authority to determine is whether the information is subject to an exemption contained in Pt 2 of FOISA. It is for the Keeper to determine whether a fees notice should be issued, whether the request is vexatious or repeated or whether the cost of complying with it would be excessive.

In normal circumstances, where an authority determined that it did not have to comply with the request for any of these reasons, it would not then have to consider whether the information was exempt. Yet, by virtue of these special provisions, even where the Keeper would not intend to comply with the request (because it is vexatious etc), it would appear that s 22(2) requires that a copy of request be forwarded for exemptions to be considered: "The Keeper *must*, as soon as practicable after receiving a request for information to which this subsection applies send a copy of that request to the authority which transferred the information."

Such a case appears not yet to have arisen.

---

83 Many of the functions and responsibilities of the Scottish Office were devolved to the Scottish Executive and the Scottish Parliament under the terms of the Scotland Act 1998. Some reserved matters and other functions are conducted by the Scotland Office (a constituent office of the UK Government's Ministry of Justice), which was established on 1 July 1999, with the Minister responsible retaining the title of "Secretary of State for Scotland".

Publication schemes

23 Publication schemes

(1) A Scottish public authority must –
   (a) adopt and maintain a scheme (in this Act referred to as a "publication scheme") which relates to the publication of information by the authority and is approved by the Commissioner;
   (b) publish information in accordance with that scheme; and
   (c) from time to time review that scheme.

Published information is that which is readily available to anyone at the point of request – it should not have to be created in response to the request.   1.186

The requirement on authorities to adopt and maintain a publication scheme was clearly intended to ensure that a proactive approach was taken to the provision of information, especially that of wide interest, rather than simply responding to individual information requests.   1.187

Although the onus is on authorities to draw up their own schemes (sometimes called "bespoke" schemes to distinguish them from model publication schemes) and in so doing determine what commitments to publication they will make, the Commissioner has taken a robust approach to the approval of schemes. This has included setting out a timetable to receive schemes and indicating what elements are expected to be included in submitted schemes. Approval has been for a time-limited period.   1.188

Publication schemes – s 23(2)(a)

(2) A publication scheme must specify –
   (a) classes of information which the authority publishes or intends to publish;

There is no definition in the legislation of what constitutes a "class" of information. However, it was not intended that publication schemes should be a catalogue or index of all material published. A class is a descriptor of information by coherent type of content, often reflecting functions within the authority or a strand of governance. The class may be amplified by sub-classes of documents which clearly indicate the nature of the information which is published. So, for example, the class could be "Human resources" with sub-classes such as "Policies,   1.189

procedures and other documents for recruiting, managing and developing staff" and "Details of jobs, responsibilities, rewards and benefits".

Publication schemes – s 23(2)(b)

(b) the manner in which information of each class is, or is intended to be, published;
and

1.190   The information may be, for example:

- commercially printed in bulk;
- photocopied for distribution;
- printed from an electronic file on request.

1.191   Much of the information contained in publication scheme classes should be capable of being published online for the public to locate and download directly. (Authorities are expected to ensure, however, that they have adequate provision in place to support people who are unable to access web-based information.)

Publication schemes – s 23(2)(c)

(c) whether the published information is, or is intended to be, available to the public free of charge or on payment.

1.192   Authorities are guided to specify in their publication schemes the charges, or the basis of the charges, which will be applied to information in the scheme. This provides the public with a guide to what to expect when requesting information. (If individual charges or the full charging policy appear unreasonable, the Commissioner may refuse to approve a publication scheme.)

Publication schemes – s 23(3)

(3) In adopting or reviewing its publication scheme the authority must have regard to the public interest in –
(a) allowing public access to information held by it and in particular to information which –
(i) relates to the provision of services by it, the cost to it of providing them or the standards attained by services so provided; or
(ii) consists of facts, or analyses, on the basis of which decisions of importance to the public have been made by it;
(b) the publication of reasons for decisions made by it.

Parliament was wary of specifying what should be published and   1.193
included in a scheme but has clearly indicated that particular attention
should be given to information which assists the public in knowing
and understanding how significant decisions have been taken, how
services are performing and the costs involved in providing those
services. Having regard to the public interest includes considering
the publication of information of specific interest to sectors such as
trade unions and employees, users and providers of services, voluntary
organisations etc.

Public interest may be expressed in frequent requests for the same   1.194
information. Although these may initially be dealt with under s 1 of
FOISA, authorities should consider publishing information which is
frequently requested of them.

Publication schemes – s 23(4) and (5)

(4) The authority must publish its publication scheme but
     may do so in such manner as it thinks fit.
(5) The Commissioner may –
     (a) when approving a publication scheme, provide that
         the approval expires at the end of a specified period;
         and
     (b) at any time give notice to an authority revoking, as
         from the end of the period of six months beginning at
         that time, approval of its publication scheme.

Schemes are usually approved for a period of 4 years. Certain revisions   1.195
to the scheme within that period can be made. Where these changes
are substantive (for example, removing a class of information which
is no longer to be published; or adding a new class for which a charge
for the information is to be made) then authorities need to secure the
prior approval of the Commissioner.

Publication schemes – 23(6)

(6) The Commissioner, when –
     (a) refusing to approve a proposed publication scheme; or
     (b) revoking approval of a publication scheme,
     must state the reason for doing so.

The Commissioner has not, to date, refused to approve any publication   1.196
scheme, or revoked any current scheme. However, an authority may

be without an approved scheme where the approval for a scheme has lapsed and a new scheme was not yet been approved, for example because the Commissioner was not satisfied with its provisions. In such cases the authority is without a functioning scheme within the scope of this section. (The issues concerning publication schemes and the initiative taken by the Commissioner to encourage a move away from bespoke schemes to a single model scheme is considered more fully in Chapter 11 (Publication Schemes).)

24 Model publication schemes

(1) **The Commissioner may, in relation to Scottish public authorities falling within particular classes –**
   (a) **prepare and approve model publication schemes; or**
   (b) **approve such schemes prepared by other persons.**

1.197   Model publication schemes are schemes which have a common framework which can be adopted by one or more public authorities with very similar functions (for example, general medical practitioners, or police services). The Commissioner has the power to develop model schemes or to approve model schemes which have been submitted by other parties. Once a model scheme is approved, it can be adopted by any authority which falls within its scope.

1.198   The expected benefits of a model scheme are:

- a high common standard across authorities in a sector;
- ease of adoption by authorities; and
- a consistent approach to the publication of information across a sector.

1.199   Model schemes have been approved for:

- NHS Health Boards;
- general dental practitioners;
- general practitioners;
- community pharmacists;
- assessors;
- Chief Constables of police forces in Scotland;
- Fire and Rescue Boards;
- local authorities;
- Scottish further education institutions;
- Scottish higher education institutions;
- Joint Valuation Boards.

In 2011, the Commissioner published a "single model scheme" for   1.200
adoption by bodies listed in Pt 7 of Sch 1 to FOISA (which includes non-
departmental public bodies) and publicly owned companies. A single
model suitable for adoption will be made available to other sectors as
their current schemes expire.

Model publication schemes – s 24(2)

(2) If an authority which falls within the class to which an
    approved model publication scheme relates adopts that
    scheme without modification, no further approval of the
    Commissioner is required so long as that model scheme
    remains approved; but the approval of the Commissioner
    is required in relation to any modification of the scheme
    by an authority.

If the scheme is adopted by the authority "off the shelf" then the   1.201
specific approval of the Commissioner is not required. Instead,
authorities need simply notify the Commissioner that they have
adopted the scheme.

Some authorities have, however, broadly adopted model schemes,   1.202
but then modified (by adding to, altering or deleting) the approved
model provisions. In such cases the authority has to submit the
modifications for approval.

Model publication schemes – s 24(3)

(3) The Commissioner may –
    (a) when approving a model publication scheme, provide
        that the approval expires at the end of a specified
        period; and
    (b) at any time publish, in such manner as the Commis-
        sioner thinks fit, a notice revoking, as from the end
        of the period of six months beginning at that time,
        approval of such a scheme.

The Commissioner approves model schemes for 4 years.   1.203

Model publication schemes – s 24(4)

(4) The Commissioner, when –
    (a) refusing to approve –
        (i) under subsection (1)(b), a proposed model scheme;
            or

(ii) any such modification as is mentioned in sub-
        section (2),
    must state the reason for doing so; or
(b) revoking approval of a model publication scheme,
        must include in the notice under subsection (3)(b) a
        statement of the reason for doing so.

Part 2

EXEMPT INFORMATION

25 Information otherwise accessible

(1) **Information which the applicant can reasonably obtain
        other than by requesting it under section 1(1) is exempt
        information.**

1.204   This is an absolute exemption. If it applies, there is no need to consider
        the "public interest" test and it lasts in perpetuity (ie it is applicable
        regardless of the age of the information sought).

1.205   Subsection (1) sets out the basic exemption and confirms that
        information which an applicant can reasonably obtain other than
        by making an information request for it is exempt. Subsections (2)
        and (3) expand on this, and give examples of when information is
        deemed to be reasonably obtainable, most noticeably as a result of
        being contained in an authority's publication scheme and when
        information *may be* reasonably obtainable. (These are addressed in
        more detail below.)

1.206   Unless the conditions in subss (2) or (3) apply, this exemption
        requires a judgement as to what is reasonably obtainable by the
        particular applicant. In this respect, it is far from being "applicant
        blind" in that the circumstances of the applicant may mean that this
        exemption can be claimed in response to requests from some, but not
        others, who have asked for the same information. Most obviously, an
        individual applicant may have already been provided with or be known
        to hold a copy of the information requested whereas another may not.
        On the other hand, information which may be readily available to most
        people may not be available to certain applicants, for example someone
        with no ability to access information which is only made available on
        the website of an authority.

The clear purpose of this exemption is not to withhold information,   1.207
but to point the applicant to where the information can be readily
found. It should not be used by an authority to deflect a request
for information it holds towards another authority if it can only be
obtained from that other authority by making a s 1 request under
FOISA.

If authorities intend to claim this exemption it is not enough to   1.208
assert that the information is in the public domain or on a website
(whether that of the authority or some other body). Rather, the
authority should, by virtue of its duty under s 15, direct the applicant
to where the information can be found.

Information otherwise accessible – s 25(2)(a)

(2) For the purposes of subsection (1), information –
   (a) may be reasonably obtainable even if payment is
       required for access to it;

Information which is held by the public authority *may* be covered by   1.209
this exemption if it can reasonably be obtained without making a s 1(1)
request, even if this requires the information to be paid for. For instance,
if the information requested is a book or map, it may be reasonably
obtainable by commercially purchasing it elsewhere. The onus is on
the authority is to demonstrate that it is reasonably obtainable at the
time of the request.

Information otherwise accessible – s 25(2)(b)

(b) is to be taken to be reasonably obtainable if –
   (i) the Scottish public authority which holds it, or any
       other person, is obliged by or under any enactment
       to communicate it (otherwise than by making it
       available for inspection) to; or
   (ii) the Keeper of the Records of Scotland holds it and
       makes it available for inspection and (in so far as
       practicable) copying by,
   members of the public on request, whether free of charge
   or on payment.

Subsection (2)(b) sets out some circumstances in which information   1.210
is covered by the exemption. The provision in subs 2(b)(i) concerning information which an authority is "obliged by or under
any enactment to communicate" would apply, for example, to the

antisocial behaviour strategies of local authorities (which they are required to publish under the Antisocial Behaviour etc (Scotland) Act 2004). ("Any enactment" refers to primary legislation (Acts of the Scottish Parliament and Acts of the UK Parliament) and secondary legislation (orders, rules or regulations, also often known as statutory instruments, made under an Act of Parliament.) However, the exemption will not automatically apply to any such information made available for inspection only.

1.211   Any information held by the Keeper of the Records of Scotland (ie by the National Archives of Scotland) which is made available to members of the public for inspection and (in so far as practicable) copying, is deemed to be exempt under s 25, *even* if it would not be practical for someone to visit the National Archives to obtain a copy of the information.

Information otherwise accessible – s 25(3)

(3) **For the purposes of subsection (1), information which does not fall within paragraph (b) of subsection (2) is not, merely because it is available on request from the Scottish public authority which holds it, reasonably obtainable unless it is made available in accordance with the authority's publication scheme and any payment required is specified in, or determined in accordance with, the scheme.**

1.212   A Court of Session opinion had this to say:

"Section 25(3) does not readily yield its meaning, but becomes clearer if its clauses are put in a different order: information which does not fall within subsection (2)(b) is not reasonably obtainable by the applicant merely because the information is available on request from the public authority which holds it, unless it is made available in accordance with the authority's publication scheme and any payment required is specified in, or determined in accordance with, the scheme."[84]

1.213   Under subs (3), information is not deemed to be reasonably obtainable merely because it is available on request from a public authority, but it will be deemed to be reasonably obtainable if it is made available in accordance with the authority's publication scheme. A charge may be

---

84 *Glasgow City Council and Dundee City Council v Scottish Information Commissioner* [2009] CSIH 73.

made for the information, but any charges made must be provided for by the scheme.

If a public authority refuses a request for information on the ground that it is otherwise accessible, it should send the applicant a refusal notice which acknowledges that it holds the information and explains why the exemption applies. (For information on refusal notices, see s 16.) Before doing so, the authority should have established that the information the applicant has asked for is in fact available elsewhere, or it should otherwise be able to show why it believes the information is "reasonably obtainable". The authority should not assume that the applicant will know where and how the information can otherwise be obtained, and if the information is already publicly available (for example, under other legislation) the authority should tell the applicant how to access it. In all cases the authority should bear in mind its general duty to provide advice and assistance to applicants (see s 15). **1.214**

26 Prohibitions on disclosure

Information is exempt information if its disclosure by a Scottish public authority (otherwise than under this Act) –

(a) is prohibited by or under an enactment;

(b) is incompatible with a Community obligation; or

(c) would constitute, or be punishable as, a contempt of court.

This is an absolute exemption, so, if it applies, there is no need to consider the "public interest" test. It lasts in perpetuity with the consequence that it applies regardless of the age of the information sought, so long as the enactment prohibiting disclosure is still in place. **1.215**

Prohibited by enactment

There is no helpful list of enactments prohibiting disclosure (an "enactment" being any primary or secondary legislation of the UK Parliament or Scottish Parliament). However, measures have been taken to remove statutory bars in the following legislation: **1.216**

- Factories Act 1961;
- Offices, Shops and Railway Premises Act 1963;
- Medicines Act 1968;

- Health and Safety at Work etc Act 1974;
- Diseases of Fish Act 1983.[85]

1.217   An authority that uses s 26(a) to justify withholding information in response to an FOI request will be expected to state in the refusal notice what enactment applies and which specific provision within that enactment (section, subsection or paragraph number) prohibits disclosure.

1.218   Some prohibitions on disclosure are wide ranging, for example prohibiting the disclosure of information obtained in the course of their duties by bodies established to deal with complaints. The prohibition applies whether or not there would be any adverse consequence resulting from disclosure or whether it may be thought that disclosing information derived from casework is in the public interest. Both the Scottish Public Services Ombudsman ("SPSO") and the Scottish Criminal Cases Review Commission ("SCCRC") have successfully argued that specific provisions of the enactments concerning their functions absolutely prohibit disclosure.[86]

1.219   In determining whether disclosure is prohibited, in practice, a key factor has been whether or not the prohibition is absolute or whether there is discretion, even in limited circumstances, to disclose information and the circumstances in which such discretion can be used.

1.220   In the SPSO and SCCRC cases above, the legislation did allow information to be disclosed but only in specified circumstances (which did not apply in those cases) so the prohibition still applied.

General duty to comply with FOISA does not override statutory prohibition

In 2006, Dumfries and Galloway Council appealed a decision by the Commissioner ordering it to disclose information which it had withheld under s 26(a). The authority claimed that Pt 9 of the Enterprise Act (EA) prohibited it from disclosing the information.

The Commissioner had taken the view that, because the Council had a discretion to disclose information under the EA for the purpose

---

85   SSI 2008/339: http://www.opsi.gov.uk/legislation/scotland/ssi2008/ssi_20080339_en_1.
86   Decision 031/2010: Mr Arthur McFarlane and the Scottish Public Services Ombudsman; and Decision 134/2008: Mr Bill Kidd, MSP and the Scottish Criminal Cases Review Commission.

of facilitating the exercise of a statutory function of that authority (ie complying with FOISA), the prohibition did not apply. The Court of Session disagreed, and found that, to the extent that any part of the EA afforded the authority discretion over its actions, such discretion had to be carried out in a manner consistent with s 237 of the EA, which "expressly prohibits disclosure of that information. In that event, exercise of a power or performance of a duty under FOISA to disclose that information would be inconsistent with the provisions of Part 9".[87]

The outcome can be different where there is a general discretionary power which allows the authority to choose whether or not to disclose information which is otherwise prohibited.   1.221

For example, the Scottish Ministers argued that the Agriculture Act 1947 prohibited the disclosure of information obtained under other sections of the 1947 Act (which allow the Ministers to require that farmers provide them with certain information). However, the Commissioner noted that s 80(c) of the 1947 Act allowed limited information (including details of farm owners) to be disclosed, provided that the Ministers considered disclosure of that information to be in the public interest. Given this discretion, he concluded that there was no prohibition on the disclosure of the information and the exemption in s 26(a) could not apply.[88]   1.222

(This distinction between an outright prohibition and a discretionary power is also drawn by commentators discussing the equivalent UK provision: s 44 of FOIA. They observe that "there is no scope for continued reliance on statutory provisions which give the public authority a discretion whether to disclose information or not"[89] and "if an enactment, Community obligation, rule of court or court order only gives a public authority a discretion as to whether or not to disclose certain information, the information will not be exempt under Section 44".[90])   1.223

It is important to note that there is no equivalent provision in the Environmental Information Regulations regarding prohibitions on disclosure. Determining whether information is environmental or not can have a very significant bearing upon whether it can be disclosed   1.224

87   *Dumfries and Galloway Council v Scottish Information Commissioner* [2008] CSIH 12.
88   Decision 132/2007: Mr John Stewart and the Scottish Executive.
89   P Coppel, *Information Rights* (2004), p 695.
90   Macdonald and Jones, *The Law of Freedom of Information* (2003), p 172.

(as the case study in Chapter 2 concerning disclosure of information about an Orkney fish farm makes clear).

Incompatible with Community obligation

1.225   "Community obligation" means an obligation created by, or arising under, any of the European Union (EU) Treaties, whether enforceable or not. Treaty articles, European Directives, Regulations and Decisions are all examples of Community obligations. (By contrast, the Convention for the Protection of Human Rights and Fundamental Freedoms is not a Community obligation as it is an initiative of the Council of Europe.)

1.226   So far, the Commissioner has not upheld the application of this exemption in the few cases which have come to him. All of these have concerned the Scottish Ministers, who have sought to withhold details of payments made under various integrated administration and control systems for certain Community aid schemes. Ministers argued that they were obliged to withhold details of payments under the Common Agricultural Policy and the Farm Woodland Premium Scheme, under a Council Regulation which states, in relation to information of this type, that "The member states shall take all measures necessary to ensure the protection of the data collected".[91] However, the Commissioner took the view that the obligation applied to data provided in the aid applications, not to information regarding payments made in respect of such applications, and, having concluded that disclosure would not contravene any of the data protection principles, determined that the exemption did not apply.[92]

Contempt of court

1.227   Contempt of court includes:

- statutory contempts regulated by the Contempt of Court Act 1981 (the "1981 Act") which prohibits disclosure of information that would prejudice the administration of justice once proceedings are "active". For example, it is likely to be contempt of court for an authority which, knowing that proceedings have been instituted

---

91   Council Regulation EEC 3508/92, Arts 9 and 9a.
92   See Decision 224/2006: Mr Alex Gordon-Duff and the Scottish Executive. The disclosure of information about CAP payments etc under the European Directive which required the publication of the names of recipients of aid (brought into force after these decisions of the Commissioner were issued) has been the subject of a judgment by the European Court of Justice: *Volker und Markus Schecke GbR v Land Hessen* (C-92/09 and C-93/09).

against someone, discloses information that is likely to prejudice those proceedings. (Statutory contempts of court, being covered by an enactment, could be exempt under either s 26(a) or (c));

- common law contempts which cover a wide variety of actions not covered by the 1981 Act. The most relevant here are the failure to obey an order of any court, whether criminal or civil; and publication of information where court proceedings are not yet "active" but imminent. The public authority will usually have to wilfully or deliberately flout judicial authority to be punished for contempt of court under common law, ie the publisher of the information must be shown to have intended to impede or prejudice the administration of justice. An authority which knowingly discloses information in the face of a court order, in response to a request under FOISA, is likely to show sufficient intent.

Contempt of court is a concept covering not only courts but a range   **1.228**
of tribunals or bodies "exercising the judicial power of the state". This definition includes justice of the peace courts, sheriff courts, the High Court of Justiciary and the Court of Session. Other bodies that have been judged to fall under the scope of contempt legislation include the children's hearings system, the Mental Health Review Tribunal and employment tribunals.

As yet, no cases citing contempt of court have come before the   **1.229**
Commissioner.

27 Information intended for future publication

(1) Information is exempt information if –
  (a) it is held with a view to its being published by –
    (i) a Scottish public authority; or
    (ii) any other person,
  at a date not later than twelve weeks after that on which the request for the information is made;
  (b) when that request is made the information is already being held with that view; and
  (c) it is reasonable in all the circumstances that the information be withheld from disclosure until such date as is mentioned in paragraph (a).

If an authority holds information which is going to be published in   **1.230**
the near future, then this exemption protects against premature

disclosure and allows for orderly general publication, so long as it is reasonable in the circumstances to delay disclosure. It needs to be clear that the information is being *published*. The Commissioner has queried an authority's claim that making information available on its intranet constituted publication.[93]

1.231   The key considerations are:

- *at the time a request for information is received, has the decision to publish the information already been taken?* The decision to publish cannot be taken *in response* to the request, with the effect or intention of delaying the information being given to the applicant. The exemption may not apply even where publication is being contemplated but not confirmed. (For instance, the Scottish Ministers were considering, but had still not decided, whether to publish an information pack regarding the tendering of ferry services, when they received a request for specific information regarding the tender. The Commissioner concluded that the exemption for future publication did not apply;)[94]

- *will publication take place within 12 weeks?* The authority needs to have reasonable certainty that publication will take place in that period. The publication date may need to be confirmed by a third party, as the exemption can apply to information held by the authority but due to be published by another person. For instance, the authority may have been given sight of a draft for comment prior to publication by another body;

- *even if it is to be published in this period, is it reasonable in all the circumstances that the information should not be disclosed before then?* Although it might generally be reasonable to withhold until publication, there may be specific reasons for disclosing the information. For instance, although there may have been an intention to publish the information within 12 weeks of application, the authority may be aware that publication is going to be considerably delayed, in which case withholding the information would be unreasonable. Or there may be specific information within that to be published which is of particular and urgent relevance to a matter to be determined prior to publication, for example a planning application. In the circumstances, it may be reasonable to disclose that particular

---

93   Decision 030/2008: Mr Mark Nixon and Glasgow City Council.
94   Decision 098/2006: Mr Jim Mather, MSP and the Scottish Executive.

information, even if the remaining material is withheld until the due publication date.

An applicant has no right automatically to be given the information once it has been published, and may have to make a fresh request. (However, it would be good practice, if an authority is about to publish the information, to retain the applicant's details and to make the information available once it is published.) If the authority fails to meet its commitment to publish the information within the 12-week period, then, in line with its duty to advise and assist contained in s 15 of FOISA, it should contact the applicant and explain the reason for the delay. It should give the revised date of publication if this is known.   **1.232**

Furthermore, there is no provision for the applicant automatically to be given the information as soon as a delay in publication exceeds the 12-week time limit, but a significant delay may make it more difficult for the authority to continue to claim that it is reasonable to withhold the information.   **1.233**

An applicant who was originally content to accept the authority's decision to withhold the information until the date of publication may now find that, as a result of the delay in publication, the deadline in FOISA for challenging the original decision has passed. (Reviews must be requested within 40 working days of the authority's response to the original request.) However, public authorities can deal with a requirement for review outwith the 40-working-day period if they consider it appropriate, and a late requirement for review in such circumstances may be thought to warrant the discretionary provision being exercised.[95]   **1.234**

Information intended for future publication – s 27(2)

(2) Information obtained in the course of, or derived from, a programme of research is exempt information if –

    (a) the programme is continuing with a view to a report of the research (whether or not including a statement of that information) being published by –

       (i) a Scottish public authority; or

      (ii) any other person; and

    (b) disclosure of the information before the date of publication would, or would be likely to, prejudice substantially –

---

95   As provided for by FOISA, s 20(6).

> (i) the programme;
> (ii) the interests of any individual participating in the programme;
> (iii) the interests of the authority which holds the information; or
> (iv) the interests of the authority mentioned in sub-paragraph (i) of paragraph (a) (if it is a different authority from that which holds the information).

1.235 This provision was added relatively late in the legislative process largely due to representations made by universities concerned that academic research which is being conducted with a view to publication would not be protected by the provisions of s 27(1). There is no equivalent of s 27(2) in the UK FOIA.[96]

1.236 Public authorities seeking to apply this exemption have to establish that:

- the information comes from a programme of research;
- the research is still under way; and
- it is intended that the result of that research will be published.

1.237 The "harm" test applies to this subsection, so authorities must demonstrate that substantial prejudice would, or would be likely to, occur if the information was released. The harm could be to the research programme, the interests of any individual participating in the programme, to the authority which holds the information or the Scottish public authority which intends to publish the research (if that is different from the authority which holds it).

1.238 There is no definition of a "programme of research" but it is clear that this exemption is intended to protect genuine academic research, which is conducted as part of a systematic programme of investigation, the findings of which are intended for publication. It may be the case that certain information gathered in the course of the research is not ultimately published but, so long as the research is under way, all of the information obtained as part of programme may be exempt, subject to the "harm" and "public interest" tests.

---

96 Despite the concerns expressed by Universities Scotland, no valid cases citing this exemption have so far come before the Commissioner.

The exemption is not intended to apply to investigations or data   1.239
analysis conducted by public authorities generally.

28 Relations within the United Kingdom

(1) Information is exempt information if its disclosure
     under this Act would, or would be likely to, prejudice sub-
     stantially relations between any administration in the
     United Kingdom and any other such administration.
(2) In subsection (1), "administration in the United Kingdom"
     means –
     (a) the Government of the United Kingdom;
     (b) the Scottish Administration;
     (c) the Executive Committee of the Northern Ireland
         Assembly; or
     (d) the National Assembly for Wales.

The term the "Scottish Administration" is not used colloquially in   1.240
Scotland. The Scotland Act 1998 provided for "the establishment of
a Scottish Parliament and Administration". The Administration is
headed by a Scottish Executive, the members of which are collectively
known as the "Scottish Ministers". When the Scottish National Party
came to power in 2007, it rebranded the Scottish Executive as the Scottish
Government, although this did not alter any statutory references. The
obligation to comply with FOISA falls upon the Scottish Ministers (by
virtue of being listed in Sch 1 to FOISA).

Although the exemption focuses on the harm to relations   1.241
among UK administrations, its use is not restricted to information
held by the Scottish Ministers. There may be cases where Scottish
public authorities (other than the Scottish Ministers) hold
information, the disclosure of which could harm relations between
administrations.

It is not necessary for the information to have been supplied by   1.242
another UK administration or Scottish public authority for it to be
covered by this exemption; an internally produced document could
also fall within its scope. However, special considerations may apply
where the information requested is held by the Scottish Ministers and
was supplied to it by another UK administration.

Following devolution, a series of agreements, known as concordats,   1.243
were drawn up among the four administrations (quadrilateral
concordats) or between two administrations (bilateral) to facilitate co-
operation among the UK Government and the devolved administrations

on both reserved and devolved matters. The provisions of an overarching concordat, the Memorandum of Understanding ("MoU"), are implicit in all other concordats or supplementary agreements.[97]

1.244   The MoU sets out the broad principles that govern inter-administration policy co-operation and consultation; in particular, the need for timely exchange of information and consultation and, where appropriate, for confidentiality.

1.245   The MoU states that:

> "Each administration will wish to ensure that the information it supplies to others is subject to appropriate safeguards in order to avoid prejudicing its interests. The [four] administrations accept that in certain circumstances a duty of confidence may arise and will between themselves respect legal requirements of confidentiality. Each administration can only expect to receive information if it treats such information with appropriate discretion."[98]

1.246   However, the concordats do not create legal obligations, and decisions on disclosure of information held by an administration need to be taken in accordance with the provisions of FOISA. (It may well be that, if information is said to be held in confidence, the provisions of s 3(2)(a)(ii) apply. This provides that information is not held for the purposes of FOISA if it is held in confidence, having been supplied by a Minister of the Crown or by a Department of the Government of the United Kingdom.)

1.247   The key consideration, so far as the s 28 exemption is concerned, is not whether the information has come from another administration in the UK, but the degree of harm to relations which would, or would be likely to, occur if the information was publicly disclosed following a request.

1.248   Authorities must consider the *content* of the information when determining whether the exemption applies – some information from an authority on a subject may be exempt (for example, detailing ongoing sensitive negotiations) while other information provided at the same time on the same subject would not be exempt (for example, prior warning of the content of a press statement, which has subsequently been released).[99]

---

97 Devolution – Memorandum of Understanding and Supplementary Agreement (Cm 7864, March 2010): http://www.cabinetoffice.gov.uk/resource-library/devolution-memorandum-understanding-and-supplementary-agreement.

98 *Ibid*, para 12.

99 See, eg, Decision 022/2008: Mr Peter McMahon and the Scottish Ministers.

Matters which authorities could consider include: 1.249

- the age of the material, as sensitivity is likely to erode over time;
- whether negotiations or discussions on a matter are ongoing or concluded at the time of the request;
- what is now in the public domain on the issue and the stance taken by respective administrations;
- whether views held by one administration were known to another;
- the degree of harm which would, or would be likely to, occur.[100] (Disclosure might cause annoyance but might not substantially prejudice relations);
- the effect of any change in the composition of the administrations since the material was exchanged or views were expressed.

The exemptions in s 28 cannot be applied to information in a "historical   1.250
record". Historical records are as defined in s 57 of FOISA.

29 Formulation of Scottish Administration policy etc.

This is what is often referred to as a "class-based" exemption – a term   1.251
which was adopted during the consultation process for the proposed
Scottish freedom of information legislation. Where an exemption
is "class based", an authority has to consider only whether the
information falls within the description specified in the exemption
when assessing whether the exemption may be applied. As a result,
even innocuous information may be covered by this exemption as
there is no need to consider whether any harm would occur from
release, as would be the case before many other FOISA exemptions
apply.

However, in practice, the extent of harm from disclosure is likely   1.252
to be taken into account when considering the "public interest"
test.

This exemption applies only to information held by the Scottish   1.253
Ministers and not to other bodies, such as local authorities, which also
formulate policy.

---

100 It is worth noting that the UK FOIA contains a similar but not identical exemption to which a lower "harm" test of simple "prejudice" applies. It is possible that information will be exempt if requested from a UK authority, which would not meet the "substantial prejudice" test of the Scottish legislation.

29 Formulation of Scottish Administration policy etc.

(1) Information held by the Scottish Administration is exempt information if it relates to –

(a) the formulation or development of government policy;

(b) Ministerial communications;

(c) the provision of advice by any of the Law Officers or any request for the provision of such advice; or

(d) the operation of any Ministerial private office.

Formulation or development of government policy

1.254   The exemption applies to information relating to the formulation and development of policy not only of the post-devolution Scottish Administration but also of the pre-devolution UK Government.

1.255   Although the scope of this exemption can be wide ranging, it cannot be taken to mean that any information regarding a policy area of the Scottish Administration (for example, health or justice) is within its scope. There is a distinction to be made between the *drawing up of* or *expanding upon* a policy, which may well be within the scope of this exemption, and the *implementation* or *administration* of that policy, which are less likely to qualify as formulation or development of policy. Sometimes insufficient recognition is given to the component elements of policy activity.

1.256   It has been held that:

> "The formulation of government policy suggests the early stages of the policy process where options are identified and considered, risks are identified, consultation takes place and recommendations and submissions are presented to Scottish Ministers. Development suggests the processes involved in reviewing, improving upon or amending already existing policy and could involve piloting, monitoring, analysing, reviewing or recording the effects of existing policy."[101]

1.257   (The extent to which information comes within the scope of this exemption and the application of the "public interest" test is considered in more detail in Chapter 5 (Key Issue 3: Government Information).)

---

101 See, eg, Decision 130/2006: Mr Paul Hutcheon of *The Sunday Herald* and the Scottish Executive, para 17. This wording derives directly from guidance issued by the UK Information Commissioner as to the interpretation of a similar exemption in FOIA at s 35(1).

Ministerial communications

However, in respect of ministerial communications, the exemption applies only to information relating to communications between Ministers in the post-devolution Scottish Administration. So, information communicated between Scottish Office Ministers, even immediately prior to devolution, does not come within the scope of the exemption.[102]

1.258

This exemption is not limited to written communications between Ministers, such as a letter or an e-mail from one Minister to another, but could also cover records of discussions between Ministers in a minute of a meeting. It also includes correspondence between Ministers' private secretaries, when corresponding on their respective Ministers' behalf.

1.259

However, a communication from a Minister giving their views is not sufficient for the exemption to apply. The key issue is whether there has been communication between two or more Ministers. So, a memo from a Minister to an official is not within the scope of this exemption.[103]

1.260

Advice from Law Officers

It is highly likely that advice given to Ministers from the Law Officers would also attract the exemption at s 36(1) concerning legal professional privilege.

1.261

Can advice from the Law Officers on matters other than policy formulation be exempt under s 29?

When a journalist sought a breakdown of occasions on which Ministers or Deputy Ministers had consulted the Law Officers in relation to civil legal proceedings, he argued that, as this was advice given to Ministers in a personal capacity, the exemption at s 29(1)(c) could not apply, on the basis that s 29 of FOISA is headed "Formulation of Scottish Administration Policy etc".

There is a degree of conflict in the authorities on statutory interpretation on the use of headings etc in construing words in a statutory provision. In *Cross on Statutory Interpretation* the authors explain that if a judge has doubt as to the meaning of a provision in a statute and the sole cause of the doubt is a disparity between clear

---

102 See Decision 057/2005: Mr William Alexander and the Scottish Executive, paras 58–59.
103 Decision 143/2007: Mr Barry Winetrobe and the Scottish Executive.

unambiguous words in the provision and a heading or title, the judge must disregard his doubts and apply the otherwise clear words. The authors go on to state:

> "If, however, the judge has doubts about the meaning of a statutory provision he is considering for some other reason, such as its lack of clarity or apparent pointlessness, he may take the title, preamble, heading or side-note into consideration in determining how those doubts should be resolved."[104]

In *Bennion on Statutory Interpretation*[105] it is suggested that most modern judges consider it not only their right but also their duty to take account of headings in Acts. Indeed, as *Bennion* points out, there is authority for the proposition that where general words are preceded by a heading indicating a narrower scope, it is legitimate to treat the general words as cut down by the heading.[106]

In the case in question, the Commissioner took account of the actual wording of the heading to s 29, which is "Formulation of Scottish Administration policy *etc*" (emphasis added). Given that s 29(1) of FOISA contains four distinct exemptions relating to the operation of the Scottish Administration, the word "etc" in the title of s 29 clearly suggested to the Commissioner that the exemptions contained within it relate to matters other than policy formulation.

Decision 090/2008: Mr Tom Gordon and the Scottish Ministers

Formulation of Scottish Administration policy etc. – s 29(2) and (3)

(2) Once a decision as to policy has been taken, any statistical information used to provide an informed background to the taking of the decision is not to be regarded, for the purposes of –

    (a) paragraph (a) of subsection (1), as relating to the formulation or development of the policy in question; or

    (b) paragraph (b) of that subsection, as relating to Ministerial communications.

(3) In determining any question under section 2(1)(b) as respects information which is exempt information by virtue of subsection (1)(a), the Scottish Administration

---

104 Cross, *Statutory Interpretation* (3rd edn; eds R Cross, J Bell and G Engle) (1995), pp 124–125.
105 F Bennion, *Statutory Interpretation* (4th edn, 2002), s 256.
106 Per *Inglis v Robertson and Baxter* [1898] AC 616.

must have regard to the public interest in the disclosure of factual information which has been used, or is intended to be used, to provide an informed background to the taking of a decision.

This exemption is entirely subject to the "public interest" test. However, s 29(3) gives particular emphasis to the public interest in the disclosure of factual information which has informed the formulation or development of government policy, although it does not provide any definition of what is to be regarded as factual information.[107]   1.262

Formulation of Scottish Administration policy etc. – s 29(4) and (5)

(4) In this section –
"government policy" means –
(a) the policy of the Scottish Administration; and
(b) in relation to information created before 1st July 1999, the policy of the Government of the United Kingdom;
"the Law Officers" means the Lord Advocate, the Solicitor General for Scotland, the Advocate General for Scotland, the Attorney General, the Solicitor General and the Attorney General for Northern Ireland;
"Ministerial communications" means any communications between Ministers and includes, in particular, communications relating to proceedings of the Scottish Cabinet (or of any committee of that Cabinet); and
"Ministerial private office" means any part of the Scottish Administration which provides personal administrative support to a Minister.

(5) In the definitions of "Ministerial communications" and "Ministerial private office" in subsection (4), "Minister" means a member of the Scottish Executive or a junior Scottish Minister.

30 Prejudice to effective conduct of public affairs

Information is exempt information if its disclosure under this Act –
(a) would, or would be likely to, prejudice substantially the maintenance of the convention of the collective responsibility of the Scottish Ministers;

---

107 There is an equivalent provision in the UK FOIA at s 35(4).

1.263   Whatever their individual views on a matter may be, the Scottish Ministers are understood to make collective decisions and are then required to abide by and defend those decisions, presenting a united front.

1.264   It is said that "the classic expression of collective responsibility remains that of Lord Salisbury" in making it clear that "For all that passes in Cabinet every member who does not remain is absolutely and irretrievably responsible and has no right afterwards to say that he agreed in one case to a compromise, while in another he was persuaded by his colleagues".[108] In this way Ministers are jointly responsible to Parliament.

1.265   The convention is said to apply to Ministers, Junior Ministers, Deputy Ministers and the Lord Advocate (except for decisions taken by the Lord Advocate when acting as head of the systems of criminal prosecution and investigation of deaths in Scotland). It covers all the business of the Scottish Government, including decisions, announcements, expenditure plans, proposed legislation and appointments. There is no statutory basis for the convention of collective responsibility, but it is formalised in the Scottish Ministerial Code[109] which provides additional guidance. (It indicates, for example, that "the issue of collective responsibility is particularly acute where the portfolio Minister is likely to take a decision that will be unpopular in another Minister's constituency. Once a decision has been reached, the constituency Minister must be prepared to defend that decision, even if individually, he/she would have argued against it in private, or, in the case of a constituency issue, had made representations as a constituency MSP".[110])

1.266   However, as this is not a class exemption, it is not sufficient to assert that simply because the information contains the views of a Minister, the exemption should apply. Rather, consideration must be given to matters such as the context in which the views were expressed, the significance of those views, and the effects of disclosure in current circumstances, before coming to a view as to whether the convention of collective responsibility would, or would be likely to, be prejudiced substantially by disclosure.

1.267   The Commissioner has determined that:

  • the ministerial views expressed should have significance. This might be the case where the view expressed by the Minister was

---

108 H Barnet, *Constitutional and Administrative Law* (5th edn, 2004), p 289.
109 Scottish Ministerial Code: A code of conduct and guidance on procedures for Members of the Scottish Government and Junior Scottish Ministers (http://www.scotland.gov.uk/Publications/2009/06/18095600/3).
110 *Ibid*, para 2.5.

at variance with the final policy; or was on a matter which was not the Minister's responsibility; or where there was strongly expressed disagreement between Ministers;[111]

- the knowledge that Ministers offered different opinions when asked for their views may not, in itself, breach the convention of collective responsibility;[112]
- the effects of disclosing the information may weaken with the passage of time or through changes in circumstances, such as a new ministerial appointment;[113]
- the exemption does not apply only in situations where Ministers disagree;[114]
- the release of information which relates to a matter of substance but is itself routine or mundane – for example, expressing a view on meeting arrangements or a deadline – is unlikely to cause the harm required for the exemption to apply;[115]
- of itself, disclosure of information showing that a Minister approved a proposal from officials, or required certain changes to draft documents is unlikely to undermine the convention of collective responsibility.[116] (The onus lies upon the authority to demonstrate the significance of actions which do not self-evidently appear to have a bearing on collective responsibility.)

Prejudice to effective conduct of public affairs – s 30(b)

(b) would, or would be likely to, inhibit substantially –
  (i) the free and frank provision of advice; or
  (ii) the free and frank exchange of views for the purposes of deliberation; or

Sections 30(b)(i) and (ii) are among the most frequently used and most strongly contested exemptions (featuring in 9 per cent of the Commissioner's decisions). Often, but not always, they are both claimed in respect of the same information   **1.268**

Often at issue is how readily it should be accepted that the disclosure of information would, or would be likely to, inhibit substantially the provision of advice or exchange of views *in the*   **1.269**

---

111 Decision 053/2007: Mr Mark Latham, *Shetland Times*, and the Scottish Executive.
112 *Ibid.*
113 *Ibid.*
114 Decision 039/2007: Mr Michael Matheson, MSP and the Scottish Executive.
115 Decision 076/2006: Mr Paul Hutcheon and the Scottish Executive.
116 *Ibid.*

future. The "harm" test involves a judgement not of *prejudice* but rather of the degree of *inhibition* (terminology which occurs only in this subsection).

1.270   In this context, to "inhibit" means to restrain, decrease or suppress the freedom with which advice is given and opinions or options are expressed; while the use of the word "substantial" means that the degree to which a person will be, or is likely to be, inhibited in expressing themselves has to be of real and demonstrable significance.

1.271   The judgement may take into account:

- the subject-matter of the advice or opinion;
- the content of the advice and opinion;
- the manner in which the advice or opinion is expressed;
- whether relevant information is already in the public domain; and
- whether the timing of release would have any bearing.

Broadly, it might be said that releasing advice or opinion while a decision is being considered, and for which further views are still being sought might be more inhibiting than disclosure once a decision has been taken.

1.272   The inhibition might also be greater when it involves an individual who is expected to contribute further advice on an issue, than a general inhibition felt by officials who are simply wary that information of that type will be disclosed.

1.273   Set against that, the seniority and professional capacity in which those involved are acting may also have a bearing as to whether they are likely to be constrained. In a case concerning advice to a Minister from a principal planner the Commissioner held that "The author's role is to advise the Minister on the planning aspects pertinent to this case with reference to relevant legislation and policy where appropriate" and in carrying out this expert role found that "As the author is acting in a professional capacity he or she will be obliged to give open, clear and full advice. To do otherwise, it seems to me, would be contrary to their professional responsibilities".[117]

1.274   For the exemption to be warranted it needs to be demonstrated why disclosure is likely to lead to substantial inhibition and who is likely to feel inhibited as a result of disclosure. In the absence of submissions

---

117 Decision 231/2006: Jim Thomson and the Scottish Executive, paras 54–55.

on the effect of disclosure *of the particular information* in dispute, the Commissioner may conclude that no evidence has been provided to suggest that specific officials, or officials generally, would, or would be likely to, be inhibited substantially in giving future advice, as a result of disclosure.[118]

What is clear, however, is that authorities cannot simply claim that the exemption applies by virtue of the fact that the information requested consists of advice or the exchange of views. This class-based approach, which fails to consider the content of the information, has been rejected by the courts.[119]   **1.275**

Decisions therefore turn upon the circumstances of each case and, in particular, whether the degree of harm claimed would be likely to come about.   **1.276**

For example, the "harm" test was not met where: **1.277**

- the notes of a meeting revealed no disagreement or controversy and the information was similar in character to minutes of the meeting already released to the requesters, then the mere fact that the notes recorded that an exchange of views took place would not have a substantially inhibiting effect on future exchanges;[120]

- given that views and advice on the location of the National Theatre of Scotland had not been exchanged with any particular frankness or freedom, the release of the information would not have a substantially inhibiting effect.[121]

By contrast, the "harm" test was met where: **1.278**

- certain legal and commercial issues remained ongoing at the time of a request for information about potential claims relating to its construction of the Scottish Parliament building. Disclosure would have led the Scottish Parliamentary Corporate Body's advisers to be extremely cautious about the way in which further advice was conveyed, for fear that the SPCB's legal or negotiating position would be compromised by further disclosure.[122]

---

118 Decision 013/2009: Prestoungrange Arts Festival (2006) and Historic Scotland, para 24.
119 *Scottish Ministers v Scottish Information Commissioner* [2006] CSIH 8, para 9: http://www.scotcourts.gov.uk/opinions/2007CSIH08.html.
120 Decision 088/2006: Mr and Mrs G Bonelle and West Lothian Council.
121 Decision 039/2007: Mr Michael Matheson, MSP and the Scottish Executive.
122 Decision 016/2008: Mr Tom Gordon and the Scottish Parliamentary Corporate Body.

- free and frank views were expressed by an individual within a local authority in the early stages of considering options for school closure, disclosure would be likely to inhibit substantially similar frankness when views were canvassed in further school closure assessments.[123]

Prejudice to effective conduct of public affairs – s 30(c)

(c) would otherwise prejudice substantially, or be likely to prejudice substantially, the effective conduct of public affairs.

1.279   Section 30(c) sets out that information will fall within the scope of the exemption where it will *otherwise* prejudice substantially, or be likely to prejudice substantially, the effective conduct of public affairs. This means that where information is claimed to be exempt under s 30(a) or (b), it is not appropriate also to apply the exemption under s 30(c) on the same grounds.

1.280   The potential scope of this exemption is wide, but its application tends to focus on adverse effects resulting from disclosure upon the operational activity of an authority, and whether procedures, routines, professional duties, relationships with external bodies etc will be significantly undermined.

1.281   For instance, the Commissioner has found that the exemption applied where disclosing information relating to the content, scoring and appeal process for psychometric testing relevant to the Core Sex Offender Treatment Programme used by the Scottish Prison Service would have allowed those undergoing such testing to manipulate the outcome.[124]

1.282   The contact information for all landlords registered with a local authority was also exempt, on the ground that mass disclosure would be contrary to the assurances expressly given that access to the landlords register would be controlled so as not to support undesirable purposes such as trawling the register. Disclosure would also prevent the Council from considering on an individual basis (in terms of s 88A(4) of the Antisocial Behaviour (Scotland) Act 2004) whether specific information should be withheld because its disclosure would be likely to jeopardise the safety or welfare of any person; or the security of any premises.[125]

---

123 Decision 081/2009: Mr Bruce Pattullo and Angus Council.
124 Decision 144/2010: Mr P and the Scottish Prison Service.
125 Decision 063/2011: Mr Paul Giusti and North Lanarkshire Council.

However, in the decision which caused unadjusted surgical   1.283
mortality rates for all of Scotland's hospital clinicians to be released,
the Commissioner concluded that release of the information did not
have the capacity to impact adversely upon the collection of clinical
performance data.[126]

National security and defence – s 31(1)

(1) **Information is exempt information if exemption from
section 1(1) is required for the purpose of safeguarding
national security.**

The onus is upon authorities to indicate why national security would   1.284
be safeguarded by withholding the information. It is not enough
that the information *relates* to national security; it can be exempted
only if exemption is required for the *purpose* of safeguarding national
security. The distinction was highlighted when a journalist asked for
information contained in files concerning the release of radionucleides
in drinking water. While some of the information related to measures
to protect essential services, withholding the information was not
necessary for the purpose of safeguarding those services or national
security.[127]

National security and defence – s 31(2)

(2) **A certificate signed by a member of the Scottish Executive
certifying that such exemption is, or at any time was,
required for the purpose of safeguarding national security
is conclusive of that fact.**

The signing of such a certificate has the practical effect of creating a   1.285
class-based exemption for any information which falls within the
scope of the certificate. It is "conclusive of the fact" that disclosure is
a threat to national security and accordingly the exemption cannot
be challenged. There is no appeal procedure under FOISA against the
imposition of such a certificate.[128]

In order for s 31(2) to apply, the certificate must be signed by a   1.286
member of the "Scottish Executive". The Scotland Act 1998 defines the
"Scottish Executive" as:

---

126 Decision 066/2005: Mr Peter MacMahon of *The Scotsman* and the Common Services Agency
for the Scottish Health Service.
127 Decision 151/2007: Rob Edwards and the Scottish Executive.
128 However, such a certificate may be capable of being challenged by judicial review.

(a) the First Minister;
(b) such Ministers as the First Minister may appoint under s 47 of the Scotland Act 1998; and
(c) the Lord Advocate and Solicitor General for Scotland.

1.287   Where such a certificate exists, an authority, in responding to a request, must consider whether the information it holds falls within the scope of the certificate. If it does, the information is exempt. However, as this is a qualified exemption, the public interest in maintaining the exemption has to be considered and dissatisfaction with the outcome could form the basis of an application to the Commissioner.

National security and defence – s 31(3)

(3) **Without prejudice to the generality of subsection (2), a certificate under that subsection may identify the information to which it applies by means of a general description and may be expressed to have prospective effect.**

1.288   There is provision for the scope of certificates to vary widely. The certificate may, for example, identify the specific material to be withheld, and may be drawn up on a case-by-case basis, in response to a specific request. Alternatively, a *prospective* certificate can apply to any information relating to a particular subject or issue, even before any request has been made, and apply to *future* information relating to that issue (as well as to information existing when the certificate was drawn up).

1.289   There is no provision in FOISA which requires the certificate to be reviewed, or causes it to expire after a period of time.

National security – ministerial certificate

When the G8 Summit was due to take place in Scotland in July 2005, security was intense. Leaders from the world's strongest economies, including President George W Bush, were due to meet in Gleneagles, Perthshire, and large numbers of protesters were expected to gather both there and in Edinburgh. Previous G8 gatherings in Genoa and Evian had been marked by violent clashes between security forces and some protesters. A temporary fence, 5 miles long, was built around Gleneagles Hotel, and a "no-fly" zone was imposed above it.

Security was provided by thousands of police officers – many drafted from across the UK.

Against that background the first – and so far only – ministerial certificate under s 31(2) was signed on 29 April 2005 by Margaret Curran, a Scottish Executive Minister. This was a *prospective* certificate applying to information held in connection with the preparation and provision of security arrangements for the Summit. The certificate set out seven categories of information: resources to be deployed; security to be deployed; event-related intelligence; information communications technology; briefing information; certain financial information; and details of police forces. The certificate also provided a non-exhaustive list of specific information within each of the categories.

Ministers indicated in October 2005 that the need for the certificate would be reviewed, but it remained in force. The certificate was finally withdrawn on 6 April 2010.

National security and defence – s 31(4)

(4) **Information is exempt information if its disclosure under this Act would, or would be likely to, prejudice substantially –**
   (a) **the defence of the British Islands or of any colony; or**
   (b) **the capability, effectiveness or security of any relevant forces.**[129]

Whether or not information is exempt depends entirely upon the degree of harm from its disclosure.   **1.290**

The Official Secrets Act 1989 states that disclosure of information relating to defence is damaging if it: **1.291**

- damages the capability of the armed forces of the Crown to carry out their tasks;
- leads to loss of life or injury to members of those forces;
- leads to serious damage to the equipment or installations of those forces;
- endangers the interests of the United Kingdom abroad;
- seriously obstructs the promotion or protection by the United Kingdom of those interests;

---

129 The Commissioner has not made any decisions where the exemption at s 31(4)(a) or (b) has been cited.

- endangers the safety of British citizens abroad; or
- would be likely to have any of these effects.[130]

1.292   It is up to Scottish authorities, however, to determine whether the disclosure of information would, or would be likely to, substantially prejudice the defence of the nation or the capability, effectiveness or security of British forces or allied forces working with them. Consideration may need to be given to the current political and military climate: the extent to which information might need to be withheld to ensure the defence of the nation will depend on whether the nation is in peacetime, preparing for war, in actual hostilities, or whether the hostilities are over. Such factors will also be relevant when considering whether release would harm the capability, effectiveness or security of the armed forces.

1.293   Consideration should also be given to what information is already in the public domain. Where the same information has been released by another official source, it is unlikely to be possible to argue that disclosure under FOISA would cause substantial prejudice.

National security and defence – s 31(5)

(5) In subsection (4) –
   (a) in paragraph (a), "British Islands" and "colony" are to be construed in accordance with Schedule 1 to the Interpretation Act 1978 (c.30); and
   (b) in paragraph (b), "relevant forces" means –
       (i) the armed forces of the Crown; and
       (ii) any forces co-operating with those forces,
   or any part of the armed forces of the Crown or of any such co-operating forces.

1.294   "British Islands", therefore, should be taken to mean the United Kingdom, the Channel Islands and the Isle of Man. A "colony" means any part of Her Majesty's dominions outside the British Islands except:

(a) countries having fully responsible status within the Commonwealth;
(b) territories for whose external relations a country other than the United Kingdom is responsible; and
(c) associated states.

---

130 Official Secrets Act 1989, s 2(a)–(c).

The expression "armed forces of the Crown" is not defined, but   1.295
should be considered to include the regular, reserve and auxiliary
naval, military and air forces of the Crown. The phrase "any forces
co-operating with ..." is potentially very broad. It would include,for
example, foreign forces co-operating with UK forces on United Nations
peacekeeping missions or joint NATO operations. However, there is no
requirement that these co-operating forces are either armed or foreign
and so it might be argued that domestic or foreign police or security
forces are included.

32 International relations

(1) Information is exempt information if –
   (a) its disclosure under this Act would, or would be likely
       to, prejudice substantially –
       (i) relations between the United Kingdom and any
           other State;
       (ii) relations between the United Kingdom and any
            international organisation or international court;
       (iii) the interests of the United Kingdom abroad; or
       (iv) the promotion or protection by the United
            Kingdom of its interests abroad; or
   (b) it is confidential information obtained from –
       (i) a State other than the United Kingdom; or
       (ii) an international organisation or international
            court.

While UK foreign policy is a reserved matter under the Scotland Act   1.296
1998 (which established the powers of the Scottish Parliament), this
does not mean that Scottish authorities will not be engaged in, or
hold information on, international relations. There are over 40 foreign
consulates in Scotland and international relations are prominent in
Scottish Government strategies concerning business and investment,
tourism, sport and cultural activities. Scotland House in Brussels is a
base from which the Scottish Government's interests in the European
Union are promoted, and it is also home to Scotland Europa, the
Highland and Islands EU partnership and the Scottish Parliament's
representation. The Scottish Government includes a Minister for
External Affairs.

When considering this exemption, the issue to be addressed is   1.297
not whether the information concerns international relations, or the
interests, of the Scottish Government. Rather, it is whether disclosure

would, or would be likely to, prejudice substantially relations between the *United Kingdom* and any other state, international organisation (such as the European Union) or international court (such as the European Court of Human Rights), or whether it would prejudice substantially the interests of the UK abroad, or the protection or promotion of such interests. It is the interests of the UK, not of a component nation or region within the UK, and not the interests of the public authority which holds the information, which need to be considered.

1.298   So far, only the Scottish Ministers have claimed the international relations exemption in cases where an application has been made to the Commissioner. These have concerned requests for information on a range of issues including: a meeting between the First Minister of the Scottish Government and the US Secretary of State; details of infraction proceedings being taken by the European Commission against the UK; and the bid to locate the European Maritime Safety Agency in Glasgow. In most cases, the Commissioner has found that the nature of the substantial prejudice to the international relations or interests of the UK had not been specified, and so the exemption did not apply. However, the Commissioner accepted that disclosure of certain information relating to the proposed introduction of Giant Pandas to Edinburgh Zoo could harm UK–Chinese relationships.[131]

International relations – s 32(2)

(2) For the purposes of subsection (1), information obtained from a State, organisation or court is confidential at any time while –

(a) the terms on which that information was obtained require it to be held in confidence; or

(b) the circumstances in which it was obtained make it reasonable for the State, organisation or court to expect that it will be so held.

1.299   This makes clear that, in respect of information obtained from a state etc, the exemptions under s 32(1)(b) do not require the breach of confidence to be "actionable" before information can be exempted (unlike the general exemption relating to confidentiality under s 36(2)).

1.300   Authorities may be able to demonstrate that the terms on which information was obtained required confidentiality by producing

---

131 Decision 051/2009: Advocates for Animals and the Scottish Ministers.

evidence of a formal agreement between parties, or a statement by the supplier indicating that confidentiality is required. Alternatively, the document may be clearly marked as "confidential" by the state or international body supplying it.

Where an authority wishes to argue that there is a reasonable expectation on the part of the state or body supplying the information that it will be held in confidence, this might potentially be evidenced by demonstrating that equivalent information provided under similar circumstances was done so under terms requiring confidentiality, or by clearly demonstrating that confidentiality is presumed in the relationship in question.   1.301

A claim by Scottish Ministers that this exemption applied to information contained in a database concerning details of EU Infraction proceedings was dismissed by the Commissioner on the grounds that: (a) most of the information had not been obtained from the European Commission but had been internally generated; and (b) it was not demonstrated that there was any expectation on the part of the Commission that the information which it had supplied should be held in confidence by the Member State.[132]   1.302

International relations – s 32(3)

(3) In subsection (1) –
    "international court" means an international court which–
    (a) is not an international organisation; and
    (b) is established –
        (i) by a resolution of an international organisation of which the United Kingdom is a member; or
        (ii) by an international agreement to which the United Kingdom is a party;

This means that for a court to be defined as an "international court" under FOISA, the United Kingdom must be either a member of the international organisation responsible for establishing the court or a party to the international agreement which established it. This definition is slightly more restrictive than that for "international organisations".   1.303

It is worth noting that a number of generally recognised international courts also fulfil the criteria of "international organisations"   1.304

---

132 Decision 196/2007: Mr Rob Edwards and the Scottish Ministers.

(for example, the European Court of Human Rights, the International Court of Justice and the International Criminal Court). In general, however, the application of either exemption under s 32 will be the same regardless of whether the body falls within the definition of "international organisation" or "international court".

International relations – s 32(3) (cont'd)

"international organisation" means –
(a) an international organisation whose members include any two or more States; or
(b) an organ of such an international organisation;

1.305   There is no fixed meaning of "international organisation" in international law. However, it is generally recognised that the core attributes of an international organisation are that it:

- is created by a treaty between two or more states;
- possesses a constitution;
- is a legal entity in international law; and
- generally has an exclusive membership of states or governments.

1.306   Organisations covered by this definition would include the Council of Europe, the European Court of Human Rights, the European Union and its organs, the International Atomic Energy Agency, NATO, the United Nations and the World Trade Organization.

International relations – s 32(3) (cont'd)

"State" includes –
(a) the government of any State; and
(b) any organ of such a government,
and references to a State other than the United Kingdom include references to any territory outwith the United Kingdom.

1.307   The definition of "state" therefore includes the *Government* of any state outwith the United Kingdom, along with all *organs* of that Government. An "organ" can be defined as "a person, body of people or thing by which some purpose is carried out or some function is performed". An organ of Government would therefore include a state's legislature and executive bodies, as well as other governmental bodies carrying out functions on behalf of the state.

As the definition of "state" also includes all territories outwith the   1.308
United Kingdom which are not recognised as states in international
law, but "belong to, or are under the dominion of, a ruler of State", this
exemption encompasses all British territories, such as Bermuda, the
Falkland Islands, Gibraltar and the British Antarctic Territory, as well as
those territories belonging to any other state.

33 Commercial interests and the economy

(1) Information is exempt information if –
    (a) it constitutes a trade secret; or

What constitutes a trade secret is not defined, but may be readily   1.309
apparent. The courts have noted, for example, that secret processes
of manufacture provide obvious examples.[133] A Scottish flavour to
this approach was given by the Justice Minister when this section
was being debated in the Scottish Parliament, when he said that "The
recipes for Drambuie and Irn Bru are examples of trade secrets that
people would readily recognise as being of a different quality from
commercial interests". He went on to point out that, while some trade
secrets attract legal protection, such as a patent or copyright, often the
only protection for businesses is in maintaining their secrecy.[134]

Whether it is a secret formula, a unique technology or an undisclosed   1.310
resource, the key requirements in applying this exemption are:

- the information must be used in trade or business;
- the owner of the information must not have permitted or
  encouraged dissemination of the information (beyond, say, a
  restricted group of individuals involved in the business);
- if the information was disclosed to a competitor it would cause
  real or significant harm to the owner.[135]

Effectively, then, the nature and extent of harm from disclosure are   1.311
implicit in considering whether information is a trade secret, even
though there is no explicit test of substantial prejudice in FOISA.

So far, the Commissioner has not upheld any arguments made by   1.312
public authorities seeking to apply this exemption. Where the cases
involved tenders for contracts he drew attention to a decision of the
Irish Information Commissioner which looks at the case law on trade

---

133 *Faccenda Chicken Ltd* v *Fowler* [1987] 1 Ch 117, [1986] 1 All ER 617.
134 Jim Wallace, MSP, in Justice Committee 1, 28 February 2002, cols 325–506.
135 See *Lansing Linde Ltd* v *Kerr* [1991] 1 All ER 418, [1991] 1 WLR 251.

secrets and confidentiality from a number of jurisdictions.[136] While accepting that prices quoted in tenders could be trade secrets, the Irish Commissioner took the view that only in exceptional circumstances would historic price information qualify as a trade secret, noting also a key requirement that the information in question must be in current use in the trade. Finally, the Irish Commissioner placed considerable importance on whether the information was of value to competitors.

1.313   In addition to the above considerations, the Scottish Information Commissioner has taken into account the fact that, while secrecy may have existed, it may be short lived, and its sensitivity or continued secrecy may diminish over time. The extent to which competitors can discover or reproduce the information for themselves will also influence whether or not the information is a trade secret at the time a request is made for it.[137]

Commercial interests and the economy – s 33(1)(b)

(b) its disclosure under this Act would, or would be likely to, prejudice substantially the commercial interests of any person (including, without prejudice to that generality, a Scottish public authority).

1.314   The first consideration here is to identify whether commercial interests exist in relation to the information, and whose interests these are. "Any person" includes any individual, company, partnership etc as well as a public authority's own commercial interests, or those of any other public authority.

1.315   Typically, the interests will be those of a third party which is tendering for or carrying out work under contract to an authority. Applications dealt with by the Commissioner include tenders and contracts for, variously, IT systems, roof repairs, catering products, and the entire PFI contract for a private prison.

1.316   A commonly encountered difficulty lies in establishing whether an authority's own interest in the information is commercial, or simply financial. Commercial interests will include trading activity within a competitive environment (for example, the ongoing sale and purchase

---

136 Cases 98049, 90056, 98057: Henry Ford & Sons, Nissan Ireland and Motor Distributors Ltd and the Office of Public Works (http://www.oic.gov.ie/en/DecisionsoftheCommissioner/LongFormDecisions/Name,1450,en.htm).

137 See, eg, Decision 180/2006: Mr Alfred Weir and Fife Council; Decision 034/2006: Mr David Smith of Pentland Homeowners Association and Dundee City Council.

of goods and services), commonly for the purpose of profit or revenue surplus, but these are indicators, not requirements.

Commercial interests can exist where the purpose of the activity is explicitly not for profit. For example, the Commissioner has determined that the ferry operators Caledonian MacBrayne were actively engaged in the sale and purchase of services within a competitive environment and, as such, held commercial interests in relation to those services, even though the body is clearly established as a not-for-profit organisation, and is subsidised from the public purse.[138]   1.317

In another case, the fundraising strategy of the Trustees of the National Galleries of Scotland was largely concerned with the financial interests of the authority but included elements which could be considered commercial, such as increasing retail sales and offering business opportunities to commercial sponsors. Consequently, the cash flow projections of the authority were adjudged to engage its commercial interests.[139]   1.318

Judging whether the activity is commercial as opposed to simply revenue raising can determine whether the exemption applies.   1.319

An authority argued that its commercial interests would be harmed if it had to disclose details of the payments which it made to consultants reviewing certain academic course materials. The payment was funded by a grant from the Scottish Government and any surplus resulting from an underspend would benefit the authority. In effect, it was being argued that if the authority had to pay more as a result of disclosing rates, then the capacity to generate a surplus in future would be diminished. In the Commissioner's view, while financial considerations may have been factored into any bid for funding, and taken into account when negotiating payments made to the writers and reviewers, generating surplus income was not the objective of the project and these financial considerations did not amount to commercial interests.[140]   1.320

The distinction between commercial and financial interests has also been considered by the UK Information Tribunal. The Student Loans Company ("SLC"), which has a responsibility for recovering loan payments from students, argued that disclosure of a training   1.321

138 Decision 061/2005: Mr Carl Reavey and Caledonian MacBrayne Ltd.
139 Decision 047/2010: Mr Alan Davidson and the Board of Trustees for the National Galleries of Scotland.
140 Decision 096/2008: Mr B and the Scottish Further Education Unit.

manual used for staff who deal with defaulting borrowers would help borrowers to delay or avoid complying with their obligations. In consequence it would receive less money from borrowers and would incur greater costs of collection. The UK Commissioner argued that the SLC was not participating competitively in the purchase and sale of goods or services, and any detrimental financial effect of the kind feared by SLC would not constitute prejudice to the "commercial interests" of SLC. However, the Tribunal took the view that "It does not seem to us to be a misuse of ordinary English to describe debt collection as a commercial activity, even when carried on by a company supported by public funds".[141]

1.322   The reasoning in that case had a bearing on a subsequent Scottish application. When the City of Edinburgh Council was asked for the amount which it had paid under contract to an international private consultancy it argued "that commercial interests should be considered to encompass the interests of any party to a contract in obtaining the best deal available in the common marketplace, and so the Council can have commercial interests without engaging in what the Commissioner might perceive as commercial activities".[142] In coming to a decision, account was taken of the Tribunal's view that "'Commercial' is an ordinary English word. While its meaning is well known, the boundaries of its meaning are not precise. It takes colour from the context in which it is used … In this context we do not consider it appropriate to tie its meaning directly or indirectly to competitive participation in buying and selling goods or services and to exclude all other possibilities".[143]

1.323   Regarding the City of Edinburgh Council, the Commissioner concluded that "the commercial procurement of resources (including services) required for the purposes of under-taking its core (non-commercial) activities can be considered to be a commercial activity, and that it has commercial interests in this respect".[144]

1.324   The second consideration is whether disclosure of the information in question would be harmful to such an extent as to cause substantial prejudice to those commercial interests. In making a case for this, the onus is on the authority to establish the precise nature of the harm, and set out how likely it is to occur.

1.325   Common deficiencies in the arguments put by authorities are:

---

141 *Student Loans Company v ICO* (EA/2008/0092).
142 Decision 074/2011: Ms Caroline Gerard and City of Edinburgh Council, para 18.
143 *Student Loans Company v ICO* (EA/2008/0092), para 42.
144 Decision 074/2011: Ms Caroline Gerard and City of Edinburgh Council, para 21.

- claiming the exemption in respect of everything in a class of information – for example, tenders or contracts. This is a contents-based exemption and while such documents may contain information which is sensitive, other elements may be appropriate for release;
- failing to take into account that the passage of time may have diminished the capacity for harm from disclosure;
- failing to recognise that the information may already be in the public domain;
- failing to indicate how harm could come about.

Evidencing real harm to commercial interests from disclosure

The Scottish Prison Service ("SPS") was asked for certain monthly statistics relating to the performance of its contractor, Reliance Secure Task Management Ltd, the provider of prisoner escort and court custody services. The information was withheld, with the SPS arguing that negative reaction to the release of similar information in 2004 had contributed to a reduction in Reliance's share price, and had a major impact on its recruitment in Scotland. (The company had been criticised following the high-profile escape from its custody of a convicted murderer.)

The Commissioner rejected the application of the exemption at s 33(1)(b) because:

- the evidence that media comment had an immediate negative impact on Reliance's share price appeared to be anecdotal;
- even if a causal link could be established, no indication had been given of the degree of harm suffered by the company, or of its duration;
- adverse media comment was not inevitable, as the information requested need not be regarded as inherently negative in its nature and impact;
- the release of further information might provide an opportunity to rectify misconceptions about the contract, and place the provider in a better light.

The Commissioner went on to say that, even if the exemption did apply, there would have been strong public interest arguments in favour of disclosure. Any adverse media comment (and any subsequent impact on the company's commercial interests) would

> come about where the company had failed to meet its performance targets. The public deserved to be given information on matters which affected the safety and welfare of all those involved, and it was in the public interest to know whether the sanctions provided in the contract in the event of service failure were being applied.[145]
>
> *Decision 053/2006: Professor Sheila Bird and the Scottish Prison Service*

1.326   There are instances of clear evidence of commercial harm which warrant the exemption being applied.

1.327   When a company asked the Scottish Qualifications Authority for copies of the tender submission and pre-qualifying questionnaire submitted by a rival for the contract to publish past examination papers, the authority was entitled to withhold information which was very specific to the unique approach the successful bidder would take to implementing its strategies. Release of the information would have presented a clear risk to its ability to generate income from its product, therefore this would have been detrimental to its commercial interests.[146]

Commercial interests and the economy – s 33(2)

(2) **Information is exempt information if its disclosure under this Act would, or would be likely to, prejudice substantially –**

  (a) **the economic interests of the whole or part of the United Kingdom; or**

  (b) **the financial interests of an administration in the United Kingdom.**

Economic interests

1.328   There is no definition of "part" in FOISA, but it is likely to include not just the separate countries making up the United Kingdom, but also the regions within those countries. The exemption seeks to protect collective interests as opposed to those of individuals, and may be

---

145 *Decision 053/2006: Professor Sheila Bird and the Scottish Prison Service.*
146 Decision 005/2010: Leckie and Leckie Ltd and the Scottish Qualifications Authority.

applied to any information where release would, or would be likely to, cause substantial harm to the economy of the UK, either as a whole or in part. The exemption may potentially also apply in relation to information relating to an individual company, in circumstances where that company's performance would have a major influence on the national or local economy. The exemption will not apply to information relating to the economic interests of states other than the UK, unless the release of that information would also impact on the UK economy.

This exemption has not so far been claimed successfully. When Glasgow City Council argued that releasing details of the travel and hotel costs associated with Glasgow's bid to stage the 2014 Commonwealth Games would be likely to damage the city's chances of success, the Council argued that release would prejudice the delivery of economic benefits to Glasgow, the West Coast of Scotland, and Scotland as a whole. The Commissioner simply did not agree that disclosure would affect the bid, or have the substantially adverse economic consequences claimed.[147]   1.329

Financial interests

An administration's financial interests will generally concern the management of its financial resources, and information falling within the scope of the exemption will be that where release will have a significant detrimental impact on, for example, the funding of the administration, the revenue raised through taxation, or the availability and cost of borrowing to the administration.   1.330

In order for the exemption to be appropriately applied, therefore, an authority is likely to have to show that release would affect the administration to the point where there would be a detrimental impact on, for example, overall public spending levels or taxation. The anticipated prejudice must also be demonstrated to affect the financial interests of the administration as a whole, as opposed to only a department, agency or other component part of that administration.   1.331

Public authorities have argued in a handful of cases that s 33(2)(b) applied to withheld information, but never successfully. Most recently, the City of Edinburgh Council argued that the disclosure of how much money it had paid to Experian, a global information services company, in relation to an analysis of council tax debt, would, or would be likely to, prejudice substantially the   1.332

---

147 Decision 023/2008: Mr Paul Drury and Glasgow City Council.

financial interests of the Government of the United Kingdom or of the Scottish Government. The Council maintained that if it was unable to obtain best value from the marketplace when tendering for goods and services, then the financial shortfall must be made up by either Westminster or Holyrood. However, the Commissioner had already determined that the disclosure of the information would not prejudice substantially the Council's commercial interests and that disclosure would not harm its ability to achieve best value through its procurement processes. He therefore concluded that it was not credible that disclosure of the sum paid to Experian would so dislocate the Council's ability to control its budget that it would have significant consequences for the financial interests of either Westminster or Holyrood.[148]

Commercial interests and the economy – s 33(3)

(3)   In subsection (2), "administration in the United Kingdom" has the same meaning as in section 28(2).

1.333   "Administration in the United Kingdom" means:

- the Government of the United Kingdom;
- the Scottish Administration;
- the Executive Committee of the Northern Ireland Assembly; or
- the National Assembly for Wales.

1.334   The "Scottish Administration" is further defined in s 126(6) and (7) of the Scotland Act 1998 as:

- members of the Scottish Executive and junior Scottish Ministers and their staff; and
- non-ministerial office holders of the Scottish Administration and their staff.

1.335   So, the exemption in s 33(2)(b) cannot be used where the financial interests of any other authority are affected.

34 Investigations by Scottish public authorities and proceedings arising out of such investigations

1.336   There are nine distinct elements to this exemption but, in essence, the common purpose is to protect information gathered in the course of

---

148 Decision 074/2011: Ms Caroline Gerard and City of Edinburgh Council.

an investigation, where that investigation may result, or has resulted, in legal proceedings or inquiries. It is important to note that in some instances it applies to information held *at any time* for the listed purposes, so that even where investigations, inquiries or proceedings are completed, the exemption still applies. This is a class-based exemption, so any information within its scope is exempt (but the "public interest" test will then apply).

34 Investigations by Scottish public authorities and proceedings arising out of such investigations

(1) Information is exempt information if it has at any time been held by a Scottish public authority for the purposes of –
   (a) an investigation which the authority has a duty to conduct to ascertain whether a person –
      (i) should be prosecuted for an offence; or
      (ii) prosecuted for an offence is guilty of it;

The need for this exemption was set out by the Lord Advocate when this exemption was being debated in Parliament. Without it, the practical consequence would be that witnesses and people under investigation would be inhibited from co-operating in criminal investigations by the possibility that the information provided might be disclosed, and their identity might be revealed to the public, outwith the protection of the court.   1.337

It is most commonly applied to information gathered by the police in relation to the investigation of a crime. The key tests which police investigations must meet where they hold the information are: 1.338

- it was gathered for the *purpose* of an investigation they carried out;
- they had a *duty* to carry out the investigation; and
- the information was gathered to *consider* whether a person or persons should be prosecuted for an offence. (There is no require-ment that the information has subsequently been supplied to the procurator fiscal or that any court action has been taken.)

Was information gathered for the *purpose* of an investigation?

The police gather intelligence from a variety of sources for crime prevention and detection, including from informants who may be paid for their assistance. Although the information provided by what

> are officially termed "Covert Human Intelligence Sources" may have
> been gathered for the purpose of an investigation, details such as
> the total amount paid by police forces to such informants is not. The
> Commissioner found that collating the amount of individual payments
> into a total was done for accounting, not investigative purposes, and
> so was not exempt under s 34(1)(a).[149]

Investigations by Scottish public authorities and proceedings arising out of such investigations – s 34(1)(b)

(b) an investigation, conducted by the authority, which
in the circumstances may lead to a decision by the
authority to make a report to the procurator fiscal
to enable it to be determined whether criminal proceedings should be instituted; or

1.339   The exemption within s 34(1)(b) has a wider scope than s 34(1)(a) in
that the authority does not need to have a statutory or common law
duty to carry out the investigation in order for the exemption to apply.

1.340   Local authorities, for example, are responsible for investigating
offences relating to trading standards, planning and environmental
health matters and serious breaches may lead to a report to the
procurator fiscal. The main factors here are that an investigation
must be conducted by the authority and the information must be
gathered in order to make a decision on reporting to the procurator
fiscal. Again, whether the procurator fiscal is subsequently informed
is irrelevant.

Investigations by Scottish public authorities and proceedings arising out of such investigations – s 34(1)(c)

(c) criminal proceedings instituted in consequence of a
report made by the authority to the procurator fiscal.

1.341   Once again, a dual test is to be applied, namely: has the information
been held by a Scottish public authority *at any time* and was it for the
purpose of criminal proceedings instituted in consequence of a report
made by the authority to the procurator fiscal?

---

149 Decision 037/2009: Mr Stephen Stewart of the *Daily Record* and the Chief Constables of
Central, Grampian, Lothian and Borders, Strathclyde and Tayside Police.

Investigations by Scottish public authorities and proceedings arising out of such investigations – s 34(2)

(2)   Information is exempt information if –
  (a) held by a Scottish public authority for the purposes of an inquiry instituted under the Fatal Accidents and Sudden Deaths Inquiry (Scotland) Act 1976 (c.14) but not for the time being concluded; or
  (b) held at any time by a Scottish public authority for the purposes of any other investigation being carried out–
    (i) by virtue of a duty to ascertain; or
    (ii) for the purpose of making a report to the procurator fiscal as respects,
  the cause of death of a person.

The Fatal Accidents and Sudden Deaths Inquiry (Scotland) Act 1976   **1.342**
provides for the holding of two types of inquiry: mandatory and discretionary.

Mandatory inquiry: provision is made for a mandatory inquiry in the case of a death in Scotland of an employee, employer or self-employed person apparently resulting from an accident sustained at work or occurring during the time in which the person who died was in legal custody.

Discretionary inquiry: apart from mandatory inquiries, the decision to hold a public inquiry is at the discretion of the Lord Advocate. The test which applies is whether or not it appears to be expedient in the public interest to hold an inquiry into the circumstances of a death occurring in Scotland on the ground that it was sudden, suspicious or unexplained, or has occurred in circumstances such as to give rise to serious public concern.

In certain cases, the procurator fiscal may require that a post mortem   **1.343**
or further investigation is carried out to establish the cause of death. The procurator fiscal can also instigate a criminal investigation if the death is suspicious.

Given that the holding of a fatal accident inquiry (an "FAI") does not   **1.344**
preclude criminal proceedings, this exemption is to avoid any possible prejudice to a criminal trial.

In relation to investigations relating to the cause of death, the then   **1.345**
Justice Minister, Jim Wallace, had this to say during the debate on s 34(2)(a):

"Information collected during the investigations into the cause of the death of a person is invariably sensitive ... much of the information collected during an investigation into a cause of death is inappropriate for general public disclosure, given the distress that might be caused ... Relatives of a victim will often have legitimate interest in information and it may be entirely appropriate to make that information available in private ... That practice will be unaffected by the legislation."[150]

1.346   This exemption acknowledges the right of the family and relatives to maintain privacy in relation to information of a personal and medical nature of deceased persons, which was generally considered to outweigh any public interest in disclosure. (The exemption affords protection to the rights of the family and relatives, under Art 8 of the European Convention on Human Rights.)

Role of the procurator fiscal

The Crown Office and Procurator Fiscal Service is part of the Scottish Government, headed by the Lord Advocate. Procurators fiscal have two main functions: as public prosecutors in criminal cases and as investigators of sudden or suspicious deaths. Reports may be made to the procurator fiscal on either of these matters.

The role of the procurator fiscal in criminal cases

In relation to the exemptions contained in s 34(1) it is important to know that it is the procurator fiscal who is responsible for investigating and prosecuting crime in his or her district. In most cases, initial investigations are carried out by the police, who will carry out work to identify the person believed to be responsible for a crime and gather evidence demonstrating guilt. (Other authorities may also be responsible for this investigation. Over 50 specialist reporting agencies, other than the police, report cases to the procurator fiscal each year. The list of reporting agencies includes the Health and Safety Executive, the Scottish Environment Protection Agency (SEPA) and the Maritime and Coastguard Agency, as well as local authority departments such as environmental health and trading standards.[151])

Once initial investigations have been undertaken, the investigating authority will make a report to the procurator fiscal, outlining

---

150 Scottish Parliament Justice Committee 1 Meeting, 28 February 2002, col 3269.
151 http://www.crownoffice.gov.uk/about/specialist-prosecutors.

the charges against the accused and the evidence gathered. The procurator fiscal may then conduct or direct further investigations in order to decide whether a prosecution should be taken forward.

The role of the procurator fiscal in relation to sudden or suspicious deaths

Another key function of the procurator fiscal is to investigate all sudden and suspicious deaths in his or her area. In a small number of cases, a fatal accident inquiry will be held. A fatal accident inquiry is a public inquiry into the circumstances of death, heard before a sheriff. It is instigated by an application from the procurator fiscal to the sheriff for the area most closely associated with the death.

Investigations by Scottish public authorities and proceedings arising out of such investigations – s 34(3)

(3) Information held by a Scottish public authority is exempt information if –
   (a) it was obtained or recorded by the authority for the purposes of investigations (other than such investigations as are mentioned in subsection (1)) which are, by virtue either of Her Majesty's prerogative or of powers conferred by or under any enactment, conducted by the authority for any purpose specified in section 35(2); and
   (b) it relates to the obtaining of information from confidential sources.

All the provisions must be satisfied if this exemption is to apply – 1.347 that is, the information must have been obtained or recorded for the purposes of certain investigations which are conducted:

(a) to ascertain whether a person has failed to comply with the law;
(b) to ascertain whether a person is responsible for conduct which is improper;
(c) to ascertain whether circumstances which would justify regulatory action in pursuance of any enactment exist or may arise;
(d) to ascertain a person's fitness or competence in relation to –
   (i) the management of bodies corporate; or

      (ii) any profession or other activity which the person is, or seeks to become, authorised to carry on;

(e) to ascertain the cause of an accident;

(f) to protect a charity against misconduct or mismanagement (whether by trustees or other persons) in its administration;

(g) to protect the property of a charity from loss or mis-management;

(h) to recover the property of a charity;

(i) to secure the health, safety and welfare of persons at work; or

(j) to protect persons, other than persons at work, against risk to health or safety where that risk arises out of, or in connection with, the actions of persons at work.

1.348 Specifically, it applies only to the *obtaining* of information from *confidential* sources. The Commissioner has taken the view that the purpose of s 34(3) is not to protect information gathered from confidential sources, or necessarily the confidentiality of the source itself. Rather, information is exempt if it is about the *process* of gathering the information – how such information is gathered, how informants are recruited and how information obtained from confidential sources is transmitted.[152] Further, it has to be demonstrated that the sources are indeed confidential – clearly, if they are not, the exemption does not apply even if the other elements are present.[153]

Royal Prerogative

1.349 Certain powers exercisable by Ministers of the Crown under the Royal Prerogative were transferred to the Scottish Ministers "so far as they are exercisable within devolved competence" by virtue of s 53 of the Scotland Act 1998.

1.350 These powers included the right to call independent public inquiries. It is less likely that the Royal Prerogative would now be required for this purpose, given that the Inquiries Act 2005 established "a comprehensive new statutory framework for inquiries set up by Ministers – including Ministers of the devolved administrations, where appropriate – to look into matters of public concern".[154]

---

152 Decision 057/2007: Mrs Lillian Gordon and the Chief Constable of Grampian Police.

153 Decision 059/2007: Mr David Ferguson and the Chief Constable of Grampian Police.

154 Ministry of Justice, *The Governance of Britain – Review of the Executive Royal Prerogative Powers: Final Report* (October 2009), para 90 (http://www.justice.gov.uk/publications/docs/royal-prerogative.pdf).

However, a review of the Royal Prerogative by the UK Ministry   1.351
of Justice found that although the Inquiries Act "replaced over 30
different pieces of legislation on Inquiries, consolidated much of
the previous legislation and codified past practice, it did not
repeal the Secretary of State's non-statutory powers to set up
Inquiries".[155]

Investigations by Scottish public authorities and proceedings arising out of such investigations – s 34(4)

(4) Information is exempt information if obtained or recorded by a Scottish public authority for the purposes of
civil proceedings, brought by or on behalf of the authority,
which arise out of such investigations as are mentioned in
subsection (1) or (3).

What matters here is whether civil proceedings have been brought,   1.352
therefore authorities have to indicate the nature of the proceedings
and demonstrate that they have been brought. Furthermore, the
information must have been obtained or recorded for the purposes of
the proceedings and not for some other purpose.[156]

35 Law enforcement

(1) Information is exempt information if its disclosure
under this Act would, or would be likely to, prejudice substantially –
(a) the prevention or detection of crime;

This could relate to a specific crime (actual or anticipated) or wider   1.353
strategies for crime reduction and detection, and could also include
information which is received from an informant.

Law enforcement – s 35(1)(b)

(b) the apprehension or prosecution of offenders;

This relates to all aspects of the process of identifying, arresting or   1.354
prosecuting anyone suspected of being responsible for criminal
activity.

---

155 Ministry of Justice, *The Governance of Britain – Review of the Executive Royal Prerogative Powers: Final Report* (October 2009), para 90 (http://www.justice.gov.uk/publications/docs/royal-prerogative.pdf).
156 Decision 059/2007: Mr David Ferguson and the Chief Constable of Grampian Police.

Law enforcement – s 35(1)(c)

(c) the administration of justice;

1.355   The phrase "administration of justice", although not defined, could refer widely to matters related to the working of courts and tribunals and other non-adversarial mechanisms such as children's panels. This could include the protection of basic principles such as the right to a fair trial and ensuring that individuals have access to justice.

Law enforcement – s 35(1)(d)

(d) the assessment or collection of any tax or duty (or of any imposition of a similar nature);

1.356   The phrase "tax or duty" includes taxes raised at local level (such as council tax) as well as those raised at national level such as vehicle excise duty (road tax), income tax, stamp duty on property and national insurance contributions.

Law enforcement – s 35(1)(e)

(e) the operation of the immigration controls;

1.357   The phrase "immigration controls" can be interpreted as incorporating both the physical controls at points of entry to the UK and the procedural mechanisms for controlling entry to and residency in the UK.

Law enforcement – s 35(1)(f)

(f) the maintenance of security and good order in prisons or in other institutions where persons are lawfully detained;

1.358   As well as prisons, people might be lawfully detained in, for example, young offenders' institutions, local authority secure accommodation, secure hospitals or immigration detention and removal centres. This exemption refers to the maintenance of both security *and* good order in such institutions.

1.359   The term "security" implies:

- the safe, secure and effective custody of prisoners;
- the safety of people in or around an institution; and
- the detection and prevention of activity not permitted within an institution.

The term "good order" suggests information about the smooth   1.360
running of institutions, and the promotion of a safe and orderly
regime.

Law enforcement – s 35(1)(g)

(g) **the exercise by any public authority (within the meaning of the Freedom of Information Act 2000 (c.36)) or Scottish public authority of its functions for any of the purposes mentioned in subsection (2);**

The exemption applies when harm will be caused to the *exercise* of   1.361
the relevant function of the authority, rather than to the purpose
for which the function is carried out. It applies to the exercise by all
authorities in the UK and English public authorities of their function,
not just by Scottish public authorities.

For this exemption to apply, public authorities must be able to   1.362
show that they have one (or more) of the functions listed in s 35(2).
A public authority's functions are those things that it has a power,
or an obligation, to do. These functions may be set out in statute or
they may derive from the constitutional powers of the Crown (Her
Majesty's Prerogative). Any public authority wishing to rely on this
exemption must be able to show that it does in fact have the power
or obligation to carry out the relevant function. The function will be
specifically entrusted to the public authority to fulfil, as opposed to
being a general duty imposed on all public authorities.

A general duty is not a specific function

When a clinician improperly accessed patients' health details, a
health board submitted that a subsequent report into this security
breach should be withheld under s 35(1)(g) The basis for this
claim was that it had a responsibility, if it discovered that any of its
employees had, or may have, committed a crime, to report this to the
police. The Commissioner held that this was not sufficient to engage
the exemption; while the health board, like any other employer, has a
duty to ensure that there is no improper conduct or failure to comply
with the law among its employees, it was not a statutory function
specifically entrusted to the public authority to fulfil.

Decision 045/011: Mr Christopher Johnstone and Fife NHS Board

Law enforcement – s 35(1)(h)

(h) any civil proceedings –
  (i) brought; and
  (ii) arising out of an investigation conducted, for any
      such purpose,
by or on behalf of any such authority, by virtue either of
Her Majesty's prerogative or of powers conferred by or
under any enactment.

1.363 "Civil proceedings" can refer to any non-criminal case heard before a court or tribunal, but these must arise out of an investigation conducted by public authorities as defined by UK FOIA and FOISA.

Law enforcement – s 35(2)(a)

(2) The purposes are –
  (a) to ascertain whether a person has failed to comply
      with the law;

1.364 The failure could relate to a criminal matter, such as a theft by an employee, or a civil matter, such as whether a body has complied with its legal duties (for example, in relation to FOISA).

Law enforcement – s 35(2)(b)

(b) to ascertain whether a person is responsible for
    conduct which is improper;

1.365 Improper conduct includes that which is contrary to an expected standard, including any legal requirement or standard set for public office holders.

Law enforcement – s 35(2)(c)

(c) to ascertain whether circumstances which would
    justify regulatory action in pursuance of any enact-
    ment exist or may arise;

1.366 Regulatory activity is usually carried out by a person or organisation given powers to do so by, for example, a local authority's environmental health, trading standards or planning service.

Law enforcement – s 35(2)(d)(i)

(d) to ascertain a person's fitness or competence in
    relation to –
  (i) the management of bodies corporate; or

This would include investigations ascertaining the competence of, company directors, shadow directors and company secretaries who are involved in the management of corporate bodies.

1.367

Law enforcement – s 35(2)(d)(ii)

(ii) any profession or other activity which the person is, or seeks to become, authorised to carry on;

Approving an application to practise in a particular profession, or investigating complaints about the fitness or competence of a member of a profession or any *other activity* requiring authorisation, such as a licence, permit or certificate of fitness, from the public authority or another body, is within scope of this subsection. (For this purpose to apply, the granting of the authorisation must be subject to considerations of fitness and competence.)

1.368

Law enforcement – s 35(2)(e)

(e) to ascertain the cause of an accident;

This purpose relates to any sort of accident investigation, from a routine "slip or trip" to major accident investigations carried out, for example by the police, the Health and Safety Executive etc.

1.369

Law enforcement – s 35(2)(f)–(h)

(f) to protect a charity against misconduct or mis-management (whether by trustees or other persons) in its administration;
(g) to protect the property of a charity from loss or mismanagement;
(h) to recover the property of a charity;

These purposes could have wide application given the range of bodies with charitable status, including some which are public authorities for the purposes of FOISA (for example, universities or arm's-length bodies such as former local authority culture and leisure bodies).

1.370

Law enforcement – s 35(2)(i)

(i) to secure the health, safety and welfare of persons at work; and

This purpose relates to the legal and regulatory framework which requires employers (including public authorities) to ensure the health and safety of their employees at work.

1.371

Law enforcement – s 35(2)(j)

(j) **to protect persons, other than persons at work, against risk to health or safety where that risk arises out of, or in connection with, the actions of persons at work.**

1.372   This encompasses physical or mental health, in this case as it is affected by the actions of persons at work. "Safety" should be given its natural meaning and relates principally to physical integrity.

1.373   In its practical application, the issue which most often has to be determined by the Commissioner is whether the scale of harm envisaged by the authority if the information is disclosed is justified or overstated. Instances where the exemption has been upheld include:

- a police report into the prevention of terrorism, the release of which might prejudice substantially the prevention or detection of crime;[157]
- information about maintaining health and safety in a prison, disclosure of which might prejudice good order in prison and the safety of prison staff.[158]

1.374   However, the degree of harm has also been overstated, and information was ordered to be disclosed on:

- the number of sex offenders in specified geographical areas, which in the Commissioner's view would not cause public disorder or cause registered sex offenders to go underground, making it more difficult to prevent or detect crime;[159]
- the number of police on duty at a particular football match.[160]

1.375   In some cases authorities appear to have taken a collective class-based approach, which has failed to distinguish between the degree of harm which would be likely given differing circumstances. When information about payments to police informants was requested (as outlined at s 34(1)), the Commissioner accepted that if this could lead to their identification (and thus either inhibit the source of

---

157 Decision 186/2007: Mr Richard Haley and the Chief Constable of Tayside Police.
158 Decision 097/2006: Mr H and the Scottish Prison Service.
159 Decision 222/2006: Mr Murdo McLeod of *Scotland on Sunday* and the Chief Constable of Northern Constabulary.
160 Decision 071/2008: Mr S and the Chief Constable of Strathclyde Police.

information or endanger their safety), it could be withheld. However, where the payments could not be linked to an individual or an event, then the information could be disclosed. The prospect of this harm varied, and was not the same irrespective of size of force and aggregated amount paid.[161] As a result, information about payments to informants was required to be disclosed by the two largest forces in Scotland: Lothian and Borders and Strathclyde, the latter of which it was reported paid £762,459 between 2004 and 2008.[162] Comparable information on payments for the remaining, smaller, forces was allowed to be withheld.

Confidentiality

36 Confidentiality

(1) **Information in respect of which a claim to confidentiality of communications could be maintained in legal proceedings is exempt information.**

In general, it can be said that s 36 incorporates the law of confidence into FOISA.   1.376

The phrase "confidentiality of communications" will include information which attracts legal professional privilege ("LPP"). Such information can broadly be defined as those communications with a legal adviser where advice is being sought or given (known as "legal advice privilege"), and also documents created in contemplation of legal proceedings (known as "litigation privilege").   1.377

Legal advice privilege

Relevant considerations regarding legal advice privilege are:

- the withheld information must relate to communications with a legal adviser – it should be noted, however, that the exemption may not apply in circumstances where "waiver" is relevant (see Box below);   1.378
- the legal adviser must be acting in a professional capacity and the communications must occur in the context of the professional

161 Decision 037/2009: Mr Stephen Stewart of the *Daily Record* and the Chief Constables of Central, Grampian, Lothian and Borders, Strathclyde and Tayside Police.
162 P Lewis, "Police force paid informants £750,000 in four years", *The Guardian*, 8 May 2009.

relationship with the client. The legal adviser may be either in private practice or an in-house solicitor.[163] (Communications with a legal executive, trainee solicitor etc will also be covered, provided the communications are supervised by a qualified solicitor);

- the information must be confidential: before information can attract legal advice privilege, the document must have been, and must continue to be, confidential between a legal adviser and his or her client. The privilege will not, therefore, apply to information known to the legal adviser through sources other than the client, or to information which is not actually confidential.

1.379   It could apply to information which records:

- discussions regarding how best to present evidence;
- communications seeking legal advice (including copying the adviser into correspondence relevant to the advice being sought);
- notes of phone calls summarising advice provided orally by a legal adviser.

1.380   Legal advice privilege continues to operate even after the professional relationship between the lawyer and the client has terminated.[164]

Litigation privilege

1.381   Litigation privilege (applying to what are known as "communications *post litem motam*") is a distinct aspect of LPP, extending beyond communications between solicitor and client. It applies to documents created in contemplation of litigation (legal action). It relates to communications at the stage when litigation is either pending or being considered.

1.382   Litigation privilege will apply to documents created by the party contemplating the potential litigation, expert reports prepared on their behalf[165] and legal advice given in relation to potential litigation. Litigation does not actually need to take place in order for the privilege

---

163 The judgment of the European Court of Justice in *Akzo Nobel Chemicals Ltd v Commission* (C-550/07 P) [2010] confirmed that legal professional privilege does not protect communications between an undertaking and its in-house lawyers in European Commission anti-competitive investigations. However, this does not affect domestic proceedings in Scotland (or in any Member State which recognises LPP for in-house lawyers).

164 *Hunter v Douglas Reyburn & Co Ltd* 1993 SLT 637.

165 See Decision 016/2008: Mr Tom Gordon and the Scottish Parliamentary Corporate Body.

to apply, and the privilege continues to apply after any litigation has been concluded.

It is only the client who has sought or received advice, or on whose behalf documents have been prepared in contemplation of litigation, who can claim LPP. LPP cannot be claimed by the legal adviser who gave the advice or prepared the document, and the adviser cannot refuse to disclose it if his or her client is content to see that material released.

1.383

In considering whether there has been waiver of LPP, further factors are:

1.384

- only the person to whom the privilege belongs can waive it. Privilege will not be waived where information is released by a solicitor without the permission of the client;
- there does not have to be a deliberate intention to waive privilege for privilege to be waived;
- privilege may not be waived where privileged information has been disclosed for a particular, limited purpose. For example, where the limited disclosure of privileged information is made by one authority to another on the condition that the information remains confidential, it is likely that an authority will still be able to rely on the exemption in s 36(1) when responding to a request for that information;
- parties can disclose privileged information to others with a common interest in the information without waiving privilege.[166]

Limited waiver of legal privilege

If legal professional privilege has been waived, the exemption in s 36(1) will not apply. The question of whether privilege has been waived is likely to arise where legal advice or a document prepared in preparation of litigation has been "deployed", ie has been disclosed in order to support the position being taken by the relevant party.

In *Decision 002/2008: Ms Diana Cairns and the City of Edinburgh Council*, the Commissioner found that part of the legal advice under consideration had been publicly summarised in support of its position. He went on to find that the effect of this disclosure was to waive privilege in the legal advice as a whole. In that case, the Commissioner said "... a party cannot 'cherry pick' or put part of a

---

166 Decision 020/2008: Mr Robert Henery and the Scottish Ministers.

> privileged document or series of documents [where these relate to the same issue] into the public domain without waiving the privilege in the remainder".
>
> However, the extent to which privilege can be said to have been waived was interpreted more narrowly in *Decision 056/2010: Mr William Lonsdale and the Scottish Further and Higher Education Funding Council*. Noting that the rule against cherry picking had been established in Scots law in the context of court proceedings, the Commissioner took a more limited view of the extent to which deployment can be said to waive legal privilege more generally. He concluded that confidentiality and the associated privilege in the information under consideration had only been lost in relation to those parts of the legal advice which had been summarised to Mr Lonsdale. Parts which had not been summarised retained their confidential (and so, privileged) nature.

Public interest regarding confidentiality of communication

1.385   The exemption at s 36(1) is subject to the "public interest" test. However, the courts have recognised that there is a strong public interest in maintaining the right to confidentiality of communications between a legal adviser and their client. Many of the arguments in favour of maintaining confidentiality of communications were discussed in the House of Lords case *Three Rivers District Council v Governor and Company of the Bank of England*, which recorded the Court of Appeal's pithy opinion that "communications between clients and lawyers, whereby the clients are hoping for the assistance of the lawyers' legal skills in the management of their (the clients') affairs, should be secure against the possibility of any scrutiny from others, whether the police, the executive, business competitors, inquisitive busy-bodies or anyone else"[167] and confirmed the view taken in *Balabel v Air India* that "legal advice is not confined to telling the client the law; it must include advice as to what should prudently and sensibly be done in the relevant legal context".[168] The Commissioner has reflected that view in his decisions, observing that, while each

---

167 *Three Rivers District Council v Governor and Company of the Bank of England* [2004] UKHL 48, per Lord Taylor of Foscote at 34.

168 *Balabel v Air India* [1988] Ch 317, per Lord Taylor at p 330.

case will be considered on an individual basis, he is likely to find that the public interest in the release of such communications is justified only in highly compelling cases.[169]

However, this is not a quasi-absolute exemption and in each case **1.386** the balance of the public interest must be assessed and may well favour disclosure. As an English High Court decision observed of the equivalent provisions in UK FOIA:

> "Section 42 is not to be elevated 'by the back-door' to an absolute exemption … it is for the public authority to demonstrate on the balance of probability that the scales weigh in favour of the information being withheld. That is as true of a case in which section 42 is being considered as it is in relation to a case which involves consideration of any other qualified exemption under FOIA. Section 42 cases are different simply because the in-built public interest in non-disclosure itself carries significant weight which will always have to be considered in the balancing exercise once it is established that legal professional privilege attaches to the document in question."[170]

Confidentiality – s 36(2)

(2) Information is exempt information if –
   (a) it was obtained by a Scottish public authority from another person (including another such authority); and
   (b) its disclosure by the authority so obtaining it to the public (otherwise than under this Act) would constitute a breach of confidence actionable by that person or any other person.

This exemption often comes into consideration when contract or **1.387** other commercial information is involved. However, it is simply not the case that the exemption can be claimed by stamping each page of a document "Commercial – in confidence". It has to be established that:

   (i) the information been obtained from *another* person. It cannot be claimed where information is provided "in

169 Decision 023/2005: Mr David Emslie and Communities Scotland. While that case related to legal advice privilege, the Commissioner has taken a similar view in relation to litigation privilege.
170 Williams J in *Department for Business, Enterprise and Regulatory Reform v O'Brien and the Information Commissioner* [2009] EWHC 164 (QB).

confidence" internally, for example, from one department of a large authority to another;

(ii) the information has actually been *obtained*. Information may not have been obtained where it is the product of a negotiated agreement between the authority and a third party (see Box);

(iii) even if there was a breach of confidence, would it be an *actionable* breach – that is, would a person taking such an action have a reasonable expectation of winning the action in court?

Has information been obtained?

Information may not have been *obtained* where it is the product of a negotiated agreement between the authority and a third party, such as an agreed contract. In such circumstances, information passes between the parties and in practice the concluded contract may contain information which has originated from the authority and not from another person.

The UK Information Tribunal had this to say about such an agreement between Derry City Council and Ryanair:

> "It might be said that the effect of any contract is that each contracting party informs the other of the obligations which it will undertake and of its agreement to accept the counterparty's obligations in return. Such a two-way flow might be characterised as a process by which the public authority obtained information from the other party. However, we think that this imposes too great a strain on the language of the Act and that the correct position is that a concluded contract between a public authority and a third party does not fall within section 41(1)(a) of the Act."[171]

(The provisions in UK FOIA at s 41(1)(a) are almost identical to FOISA, s 36(2)(a).)

The Commissioner came to a similar view in respect of a contract entered into by VisitScotland, after he established that the draft contract had been drawn up by the authority's solicitors and was then adjusted in negotiation with other parties to the agreement.[172]

---

171 Decision EA/2006/0014 from the Information Tribunal in the case of Derry City Council and the Information Commissioner.

172 Decision 088/2007: Mr Alan Keith, Chairman of the Association of Dumfries and Galloway Accommodation Providers, and VisitScotland.

For an action to be successful: 1.388

- the information must have the "necessary quality of confidence";
- the public authority must have received the information in circumstances which imposed an obligation on the authority to maintain confidence;
- unauthorised disclosure must be to the detriment of the person who communicated the information in confidence.

There are defences to breach of confidence which bear upon the   1.389
prospect of a successful action:

- the obligation relates to information that is useless or trivial;
- it can be shown that the information in question was known to the recipient before it was communicated to him or her in confidence;
- the information has subsequently become public knowledge; or
- it would be contrary to the public interest to withhold the information. (So while this is an absolute exemption not subject to the "public interest" test in s 2(1)(b), nevertheless the public interest in disclosing the information may be taken into account, although there would be no presumption in favour of disclosure when weighing competing interests.)

While authorities have been able to demonstrate that information   1.390
is held in confidence, in several cases their arguments have failed
because:

- the necessary quality of confidence did not exist – when an applicant sought information on the number of deaths in custody the Commissioner questioned whether this information had the necessary quality of confidence, since it was impossible to conceive of circumstances in which any incident of death in custody would not be reported in the public domain;[173]
- no harm from disclosure had been demonstrated.[174]

Court records

Courts and judges are not public authorities for the purposes of FOISA   1.391
and so are not required to make information available in response to

---

173 Decision 053/2006: Professor Sheila Bird and the Scottish Prison Service.
174 Decision 073/2007: Orkney Pre-School and Play Association and Orkney Islands Council.

FOISA requests. (While the Scottish Court Service is covered by FOISA, it is responsible only for the administration of Scottish courts.)

1.392   Section 37 of FOISA ensures that existing procedures which govern access to information generated by or used in court (and other legal dispute resolution) proceedings are not overridden by FOISA. The exemption ensures that where authorities hold information solely because of their involvement in court proceedings, they are not required to release it outwith those proceedings.[175]

1.393   Section 37 is an absolute exemption.

37 Court records, etc.

(1) Information is exempt information if it is contained in –
(a) a document –
(i) lodged with, or otherwise placed in the custody of, a court for the purposes of proceedings in a cause or matter;
(ii) served on, or by, a Scottish public authority for the purposes of such proceedings; or
(iii) created by a court or a member of its administrative staff for the purposes of, or in the course of, such proceedings; or
(b) a document –
(i) lodged with, or otherwise placed in the custody of, a person conducting an inquiry or arbitration, for the purposes of that inquiry or arbitration; or
(ii) created by such a person for such purposes,
and a Scottish public authority holds the information solely because it is contained in such a document.

1.394   A range of formal documents might be lodged with (or otherwise be placed in the custody of) a court, including indictments (documents

---

175 It has been presumed that this exemption applies even where the court proceedings or inquiry in question has or have come to an end. However, that has been brought into question by the judgment of the (English and Welsh) Court of Appeal in the case of *Kennedy v The Information Commissioner and the Charity Commission* [2011] EWCA Civ 367, which considered the UK FOIA equivalent of s 37. The case involved a request for information held by the Charity Commission in relation to two inquiries it had carried out into the "Mariam Appeal", launched by George Galloway in 1998. While the judges appeared to be willing to accept – albeit reluctantly – that the exemption did continue to apply after the inquiries had been concluded, at the last moment they acceded to the arguments made on behalf of Mr Kennedy that there was an Art 10 ECHR (freedom of expression) point which required to be considered. The court therefore referred the case back to the Information Tribunal to determine whether Art 10 could be engaged.

setting out charges in criminal cases), written pleadings outlining the arguments to be put before a court and affidavits (signed statements taken under oath). Alongside such formal and procedural documents, other relevant documents can be lodged by the parties to a court action in support of their case. Similarly, a wide range of documents might be lodged with or placed in the custody of a person conducting an inquiry or arbitration. This means that the potential scope of the exemption in s 37 is wide.

However, two essential circumstances must exist in order for this exemption to apply. First, court, inquiry or arbitration proceedings must have *commenced*. The exemption does not apply to information held in contemplation of such proceedings which have not commenced. The authority must be able to demonstrate that this is the case.   **1.395**

Second, the information must be held *solely* because it is contained in a document falling within the categories of s 37(1)(a) or (b). If information has been created or held for another purpose, then, even if it is lodged with a court etc, it is not exempt. This was the case where the Commissioner has found that statements of reasons, relating to the refusal of a licence by a local authority for a house of multiple occupation had been lodged in court for the purposes of an appeal hearing, but had been created prior to those proceedings for another statutory purpose. As such, they were not held solely because they were contained in the document lodged in court.[176]   **1.396**

Court records, etc. – s 37(2)

(2)   In this section –
   "court" includes a tribunal or body exercising the judicial power of the State; and

This definition follows that contained in s 19 of the Contempt of Court Act 1981 and includes justice of the peace courts, sheriff courts, the High Court of Justiciary and the Court of Session.   **1.397**

Tribunals falling within the definition of "court" for the purposes of this exemption are listed in Sch 1 to the Tribunals and Inquiries Act 1992, and include, for example, children's hearings, the Mental Health Tribunal Scotland, Employment Tribunals and the Lands Tribunal for Scotland.   **1.398**

Court records, etc. – s 37(2) (cont'd)

   "inquiry" means an inquiry or hearing held under a provision contained in, or made under, an enactment.

---

176 Decision 116/2008: Andrew Montgomery and Glasgow City Council.

1.399   The term "inquiry" refers in this exemption only to statutory inquiries. Statutory inquiries can be instigated under provisions contained in a range of legislation. For example, the one-off inquiries into the Dunblane school killings and Harold Shipman murders were established under the Tribunals of Inquiry (Evidence) Act 1921 (now repealed by the Inquiries Act 2005). Planning inquiries are also statutory inquiries.

Court records, etc. – s 37(3)

(3) **This section does not apply to information held by a Scottish public authority for the purposes of an inquiry instituted under the Fatal Accidents and Sudden Deaths Inquiry (Scotland) Act 1976 (c.14).**

1.400   Section 37 does not apply to information held by a public authority for the purposes of a fatal accident inquiry established under the provisions of the Fatal Accidents and Sudden Deaths Inquiry (Scotland) Act 1976. The exemption under s 34 of FOISA should instead be considered in relation to such information.

1.401   However, the Commissioner has found that an audio recording of a fatal accident inquiry was not held for the *purposes* of an FAI. He concluded that "the audio recording was a product of occurrence of the FAI (as a record of what took place) and that this information can be distinguished from information which was created with the intention of being analysed during the process of the inquiry itself. He is therefore satisfied that the audio recording was created 'in the course of' an inquiry instituted under the FAI Act and not 'for the purposes' of such an inquiry". Accordingly s 37(3) did not apply.[177]

1.402   As a result, the recording was found to be exempt from disclosure under s 37(1)(a)(iii) of FOISA, on the basis that it had been created by a member of the court's administrative staff in the course of the FAI.

Personal information

1.403   Section 38 contains a number of different exemptions dealing with personal information. It regulates the interaction between the Data Protection Act 1998 ("DPA") and FOISA. DPA governs how the personal data of living individuals should be handled by organisations, while providing individuals with a right to access their own personal data. FOISA, on the other hand, provides a general right to the information

---

177 Decision 010/2011: Mr Keith Knowles and the Scottish Court Service, para 50.

held by public authorities, provided that the information is not exempt from disclosure. Section 38 of FOISA sets out the circumstances in which an individual's personal information can be disclosed under FOISA.

For information to be exempt from disclosure under s 38(1)(a) and (b), it must be "personal data" for the purposes of DPA. Deciding whether information is personal data is not always easy – and, since FOISA came into force, has proved to be particularly difficult when dealing with requests for statistics (for example, the number of children diagnosed with leukaemia in a particular area; the number of registered sex offenders living in a particular postcode; or the number of late abortions carried out over a particular time period). The issues involved in determining whether information is personal data are considered in Chapter 6 (Key Issue 4: Personal Information). **1.404**

38 Personal information

(1) **Information is exempt information if it constitutes –**
      (a) **personal data of which the applicant is the data subject;**

This exemption applies where someone makes an information request which is for, or which includes, their own personal data. Although it is an absolute exemption, this does not mean that individuals are precluded from accessing their own personal data; individuals have a right to request their own personal data under DPA. Such requests are commonly known as "subject access requests".[178] **1.405**

Although s 38(1)(a) appears straightforward, there are some pitfalls to be aware of, and it might not always be clear whether the request should be dealt with under FOISA or under DPA. **1.406**

For example, if a request is for a third party's personal data, but the person making the request is acting on behalf of the data subject, this should be treated as a subject access request and s 38(1)(a) applied. (This commonly happens where a solicitor makes a request to a public authority on behalf of a client.) **1.407**

The same issue may arise where a request is made for information which constitutes the personal data of the applicant and of a third party. Where the personal data of both parties is inextricably linked, the Commissioner considers that the appropriate way to deal with **1.408**

---

178 Section 7 of DPA gives individuals the right to be informed by a data controller whether their personal data is being processed by or on behalf of the data controller; to be given a description of the data and to have communicated to them in an intelligible form, the information constituting the data.

the request is to treat the request as a subject access request and to apply the exemption in s 38(1)(a). This will allow the public authority to consider whether to disclose the third-party data in line with s 7(4)–(6) of DPA.[179] However, if the personal data of the applicant and of the third party can be separated (for example, if different sections of a document deal with the different parties), then the Commissioner considers that the third-party data should be dealt with separately under the exemptions in s 38(1)(b) of FOISA.

Personal information – s 38(1)(b)–(d)

(b) personal data and either the condition mentioned in subsection (2) (the "first condition") or that mentioned in subsection (3) (the "second condition") is satisfied;

(c) personal census information; or

(d) a deceased person's health record.

1.409   A description of the types of information which are exempt under these sections is included below.

Personal information – s 38(2)–(4)

(2) The first condition is –

(a) in a case where the information falls within any of paragraphs (a) to (d) of the definition of "data" in section 1(1) of the Data Protection Act 1998 (c.29), that the disclosure of the information to a member of the public otherwise than under this Act would contravene –

(i) any of the data protection principles; or

(ii) section 10 of that Act (right to prevent processing likely to cause damage or distress); and

(b) in any other case, that such disclosure would contravene any of the data protection principles if the exemptions in section 33A(1) of that Act (which relate to manual data held) were disregarded.

---

179 Section 7(4) of DPA allows information relating to another identifiable individual to be disclosed where that individual has consented to the disclosure of the information to the person making the request or it is reasonable in all the circumstances to comply with the request without the consent of the individual. In terms of s 7(6), in determining whether disclosure would be reasonable, the data controller should have regard to matters such as any duty of confidentiality owed to the other individual and any express refusal of consent by the other individual.

(3) The second condition is that, by virtue of any provision of Part IV of that Act, the information is exempt from section 7(1)(c) of that Act (data subject's right of access to personal data).

(4) In determining for the purposes of this section whether anything done before 24th October 2007 would contravene any of the data protection principles, the exemptions in Part III of Schedule 8 to that Act are to be disregarded.

Third-party personal data is exempt from disclosure in three different circumstances under FOISA. These are: **1.410**

- where disclosure would contravene any of the data protection principles set out in Sch 1 to DPA (this is an absolute exemption).[180] This is a complex, but common, exemption (at the time of writing, the Commissioner has published over 250 decisions which look at how this particular exemption has been used). The exemption is considered in detail in Chapter 6 (Key Issue 4: Personal Information);
- where disclosure would contravene s 10 of DPA. The DPA allows data subjects to object to their personal data being processed where the processing is likely to cause unwarranted and substantial damage or distress. The data subject sends a notice, in writing, to the data controller, requiring it to stop, or not to begin, processing their personal data within a reasonable time. The notice must specify why the processing will, or will be likely to, cause damage or distress. On receipt of the notice, the data controller must write to the data subject either confirming that it will comply with the notice or setting out why it considers the notice to be unjustified;

     Where a public authority has accepted a s 10 notice, and an information request is made for personal data caught by the notice, the exemption will apply. However, this particular exemption is subject to the "public interest" test, and so the personal data must be disclosed unless the public interest in maintaining the exemption outweighs the public interest in disclosing the information.

---

180 Where the personal data falls within definitions (a)–(d) of "data" in s 1(1) of DPA, the exemption which applies is s 38(1)(b) as read with s 38(2)(a)(i). Where the personal data is unstructured and falls within definition (e) of "data", the exemption which applies is s 38(1)(b) as read with s 38(2)(b). Most public authorities fail to recognise this distinction.

This exemption[181] has been considered by the Commissioner on only a handful of occasions. In one case, a journalist asked the Chief Constable of Central Scotland Police for the names of police officers against whom race-related complaints had been made. After the request was made, the Chief Constable received s 10 notices from the officers in question. The Commissioner accepted that the Chief Constable was entitled to apply the exemption, although the notices had not been received until after the request was made. He also found that, on balance, the public interest lay in withholding the names of the officers involved, on the basis that ordering the names to be disclosed might reduce the likelihood of such complaints being made in the future;[182]

- where, if the data subject made a subject access request for the information, they would not be entitled to receive the information because of one or more of the exemptions contained in Pt IV of DPA (for example, national security; crime; health, education and social work records; and the exercise of certain regulatory functions). This particular exemption is subject to the "public interest" test. The Commissioner has yet to consider an application which involves this exemption.[183]

Personal information – s 38(5)

(5) **In this section –**
"the data protection principles" means the principles set out in Part I of Schedule 1 to that Act, as read subject to Part II of that Schedule and to section 27(1) of that Act;
"data subject" and "personal data" have the meanings respectively assigned to those terms by section 1(1) of that Act;

1.411   The Data Protection Act 1998 defines "data subject" and "personal data" as follows:

- "personal data" means data which relate to a living individual who can be identified –
  (a) from those data, or

---

181 ie s 38(1)(b) as read with s 38(2)(a)(ii) of FOISA.
182 Decision 054/2005: Paul Hutcheon of *The Sunday Herald* and the Chief Constable of Central Scotland Police.
183 ie s 38(1)(b) as read with s 38(3) of FOISA.

(b) from those data and other information which is in the possession of, or is likely to come into the possession of, the data controller,

and includes any expression of opinion about the individual and any indication of the intentions of the data controller or any other person in respect of the individual;

- "data subject" means an individual who is the subject of personal data.

Personal information – s 38(5) (cont'd)

"health record" has the meaning assigned to that term by section 1(1) of the Access to Health Records Act 1990 (c.23); and

Accordingly a "health record" means a record which: 1.412

(a) consists of information relating to the physical or mental health of an individual who can be identified from that information, or from that and other information in the possession of the holder of the record; and

(b) has been made by or on behalf of a health professional in connection with the care of that individual.

It should be noted that the term "health professional" is itself defined   1.413
in s 69 of DPA and includes professions such as registered medical practitioners, dentists, opticians and chemists. In most cases, the exemption covering health records[184] will not cover social work or special educational needs records, or an employment record which details medical conditions, given that these records are unlikely to have been made by or on behalf of a registered medical practitioner. This particular exemption is absolute.[185]

Personal information – s 38(5) (cont'd)

"personal census information" means any census information –
(a) as defined in section 8(7) of the Census Act 1920 (c.41); or

---

184 FOISA, s 38(1)(d).
185 Although this is an absolute exemption under FOISA, the Access to Health Records Act 1990 gives the patient's personal representative and any person who may have a claim arising out of the patient's death certain rights to access the records.

> (b) acquired or derived by virtue of sections 1 to 9 of the
>   Census (Great Britain) Act 1910 (c.27),
> which relates to an identifiable person or household.

1.414   Section 8(7) of the Census Act 1920 defines "personal census informa-
         tion" as any census information which relates to an identifiable person
         or household.

Personal information – s 38(6)

> (6) In section 8(7) of the Census Act 1920 (penalties), in the
>   definition of "personal census information", at the end
>   there is added "but does not include information which,
>   by virtue of section 58(2)(b) of the Freedom of Information
>   (Scotland) Act 2002 (asp 13) (falling away of exemptions
>   with time), is not exempt information within the meaning
>   of that Act".

1.415   The effect of this is to allow that census information which relates to
         an identifiable person or household is not exempt information where
         the information is more than 100 years old. The exemption for personal
         census information[186] is an absolute exemption.

39 Health, safety and the environment

> (1) Information is exempt information if its disclosure under
>   this Act would, or would be likely to, endanger the physical
>   or mental health or the safety of an individual.

1.416   "Safety" refers to a person's well-being or to their security. It suggests
         freedom from danger as well as protection from, or not being exposed
         to, the risk of harm or injury.

1.417   The term "endanger" is not defined in FOISA, but the Commis-
         sioner's view is that the term is broad enough to apply where there is
         a threat to the health or safety of a person which would foreseeably
         arise in the future as well as the prospect of immediate harm, since the
         exemption does not specify that any threat should be imminent before
         it applies. There must, however, be some well-founded apprehension
         of danger.

1.418   The apprehension of danger may be reasonably demonstrable
         where the authority is aware of specific threats to individuals or
         generally to staff working in a particular role. (Where authorities have

---

186 FOISA, s 38(1)(c).

such knowledge, it is advisable to share this with the Commissioner. On more than one occasion, the Commissioner has found that the case made to him by the authority lacked substance and only after a decision had been issued and appealed by the authority was he then provided with specific information regarding previous activity which justified a well-founded apprehension of danger.[187])

There does not have to be specific knowledge of a direct threat or imminent danger, however. The nature of the information, combined with generally applicable concerns, may be sufficient. This was the case where the general arrangement plans for a ferry were requested from Caledonian MacBrayne. Had the plans (which would show restricted areas of the ship) been made generally available, the ship would have been vulnerable to terrorism or vandalism, thus endangering passengers and crew.[188]   1.419

In other cases the likelihood of endangerment has been found to be remote or overstated. Claims that disclosure of information regarding mobile safety cameras, policing arrangements at a football match, or MSPs' expenses would endanger the safety of the public or specific individuals have all been rejected as ill founded.   1.420

The floor plans of three schools were also found not to be exempt under s 39(1). The local authority had withheld the plans, with reference to the shootings at Dunblane Primary School and the Beslan school hostage crisis in which school pupils had been killed. However, the Commissioner came to the conclusion that the local authority had failed sufficiently to identify specific concerns surrounding the disclosure of the plans. While he understood the precautionary approach being taken by the authority, he considered that the disclosure of the plans would not increase or extend the probability of such events happening,[189] especially since virtually identical plans of a similar school were already available online.[190]   1.421

---

187 Eg, Decision 024/2006: Mr F and the Scottish Ministers. The Commissioner agreed that the original decision should be quashed, after additional information concerning endangerment was supplied by the authority, and a new decision was issued, finding that the information requested was exempt from disclosure by virtue of s 39(1).

188 Decision 055/2005: Russ McLean, Chief Executive of Argyll Group plc, and Caledonian MacBrayne Ltd.

189 In dealing with the same exemption under the Freedom of Information Act 2000, the Information Tribunal held that, in order for the exemption to apply, the disclosure must, on the balance of probabilities, increase the risk of endangerment: People for the Ethical Treatment of Animals Europe and the Information Commissioner and the University of Oxford (EA/2009/0076).

190 Decision 086/2011: Mr B and Scottish Borders Council.

1.422   Where the exemption is applied to prevent endangerment to mental health, it may be difficult to evidence the likely harm or to demonstrate that the authority has the competence to come to a view as to the mental health consequences for an individual or a group of individuals in the absence of professionally qualified opinion.

1.423   Some other legislation does allow information to be withheld if disclosure would harm mental health. Under the Access to Medical Reports Act 1988, a patient may be prohibited from viewing all or part of the report if viewing it is likely to cause serious harm to the physical or mental health of the patient.[191] However, for this to happen, a qualified medical practitioner would have to be of the opinion that the recipient of the information, ie the patient, would be harmed by disclosure. That is quite different from an authority asserting that third parties, for example relatives or even the general public, would be harmed.

1.424   The exemption under FOISA should not be relied upon to withhold information which an authority considers to be "distasteful", on the basis of a general claim that one or more members of the public or staff may be upset by the disclosure of the information:

Health, safety and the environment – s 39(2) and (3)

(2) Information is exempt information if a Scottish public authority –
(a) is obliged by regulations under section 62 to make it available to the public in accordance with the regulations; or
(b) would be so obliged but for any exemption contained in the regulations.
(3) Subsection (2)(a) is without prejudice to the generality of section 25(1).

1.425   In short, where information is environmental information and so must be considered for disclosure under the Environmental Information (Scotland) Regulations 2004 (as provided for by s 62 of FOISA), then s 39(2) provides that the information is exempt under FOISA. This is essentially a technical exemption, designed to allow authorities to manage the relationship between these two laws, both of which give individuals rights to request environmental information. By using the exemption under s 39(2), an authority can go on to consider solely in terms of the EIRs whether the information needs to be disclosed. (The

---

191 Access to Medical Reports Act 1988, s 7(1).

interplay is dealt with in more detail in Chapter 2 but it is clear that there is no scope for the authority to choose to consider a request for environmental information solely under FOISA.)

However, the way in which the exemption is framed may give rise to confusion and unnecessary considerations. As has been established, authorities are not required to claim an exemption and the definition of "information" in s 74 of FOISA does not exclude environmental information. If an authority fails or chooses not to claim s 39(2), the consequence is that a request for environmental information has to be considered under both FOISA and the EIRs. There is no obvious benefit to the authority in doing so: if the information can be withheld under one regime, but must be disclosed under the other, then it must be disclosed.[192]   **1.426**

Even if an authority claims this exemption to allow a request to be considered under the EIRs alone, the "public interest" test has still to be applied to the exemption. So far, the Commissioner has accepted that, since there is a separate statutory right of access to environmental information, the public interest lies in maintaining the s 39(2) exemption in FOISA.[193]   **1.427**

40 Audit functions

Information is exempt information if its disclosure under this Act would, or would be likely to, prejudice substantially the exercise of a Scottish public authority's functions in relation to –

(a) the audit of the accounts of other Scottish public authorities; or

(b) the examination of the economy, efficiency and effectiveness with which such authorities use their resources in discharging their functions.

This exemption covers information relating to audits of Scottish public authorities. "Audit function" has a very specific meaning relating to *statutory* functions (ie as set down in law) of an auditing body. When considering whether the exemption applies, reference should be made to the legislation which gives the auditing body its powers.   **1.428**

In Scotland, the audits of accounts of public authorities are mostly carried out by Audit Scotland, a statutory public body that provides services to the Auditor General for Scotland and the Accounts   **1.429**

---

192 See, eg, Decision 182/2006: Mr Bruce Sandison and the Fisheries Research Services.
193 See Decision 230/2007: Mr Gordon Watson and Scottish Water.

Commission. Audit Scotland carries out or commissions audits of over 200 public bodies throughout Scotland, including the NHS, police and fire boards, further education colleges, and central and local government, and employs a number of in-house personnel to carry out these audits. However, such audits are also carried out by private firms appointed by the Auditor General or the Accounts Commission, whose fees are paid by Audit Scotland. This has a bearing on information which can be said to be "held" by Audit Scotland. The Commissioner has found that information obtained and held by one of these private firms in the course of its audit of a Scottish local authority was not, however, held on behalf of Audit Scotland. It was established that, while Audit Scotland provides guidance and support to these appointed auditors and monitors their performance, appointed auditors act independently in carrying out the audit.[194]

1.430   The exemption covers the audit of financial accounts, but also other audits (such as "Best Value" audits) which look at how efficiently and effectively a public authority is employing its resources in the pursuit of its objectives.

1.431   However, the exemption will not cover *internal* audits of public bodies or audits of bodies which are not Scottish public authorities but which are carried out by public authorities. Equally, where an audit is being carried out, but only part of the audit falls under the types of audit covered by s 40, only that part of the audit can be considered under this exemption.

1.432   This exemption can apply to any information held by the authority, provided that its disclosure would, or would be likely to, substantially prejudice a public authority's audit functions. This could include (but will not be confined to) background papers, supporting data, draft and final reports. Section 40 can also apply at any point of an audit – before it commences, during the audit, or after it is completed. A public authority relying on this exemption will be expected to show that the body carrying out the audit has a statutory function in relation to audit.

41 Communications with Her Majesty, etc. and honours

Information is exempt information if it relates to –

(a) communications with Her Majesty, with other members of the Royal Family or with the Royal Household;

---

194 Decision 126/2008: Mr William Stewart and Audit Scotland.

By way of definition: **1.433**

- "Her Majesty" means the reigning monarch.
- The expression "Royal Family" carries no strict legal definition but, for the purposes of FOISA, the "Royal Family" can be taken to include any person who has held the title of "HRH" during the last 30 years (ie the period covered by the exemption).
- It should be noted that the exemption will apply to communications with those who have been members of the Royal Family even for a limited period of time, but only for the time that they were members of the Royal Family.
- The Royal Household comprises all members of the Royal Family's staff. It should generally be taken to include those individuals who are authorised to act on behalf of a member of the Royal Family (for example, their employees, servants or agents) in fulfilling public, official and constitutional roles.

The exemption applies both to information which records *direct* com-   **1.434**
munications with the Queen, the Royal Family or the Royal Household,
and to information *relating* to those communications.

So, the exemption applied where a specific request was made for   **1.435**
documentation detailing the attitude of the Royal Family and the Royal
Household to the Holyrood Project (that is, the design and construction
of the Scottish Parliament building).[195] It was confirmed that a number
of documents fell within the scope of the request, some of which were
direct communications from members of the Royal Family or the Royal
Household and others related to these communications.

Where a general request was made for the Minutes of the then   **1.436**
Scottish Executive's Management Group, these contained a single item
within the scope of this exemption. However, as this was seen to be
very brief and routine in content, the Commissioner was not persuaded
by the Executive's submission that disclosure of this information
would harm the political neutrality of the monarchy and found that
the public interest lay in disclosing the information.[196]

In another instance, the Scottish Government refused to confirm or   **1.437**
deny whether information was held regarding communications by HRH
The Prince of Wales on certain environmental topics. That request was
dealt with under the quite different provisions of the EIRs concerning

---

195 Decision 051/2006: Mr Peter MacMahon, *The Scotsman* newspaper, and the Scottish Executive.
196 Decision 105/2007: Mr Paul Hutcheon and the Scottish Executive.

personal information.[197] However, the basis of general argument made in that case might also be used as justification for neither confirming nor denying whether non-environmental information is held concerning communications with Her Majesty, the Royal Family or members of the Royal Household (by virtue of the provisions of s 18 of FOISA, in respect of information which might be exempt under this exemption).[198] In that case: "The Ministers (having consulted the Royal Household about this matter) have highlighted that there is a strong expectation of confidentiality with respect to communications between members of the Royal Family and the Royal Household and government" and that "the rights of the Sovereign could not be exercised effectively without this expectation of confidentiality, and that, if the content of these consultations became known, it would undermine the appearance of the political neutrality of the Sovereign". Arguing that only a uniform approach of neither confirming nor denying whether the Prince of Wales had corresponded on particular topics could provide adequate protection, they maintained that "the Prince of Wales knows that the decisions he takes about whether to correspond on any topic and with which Ministers are protected, and that no unwarranted inference can be drawn from the existence or absence of correspondence with any individual member of the government or from the existence or absence of correspondence on a particular topic".[199]

1.438   The Commissioner recognised that, as a result of constitutional conventions, expectations of confidentiality did exist. However, within his role as heir to the throne, the Prince of Wales had spoken publicly on a range of public policy issues over a number of years, influencing and at times shaping public debate. "In doing so, his actions have raised legitimate questions about the role of the future monarch in public life."[200] In the circumstances of that case, which dealt with issues on which the Prince of Wales had made comments which "have been intentionally high profile and apparently made with a view to encourage action", the Commissioner considered there to be "a weighty competing legitimate and public interest in understanding

---

197 There is no equivalent of s 41 in the EIRs; the information was withheld under the general provisions of reg 11(6) concerning personal information.

198 Under FOISA, s 18, where an authority considers that to reveal whether the information exists or is held would be contrary to the public interest then it can issue a refusal notice. However this applies only to information which could be exempt under ss 28–35, 39(1) or 41 and, unlike the EIRs, not to personal information exempt under s 38.

199 Decision 039/2011: Mr Dominic Kennedy of *The Times* and the Scottish Ministers, para 57.

200 *Ibid*, para 72.

the role of the Prince of Wales, and topics on which he corresponds with government Ministers on matters of environmental policy, at least on those matters of public advocacy and expressed views".[201]

Communications with Her Majesty, etc. and honours – s 41(b)

(b) the exercise by Her Majesty of Her prerogative of honour.

The conferment of honours is the Queen's prerogative, in large part acting on the advice of the Prime Minister who in turn is advised by an Honours Advisory Committee.   1.439

This exemption would apply to information discussing the merits and achievements of those who might be nominated for an honour, or setting out reasoning for decisions as to why specific individuals were, or were not, ultimately nominated to receive an honour.   1.440

Should the exemption apply, the "public interest" test must be considered. In general, there is a significant public interest in preserving the integrity of the process by which people are nominated for honours, by allowing private deliberations based on detailed (and personal) information and fully expressed views. This weighed against disclosure in a case concerning a request for the names of those who had recommended a serving high-ranking police officer to receive a Queen's Police Medal.[202]   1.441

However, the passage of time can erode such sensitivities, and the Commissioner concluded that the public interest favoured the disclosure of the information in a file regarding the late Jock Stein, former manager of Celtic Football Club. The information was contained in documents created around 40 years previously; the subject of the information had died in 1985; and the individuals involved in deliberation over the award were almost certainly no longer involved in such deliberations. In the circumstances, the Commissioner decided that the information concerned a matter of largely historical public interest, and should be disclosed.[203]   1.442

201 Decision 039/2011, para 75.
202 Decision 221/2007: Mr Alistair Gemmell and the Scottish Ministers.
203 Decision 079/2007: Kathleen Nutt and the Keeper of the Records in Scotland. The documents, detailing why Jock Stein was removed from the New Years Honours List, when he was due to be recognised for his achievement in leading the first British team to win the European Cup, were subsequently published by the National Archives of Scotland: http://www.nas.gov.uk/about/070629new.asp.

Part 3

THE SCOTTISH INFORMATION COMMISSIONER

1.443   Significant amendments to this part of FOISA were made as a result of the Scottish Parliamentary Commissions and Commissioners etc Act 2010, which came into effect on 1 April 2011. The text below incorporates those amendments. The effect of these is largely to provide the Parliamentary Corporation (the Scottish Parliament Corporate Body ("SPCB")) with certain powers of direction and generally to require greater accountability by the Commissioner to the SPCB.

1.444   The stated intention is not to undermine the independence of the Commissioner, especially in coming to decisions on applications (which could after all concern the SPCB as a public authority to which FOISA applies), but to require greater accountability, especially for the expenditure of public funds. These are not entirely separate matters. For instance, the Commissioner is not provided with a legal contingency fund with which to defend appeals against his decisions. The capacity of the Commissioner to secure independent legal advice and representation on cases which come before the courts therefore depends upon the SPCB giving approval for the allocation of additional funds.

42 The Scottish Information Commissioner

(1)   For the purposes of this Act there is to be an officer known as the Scottish Information Commissioner (in this Act referred to as the "Commissioner") who is to be an individual appointed by Her Majesty on the nomination of the Parliament.

(1A)   A person is disqualified from appointment as the Commissioner if the person is, or holds office in, or is an employee or appointee of, another Scottish public authority.

(1B)   The Commissioner may not, without the approval of the Parliamentary corporation, also be, or hold office in, or be an employee or appointee of, another Scottish public authority.

(2)   The Commissioner is entitled to –
(a) a salary of such amount; and

(b) such allowances,

as the Parliamentary corporation may determine.

(3) Subject to subsection (4), the Commissioner is to hold office for such period not exceeding eight years as the Parliamentary corporation, at the time of appointment, may determine.

Previously, FOISA provided that the Commissioner would hold office for   **1.445**
a period not exceeding 5 years. The period has been extended to 8 years, but there is no provision for re-appointment at the end of that term (see s 42(5) below). It is suggested that the effect of this arrangement is to strengthen the independence of the Commissioner, as it takes away the opportunity for Parliament to remove a Commissioner simply by declining on a majority to reappoint.

The Scottish Information Commissioner – s 42(3A)–(4A)

(3A) The Commissioner is to hold office otherwise on such terms and conditions as the Parliamentary corporation may determine.

(3B) Those terms and conditions may, without prejudice to subsection (1A) –
   (a) prohibit the Commissioner from holding any other specified office, employment or appointment or engaging in any other specified occupation,
   (b) provide that the Commissioner's holding of any such office, employment or appointment or engagement in any such occupation is subject to the approval of the Parliamentary corporation.

(3C) In subsection (3B), "specified" means specified in the terms and conditions of office or within a description so specified.

(4)[204] The Commissioner –
   (a) may be relieved of office by Her Majesty at that officer's request;
   (c) may be removed from office by Her Majesty if subsection (4A) applies

(4A) This subsection applies if –

---

204 The provision in FOISA, s 42(4)(b) that "the Commissioner vacates office on 31st December in the year in which that officer attains the age of 65" was repealed by the Employment Equality (Age) Regulations 2006 (SI 2006/1031).

(a) the Parliamentary corporation is satisfied that the Commissioner has breached the terms and conditions of office and the Parliament resolves that the Commissioner should be removed from office for that breach, or

(b) the Parliament resolves that it has lost confidence in the Commissioner's willingness, suitability or ability to perform the functions of the Commissioner,

and, in either case, the resolution is voted for by a number of members not fewer than two thirds of the total number of seats for members of the Parliament.

1.446   This subsection provides that if the Commissioner is removed from office it must be on stated grounds such as breaching the terms and conditions of office or failing to demonstrate a sufficient willingness, suitability or ability to carry out the role. Previously, Parliament could simply resolve to remove the Commissioner without any stated reason.

The Scottish Information Commissioner – s 42(5)

(5) A person who has held office as Commissioner is ineligible for reappointment at any time.

1.447   As a *quid pro quo* for a longer term of appointment, the Commissioner is no longer eligible for re-appointment for a second term. (Previously, the Commissioner was eligible to be re-appointed for a further term not exceeding 5 years.)

1.448   There are no exceptions to this. Prior to this amendment of FOISA, provision was made for re-appointment for a further, third, term if special circumstances existed which made this desirable in the public interest. This might have been applied, for example, to allow a short-term appointment to bridge any vacant period between the scheduled departure of an outgoing Commissioner and the date by which a new Commissioner could take up office. This is no longer possible. Short-term appointments, if required, would be made from the outgoing Commissioner's staff or from external appointees (s 42(8)).

The Scottish Information Commissioner – s 42(6)

(6) The validity of any actings of the Commissioner is not affected by a defect in the nomination by the Parliament for that officer's appointment.

So long as the Commissioner has been appointed by Her Majesty, then   **1.449**
decisions on applications taken by the Commissioner are enforceable,
even if there has been some inadequacy in the process of nomination
by the Parliament:

The Scottish Information Commissioner – s 42(7)

(7) **The Commissioner, in the exercise of that officer's
functions (except the function of preparing accounts), is
not subject to the direction or control of the Parliamentary
corporation, of any member of the Scottish Executive or of
the Parliament; but this subsection is without prejudice
to sections 42(9C) and 46(2A) and paragraphs 3(4), 4A,
6(2), 7 and 8 of schedule 2.**

This section provides that the Commissioner is not subject to the   **1.450**
direction or control of the SPCB, but then indicates the considerable
exceptions to this general claim, largely as a result of amendments
made by the Scottish Parliamentary Commissions and Commissioners
etc Act 2010.

So, the actions of the Commissioner are not subject to the direction   **1.451**
or approval of the SPCB, except that:

- payments for advisers, assistance or services need to be approved
  by SPCB (s 42(9C));
- the SPCB can direct the form and content of the Commissioner's
  annual report to Parliament (s 46(2A));
- the Commissioner requires SPCB approval for the appointment of staff and the terms of their payment (para 3(4) of
  Sch 2);
- the Commissioner must prepare a budget and send it to the
  SPCB for approval (para 4A of Sch 2);
- the SPCB must approve the acquisition or disposal of land by the
  Commissioner (para 6(2) of Sch 2).

The Commissioner must comply with any direction given by the   **1.452**
SPCB as to the location of the Commissioner's office (para 7 of Sch 2)
or any direction to share premises, staff, services, etc. with any other
officeholder or any public body (para 8 of Sch 2).

The Scottish Information Commissioner – s 42(8)

(8) **Where the office of Commissioner is vacant, the Parliamentary corporation may appoint a person (who may**

or may not be a member of the Commissioner's staff) to discharge the functions of that office until a new Commissioner is appointed.

1.453 A temporary appointment can be made by the SPCB to fulfil the role of Commissioner in the event of an unfilled vacancy.

The Scottish Information Commissioner – s 42(9)

(9) A person appointed under subsection (8) –
   (a) may be relieved of that appointment at that person's request;
   (b) may be removed from office by the Parliamentary corporation by notice in writing given by it;
   (c) in other respects, holds office on such terms and conditions as the Parliamentary corporation may determine; and
   (d) while holding that appointment, is to be treated for all purposes, except those of subsections (1) to (6) and those of paragraph 2 of schedule 2, as the Commissioner.

1.454 A temporary Commissioner can be removed from office by the SPCB without reference to Parliament.

The Scottish Information Commissioner – s 42(9A)–(9C)

(9A) The Commissioner may obtain advice, assistance or any other service from any person who, in the opinion of the Commissioner, is qualified to give it.
(9B) The Commissioner may pay to that person such fees and allowances as the Commissioner determines.
(9C) Any payment under subsection (9B) is subject to the approval of the Parliamentary corporation.

1.455 This could apply to the appointment of legal advisers, internal auditors or assessors; but "any other service" can be read very widely. The practical effect of these provisions is not yet clear, but an agreement between the Commissioner and the SPCB would be expected to ensure that the need to secure approval for any payments would not inhibit the capacity for the Commissioner timeously to respond to or pursue legal actions in the Court of Session or otherwise.

The Scottish Information Commissioner – s 42(10)

(10) Any function of the Commissioner may be exercised on behalf of that officer by any person (whether or not a member of that officer's staff) authorised by the Commissioner to do so (and to the extent so authorised).

The Commissioner has drawn up a Scheme of Delegation which authorises members of staff to exercise certain functions, for example approving decisions or payments. The Scheme also limits the extent to which delegation is permitted, for example limiting the authorisation to cases of a certain type or to payments which do not exceed a certain amount.   1.456

The Scottish Information Commissioner – s 42(11)–(11C)

(11) The Parliamentary corporation is to pay –
   (a) the salary and allowances of the Commissioner;
   (b) any expenses properly incurred by that officer in the exercise of functions under this Act so far as those expenses are not met out of sums received and applied by that officer under section 43(6); and
   (c) any sums payable by virtue of subsection (9)(a) to (c) to, or in respect of, a person who-
      (i) is appointed under subsection (8); or
      (ii) has ceased to hold office by virtue of having been so appointed.

(11A) Subsection (11)(b) does not require the Parliamentary corporation to pay any expenses incurred by the Commissioner which exceed or are otherwise not covered by a budget or, as the case may be, revised budget approved under paragraph 4A of schedule 2.

(11B) However, the Parliamentary corporation may pay those expenses.

(11C) The Parliamentary corporation is to indemnify the Commissioner in respect of any liabilities incurred by the Commissioner in the exercise of the Commissioner's functions under this Act.

The issue of indemnity is linked to the clarifying amendment made to the status of the Commissioner under para 1(2) of Sch 2 which provides that "The Commissioner is … to be regarded as a juristic person distinct from the natural person holding the office".   1.457

There had been a concern shared among Commissioners and the Ombudsman as to the lack of clear distinction between the person and the office. This may have meant that obligations as an employer or under leases, contracts etc entered into by one Commissioner may not transfer to the subsequent appointee and that, in the event of dispute, a landlord or contractor may pursue the original signatory in their personal capacity, rather than the present incumbent office-holder.

1.458   In combination these provisions are clearly an attempt to clarify the position and avoid any personal liability arising from the exercise of the Commissioner's functions.

The Scottish Information Commissioner – s 42(12)

(12)   Schedule 2 to this Act has effect with respect to the Commissioner.

43   General functions of Commissioner

(1)   The Commissioner, with a view in particular to promoting the observance by Scottish public authorities of the provisions of –
(a) this Act; and
(b) the codes of practice issued under sections 60 and 61,
is to promote the following of good practice by those authorities.

1.459   The primary means of promoting good practice by authorities have been: the production of briefing materials on the interpretation of exemptions and other provisions of FOISA; the publication of all of the Commissioner's decisions on a website; organising conferences and seminars on current issues; and circulating regular updates to FOI specialists within public authorities, highlighting key decisions and recent developments in Scotland and internationally.

General functions of Commissioner – s 43(2)

(2)   The Commissioner –
(a) must determine what information it is expedient to give the public concerning the following matters –
(i) the operation of this Act;
(ii) good practice;
(iii) other matters within the scope of that officer's functions,

and must secure the dissemination of that information in
an appropriate form and manner; and

(b) may give advice to any person as to any of those
    matters.

The primary means of doing so have been the distribution of tens of   1.460
thousands of *Your Right to Know* guides; media campaigns targeted at
local and national press; training journalists, voluntary organisations,
youth groups, and advisory bodies on the provisions of FOISA; and
maintaining a telephone enquiry service.

General functions of Commissioner – s 43(3)

(3) The Commissioner may assess whether a Scottish public
    authority is following good practice.

Practice assessments are conducted by the Commissioner into   1.461
the following of good practice by an authority as a whole or, in the
case of large authorities, directed towards particular organisational
functions. While general compliance and practice are assessed, specific
attention is given to aspects of practice which may have given rise to
concern, based primarily upon the Commissioner's prior experience
of the authority's performance through investigation of applications
made to him and response to a pre-assessment questionnaire. An
assessment may lead to a practice recommendation (see s 44). More
often, however, it results in the Commissioner making proposals for
improvement which the authority undertakes to implement by way
of a voluntary work plan agreed with the Commissioner.

General functions of Commissioner – s 43(4)

(4) The Commissioner may from time to time make proposals
    to the Scottish Ministers for the exercise by them of their
    functions under sections 4 and 5 of this Act.

The Commissioner has proposed to Ministers that a range of bodies   1.462
such as local authority trusts, housing associations and private
contractors carrying out certain public functions should be brought
within the scope of FOISA by way of designation under s 5.

Although Ministers indicated that they were minded to designate   1.463
many of the bodies proposed by the Commissioner, and consulted (as
required by statute) on whether coverage of FOISA should be extended

to one or more of these under s 5, they eventually determined in January 2011 not to designate any additional bodies.

General functions of Commissioner – s 43(5)–(7)

(5) The Commissioner may determine and charge reasonable sums for anything done or provided by the Commissioner in the performance of, or in connection with, the Commissioner's functions.

(6) Any sum received by the Commissioner by virtue of subsection (5) is to be retained by that officer and applied to meet expenditure incurred in doing or providing whatever is charged for.

(7) The Commissioner must from time to time consult the Keeper of the Records of Scotland about the promotion under subsection (1) of the observance by Scottish public authorities of the provisions of the code of practice issued under section 61.

1.464   Consultation with the Keeper has been focused primarily on measures to strengthen records management practice by Scottish public authorities and in particular on securing an improved statutory framework. The Public Records (Scotland) Act 2011 goes beyond the Code of Practice issued under s 61 by:

- requiring authorities to produce Records Management Plans ("RMPs") covering all their public records;
- defining "public records" for the purposes of the Act, to include records produced by an authority and records produced by contractors who deliver functions on behalf of the authority;
- establishing a role for the Keeper of the Records of Scotland in approving and monitoring the use of RMPs.

General functions of Commissioner – s 43(8)

(8) In this section "good practice", in relation to a Scottish public authority, means such practice in the discharge of its functions under this Act as appears to the Commissioner to be desirable, and includes (but is not limited to) compliance with the requirements of this Act and the provisions of the codes of practice issued under sections 60 and 61.

A revised Code of Practice issued under s 60 was laid before Parliament   **1.465**
in December 2010.

44 Recommendations as to good practice

(1) If it appears to the Commissioner that the practice of a Scottish public authority in relation to the exercise of its functions under this Act does not conform with the code of practice issued under section 60 or 61, the Commissioner may give the authority a recommendation (in this Act referred to as a "practice recommendation").

(2) A practice recommendation must –

(a) be in writing and specify the code and the provisions of that code with which, in the Commissioner's opinion, the authority's practice does not conform; and

(b) specify the steps which that officer considers the authority ought to take in order to conform.

So far, the Commissioner has largely chosen to agree voluntary   **1.466**
practice improvement plans with public authorities which propose improvements beyond a formal practice recommendation.

Practice recommendation

The first practice recommendation was made to Scottish Borders Council. It identified deficiencies in council practice in relation to:

- *staff training*: in that the general level of knowledge among staff in relation to obligations under FOISA, the EIRs and the relevant Codes of Practice was inadequate;

- *timeliness in dealing with requests for information*: the authority having consistently failed to respond to an acceptable percentage of requests for information within the requisite timescales;

- *monitoring*: the authority not having maintained reliable data of the number of requests refused, reviews carried out, fees charged, and instances when the time limit for reply had been exceeded;

- *refusal of requests*: the authority not having providing applicants with adequate reasons in support of its decisions to withhold information, or inform applicants of their right to apply to the Commissioner for a decision.

> The practice recommendation set out the provisions of the Codes in respect of each of these areas, detailed the Commissioner's findings of deficiency and set out recommended steps to be taken by the Council. It requested that the Council report within 3 months on the measures it had taken in response to the recommendation, with evidence of improvement.
>
> *Practice Recommendation 01/2010 EN–9003 Scottish Borders Council.*

Recommendations as to good practice – s 44(3)

(3) **The Commissioner must consult the Keeper of the Records of Scotland before giving a practice recommendation to a Scottish public authority (other than the Keeper) in relation to conformity with the code of practice issued under section 61.**

1.467   No practice recommendations of record keeping within the provisions of s 61 of the Code have been made. However, joint assessments are carried out with the Keeper when considering the records management practice of a public authority.

1.468   The Commissioner may draw deficiencies in practice to the attention of the authority within a decision notice on a specific application (see Box).

> **Records creation**
>
> An investigation which addressed the lack of recorded information falling within the scope of a request to the Water Industry Commission for Scotland ("WICS") found that:
>
> • WICS's Directors do not record information as a result of meetings or conversations and take a mental note. If actions are required, the directors will advise the appropriate staff verbally;
>
> • WICS's culture is one in which action points from a meeting may be noted (on paper), but little else; once these action points are passed on to the appropriate member of staff, then any recorded information is destroyed;
>
> • if the meeting is held with an external organisation, the chair of the meeting is responsible for the minute;

- the majority of meetings are arranged by telephone and the arrangements for the meeting are recorded in the individual's electronic calendar. These calendar entries are deleted once the expenses for the time period concerned are received.

The Commissioner regarded this as "highly unusual practice, which appears to have the consequence that it would be very difficult for it to evidence and document its work or decision making, for either internal purposes or external scrutiny". The provisions of the Code of Practice on Records Management were drawn to the attention of the authority and in particular those concerning record creation which recommend that "Each business area of the authority should have in place adequate arrangements for documenting its activities. These arrangements should take into account the legislative and regulatory environments in which the authority operates".[205]

The Code indicates that "Records of a business activity should be complete and accurate enough to allow current employees and their successors to fulfil their responsibilities to:

- facilitate an audit or examination of the business by anyone so authorised;
- protect the legal and other rights of the authority, its clients and any other person affected by its actions;
- provide proof of the authenticity of the records so that the evidence derived from them is shown to be credible and authoritative; and
- provide a true and accurate record of the principal policies and activities of the authority for ongoing public accountability and interest, as well as for the historical interest of future generations, including historians".[206]

Decision 084/2011: Mr Tommy Kane and the Water Industry Commission for Scotland

45 Confidentiality of information obtained by or furnished to Commissioner

(1) **A person who is or has been the Commissioner, a member of the Commissioner's staff or an agent of**   1.469

---

205 A Code of Practice on Records Management pursuant to s 61(6) of the Freedom of Information (Scotland) Act 2002 (November 2003), para 8.1 (http://www.scotland.gov.uk/Resource/Doc/1066/0003775.pdf).

206 *Ibid*, para 8.2.

the Commissioner must not disclose any information which –

(a) has been obtained by, or furnished to, the Commissioner under or for the purposes of this Act; and

(b) is not at the time of the disclosure, and has not previously been, available to the public from another source,

unless the disclosure is made with lawful authority.

(2) For the purposes of subsection (1), disclosure is made with lawful authority only if, and to the extent that –

(a) the disclosure is made with the consent of the person from whom the information was so obtained or by whom it was so furnished;

(b) the information was provided for the purpose of its being made available to the public (in whatever manner) under a provision of this Act;

(c) the disclosure is made for the purpose of, and is necessary for, the discharge of-

(i) a function under this Act; or

(ii) a Community obligation;

(d) the disclosure is made for the purpose of proceedings, whether criminal or civil and whether arising under, or by virtue of, this Act or otherwise; or

(e) either –

(i) in a case where the person mentioned in paragraph (a) is a Scottish public authority, had that person received on the day of disclosure a request for the information that person; or

(ii) in any other case, had the Commissioner received on that day such a request the Commissioner,

would, by virtue of section 1(1), have been under an obligation to give it.

(3) A person who knowingly or recklessly discloses information in contravention of subsection (1) is guilty of an offence.

(4) A person guilty of an offence under subsection (3) is liable–

(a) on summary conviction, to a fine not exceeding the statutory maximum; or

(b) on conviction on indictment, to a fine.

This potentially highly restrictive provision appears to owe much to s 59(1) of the Data Protection Act 1998 ("DPA"), which applies to the UK Information Commissioner.

In respect of DPA cases, the Information Commissioner has said: 1.470

"This is understood to mean all information held by the Commissioner for the purposes of and in relation to investigations that he conducts following complaints about compliance with the legislation over which he has jurisdiction."[207]

Read narrowly, the interpretation of s 45 could lead to a conclusion   1.471 that the Commissioner is severely inhibited from disclosing any information volunteered by or gathered from a third party in the course of his duties under FOISA.

Debate in Parliament clearly indicated that the purpose of this   1.472 section was to counterbalance the power of the Commissioner to "in theory require a Scottish public authority to provide [to the Commissioner] any information – without limit and regardless of sensitivity – that the authority holds".[208]

The restriction most obviously applies to information provided to   1.473 the Commissioner in coming to a decision on an application. Usually in the course of an investigation the Commissioner is provided with the information which is being withheld and with submissions by an authority. These submissions may also contain confidential information, for example personal information or details of commercial interests, which cannot be disclosed. It is possible also that the applicant will provide information in support of the application which they do not wish to make known to the public authority or more generally. For example, they may disclose that they are an employee of the authority and they wish the information in pursuit of a dispute; or they may provide personal details as to why they have a legitimate interest in a third party's personal information.

The Commissioner is not required by FOISA to provide reasons in a   1.474 decision notice (see s 49(6)) for his decision. However, there is felt to be a common-law obligation upon the Commissioner to do so. This can present a challenge in giving sufficient reasons to justify the decision without disclosing information protected by s 45.

The courts have recognised the fine line the Commissioner has   1.475 to tread. The Lord President has said in *Scottish Ministers v Scottish Information Commissioner (William Alexander's Application)* (2006):

207 The Information Commissioner's Decision Notice No FS50126668.
208 Justice Minister Jim Wallace, Scottish Parliament Justice 1 Committee meeting, 5 March 2002, col 3297.

> "... it was rightly accepted on behalf of the respondent before us that there remains a common law duty on him to give proper and adequate reasons for his decision. A number of familiar authorities were cited in that respect.
>
> It is important, in our view, when considering these authorities to bear in mind that the respondent, in giving reasons for his decision, is necessarily restrained by the need to avoid, deliberately or accidentally, disclosing information which ought not to be disclosed."[209]

1.476   However, in a later case, the Lord President made it clear that a need for such circumspection "does not absolve the respondent from giving intelligible reasons for his decision"[210] and that a failure to do so will amount to an error in law.

1.477   The Commissioner has taken the view that revealing some information to make his reasons intelligible constitutes disclosure made with lawful authority. It is made for the purpose of, and is necessary for, the discharge of a function under FOISA – in this case, to come to a decision under s 49.

1.478   A decision will therefore, wherever possible, indicate the nature of the information (for example, a report; an e-mail; a contract); the general content or purpose (for example, a policy proposal on a certain subject for approval by Ministers; an exchange between officials on administrative matters; the procurement of certain goods and services); and the submissions made by the authority and applicant (unless these contain sensitive information which should not be disclosed).

1.479   However, it is clear that in coming to his decision the Commissioner should avoid disclosing the information which is in dispute.

46 Laying and publication of reports

(1)   The Commissioner must lay annually before the Parliament a general report on the exercise during the reporting year of the functions conferred on that officer under this Act.

(1A) Each report must be so laid within 7 months after the end of the reporting year.

(1B) In this section, "reporting year" means the year beginning on 1 April.

---

209 *Scottish Ministers v Scottish Information Commissioner (William Alexander's Application)* [2006] CSIH 8 (XA2/06 and XA6/06), paras 17–18.

210 *Craigdale Housing Association and Others v Scottish Information Commissioner* [2010] CSIH 43 (XA51/09), para 28.

The Commissioner's practice had been to make an annual report on a   1.480
calendar year basis – reflecting the fact that the legislation came fully
into force on 1 January 2005. The amendments to FOISA made by the
Scottish Parliamentary Commissions and Commissioners etc Act 2010
at s 46(1A) and (1B) clearly require a change in the reporting period to
that of the financial year.

Laying and publication of reports – s 46(2)–(3)

(2) The report mentioned in subsection (1) (without prejudice
    to the generality of that subsection) must record the
    number of occasions, during the period covered by the
    report, on which the Commissioner failed to reach a
    decision on an application under section 47(1) (being an
    application on which a decision fell to be made) within the
    period of four months specified in section 49(3)(b).

(2A) In preparing a report under subsection (1), the Commis-
    sioner must comply with any direction given by the
    Parliamentary corporation as to the form and content of
    the report.

(3) The Commissioner may from time to time lay before
    the Parliament such other reports with respect to the
    functions conferred on that officer under this Act as that
    officer thinks fit.

The Commissioner has not, so far, chosen to lay any other reports   1.481
before Parliament.

Laying and publication of reports – s 46(3A)

(3A) The Commissioner must arrange for the publication of
    each report laid before the Parliament under this section.

46A Strategic plans

(1) The Commissioner must, in respect of each 4 year period,
    lay before the Parliament a plan (referred to in this section
    as a "strategic plan") setting out how the Commissioner
    proposes to perform the Commissioner's functions during
    the 4 year period.

(2) A strategic plan must, in particular, set out –
    (a) the Commissioner's objectives and priorities during
       the 4 year period,
    (b) how the Commissioner proposes to achieve them,
    (c) a timetable for doing so, and

(d) estimates of the costs of doing so.

(3) Before laying a strategic plan before the Parliament, the Commissioner must provide a draft of it to and invite, and (if any are given) consider, comments on it from—

(a) the Parliamentary corporation,

(b) the Keeper of the Records of Scotland, and

(c) such other persons as the Commissioner thinks appropriate.

(4) The reference in subsection (3)(c) to other persons includes a committee of the Parliament.

(5) The Commissioner must lay each strategic plan before the Parliament not later than the beginning of the 4 year period to which the plan relates.

(6) The Commissioner must arrange for the publication of each strategic plan laid before the Parliament.

(7) The Commissioner may, at any time during a 4 year period, review the strategic plan for the period and lay a revised strategic plan before the Parliament.

(8) Subsections (2) to (7) apply to a revised strategic plan as they apply to a strategic plan.

(9) In that application, the reference in subsection (5) to the 4 year period is a reference to the period to which the revised strategic plan relates.

(10) In this section, "4 year period" means the period of 4 years beginning on 1 April next following the coming into force of this section and each subsequent period of 4 years.

1.482   Although the Commissioner has drawn up and worked to published strategic plans since 2003, the first of these under the terms of this new section must be laid before Parliament not later than 1 January 2012 for the period April 2012–March 2016.

Part 4

ENFORCEMENT

47 Application for decision by Commissioner

(1) A person who is dissatisfied with –

(a) a notice given under section 21(5) or (9); or

(b) the failure of a Scottish public authority to which a requirement for review was made to give such a notice,

may make application to the Commissioner for a decision whether, in any respect specified in that application, the request for information to which the requirement relates has been dealt with in accordance with Part 1 of this Act.

This provides that a person who is dissatisfied with: **1.483**

- a notice (under s 21(5)) in response to a requirement for review of its actions and decisions;
- a notice (under s 21(9)) that the requirement is vexatious;
- a notice (under s 21(9)) that request for information to which the requirement for review relates was one which the authority was not obliged to comply;[211] or
- the failure of an authority to give such a notice

may apply to the Commissioner for a decision.

The application can relate to any aspect of Pt 1 of FOISA; so, for   **1.484**
example, it could be in respect of:

- the application of exemptions to refuse information;
- the consideration of the "public interest" test;
- a notice that the information is not held;
- changes made to the information following the request;
- destruction of the information following the request;
- an authority refusing to recognise a request for information as being valid;
- the charging of fees;
- the time taken to comply with the request;
- the means by which the authority has provided the information if it is contrary to the expressed preference of the applicant;
- the basis on which the authority has judged the cost of compliance to be excessive;
- the authority's view that the request of information is vexatious or repeated;

---

211 By virtue of s 14, an authority is not obliged to comply with a request for information if (a) the request is vexatious or, (b) the authority has already complied with a request from a person and a subsequent request from that person is identical or substantially similar, unless a reasonable period of time has elapsed.

- the failure of the authority properly to provide advice and assistance;
- the failure of the authority to respond to a request or requirement for review.

1.485   It is clear that an application to the Commissioner is valid only if the authority has been given the opportunity to give a notice in response to a requirement for review.

Application for decision by Commissioner – s 47(2)

(2) An application under subsection (1) must –
   (a) be in writing or in another form which, by reason of its having some permanency, is capable of being used for subsequent reference (as, for example, a recording made on audio or video tape);
   (b) state the name of the applicant and an address for correspondence; and
   (c) specify –
      (i) the request for information to which the requirement for review relates;
      (ii) the matter which was specified under sub-paragraph (ii) of section 20(3)(c); and
      (iii) the matter which gives rise to the dissatisfaction mentioned in subsection (1).

1.486   The applicant must provide certain details about the case to allow the Commissioner to check compliance with the procedures set down in FOISA, for example to ensure that a review has been sought from the authority before making an application. This also allows the Commissioner to notify the authority and give it an opportunity to comment on the application (see s 49(3)(a)). The applicant must make clear:

- what was the specific request for information to which the requirement for review relates;
- the reason(s) they were dissatisfied with the original response from the authority which led to them requesting the review (as required by s 20(3)(c)(ii)); and
- the reason(s) they remain dissatisfied, having sought a review (as provided for in the examples given at subs (1) above).

Application for decision by Commissioner – s 47(3)

(3) For the purposes of paragraph (a) of subsection (2) (and without prejudice to the generality of that paragraph), an application under that subsection is treated as made in writing where the text of the application is as mentioned in paragraphs (a) to (c) of section 8(2).

As with a request to an authority for information, the application to the Commissioner can be in a form other than writing, so long as it has some permanency. However, the Commissioner has not received applications other than by typed letters or e-mails or handwritten letters and faxes.   1.487

Application for decision by Commissioner – s 47(4) and (5)

(4) Subject to subsection (5), an application to the Commissioner under subsection (1) must be made –
   (a) where the application concerns a matter mentioned in paragraph (a) of subsection (1), before the expiry of six months after the date of receipt by the applicant of the notice complained of; or
   (b) where the application concerns a matter mentioned in paragraph (b) of that subsection, before the expiry of six months after the period allowed in section 21(1) for complying with a requirement for review has elapsed.

(5) The Commissioner may consider an application under subsection (1) made after the expiry of the time allowed by subsection (4) for the making of that application if, in the opinion of the Commissioner, it is appropriate to do so.

The Commissioner may, for example, accept a late application where the 6-month time limit has passed relatively recently and: 1.488

- the authority has misled the applicant;[212]
- the authority failed to advise the applicant of their right to refer the matter to the SIC;[213]
- reasons that the applicant might be dissatisfied with the authority's response to the request for information have only just become apparent; or

---

212 See, eg, Decision 104/2009: UNISON Scotland and the Scottish Prison Service, where the authority had extended the process of review, giving the impression that the formal FOISA process was still ongoing.
213 See, eg, Decision 059/2011: Ms Agnes McWhinnie and City of Edinburgh Council.

- where the public authority has previously promised to provide the applicant with information but fails to do so, and as a result the 6-month deadline has passed.

Application for decision by Commissioner – s 47(6)

(6) The Scottish Ministers may by regulations provide –
   (a) that a paragraph of subsection (4) is to have effect as if the reference in that paragraph to six months were a reference to such other period of months (being a period of not less than six months) as is specified in (or determined in accordance with) the regulations; and
   (b) that subsection (5) is to have effect accordingly.

1.489   To date, the Scottish Ministers have made no such provision to extend the period within which an application must be made to the Commissioner.

Application for decision by Commissioner – s 47(7) and (8)

(7) Regulations under subsection (6) may –
   (a) prescribe different periods of months in relation to different cases; and
   (b) confer a discretion on the Commissioner.
(8) This section is subject to section 48.

48 When application excluded

No application may be made to the Commissioner for a decision under section 47(1) as respects a request for review made to –
(a) the Commissioner;
(b) a procurator fiscal; or
(c) the Lord Advocate, to the extent that the information requested is held by the Lord Advocate as head of the systems of criminal prosecution and investigation of deaths in Scotland.

1.490   Information held by the Lord Advocate as head of the systems of criminal prosecution and investigation of deaths in Scotland covers all police reports – and reports by other agencies with an interest in the investigation of crime – and related statements, documents, productions etc. Essentially, if material relates to an allegation of crime and is reported to the prosecution for the purposes of the investigation and (consideration of) prosecution of crime, it falls within the ambit of information held by the Lord Advocate in that capacity, as described above.

Information held by the Lord Advocate

The extent to which information can be said to be held by the Lord Advocate as head of the systems of criminal prosecution has been raised with the Commissioner.

A request was made to the Lord Advocate for the written cases presented on behalf of all parties (including the Crown and the Advocate General for Scotland) in a case considered by the Supreme Court and which concerned the legislative competence of the Scottish Parliament.[214] The Crown Office provided details of its own case but withheld all other information under s 48(c). The applicant argued that the provision should be read narrowly and should not apply, as:

1. the prosecutions in question were long over and there had to be doubt as to whether the information was still held by the Lord Advocate in her prosecutorial capacity;
2. even if the information was still held in that capacity, it had to be unlikely that information contained in the submissions of separate parties to the proceedings (for example, the Advocate General for Scotland) is held by the Lord Advocate in the protected capacity; and
3. given the background to the cases, the information was held by the Lord Advocate in her capacity as legal adviser to the Scottish Government on devolution issues in general.

The Commissioner took the view that the provision had to be read broadly, to reflect the independence of the Lord Advocate as head of the systems of criminal prosecution. This was articulated in the Policy Memorandum referring to this provision accompanying the Freedom of Information (Scotland) Bill:

> "Under s 48 of the Scotland Act 1998, any decision taken by the Lord Advocate, as head of the systems of criminal prosecution and investigation of deaths in Scotland, is to be 'taken by him independently of any other person". Consequently, it would not

---

214 *Martin v Her Majesty's Advocate; Miller v Her Majesty's Advocate* [2010] UKSC 10.

have been competent of the Bill to provide the Commissioner with powers to require disclosure of information held by the Lord Advocate – decisions as to the disclosure of information held by the Lord Advocate, as head of the systems of criminal prosecution and investigation of deaths in Scotland can *only* be taken by the Lord Advocate ..."[215]

The Commissioner found that the information was held by the Lord Advocate in that capacity, in which case the provision applies to *any* information so held and does not provide any qualification as to the content or time period for which the information is held.

1.491   However, requests for information can be made to the Commissioner, the procurator fiscal and the Lord Advocate under FOISA and must be responded to in terms of FOISA. So, the timescales for response have to be observed, and if information is withheld, exemptions or other provisions of FOISA have to be claimed and, where required, the "public interest" test applied. If the applicant is dissatisfied with the way in which the request has been dealt with they can require the Commissioner, the PF or the Lord Advocate to review their decision.[216]

1.492   However, if, following this review, the applicant remains dis-satisfied,they do not have a right of application to the Commissioner under s 47(1). There is no equivalent provision in the UK FOIA excluding applications to the UK Information Commissioner ("UKIC") as to whether he has dealt with a request for information in accordance with that Act. As a result, several formal decisions on such applications have been made, in some of which the UKIC finds against himself and upholds the complaint.

49 Commissioner's decision

(1) The Commissioner must make a decision in relation to an application made in accordance with section 47(1) which is not excluded by section 48 unless –
   (a) in the opinion of the Commissioner, the application is frivolous or vexatious; or

---

215 Freedom of Information (Scotland) Bill – Policy Memorandum (SP Bill 36-PM) 2001, para 115.
216 This section refers to a "request for review" but that should be read as if it were a requirement for review under s 20(1).

(b) in the opinion of the Commissioner, the application appears to have been withdrawn or abandoned.

The Commissioner does not have the discretion to choose whether or not to make a decision on an application[217] except where it is frivolous or vexatious or appears to have been withdrawn or abandoned.   **1.493**

Frivolous or vexatious

Whether an application to the Commissioner is frivolous or vexatious is independent of any consideration, under s 14(1), of whether the request to the authority was vexatious. (There is no explicit provision under s 14(1) or elsewhere for authorities to claim that a request for information was *frivolous*.) There are similar provisions in other legislation, for example in Ireland[218] and in Australia (where the application is "frivolous, vexatious, misconceived, lacking in substance or not made in good faith").[219]   **1.494**

In Scotland, the Scottish Legal Complaints Commission can decide not to investigate complaints which are "frivolous, vexatious or totally without merit".[220]   **1.495**

Although the terminology is well known in law regarding cases which are manifestly hopeless and have no prospect of success, or litigation embarked upon simply to cause delay or embarrassment, these words are not defined in FOISA regarding applications to the Commissioner. The provision has been used very rarely, with only 13 applications deemed frivolous and six vexatious out of over 3,000 over a 6-year period. (This is usually where the Commissioner has already made a determination on a particular matter and another application is made on the same matter, usually by the applicant or someone connected with the applicant.)   **1.496**

Withdrawn or abandoned

An application can be said to be withdrawn when the applicant so informs the Commissioner. This may occur where: **1.497**

---

217 In contrast to the Scottish Public Services Ombudsman, for example, who can decide whether to initiate, continue or discontinue an investigation: Scottish Public Services Ombudsman Act 2002, s 2(3).
218 Freedom of Information Act 1997, s 34(9)(a)(i).
219 Freedom of Information Act 1982, s 54W.
220 Legal Profession and Legal Aid (Scotland) Act 2007, s 2(4).

- the cause of dissatisfaction has been addressed belatedly, for example where a response has been provided by the authority, information has been provided or fees have been waived;
- settlement has taken place;
- the applicant no longer wishes to receive the information;
- the applicant recognises that a decision is not necessary or will not be favourable. For example, where an application concerns the applicant's own personal data, the applicant may accept, through discussion with the investigating officer, that there is no purpose in pursuing the matter under FOISA.

1.498   An application may be deemed to have been abandoned when an applicant stops corresponding with the Commissioner's investigating officer, usually because one of the matters listed above has happened.

Commissioner's decision – s 49(2)

(2) **In a case where the Commissioner determines that subsection (1) does not require a decision to be made, that officer must give the applicant and the Scottish public authority in question notice in writing within one month of receipt of the application, or within such other period as is reasonable in the circumstances, specifying –**
  (a) **that no decision falls to be made in relation to the application; and**
  (b) **the reasons why that is the case.**

1.499   Even if, in the opinion of the Commissioner, an application is frivolous or vexatious, the applicant needs to be told of this determination and that no decision requires to be made on it. (An applicant has the right to appeal this determination to the Court of Session in terms of s 56(a) of FOISA.)

Commissioner's decision – s 49(3)

(3) **In any other case, the Commissioner must –**
  (a) **give that authority notice in writing of the application and invite its comments; and**
  (b) **if no settlement has in the meantime been effected, reach a decision on the application before the expiry of four months after receiving it, or before the expiry of such other period as is reasonable in the circumstances.**

A notice is given to the authority which identifies the applicant, the   **1.500**
substance and date of the request for information and the nature of
the dissatisfaction expressed to the Commissioner, and the authority
is also usually supplied with a copy of the application. Comments
(often referred to as "submissions") are sought. These comments can
amplify the reasons given to the applicant as to why an exemption
applies or the public interest lies in withholding the information. The
authority may give the Commissioner confidential information in
support of their position which has not been, and cannot be, divulged
to the applicant, for example concerning personal information or
commercial interests.

The effect of subs (3)(b) is to require a decision to be issued within   **1.501**
4 months unless the Commissioner considers that a longer period is
justified in the circumstances of the case. In practice, many contested
cases will take longer than 4 months. In the course of investigation
further submissions may be required to clarify a range of matters and, if
an authority is served with an information notice by the Commissioner
during the course of an investigation, it must be allowed at least 42
days in which to reply or appeal against the notice.

A small number of cases may be suspended to await the outcome of   **1.502**
an appeal to the Court of Session on a similar case or highly pertinent
point of interpretation.

Nevertheless, the 4-month timescale signals Parliament's intent   **1.503**
that cases should be dealt with expeditiously and Parliament has to
be informed of any cases where the Commissioner has taken longer
than that time to reach a decision. (In the 2010 Annual Report the
Commissioner reported that 61 per cent of cases closed that year were
closed within 4 months.)

Commissioner's decision – s 49(4)

(4) **The Commissioner may endeavour to effect a settlement
between the applicant and that authority before the
expiry of the period allowed by subsection (3) for reaching
a decision on the application.**

A settlement is a mutually agreed informal resolution of an   **1.504**
application. This most often entails the applicant receiving some
or all of the information requested, in return for withdrawing the
application, thereby not requiring the Commissioner to make a
decision. (The means by which the Commissioner endeavours to reach
a settlement are dealt with in greater detail in Chapter 9: The Conduct
of Investigations.)

1.505   The Commissioner is not required to attempt to effect a settlement. Settlement usually occurs where:

- the authority recognises that it is in a position to satisfy the request;
- the authority offers some other information or assistance which satisfies the applicant; or
- the applicant clarifies or revises the request such that the authority is able to provide a satisfactory response.

Commissioner's decision – s 49(5)

(5) **The Commissioner must give the applicant and that authority, within the time allowed by subsection (3), notice in writing (referred to in this Act as a "decision notice") of any decision under paragraph (b) of that subsection.**

1.506   The same decision notice is provided to both the applicant and the authority.

Commissioner's decision – s 49(6)

(6) **Where the Commissioner decides that that authority has not dealt with a request for information in accordance with Part 1 of this Act, the notice under subsection (5) must specify –**
   (a) **the provision of that Part with which the authority has failed to comply and the respect in which it has so failed;**
   (b) **the steps which, in the opinion of the Commissioner, the authority must take to comply with the provision; and**
   (c) **the time within which those steps must be taken.**

1.507   The decision notice will usually set out:

- the background to the application, including the substance of the request, the response from the authority and response to the request for review;
- the nature of the Commissioner's investigation, by which information was gathered to allow the Commissioner to come to a decision, and confirming that comments on the application were sought from the authority;

- the Commissioner's analysis and findings;
- the decision. In compliance with this section, the Commissioner will specify the parts of FOISA with which the authority has failed to comply; what steps should be taken to comply (for example, provide some or all information); and a date by which this should be done.

Commissioner's decision – s 49(7)

(7) **The time specified under subsection (6)(c) must not expire before the end of the period within which an appeal may be brought under section 56 against the decision of the Commissioner and, if such an appeal is brought, no step which is affected by the appeal need be taken before the cause is finally determined.**

An appeal to the Court of Session must be made within 42 days   1.508
after the date of intimation of the decision notice. Consequently, the time within which steps must be taken will be indicated by a date which is more than 42 days (usually 45 days) after the decision notice is issued.[221]

Commissioner's decision – s 49(8)

(8) **A notice under subsection (2) or (5) must contain particulars of the right of appeal conferred by section 56.**

The decision notice will inform both the applicant and the authority   1.509
that an appeal can be made to the Court of Session on a point of law only and the time (42 days) within which an appeal must be made.

Commissioner's decision – s 49(9)

(9) **This section is subject to section 52.**

Section 52 provides that the Commissioner's decision given to the   1.510
Scottish Administration can in certain circumstances cease to have effect if the First Minister lays a certificate before Parliament.

50 Information notices

(1) **Where the Commissioner –**
    (a) **has received an application under section 47(1); or**
    (b) **reasonably requires information –**

---

221 The rules governing appeals under FOISA are found in the Act of Sederunt (Rules of the Court of Session 1994) (SI 1994/1443), rr 41.18–41.22.

> (i) for the purpose of determining whether a Scottish public authority has complied or is complying with the provisions of this Act; or
>
> (ii) for the purpose of determining whether the practice of a Scottish public authority conforms with the code of practice issued under section 60 or 61,
>
> that officer may give the authority notice in writing (referred to in this Act as "an information notice") requiring it, within such time as is specified in the notice, to give the officer, in such form as may be so specified, such information relating to the application, to compliance with this Act or to conformity with the code of practice as is so specified.

1.511   The Commissioner can issue an information notice either in response to an application for a decision or on his own initiative to check on an authority's compliance with FOISA or its related Codes of Practice.

1.512   All but one of the 116 information notices issued so far have been in the context of the investigation of applications. One information notice was issued following an assessment of a local authority's practice under FOISA.

1.513   Often, when authorities are invited to provide comment on the application they are also asked to respond to specific questions concerning it. Where there is no response to this request or a reminder, then an information notice may be given to the authority.

1.514   Importantly, the Commissioner can specify the form in which information is to be provided, allowing him to require that information be given in the form of copies of original documents and records. If this were not the case, the Commissioner's powers of investigation would be much weaker, and he would have to have recourse to his powers, under Sch 3 to FOISA, to obtain a warrant to enter and search a public authority's premises, inspect and seize documents etc, on a much more regular basis.

Information notices – s 50(2) and (3)

> (2) An information notice must contain –
>
> (a) in a case mentioned in paragraph (a) of subsection (1) a statement that the Commissioner has received an application under section 47(1); or
>
> (b) in a case mentioned in paragraph (b) of that subsection, a statement of –

     (i) the purpose mentioned in that paragraph for which that officer regards the specified information as relevant;

     (ii) the officer's reasons for so regarding the information; and

     (iii) the time within which the information is to be given.

(3) An information notice must contain also particulars of the right of appeal conferred by section 56.

The right of appeal against an information notice is the same as for a decision notice: to the Court of Session within 42 days.   **1.515**

Information notices – s 50(4)

(4) The time specified under subsection (2)(b)(iii) in an information notice must not expire before the end of the period within which an appeal may be brought under section 56 against the notice; and, if such an appeal is brought, the information need not be given pending the determination or withdrawal of the appeal.

This section, by making explicit reference to the statement of time required by subs (2)(b)(iii), appears to apply only to information notices which the Commissioner has issued on his own initiative regarding compliance with FOISA or Codes of Practice. There is no explicit reference here (or elsewhere) to how long an authority must be given to respond to notices given in respect of applications received by the Commissioner. However, it is now thought sensible to allow the same period of time (42 days) as though this section did have direct application to all information notices.   **1.516**

Information notices – s 50(5)

(5) A Scottish public authority is not obliged by virtue of this section to give the Commissioner information in respect of –

     (a) a communication between professional legal adviser and client in connection with the giving of legal advice to the client with respect to that client's obligations under this Act; or

     (b) a communication between professional legal adviser and client, or between such adviser or client and

> another person, made in connection with or in contemplation of proceedings under or arising out of this Act and for the purpose of such proceedings.

1.517   Although the Commissioner does not specifically ask for such information, the authority can choose to give it, particularly if it believes that it will strengthen its submission in response to the application or to address matters raised in the notice.

Information notices – s 50(6) and (7)

> (6) In subsection (5), references to the client of a professional legal adviser include references to a person representing such client.
> (7) Subject to subsection (5), neither –
>   (a) an obligation to maintain secrecy; nor
>   (b) any other restriction on disclosure,
>   however arising or imposed, affects the duty to comply with an information notice.

1.518   An authority cannot decline to provide information in response to an information notice on the ground that it has given an undertaking not to disclose certain information, for example exchanged with or received from a third party on the condition of secrecy. Nor can it decline to comply with the notice because of any other perceived restriction on disclosure, for example where otherwise there would be a statutory prohibition on disclosure.

1.519   Some authorities have requested that an information notice be given to them where the Commissioner requires to see personal data, to avoid any breach of the Data Protection Act 1998. However, this is unnecessary. A public authority required to disclose personal data to the Commissioner for the purposes of determining an application made to him will not breach the 1998 Act, where the "processing" of the data is necessary for the exercise of functions conferred on the Commissioner by or under FOISA.[222]

Information notices – s 50(8) and (9)

> (8) The Commissioner may cancel an information notice by notice in writing given to the authority.

---

222 Data Protection Act 1998, Sch 2, condition 5(b), Sch 3, condition 7(1)(b).

(9) In this section, "information" includes unrecorded infor-
     mation.

This sometimes overlooked provision allows the Commissioner to ask   1.520
for more than the usual recorded information. As other commentators
have recognised: "In effect therefore, the Commissioner can require
individuals such as the employees of Scottish public authorities to
give the equivalent of precognitions."[223]

The same provision exists in the UK FOIA[224] and similar conclusions   1.521
have been drawn that "this means that the Commissioner may require
an authority to provide evidence of, for example, its employees'
recollection of events".[225]

Information notice requiring unrecorded information

An information notice was given by the Commissioner to Scottish
Ministers in *Decision 025/2011: Mr Simon Johnson of* The Daily
Telegraph *and the Scottish Ministers* concerning local income tax
projections. It asked *inter alia* whether, to the knowledge of each
Minister or Special Adviser, any recorded information was generated
and held at any time which would fall within the scope of the request.
It asked furthermore: "What was the understanding of Ministers and
special advisers as to whether information of relevance to the subject
matter of the request should or should not be recorded?"

An appeal against the notice, lodged at the Court of Session on
behalf of Ministers, was subsequently settled, with information in
response to questions asked in the notice being provided and the
notice being withdrawn.

---

51 Enforcement notices

(1) If the Commissioner is satisfied that a Scottish public
     authority has failed to comply with a provision of Part 1
     of this Act, the Commissioner may give the authority a
     notice (referred to in this Act as "an enforcement notice")
     requiring the authority to take, within such time as is
     specified in the notice, such steps as are so specified for so
     complying.

---

223 *Current Law Statutes* 2002, asp 13, para 13–83.
224 Freedom of Information Act 2000, s 51(8).
225 M Turle, *Freedom of Information Manual* (Sweet & Maxwell, 2005), p 188, para 1–270.

(2) An enforcement notice must contain –
   (a) a statement of the provision with which the Commissioner is satisfied that the authority has failed to comply and the respect in which it has not done so; and
   (b) particulars of the right of appeal conferred by section 56.
(3) The time specified under subsection (1) must not expire before the end of the period within which an appeal may be brought under section 56 against the notice and, if such an appeal is brought, the notice need not be complied with before the cause is finally determined.
(4) The Commissioner may cancel an enforcement notice by notice in writing given to the authority.
(5) This section is subject to section 52.

1.522   Enforcement notices are likely to be used where a public authority has systematically failed to comply with any relevant provision in Pt 1 of FOISA, or where a particular example of non-compliance is so severe that it warrants firm and immediate action. An enforcement notice may be used where a public authority has failed to comply with a practice recommendation (although the failure to comply would also have to be a breach of Pt 1, of course) and may be used where a public authority has failed to adopt a publication scheme in line with s 23 or to make information available under that scheme in line with s 24. The Commissioner has not so far found it necessary to issue such notices.

52 Exception from duty to comply with certain notices

(1) This section applies to a decision notice or enforcement notice which –
   (a) is given to the Scottish Administration; and
   (b) relates to a perceived failure, in respect of one or more requests for information, to comply with section 1(1) in respect of information which, by virtue of section 29, 31(1), 32(1)(b), 34, 36(1) or 41(b), is exempt information.
(2) A decision notice or enforcement notice to which this section applies ceases to have effect, in so far as it relates to the perceived failure, if, not later than the thirtieth working day following the effective date, the First Minister of the Scottish Executive, after consulting the other members

of that Executive, signs and gives the Commissioner a certificate stating that the First Minister has on reasonable grounds formed, after such consultation, the opinion both that –

(a) there was no such failure; and

(b) the information requested is of exceptional sensitivity.

(3) The First Minister is, by not later than the tenth working day after such a certificate-

(a) is given, to lay a copy of it before the Parliament; and

(b) is given in relation to a decision notice, to inform the person to whose application the notice relates of the reasons for the opinion formed,

except that the First Minister is not obliged to provide information under paragraph (b) if, or to the extent that, compliance with that paragraph would necessitate the disclosure of exempt information.

(4) In subsection (2), "the effective date", in relation to a notice, means –

(a) the day on which the notice was given to the Scottish Administration; or

(b) where an appeal under section 56 is brought, the day on which the cause is finally determined.

This section gives the First Minister the authority to prevent a decision or enforcement notice, given to the Scottish Administration by the Commissioner, from having effect.   1.523

For this to happen, several conditions have to be met. The notice must relate to the failure to comply with a request for information which falls within the scope of certain exemptions dealing with: 1.524

- formulation of Scottish administration policy (s 29);
- safeguarding national security (s 31(1));
- confidential information obtained from a state other than the United Kingdom, an international organisation or an international court (s 32(1)(b));
- investigations by Scottish public authorities and proceedings arising out of such investigations (s 34);
- information in respect of which a claim to confidentiality of communications could be maintained in legal proceedings (s 36(1));
- the exercise by the Queen of her prerogative of honour (s 41(b)).

1.525   The First Minister has to consult "the other members of the Executive". This has been taken to mean a collective decision by the Cabinet, rather than a requirement for consulting members individually.[226]

1.526   The First Minister has to give the Commissioner a certificate which states that he has, on reasonable grounds and after such consultation, formed the opinion that the Scottish Administration has not failed to comply with s 1(1) *and* that the information requested is of exceptional sensitivity.

1.527   The notice can be given within 30 working days of the relevant notice being given to the Administration or, if the Ministers have challenged the notice at the Court of Session, within 30 working days of any determination of the court.

1.528   The First Minister's certificate can be challenged only by judicial review.

53 Failure to comply with notice

(1) If a Scottish public authority has failed to comply with –

(a) so much of a notice given to it by the Commissioner under subsection (5) of section 49 as, by virtue of subsection (6)(b) of that section, requires steps to be taken by the authority;

(b) an information notice; or

(c) an enforcement notice,

the Commissioner may certify in writing to the court that the authority has failed to comply with the notice.

(2) For the purposes of this section, a Scottish public authority which, in purported compliance with an information notice –

(a) makes a statement which it knows to be false in a material respect; or

(b) recklessly makes a statement which is false in a material respect,

is to be taken to have failed to comply with the notice.

(3) Where a failure to comply is certified under subsection (1), the court may inquire into the matter and, after hearing any witness who may be produced against or on behalf of the authority, and after hearing any statement that may

---

226 The Justice Minister informed the Parliament's Justice Committee that "our view is that section 52 is structured to mean that the consultation would involve the Cabinet's collective decision and the decisions of the Lord Advocate and Solicitor-General for Scotland" (Justice 1 Committee, 5 March 2002, col 3306).

be offered in defence, may deal with the authority as if it had committed a contempt of court.

(4) In this section, "the court" means the Court of Session.

If an authority fails to comply with the requirements of a decision notice, an information notice or an enforcement notice, the Commissioner can certify this failure to the Court of Session, which may deal with the authority as though it had committed a contempt of court. The penalty for contempt of court in Scottish proceedings is a fine or a maximum term of imprisonment of 2 years or both.[227] There has never yet been an instance when a Scottish public authority has failed to comply with any such notice by the Commissioner (except by way of appeal as provided for by s 56).[228]

1.529

54 Powers of entry and inspection

Schedule 3, which makes provision as to powers of entry and inspection, has effect.

55 No civil right of action against Scottish public authority

(1) This Act does not confer a right of action in civil proceedings in respect of failure by a Scottish public authority to comply with a duty imposed by, under or by virtue of this Act.

(2) Subsection (1) does not affect the powers of the Commissioner under section 53(1).

The section prevents anyone dissatisfied with the way in which a public authority has dealt with their information request from taking action against the public authority in the courts instead of making an application to the Commissioner. In practice, this strengthens the role of the Commissioner as, subject to appeals against his decisions, it is left to the Commissioner to interpret the provisions of FOISA.

1.530

56 Appeal against notices under Part 4

An appeal, on a point of law, to the Court of Session may be made –

(a) against a decision by the Commissioner under subsection (2) of section 49, by the person who applied for that decision;

---

227 Contempt of Court Act 1981, s 15(2).
228 In line with the Act of Sederunt (Rules of the Court of Session Amendment No 5) (Miscellaneous) 2005, an application made under s 53(3) shall be made by petition.

> (b) against a decision by the Commissioner under
>   subsection (3)(b) of that section –
>   (i) by that person; or
>   (ii) by the Scottish public authority in respect of which
>   the decision was made; or
> (c) against the decision which resulted in the giving of-
>   (i) an information notice; or
>   (ii) an enforcement notice,
> to a Scottish public authority, by that authority.

1.531   Appeals against the Commissioner's decisions are to be made on a point of law (that is, restricted to the interpretation and application of the law). The right to bring appeals extends only to the applicant or the authority. A third party, for example a commercial firm whose interests were affected by a decision, cannot make an appeal.

1.532   Thus far, 32 appeals against decision notices have been intimated and one against an information notice.[229] Only a few cases result in a hearing in the Court of Session, with others being withdrawn or conceded prior to a hearing. Where there has been a hearing this has been heard by the Inner House of the Court of Session.

Part 5

HISTORICAL RECORDS

57 The expression "historical record"

> (1) For the purposes of this Part, a record becomes a
>   "historical record" at the end of that period of thirty years
>   which commences at the beginning of the calendar year
>   following that in which the record is created.

1.533   Although the term "30-year rule" is often used in the Scottish media, as the Keeper of Records has noted:

> "The 1958 Public Records Act exempts from its terms records of government bodies that are mainly concerned with Scottish affairs.

---

229 Of these, 26 appeals were made by authorities; and seven by applicants.

In consequence therefore, the '30 Year rule' [sic] has never applied to Scottish public records. Until 2005, Scottish Ministers adopted the 30 year closure period by administrative action, ensuring that release of public records from government files was in line with practice elsewhere in the UK."[230]

From 1 January 2005, when FOISA came into effect, a request for information could be made for records deposited within the National Archives even though they were subject to a closure period preventing their publication. In the Keeper's view, "More than any other Act therefore, FOISA has radically changed the notion of keeping records 'closed' for 30 years".[231]   **1.534**

In 2009, the Scottish Government instructed the National Archives of Scotland to make available publicly the bulk of the historic Scottish Government files it holds once the information is 15 years old. It was estimated that this would make an additional 13,000 files accessible through the public search rooms of NAS. The material has been made available in phases, with the 4,000 files released in the second tranche said to "reflect topics as diverse as the demise of the shipbuilding industry in Scotland, the BSE cattle crisis, the impact of alcohol on public health, early proposals for constructing a road bridge to Skye, and the further development of winter sports in the Highlands".[232]   **1.535**

The expression "historical record" – s 57(2)

(2) **Where records created at different dates are for administrative purposes kept together in one file or other assemblage, all the records in that file or assemblage are to be treated for the purposes of this Part as created when the latest of those records is created.**

58 Falling away of exemptions with time

(1) **Information contained in a historical record cannot be exempt information by virtue of any of sections 28 to 30, 33(1), 36, 37, 40 and 41(a).**

(2) **Information cannot be exempt information by virtue of –**
    (a) section 41(b) after the end of that period of sixty years; or

230 Response by the Keeper of the Records of Scotland, 29 February 2008, to the 30-Year Rule Review:www.30yearrulereview.org.uk/evidence/we-keeperoftherecordsofscotland.pdf.
231 *Ibid.*
232 National Archives of Scotland: http://www.nas.gov.uk/about/100115.asp.

> (b) section 34(2)(b), 35 or 38(1)(c) or (d) after the end of
> that period of one hundred years,
>
> which commences at the beginning of the calendar
> year following that in which the record containing the
> information is created.

1.536   This means that the following exemptions last for only 30 years:

- relations within the UK (s 28);
- formulation of Scottish Administration policy etc (s 29);
- prejudice to effective conduct of public affairs (s 30);
- trade secrets (s 33(1)(a));
- substantial prejudice to commercial interests (s 33(1)(b));
- confidentiality (s 36);
- court records etc (s 37);
- audit functions (s 40);
- communications with the Royal Household (s 41(a)).

1.537   The following exemption lasts for only 60 years:

- the exercise by HM The Queen of her prerogative of honour (s 41(b)).

1.538   The following exemptions last for only 100 years:

- information held for the purposes of an investigation as to the cause of death of a person (s 34(2)(b));
- law enforcement (s 35);
- personal census information (s 38(1)(c));
- a deceased person's health record (s 38(1)(d)).

1.539   All other exemptions last in perpetuity, although, in practice, the older the information, the less likely it is that disclosure will, for example, cause substantial prejudice or that it will relate to living individuals and therefore qualify as personal data.

59 Power to vary periods mentioned in sections 57 and 58

> (1) The Scottish Ministers may by order amend subsection
> (1) of section 57 or paragraph (a) or (b) of subsection (2) of
> section 58 so as to substitute for the number of years for
> the time being mentioned in the provision in question
> such other number of years (not being a number which
> exceeds that mentioned in the provision as originally
> enacted) as may be specified in the order.

(2)   An order under subsection (1) may contain such transitional provisions and savings as the Scottish Ministers think fit.

In July 2009, the Scottish Ministers issued a consultation paper[233] on reducing the lifespan of eight exemptions contained in FOISA from 30 to 15 years, applicable to all relevant information held by Scottish public authorities. **1.540**

In January 2011, the Scottish Government announced that there would be a Freedom of Information (Scotland) Act 2002 Amendment Bill. Among other actions, this Bill would reduce the lifetime of certain exemptions in s 59 of FOISA. **1.541**

Part 6

CODES OF PRACTICE

60 Code of practice as to functions under this Act

(1)   The Scottish Ministers are to issue, and may from time to time revise, a code of practice providing guidance to Scottish public authorities as to the practice which it would, in the opinion of the Ministers, be desirable for the authorities to follow in connection with the discharge of the authorities' functions under this Act.

(2)   The code must, in particular, include provision relating to–

(a)   the provision of advice and assistance by the authorities to persons who propose to make, or have made, requests for information;

(b)   the transfer of requests by one of the authorities to another by which the information requested is or may be held;

(c)   consultation with persons to whom information requested relates or with persons whose interests

233 Freedom of Information: Improving Openness: Consultation by Scottish Ministers on reducing the term of certain exemptions within the Freedom of Information (Scotland) Act 2002: http://www.scotland.gov.uk/Publications/2009/07/01094653/2.

are likely to be affected by the disclosure of such information;

(d) the inclusion in contracts entered into by the authorities of terms relating to the disclosure of information;

(e) the provision by the authorities of procedures for dealing with complaints about the handling by the authorities of requests for information; and

(f) the collection and recording by the authorities of statistics as respects the discharge by them of their functions under this Act.

(3) The code may make different provision for different Scottish public authorities.

(4) Before issuing or revising the code, the Scottish Ministers are to consult the Commissioner.

(5) The Scottish Ministers must lay the code, and any revised code made under this section, before the Parliament.

1.542   The Scottish Ministers' Code of Practice on the Discharge of Functions by Public Authorities under the Freedom of Information (Scotland) Act 2002 was laid before the Scottish Parliament on 6 September 2004.

1.543   On 15 December 2010, a revised Code was approved which not only superseded the earlier "s 60 Code" but also replaced another issued in 2006 under reg 18 of the EIRs (commonly known as the "s 62 Code of Practice").[234]

1.544   It is described as a concise document focused on the particular provisions of s 60(2) above, recommending that "Where authorities require further information on the application of FOISA and the EIRs, they should refer to the guidance published by the Scottish Information Commissioner".[235]

61 Code of practice as to the keeping, management and destruction of records

(1) The Scottish Ministers are to issue, and may from time to time revise, a code of practice providing guidance to Scottish public authorities as to the practice which it would, in the opinion of the Ministers, be desirable

---

234 The Scottish Ministers' Code of Practice on the Discharge of Functions by Scottish Public Authoritiesunder theFreedom of Information (Scotland) Act 2002 and the Environmental Information (Scotland) Regulations 2004.

235 The current Code is at Appendix 3.

for the authorities to follow in connection with the keeping, management and destruction of the authorities' records.

(2) The code may also include guidance as to the practice –
   (a) to be adopted in relation to the transfer of records to the Keeper of the Records of Scotland;
   (b) of reviewing records before they are so transferred; and
   (c) to be adopted where one Scottish public authority holds records on behalf of another such authority.

(3) In exercising their functions under this section, the Scottish Ministers are to have regard to the public interest in allowing public access to information held by Scottish public authorities.

(4) The code may make different provision for different Scottish public authorities.

(5) Before issuing or revising the code the Scottish Ministers are to consult –
   (a) the Commissioner; and
   (b) the Keeper of the Records of Scotland.

(6) The Scottish Ministers must lay the code, and any revised code made under this section, before the Parliament.

A Code of Practice on Records Management pursuant to s 61(6) of the Freedom of Information (Scotland) Act 2002 was laid before the Scottish Parliament on 10 November 2003. It has not been revised or replaced.   **1.545**

Part 7

MISCELLANEOUS AND SUPPLEMENTAL

62 Power to make provision relating to environmental information

(1) In this section "the Aarhus Convention" means the Convention on Access to Information, Public Participation in Decision making and Access to Justice in Environmental Matters signed at Aarhus on 25th June 1998.

(2) For the purposes of this section, "the information provisions" of the Aarhus Convention are Article 4, together with Articles 3 and 9 so far as relating to that Article.

(3) The Scottish Ministers may, in relation to information held by or requested from any Scottish public authority, by regulations make such provision as they consider appropriate-

(a) for the purpose of implementing the information provisions of the Aarhus Convention or any amendment of those provisions made in accordance with Article 14 of the Convention; and

(b) for the purpose of dealing with matters arising out of, or related to, the implementation of those provisions or of any such amendment.

1.546   The Environmental Information (Scotland) Regulations 2004 ("EIRs") implement the information provisions of the Aarhus Convention.[236] They were approved only in December 2004, but came into effect on 1 January 2005, on the same day as the Freedom of Information (Scotland) Act 2002 came fully into effect.

The provisions and effect of the EIRs are dealt with in Chapter 2.

Power to make provision relating to environmental information – s 62(4)(a)

(4) Regulations under subsection (3) may in particular –

(a) enable charges to be made for making information available in accordance with the regulations;

1.547   The EIRs enable an authority to charge a fee for making information available. The extent to which charges can be made under the EIRs varies from the charges which may be applied in respect of information disclosed under FOISA. In particular, the EIRs do not allow an authority to refuse to supply information solely on the basis of exceeding a certain cost. This is unlike the Fees Regulations attached to FOISA, which do not require an authority to provide any information in response to a request if the cost of doing so would exceed a certain amount (currently £600).

---

236 They also bring into effect the provisions of EU Directive 2003/4/EC.

Power to make provision relating to environmental information – s 62(4)(b)

(b) provide that any obligation imposed by the regulations in relation to the disclosure of information is to have effect notwithstanding any enactment or rule of law;

The EIRs take precedence over other legislation which would prevent the disclosure of environmental information. In effect, the EIRs do not allow for a prohibition on disclosure by virtue of other legislation. By contrast, s 26 of FOISA explicitly provides that information is exempt if its disclosure is prohibited by or under an enactment.

1.548

Power to make provision relating to environmental information – s 62(4)(c)

(c) make provision for the issue by the Scottish Ministers of a code of practice;

The Ministers issued a separate Code of Practice (the s 62 Code) but this has been revised and replaced with a Code of Practice which also meets the requirements of s 60 to provide guidance on good practice with regard to authorities' functions under FOISA (see s 60).

1.549

Power to make provision relating to environmental information – s 62(4)(d)

(d) provide for sections 43 and 44 to apply in relation to such a code with such modifications as may be specified in the regulations;

The EIRs provide that the general functions of the Scottish Information Commissioner (including that of promoting the following of good practice by authorities (s 43) and the power of the Commissioner to make recommendations as to good practice (s 44)) apply in relation to any Code of Practice regarding the EIRs issued under s 62.

1.550

Power to make provision relating to environmental information – s 62(4)(e)

(e) provide for all or any of the provisions of Part 4 to apply, with such modifications as may be so specified, in relation to compliance with any requirement of the regulations; and

1.551   Part 4 of FOISA deals with enforcement and in particular the rights of application to the Commissioner and the Commissioner's powers to issue notices. The provisions of Pt 4 apply, subject to minor modifications, to requests for environmental information dealt with under the EIRs.

Power to make provision relating to environmental information – s 62(4)(f)

(f) contain such transitional or consequential provision (including provision modifying any enactment) as the Scottish Ministers consider appropriate.

1.552   The EIRs revoke the Environmental Information Regulations 1992 and the Environmental Information (Amendment) Regulations 1998 and also modify FOISA for the purposes of the EIRs.

63 Disclosure of information to Scottish Public Services Ombudsman or to Information Commissioner

The Commissioner may disclose to –

(a) the Scottish Public Services Ombudsman any information obtained by, or furnished to, the Commissioner under or for the purposes of this Act if it appears to the Commissioner that the information relates to a matter which is, or could be, the subject of an investigation by the Ombudsman under the Scottish Public Services Ombudsman Act 2002 (asp 11); or

(b) the Information Commissioner any information so obtained or furnished if it appears to the Commissioner that the information so relates as is mentioned in paragraph (a) or (b) of section 11AA(1) of the Parliamentary Commissioner Act 1967 (c.13) (disclosure of information by Parliamentary Commissioner to Information Commissioner).

1.553   The purpose of this section is to allow (not require) the Commissioner to provide information to the Scottish Public Services Ombudsman ("SPSO") regarding a current or potential investigation and to the UK Information Commissioner ("UKIC") regarding, largely, the enforcement functions of the UKIC in respect of the Data Protection Act 1998 and UK FOIA.

It anticipates that the Commissioner may be provided with, or come across, information which is relevant to current investigations by either the SPSO or the UKIC, or which in the opinion of the Commissioner may be worthy of action by them. In respect of the role of the SPSO, this could be evidence of maladministration or service failure by a Scottish public authority. Regarding the functions of the UKIC, it could be information which suggests that access to personal data is being denied to an individual by a Scottish public authority or has been unlawfully disclosed contrary to the Data Protection Act 1998, or that a UK authority has acted contrary to the provisions of the UK FOIA, for example maintaining that information is not held even though evidence from the Scottish Information Commissioner's investigation indicates that it is. **1.554**

The effect of this section is to provide the lawful authority under s 45 of FOISA which is required for the disclosure of information "obtained by or furnished to the Commissioner under or for the purposes of this Act". So, for example, if the Commissioner had served an information notice on an authority and then passed some of the information obtained to the SPSO then without this section the Commissioner could have been guilty of an offence and liable, if convicted, to a fine. **1.555**

There are reciprocal provisions under s 19(8) of the Scottish Public Services Ombudsman Act 2002 (introduced by Sch 4 to FOISA) for the SPSO to act similarly in providing information to the Scottish Information Commissioner. **1.556**

64 Power to amend or repeal enactments prohibiting disclosure of information

(1) If it appears to the Scottish Ministers that by virtue of section 26(a) a relevant enactment is capable of preventing the disclosure of information under section 1, they may by order repeal or amend that enactment, in so far as it relates to any Scottish public authority, so as to remove or relax the prohibition.

(2) In subsection (1) –
"relevant enactment" means an Act of Parliament, or Act of the Scottish Parliament, which receives Royal Assent before the end of the calendar year in which this Act receives Royal Assent or any subordinate legislation made before the date on which this Act receives Royal Assent; and
"information" includes unrecorded information.

(3) An order under subsection (1) may do all or any of the following –
   (a) make such modifications of enactments as, in the opinion of the Scottish Ministers, are consequential upon, or incidental to, the repeal or amendment of the relevant enactment;
   (b) contain such transitional provisions and savings as appear to them to be appropriate;
   (c) make different provision in relation to different cases.

1.557   Legislation prohibiting the disclosure of information (and which has the effect of making information exempt from disclosure by virtue of s 26 of FOISA) can be repealed or amended by Scottish Ministers.

1.558   However, the power of Scottish Ministers under s 64 of FOISA only extends to legislation which pre-existed FOISA. Therefore, Scottish Ministers cannot repeal or amend an Act of Parliament or an Act of the Scottish Parliament which received Royal Assent after the end of 2002 or any secondary legislation made on or after 28 May 2002. This assumes that any subsequent legislation or secondary legislation containing a prohibition on the disclosure of information will have been passed in the full knowledge that it will prevent a right of access under FOISA. However, where the information is environmental information this power would not prevent its disclosure under the EIRs.

1.559   Scottish Ministers have lifted statutory bars to the disclosure of information contained in the following legislation:[237]

   • Factories Act 1961;
   • Offices, Shops and Railway Premises Act 1963;
   • Medicines Act 1968;
   • Health and Safety at Work etc Act 1974;
   • Diseases of Fish Act 1983.

65 Offence of altering, etc, records with intent to prevent disclosure

(1) Where –
   (a) a request for information is made to a Scottish public authority; and
   (b) the applicant is, under section 1, entitled to be given the information or any part of it,

---

237 Freedom of Information (Relaxation of Statutory Prohibitions on Disclosure of Information) (Scotland) Order 2008 (SSI 2008/339).

> a person to whom this subsection applies who, with the intention of preventing the disclosure by the authority of the information, or part, to which the entitlement relates, alters, defaces, blocks, erases, destroys or conceals a record held by the authority, is guilty of an offence.
>
> (2) Subsection (1) applies to the authority and to any person who is employed by, is an officer of, or is subject to the direction of, the authority.
>
> (3) A person guilty of an offence under subsection (1) is liable, on summary conviction, to a fine not exceeding level 5 on the standard scale.

The Commissioner has a Memorandum of Understanding ("MoU") with the Crown Office and Procurator Fiscal Service ("COPFS") and Scottish police forces in relation to the investigation of criminal offences.[238]   **1.560**

This MoU provides an agreed framework for the investigation and reporting of criminal offences under s 65. Where appropriate, each alleged offence will be fully investigated where there is *prima facie* a sufficiency of evidence. The investigation is conducted jointly by the Commissioner and the relevant police force (for the area where the alleged offence was committed). The police force has the responsibility for submitting reports of offences, where appropriate, to the COPFS. However, the power of entry, search and seizure, which it may be necessary to use in the course of an investigation, is limited to the Commissioner and his staff.[239]   **1.561**

A formal criminal investigation into an alleged s 65 offence will normally commence only when: **1.562**

- the allegation relates to a formal request for information under FOISA or the FIRs;
- the allegation is accompanied by evidence to indicate that an offence has taken place, for example reliable evidence from a credible eye witness.

Prosecutions must be raised within 6 months of the date of the offence. A person or an authority found guilty is liable to a fine not exceeding £5,000 but not to imprisonment.[240]   **1.563**

---

238 www.itspublicknowledge.info/home/AboutSIC/StrategicAgreements.
239 FOISA, Sch 3, para 2.
240 Criminal Procedure (Scotland) Act 1995, s 136.

66 Saving for existing powers of disclosure

Nothing in this Act is to be taken to limit the powers of a Scottish public authority to disclose information held by it.

1.564   There is nothing in FOISA which *requires* the authority to apply the exemptions or prevents the authority from disclosing information which has been requested if it so wishes (to the extent that it has the power to do so). For example, even though certain information may be held to be exempt because it is intended for future publication,[241] the authority need not claim the exemption and can simply disclose the information.

1.565   Similarly, even where other provisions, such as excessive cost for compliance, do not oblige the authority to comply with a request, nevertheless the authority can still choose to do so.

1.566   However, if an authority decides not to apply an exemption, it may be in breach of other legislation protecting that information from disclosure such as the Data Protection Act.

67 Protection from actions for defamation

Where, in compliance with a request for information, information supplied to a Scottish public authority by a third party is communicated by the authority, under section 1, to the applicant, the publication to the applicant of any defamatory matter contained in the information so supplied is privileged unless that publication is shown to have been made with malice.

1.567   It is possible that the authority holds information from a third party which contains comments which might be regarded a defamatory. If such information has to be disclosed to comply with a request under s 1, then the authority is not liable to legal action for defamation, unless it could be shown that the disclosure was made with malice.

1.568   Such privilege does not extend to the applicant should the information subsequently be publicly distributed by them.

1.569   In practice, it is likely that any material which is defamatory will be exempt from disclosure under s 38 (personal information) or, perhaps, s 30 (effective conduct of public affairs).

---

241 As provided for by FOISA, s 27.

68 Scottish Parliament and Scottish Administration

Section 65 and paragraph 10 of schedule 3 apply to –
(a) a member of the staff of, or a person acting on behalf
     of, the Parliament or the Parliamentary corporation; or
(b) a member of the staff of the Scottish Administration,
as they apply to any other person; but none of those bodies
is liable to prosecution under this Act.

While individual employees or others acting on behalf of the Parlia   1.570
ment, Scottish Parliamentary Corporate Body or Scottish Government
are liable to prosecution for certain offences under FOISA, the
authorities themselves are not liable to prosecution.

So, if a person is found to have altered, defaced, blocked, erased,   1.571
destroyed or concealed a record they would have committed an offence
under s 65. Also, if they intentionally obstructed a person executing
a warrant to enter and search premises, or failed to give reasonable
assistance to the person executing a warrant, then an offence would
have been committed under para 10 of Sch 3. If found guilty, the person
would be liable to a fine of up to £5,000.

However, even though they may have been acting on behalf of the   1.572
Parliament, the Scottish Parliamentary Corporate Body or the Scottish
Government, these bodies are not liable to prosecution.

This section mirrors the similar provision at s 81 of the UK FOIA for   1.573
Government Departments, the House of Commons and the House of
Lords.

(When s 68 was debated in Parliament, it was pointed out that the   1.574
Scotland Act 1998 amended s 40(2)(a) of the Crown Proceedings Act
1947 to give the "main new institutions in Scotland – the Scottish
Administration and the Scottish Parliament – the same constitutional
position as regards prosecutions as the Crown and the Crown in
Parliament have in the United Kingdom".)[242]

69 Exercise of rights by children

(1) Where a question falls to be determined as to the legal
     capacity of a person who has not attained the age of
     sixteen years to exercise any right conferred by any
     provision of this Act, any such person is to be taken to
     have that capacity who has a general understanding of
     what it means to exercise the right.

---

242 Jim Wallace, MSP, Minister for Justice, Scottish Parliament Justice 1 Committee Official
    Report, 5 March 2002, col 3346.

> (2) **Without prejudice to the generality of subsection (1), a person who has attained the age of twelve years is to be presumed to be of sufficient age and maturity to have such understanding as is mentioned in that subsection.**

1.575   Children over the age of 12 have the full rights of an applicant under FOISA. For example, they can request information and make an application to the Commissioner. Children under the age of 12 are not disqualified from being applicants solely on the basis of age: if they have a general understanding of what it means to exercise the right then they too can expect to have their requests treated like any other applicant (including being in receipt of advice and assistance from the authority).

1.576   There is no similar express provision in the UK FOIA. However, this is not novel for Scotland. Very similar wording is used in the Data Protection Act 1998 (s 66) to make explicit that children can exercise rights under that legislation.[243]

70 Amendment of Public Records (Scotland) Act 1937

> (1) **The Public Records (Scotland) Act 1937 (c.43) is amended as follows.**

1.577   There is no subs (2).[244]

Amendment of Public Records (Scotland) Act 1937 – s 70(3)

> (3) **After section 12 there is inserted –**
>
> **"12A Duty to afford facilities for inspection etc. of certain records**
>
> **It shall be the duty of the Keeper to arrange that reasonable facilities are available to the public for –**
> **(a) inspecting; and**
> **(b) obtaining copies of,**
> **such records held by the Keeper as either fall to be disclosed in accordance with the Freedom of Information (Scotland)**

---

243 That is not to say that children in England and Wales cannot exercise rights under FOIA or DPA.

244 The provisions of s 70(2), relating to the Scottish Records Advisory Council, were repealed by s 4(5) of the Public Services Reform (Scotland) Act 2010. The Scottish Records Advisory Council was established by the Public Records (Scotland) Act 1937 to advise on questions relating to the custody, preservation and cataloguing of, as well as access to, public records. It held its last meeting on 27 February 2008 after the Scottish Government announced it was to be among a number of public bodies to be dissolved.

> Act 2002 (asp 13) or comprise information which is exempt
> information (within the meaning of that Act) by virtue of
> section 25(2)(b)(ii) of that Act."

This section requires the Keeper of the Records of Scotland to make   1.578
it possible for members of the public to inspect and obtain copies of
information which they are entitled to be given under FOISA.

Information is exempt from disclosure under FOISA, by virtue of   1.579
s 25, if it is reasonably obtainable other than by requesting it under
s 1(1). Section 25(2)(b)(ii) says that "information is to be taken to be
reasonably obtainable if the Keeper of the Records of Scotland holds
it and makes it available for inspection and (in so far as practicable)
copying by, members of the public on request, whether free of charge
or on payment". Section 70(3) places a legal obligation upon the Keeper
to make reasonable arrangements to allow such requests to be met. In
practice these arrangements were already in place.

71 Amendment of Scottish Public Services Ombudsman Act 2002

(1) In Part 2 of schedule 2 to the Scottish Public Services
Ombudsman Act 2002 (asp 11) (persons listed as liable to
investigation under that Act), after paragraph 45 there is
inserted –

"45A The Scottish Information Commissioner."

The Scottish Information Commissioner may be investigated by the   1.580
Scottish Public Services Ombudsman.

Amendment of Scottish Public Services Ombudsman Act 2002 – s 71(2)

(2) Schedule 4 to this Act, which contains amendments to that
Act consequential on the provisions of this Act, has effect.

Schedule 4 allows the Ombudsman to disclose information to the   1.581
Commissioner. Effectively this is a reciprocal arrangement to that
provided under s 63 of FOISA which allows the Commissioner to
disclose information to the Ombudsman.

72 Orders and regulations

(1) Any power of the Scottish Ministers to make an order or
regulations under this Act is exercisable by statutory
instrument.

1.582   Statutory instruments are a form of subordinate legislation made by or under powers conferred by or under statute on Ministers. Section 72 specifies that where FOISA provides that Ministers can make an order or regulations then this should be done by statutory instrument.

1.583   Orders or regulations are approved by Parliament either by:

- the negative resolution procedure – by which a Minister lays an order before Parliament and unless it is rejected within 40 days of laying the order (ie is subject to annulment in pursuance of a resolution of Parliament) it is effective;

- the affirmative resolution procedure – which requires the Minister actively to seek the approval of Parliament by way of a resolution. Most of the orders or regulations made by Ministers under FOISA require the affirmative procedure.

Orders and regulations – s 72(2)(a)

(2)   **A statutory instrument –**

   (a) **made in exercise of any of the powers conferred by sections 4(1) (except in the case mentioned in subsection (3)), 13(1) or 62(3) is subject to annulment in pursuance of a resolution of the Parliament;**

1.584   On a negative resolution procedure, Ministers can:

- by amending Sch 1, add or remove a body or holder of office from the list of those subject to FOISA (s 4(1) – except in the case (as set out in s 72(3) below regarding s 7(1)) where, in adding an entry, the authority is listed only in relating to information of a specified description. Schedule 1 has been amended since FOISA came into effect;

- determine the fees which an authority may charge where the authority is willing to provide the information even though it is not obliged to (s 13(1)), because the cost of so doing exceeds the amount prescribed by Ministers. (So, if complying with a request costs more than £600, but the authority is willing to provide the information subject to payment, then Ministers can by order regulate the amount which the authority could charge – see the Freedom of Information (Fees for Disclosure under Section 13) (Scotland) Regulations 2004); and

- make or amend regulations for the purpose of implementing the information provisions of the Aarhus Convention (s 62(3)) – which they have done by virtue of the Environmental Information (Scotland) Regulations 2004.

Orders and regulations – s 72(2)(b)

(b) containing an order under section 4(1) (but only in the case so mentioned), 5(1), 7(2) or (4)(b),[245] 59(1) or 64(1) or regulations under section 9(4), 10(4), 12, 20(7), 21(6) or 47(6) is not made unless a draft of the instrument has been –
(i) laid before; and
(ii) approved by resolution of,
the Parliament.

On an affirmative resolution procedure Ministers can: 1.585

- add an authority to the list at Sch 1 but only where the authority is being listed only in relation to information of a specified description (FOISA, s 4(3));
- designate as a public authority, for the purposes of FOISA, any person who appears to the Scottish Ministers to exercise a function of a public nature or is providing, under a contract made with a public authority, any service whose provision is a function of that authority (an order under FOISA, s 5(1));
- limit the extent to which an authority is designated under Sch 1 either by limiting the entry to information of a specific description; or by removing or amending any limitation on a body which has been entered into Sch 1 with a limitation to information of a specific description (order under FOISA, s 7(2));
- shorten the period after which a record becomes a historical record; shorten the period after which certain exemptions fall away (order under FOISA, s 59(1));

---

245 In *Current Law Statutes* on the Freedom of Information (Scotland) Act 2002 (asp 13) the annotations on s 72(2) and (b) suggest that bodies can only be *added* by negative resolution procedure (para 13-109) and that an affirmative resolution procedure is required for *removing* bodies.(para 13-110). However, this appears to be based on a reading of (4)(b) in this subsection as s 4(b)(1) – which does deal with the removal of bodies – instead of s 7(4)(b) which relates to regulations dealing with publicly owned companies. Accordingly the view taken by the Commissioner is that bodies can be added and removed by negative resolution.

- amend or appeal enactments prohibiting disclosure of information (order under FOISA, s 64(1));
- determine a fee to be charged for complying with a request for information (regulations under FOISA, s 9(4) – see the Freedom of Information (Fees for Required Disclosure) (Scotland) Regulations 2004);
- alter the time within which authorities must comply with requests for information (regulations under s 10(4));
- prescribe the costs beyond which an authority need not comply with an information request on the ground of excessive cost of compliance (regulations under FOISA, s 12 – see the Freedom of Information (Fees for Required Disclosure) (Scotland) Regulations 2004);
- alter the timescales within which an applicant can require a review of refusal etc (regulations under FOISA, s 20(7));
- alter the time within which an authority has to comply with a requirement for review (regulations under FOISA, s 21(6)); and
- lengthen the period beyond 6 months within which an application can be made to the Commissioner for a decision (regulations under FOISA, s 47(6)).

Orders and regulations – s 72(3)

(3) The case is that the instrument contains an order under paragraph (a) of section 4(1) and lists an authority in the way mentioned in section 7(1).

73 Interpretation

In this Act, unless the context requires a different interpretation –

"the Commissioner" means the Scottish Information Commissioner;

"body" includes an unincorporated association;

"decision notice" has the meaning given by section 49(5);

"enactment" includes an enactment comprised in, or in an instrument made under, an Act of the Scottish Parliament;

"enforcement notice" has the meaning given by section 51(1);

"exempt information" means information which is so described in any provision of Part 2;

"fees notice" has the meaning given by section 9(1);

"information" (subject to sections 50(9) and 64(2)) means information recorded in any form;

"information notice" has the meaning given by section 50(1);

"Minister of the Crown" has the same meaning as in the Ministers of the Crown Act 1975 (c.26);

"the Parliamentary corporation" means the Scottish Parliamentary Corporate Body;

"publication scheme" has the meaning given by section 23(1)(a);

"refusal notice" has the meaning given by section 16(1) (including that section as read with section 18(2));

"requirement for review" has the meaning given by section 20(2);

"Scottish public authority" has the meaning given by section 3(1);

"subordinate legislation" has the same meaning as in the Interpretation Act 1978 (c.30) but includes an instrument made under an Act of the Scottish Parliament; and

"working day" means any day other than a Saturday, a Sunday, Christmas Day or a day which, under the Banking and Financial Dealings Act 1971 (c.80), is a bank holiday in Scotland.

Schedule 1 to the Banking and Financial Dealings Act 1971 stipulates that the following are to be bank holidays in Scotland: 1.586

"New Year's Day, if it be not a Sunday or, if it be a Sunday, 3rd January.
2nd January, if it be not a Sunday or, if it be a Sunday, 3rd January.
Good Friday.
The first Monday in May.
The first Monday in August.
Christmas Day, if it be not a Sunday or, if it be a Sunday, 26th December."

Special days can be appointed under the 1971 Act as bank holidays (either additional or in place of bank holidays which fall on a Saturday or Sunday) subject to Royal Proclamation each year. These include Boxing Day, which has been an additional bank holiday since 1978. The   1.587

1971 Act also enables the Queen to appoint substitute bank holidays in any one year by Royal Proclamation.[246]

1.588   Bank holidays should not be confused with public or local holidays in Scotland, which must not be taken into account in calculating the time limits under FOISA.

74 Giving of notice, etc.

(1)   In this Act, any reference to –
   (a) a notice being given is to be construed as a reference to its being –
      (i) delivered; or
      (ii) posted; and

1.589   The following notices are said to be given if they are either delivered (by hand, by courier) or posted:

NOTICES BY COMMISSIONER

   Revoking a publication scheme – s 23(5)(b)
   Revoking a model publication scheme – s 24(3)(b)
   Notice to an authority of application and inviting comments –
      s 49(3)(a)
   Notice that no decision falls to be made in relation to an
   application – s 49(2)
   Decision – s 49(5)
   Information – s 50
   Enforcement – s 51

NOTICES BY SCOTTISH PUBLIC AUTHORITIES

   Fees – s 9(1)
   Refusal notices under –
   • s 16(1) Exempt information; 16(4) Excessive cost; 16(5) Vexatious
     or repeated requests
   • s 18(1) Revealing whether information exists is contrary to
     public interest
   Information is not held – s 17(1)
   Response to request for review – s 21(4) and (9).

1.590   Therefore, although these notices can be transmitted electronically, it would appear that they are not said to be given unless delivered

---

246 For example, a special bank holiday to celebrate the Queen's Diamond Jubilee was announced for 2012.

or posted. In practice, this would be inconsistent with the other provisions of FOISA which clearly allow an information request etc to be made electronically and for information to be supplied to an applicant electronically. Provided that the applicant can demonstrate that they have received the refusal notice etc, the Commissioner takes the view that any defects in the service of the notice by e-mail will be cured.

Giving of notice, etc. – s 74(1)(b)

(b) a request for information, a requirement for review or an application being made, or a certificate being given, is to be construed as a reference to its being –
(i) delivered;
(ii) posted; or
(iii) transmitted by electronic means.

An applicant is considered to have made a request for information or requirement for review or an application to the Commissioner if any of these is delivered, posted or transmitted by electronic means such as e-mail or via a website.   1.591

Certificates from Ministers or the Commissioner, unlike notices, are said to be given if delivered, posted or transmitted electronically.   1.592

These are: 1.593

- a certificate signed by a Minister that exemption is required for purpose of safeguarding national security – s 31(2);
- a certificate by the First Minister – s 52(2);
- the Scottish Information Commissioner certifying failure to comply with a notice – s 53(1).

Giving of notice, etc. – s 74(2)

(2) For the purposes of any provision of this Act, a thing –
(a) posted is presumed not to be received until the third day after the day of posting; and
(b) transmitted by electronic means is presumed to be received on the day of transmission.

75 Commencement

(1) This section and sections 72 and 76 come into force on Royal Assent; and the other provisions of this Act come into force –

   (a) on such day as the Scottish Ministers may by order appoint, that day being, subject to paragraph (b), a day no later than 31st December 2005; or

   (b) if the Commissioner recommends to the Scottish Ministers that a day after 31st December 2005 and specified in the recommendation be so appointed and they accept that recommendation, then on the specified day as so appointed,

and different days may be so appointed (or as the case may be recommended and appointed) for different provisions, for different persons or categories of person and for different purposes.

1.594   Royal Assent was given for FOISA on 28 May 2002, bringing into effect this section, the power for Ministers to make orders and regulations (s 72) and the right to cite FOISA by its short title.

1.595   FOISA could have been brought into effect on any day appointed by Ministers up to 31 December 2005, or an even later day on the recommendation by the Commissioner, which was accepted by the Ministers. However, the Scottish Ministers and the Commissioner shared a commitment to match the appointed date for the UK FOIA. FOISA came into effect simultaneously with FOIA on 1 January 2005.

Commencement – s 75(2) and (3)

   (2) An order under paragraph (b) of subsection (1) may contain such transitional provisions and savings (including provisions capable of having effect after the coming into force of provisions of this Act other than this section and sections 72 and 76) as the Scottish Ministers consider appropriate.

   (3) During –

     (a) that period of twelve months which begins with the date of Royal Assent; and

     (b) each subsequent period of twelve months until all the provisions of this Act are fully in force,

the Scottish Ministers are to prepare, and lay before the Parliament, a report of their proposals (including their response to any recommendations made under subsection (1)(b)) for bringing fully into force the provisions of this Act.

76 Short title

This Act may be cited as the Freedom of Information (Scotland) Act 2002.

SCHEDULE 1

SCOTTISH PUBLIC AUTHORITIES

(introduced by section 3(1)(a)(i))

- Italic text represents added bodies or amendments to entries in   1.596
  the original Schedule.
- Strike-through text represents bodies which have been removed
  from the Schedule.

Part 1
Ministers, the Parliament

1   The Scottish Ministers.
2   The Scottish Parliament.
3   The Scottish Parliamentary Corporate Body.

Part 2
Non Ministerial Office Holders in the Scottish Administration

4   The Chief Dental Officer of the Scottish Administration.
5   The Chief Medical Officer of the Scottish Administration.
6   Her Majesty's Chief Inspector of Constabulary.
7   Her Majesty's Chief Inspector of Prisons for Scotland.
7A *The Drinking Water Quality Regulator for Scotland.*[247]
8   Her Majesty's Inspector of Anatomy for Scotland.
9   Her Majesty's *Chief* Inspector of Fire *and Rescue Authorities.*[248]
10 Her Majesty's inspectors of schools (that is to say, the inspectors of schools appointed by Her Majesty on the recommendation of the Scottish Ministers under the Education (Scotland) Act 1980 (c.44)).
11 The Keeper of the Records of Scotland.
12 The Keeper of the Registers of Scotland.

247 Added by the Freedom of Information (Scotland) Act 2002 (Scottish Public Authorities) Amendment Order 2008 (SSI 2008/297) (the "SSI 2008 No 297 FOISA Amendment Order").
248 Amended by the Fire (Scotland) Act 2005, Sch 3, para 22.

12A   *The Office of the Scottish Charity Regulator.*[249]

13   A procurator fiscal.

14   The Queen's and Lord Treasurer's Remembrancer.

15   The Queen's Printer for Scotland.

16   The Registrar General of Births, Deaths and Marriages for Scotland.

17   The Registrar of Independent Schools in Scotland.

18   A rent officer appointed under section 43(3) of the Rent (Scotland) Act 1984 (c.58).

18A   *The Scottish Court Service.*[250]

19   ~~A social work inspector appointed under section 4 of the Joint Inspection of Children's Services and Inspection of Social Work Services (Scotland) Act 2006.~~[251]

Part 3
Local Government

20   An assessor appointed under section 27(2) of the Local Government etc (Scotland) Act 1994 (c.39).

21   A council constituted by section 2 of that Act.

22   A joint board, within the meaning of section 235(1) of the Local Government (Scotland) Act 1973 (c.65).

23   A licensing board *continued in existence by or established under section 5 of the Licensing (Scotland) Act 2005 (asp 16).*[252]

24   The Strathclyde Passenger Transport Authority.

24A   *A Transport Partnership created under the Transport (Scotland) Act 2005.*[253]

Part 4
The National Health Service

25   ~~The Clinical Standards Board for Scotland.~~[254]

---

249   Added by SSI 2008 No 297 FOISA Amendment Order.
250   Amended by the Judiciary and Courts (Scotland) Act 2008, Sch 3, para 18.
251   Amended by the Joint Inspection of Children's Services and Inspection of Social Work Services (Scotland) Act 2006, Pt 3, s 8(2) and repealed by the Public Services Reform (Scotland) Act 2010 (Consequential Modifications) Order 2011 (SSI 2011/211).
252   Amended by the Licensing (Scotland) Act 2005, Sch 6, para 10.
253   Added by the Transport (Scotland) Act 2005, Sch 1, para 20.
254   Removed by SSI 2008 No 297 FOISA Amendment Order .

26   The Common Services Agency for the Scottish Health
     Service.

27   A Health Board, constituted under section 2 of the
     National Health Service (Scotland) Act 1978.

27A *Healthcare Improvement Scotland.*[255]

28   ~~The Health Education Board for Scotland.~~[256]

29   ~~The Health Technology Board for Scotland.~~[257]

29A *The National Waiting Times Centre Board.*[258]

30   ~~A local health council, established under section 7 of the
     National Health Service (Scotland) Act 1978.~~[259]

31   ~~A National Health Service trust.~~[260]

32   NHS 24.

32A *NHS Education for Scotland.*[261]

32B *NHS Health Scotland.*[262]

32C ~~NHS Quality Improvement Scotland.~~[263]

33   A person providing *primary medical services under a
     general medical services contract (within the meaning
     of the NHS (Scotland) Act (1978) or* general dental
     services, general ophthalmic services or pharmaceutical
     services under Part II of *that Act*, but only in respect of
     information relating to the provision of those services.[264]

34   A person providing *primary* medical services or personal
     dental services under arrangements made under section
     17C of that Act, but only in respect of information relating
     to the provision of those services.[265]

35   A person providing, in Scotland, piloted services within
     the meaning of the National Health Service (Primary
     Care) Act 1997 (c.46), but only in respect of information
     relating to the provision of those services.

255 Added by the Public Services Reform (Scotland) Act 2010 (Consequential Modifications)
     Order 2011.
256 Removed by SSI 2008 No 297 FOISA Amendment Order.
257 *Ibid.*
258 Added by SSI 2008 No 297 FOISA Amendment Order.
259 Repealed by the National Health Service Reform (Scotland) Act 2004, Sch 2 (not yet in
     force).
260 *Ibid.*
261 Added by SSI 2008 No 297 FOISA Amendment Order.
262 *Ibid.*
263 *Ibid.* Repealed by the Public Services Reform (Scotland) Act 2010 (Consequential
     Modifications) Order 2011.
264 Amended by the Primary Medical Services (Scotland) Act 2004, Sch 1, para 5.
265 *Ibid*, para 5(b).

36   The Post Qualification Education Board for Health Service Pharmacists in Scotland.[266]

37   The Scottish Advisory Committee on Distinction Awards.

38   The Scottish Advisory Committee on the Medical Workforce.[267]

39   The Scottish Ambulance Service Board.

40   The Scottish Council for Post Graduate Medical and Dental Education.[268]

41   The Scottish Dental Practice Board.

42   The Scottish Health Advisory Service.[269]

43   The Scottish Hospital Endowments Research Trust.[270]

44   The Scottish Hospital Trust.[271]

45   The State Hospitals Board for Scotland.

46   The Scottish Medical Practices Committee.[272]

Part 5
Educational Institutions

47   The board of management of a college of further education (expressions used in this paragraph having the same meaning as in section 36(1) of the Further and Higher Education (Scotland) Act 1992 (c.37)).

48   A central institution within the meaning of the Education (Scotland) Act 1980.

49   An institution in receipt of funding from the Scottish *Further and* Higher Education Funding Council other than any institution whose activities are principally carried on outwith Scotland.[273]

Part 6
Police

50   A chief constable of a police force in Scotland.

---

266 Removed by SSI 2008 No 297 FOISA Amendment Order.
267 *Ibid.*
268 *Ibid.*
269 *Ibid.*
270 Repealed by the Smoking, Health and Social Care (Scotland) Act 2005, Sch 3, para 1.
271 Repealed by the Public Appointments and Public Bodies etc (Scotland) Act 2003, Sch 4, para 17(a)(i).
272 Amended by the Public Appointments and Public Bodies etc (Scotland) Act 2003, Sch 4, para 17(a)(ii).
273 Amended by the Further and Higher Education (Scotland) Act 2005, Sch 3, para 12(a).

51   A joint police board constituted by an amalgamation scheme made or approved under the Police (Scotland) Act 1967 (c.77).

52   The Police Advisory Board for Scotland.

52A   The Scottish Police Services Authority, but only in respect of information relating to the provision of the police support services within the meaning of section 3(2) of the Police, Public Order and Criminal Justice (Scotland) Act 2006.[274]

Part 7
Others

53   The Accounts Commission for Scotland.

54   ~~The Advisory Committee on Sites of Special Scientific Interest.~~[275]

55   ~~The Ancient Monuments Board for Scotland.~~[276]

56   ~~An area tourist board established by virtue of section 172(1) of the Local Government (Scotland) Act 1994 (c.39).~~[277]

57   Audit Scotland.

58   The Auditor General for Scotland.

59   The Board of Trustees for the National Galleries of Scotland.

60   The Board of Trustees of the National Museums of Scotland.

61   The Board of Trustees of the Royal Botanic Garden, Edinburgh.

61A   Bord Na Gaidhlig.[278]

62   ~~The Central Advisory Committee on Justices of the Peace.~~[279]

62A   A Community Justice Authority.[280]

---

274 Amended by the Police, Public Order and Criminal Justice (Scotland) Act 2006, Sch 6(1), para 11(a).

275 Repealed by the Public Services Reform (Scotland) Act 2010, Pt 1, s 2(4).

276 Amended by the Public Appointments and Public Bodies etc (Scotland) Act 2003, Sch 4, para 17(b)(i).

277 Amended by the Tourist Boards (Scotland) Act 2006, Sch 2(1), para 8(a)(i).

278 Added by the Gaelic Language (Scotland) Act 2005, Sch 2, para 3.

279 The District Courts and Justices of the Peace (Scotland) Order 2007 repeals s 16 of the District Courts (Scotland) Act 1975, ie the section which established the Justices' Committees from which the Central Advisory Committee (CAC) membership was drawn.

280 Added by the Management of Offenders etc (Scotland) Act 2005, s 21(12).

62A   ~~The Commissioner for Public Appointments in Scotland.~~[281]

62ZA   *The Commissioner for Children and Young People.*[282]

62ZZA   *The Commission for Ethical Standards in Public Life in Scotland in the performance of its functions under section 1(7) of the Scottish Parliamentary Commissions and Commissioners etc. Act 2010 (asp 11).*[283]

62ZZZA   *Children's Hearings Scotland.*[284]

62B   ~~The Convener of the Water Customer Consultation Panels (appointed under paragraph 5(1) of schedule 1 to the Water Industry (Scotland) Act 2002 (asp 3)) and those Panels.~~[285]

62C   *Creative Scotland.*[286]

63   The Crofters Commission.

64   ~~The Deer Commission for Scotland.~~[287]

65   ~~The Fisheries Committee continued in existence by paragraph 5 of Schedule 9 to the Electricity Act 1989 (c.29).~~[288]

66   The General Teaching Council for Scotland.

66A   *Her Majesty's Chief Inspector of Prosecution in Scotland.*[289]

67   Highlands and Islands Enterprise.

67A   ~~The Historic Environment Advisory Council for Scotland.~~[290]

---

281 Added by the Public Appointments and Public Bodies etc (Scotland) Act 2003, Sch 4, para 17(c), but abolished by the Scottish Parliamentary Commissions and Commissioners etc Act 2010, s 2(3)(c) (effective as of 1 April 2011).

282 Added by SSI 2008 No 297 FOISA Amendment Order.

283 Added by the Scottish Parliamentary Commissions and Commissioners etc Act 2010, s 27(1) (effective as of 1 April 2011).

284 Added by the Ethical Standards in Public Life etc (Scotland) Act 2000 (Devolved Bodies and Stipulated Time Limit) and the Freedom of Information (Scotland) Act 2002 Amendment Order 2011 (SSI 2011/113), art 4 (effective as of 18 April 2011).

285 Added by the Water Services etc (Scotland) Act 2005, Sch 5, para 9(a), but repealed by Sch 3 to the Public Services Reform (Scotland) Act 2010 (not yet in force).

286 Added by the Public Services Reform (Scotland) Act 2010, Sch 10, para 3(a).

287 Added by SSI 2008 No 297 FOISA Amendment Order.

288 Repealed by the Public Services Reform (Scotland) Act 2010, Sch 1, para 30.

289 Repealed by the Flood and Water Management Act 2010, s 46(5) but consequential amendment not yet made to FOISA.

290 Added by the Public Appointments and Public Bodies etc (Scotland) Act 2003, Sch 4, para 17(c)(ii), but repealed by s 7(4) of Public Services Reform (Scotland) Act 2010.

68   The Historic Buildings Council for Scotland.[291]

68A   *The Judicial Appointments Board for Scotland.*[292]

69   A justice of the peace advisory committee.

70   Learning and Teaching Scotland.

71   The Local Government Boundary Commission for Scotland.

72   The Mental Welfare Commission for Scotland.

73   A National Park authority, established by virtue of schedule 1 to the National Parks (Scotland) Act 2000 (asp 10).

74   The Parole Board for Scotland.

75   A person appointed for Scotland under section 3(1) of the Local Government and Housing Act 1989 (c.42).

75A   *The Public Transport Users' Committee for Scotland.*[293]

75A   *The Police Complaints Commissioner for Scotland.*[294]

75ZA *The Public Appointments Commissioner for Scotland.*[295]

75B   *Quality Meat Scotland.*[296]

75C   *The Risk Management Authority.*[297]

76   The Royal Commission on the Ancient and Historical Monuments of Scotland.

77   The Scottish Agricultural Wages Board.

78   The Scottish Arts Council.[298]

79   The Scottish charities nominee, appointed under section 12 of the Law Reform (Miscellaneous Provisions) (Scotland) Act 1990 (c.40).[299]

80   The Scottish Children's Reporter Administration.

80A   The Scottish Civil Enforcement Commission.[300]

---

291 Repealed by the Public Appointments and Public Bodies etc (Scotland) Act 2003, Sch 4, para 17(b)(ii).

292 Added by the Judiciary and Courts (Scotland) Act 2008, Sch 1, para 21.

293 Added by the Transport (Scotland) Act 2005, Pt 3, s 41(4).

294 Added by the Police, Public Order and Criminal Justice (Scotland) Act 2006, Sch 6(1), para 11(b).

295 Added by the Scottish Parliamentary Commissions and Commissioners etc Act 2010, s 27(1) (effective as of 1 April 2011).

296 Added by SSI 2008 No 297 FOISA Amendment Order.

297 *Ibid.*

298 Repealed by the Public Services Reform (Scotland) Act 2010, Sch 10, para 3(b).

299 Removed by SSI 2008 No 297 FOISA Amendment Order.

300 Added by the Bankruptcy and Diligence etc (Scotland) Act 2007, Sch 5, para 28 (not yet in force).

80B   The Scottish Commission for Human Rights.[301]

81   ~~The Scottish Commission for the Regulation of Care.~~[302]

82   ~~The Scottish Conveyancing and Executry Services Board.~~[303]

83   The Scottish Criminal Cases Review Commission.

84   Scottish Enterprise.

85   The Scottish Environment Protection Agency.

85A   The Scottish Further and Higher Education Funding Council.[304]

85B   The Scottish Housing Regulator.[305]

86   ~~The Scottish Further Education Funding Council.~~[306]

87   ~~The Scottish Higher Education Funding Council.~~[307]

88   ~~Scottish Homes.~~[308]

89   ~~The Scottish Industrial Development Advisory Board.~~[309]

90   The Scottish Information Commissioner.

91   The Scottish Law Commission.

92   The Scottish Legal Aid Board.

92A   The Scottish Legal Complaints Commission.[310]

92B   The Scottish Local Authorities Remuneration Committee.[311]

93   Scottish Natural Heritage.

94   ~~The Scottish Prison Complaints Commission.~~[312]

95   The Scottish Public Services Ombudsman.

96   The Scottish Qualifications Authority.

97   ~~The Scottish Records Advisory Council.~~[313]

---

301 Added by the Scottish Commission for Human Rights Act 2006, Sch 1, para 17 .
302 Repealed by the Public Services Reform (Scotland) Act 2010 (Consequential Modifications) Order 2011.
303 Repealed by the Public Appointments and Public Bodies etc (Scotland) Act 2003, Sch 4, para 17(b)(iii).
304 Added by the Further and Higher Education (Scotland) Act 2005, Sch 3, para 12(b).
305 Added by the Housing (Scotland) Act 2010, Sch 2, para 9.
306 Repealed by the Further and Higher Education (Scotland) Act 2005, Sch 3, para 12(c).
307 *Ibid.*
308 Removed by the SSI 2008 No 297 FOISA Amendment Order.
309 Repealed by the Public Services Reform (Scotland) Act 2010, s 5(4).
310 Inserted by the Legal Profession and Legal Aid (Scotland) Act 2007, Sch 5, para 5.
311 Added by SSI 2008 No 297 FOISA Amendment Order.
312 Repealed by the Scottish Parliamentary Commissions and Commissioners etc Act 2010, Sch 3, para 20, but consequential amendment not yet made to FOISA.
313 Repealed by the Public Services Reform (Scotland) Act 2010, Pt 1, s 4(5)(b).

97A *The Scottish Road Works Commissioner.*[314]

98 ~~Scottish Screen.~~[315]

99 The Scottish Social Services Council.

100 The Scottish Sports Council.

101 ~~The Scottish Tourist Board.~~[316]

102 Scottish Water.

102A *Social Care and Social Work Improvement Scotland.*[317]

103 ~~Social Inclusion Partnerships.~~[318]

104 The Standards Commission for Scotland.

105 The Trustees of the National Library of Scotland.

105A *VisitScotland.*[319]

106 The Water Industry Commissioner for Scotland.[320]

SCHEDULE 2

THE SCOTTISH INFORMATION COMMISSIONER

As amended by the Scottish Parliamentary Commissions and Commissioners etc. Act 2010 – amendments are shown in italics.

Status

1 *(1)* The Commissioner and that officer's staff are not to be regarded as servants or agents of the Crown or as having any status, immunity or privilege of the Crown; and the Commissioner's property is not to be regarded as property of, or property held on behalf of, the Crown.

(2) The Commissioner is, as such, to be regarded as a juristic person distinct from the natural person holding the office.

As previously mentioned (see s 42(11C)) Commissioners and the Ombudsman were concerned that the construction of the legislation establishing their function did not provide a distinction between the individual appointee and any separate legal entity as Commissioner.

---

314 Added by the Transport (Scotland) Act 2005, Sch 2 para 4.

315 Repealed by the Public Services Reform (Scotland) Act 2010, Sch 10, para 3(b).

316 Repealed by the Tourist Boards (Scotland) Act 2006, Sch 2, para 8(a)(ii).

317 Added by the Public Services Reform (Scotland) Act 2010 (Consequential Modifications) Order 2011.

318 Removed by SSI 2008 No 297 FOISA Amendment Order.

319 Added by the Tourist Boards (Scotland) Act 2006, Sch 2, para 8(b).

320 Amended by the Water Services (Scotland) Act 2005, Sch 5, para 9(b).

The Commissioner is not an employee and is not a servant or agent of the Crown. Nor was the Commissioner a corporate entity because there is no Act, Deed or other document of incorporation. Accordingly, there was doubt as to whether one Commissioner could bind a successor to the terms of contracts or leases or could transfer staff into their employ.

1.597   In England and Wales the concept of an individual as a corporation does exist and statute refers to "corporation sole". UK legislation sometimes"translates" this concept to allow it to apply in Scotland. For instance, certain sections of the Serious Organised Crime and Police Act 2005 "shall have effect as if for the words "corporation sole" there were substituted "distinct juristic person (that is to say, as a juristic person distinct from the individual who for the time being is the office-holder)".[321] Paragraph 2 appears to have drawn upon this type of wording as a means of addressing the concerns raised by Commissioners.

Pensions, allowances, etc.

2(1)   The Parliamentary corporation may make arrangements for the payment of pensions, allowances or gratuities to, or in respect of, any person who has ceased to hold the office of Commissioner and (without prejudice to that generality) may –

(a) make contributions or payments towards provision for such pensions, allowances or gratuities; and

(b) for the purposes of this sub-paragraph, establish and administer one or more pension schemes.

(2)   The references in sub-paragraph (1) to pensions, allowances and gratuities include references to, as the case may be, pensions, allowances or gratuities by way of compensation for loss of office.

Staff

3(1)   The Commissioner may appoint such staff, on such terms and conditions, as that officer may determine.

(2)   The Commissioner may make arrangements for the payment of pensions, allowances or gratuities to, or in respect of, any person who has ceased to be a member of such staff and (without prejudice to that generality) may –

---

321 Serious Organised Crime and Police Act 2005, s 158(2F)(a).

(a) make contributions or payments towards provision for such pensions, allowances or gratuities; and

(b) for the purposes of this sub-paragraph, establish and administer one or more pension schemes.

(3) The references in sub-paragraph (2) to pensions, allowances and gratuities include references to, as the case may be, pensions, allowances or gratuities by way of compensation for loss of employment.

(4) *The exercise of a power in sub-paragraph (1) or (2) is subject to the approval of the Parliamentary corporation*

Accountable officer

4 (1) The Parliamentary corporation is to designate the Commissioner or a member of that officer's staff as the accountable officer for the purposes of this paragraph.

(2) The functions of the accountable officer are –

(a) those specified in sub-paragraph (3); and

(b) where the accountable officer is not the Commissioner, the duty set out in sub-paragraph (4),

and the accountable officer is answerable to the Parliament for the exercise of those functions.

(3) The functions referred to in sub-paragraph (2)(a) are –

(a) signing the accounts of the expenditure and receipts of the Commissioner;

(b) ensuring the propriety and regularity of the finances of the Commissioner; and

(c) ensuring that the resources of the Commissioner are used economically, efficiently and effectively.

(4) The duty referred to in sub-paragraph (2)(b) is a duty, where the accountable officer is required to act in some way but considers that to do so would be inconsistent with the proper performance of the functions specified in sub-paragraph (3), to –

(a) obtain written authority from the Commissioner before taking the action; and

(b) send a copy of that authority as soon as possible to the Auditor General.

Budget

4A (1) *The Commissioner must, before the start of each financial year, prepare proposals for the Commissioner's use of resources and expenditure during the year (a "budget")*

and, by such date as the Parliamentary corporation determines, send the budget to the Parliamentary corporation
for approval.

(2) The Commissioner may, in the course of a financial year,
prepare a revised budget for the remainder of the year and
send it to the Parliamentary corporation for approval.

(3) In preparing a budget or revised budget, the Commissioner
must ensure that the resources of the Commissioner will
be used economically, efficiently and effectively.

(4) A budget or revised budget must contain a statement that
the Commissioner has complied with the duty under sub-
paragraph (3).

Accounts

5(1) The Commissioner must –
(a) keep accounts; and
(b) prepare annual accounts in respect of each financial
year,
in accordance with such directions as the Scottish
Ministers may give that officer.

(2) The Commissioner must send a copy of the annual
accounts to the Auditor General for Scotland for auditing.

(3) The financial year of the Commissioner is –
(a) the period beginning with the date on which the
Commissioner is appointed and ending with 31st
March next following that date; and
(b) each successive period of twelve months ending with
31st March.

(4) If requested by any person, the Commissioner must
make available at any reasonable time, without charge, in
printed or in electronic form, the audited accounts, so that
they may be inspected by that person.

General powers

6(1) The Commissioner may do anything which appears
necessary or expedient for the purpose of, or in connection
with, or which appears conducive to, the exercise of
that officer's functions; and without prejudice to that
generality, may in particular –
(a) acquire and dispose of land and other property; and
(b) enter into contracts.

(2) The exercise of the power to acquire or dispose of land is subject to the approval of the Parliamentary corporation

Location of office

7   The Commissioner must comply with any direction given by the Parliamentary corporation as to the location of the Commissioner's office.

Sharing of premises, staff, services and other resources

8   The Commissioner must comply with any direction given by the Parliamentary corporation as to the sharing of premises, staff, services or other resources with any other officeholder or any public body.

Restrictions on subsequent appointments etc

9 (1) A person who has ceased being the Commissioner may not, without the approval of the Parliamentary corporation –
   (a) be employed or appointed in any other capacity by the Commissioner,
   (b) be a Scottish public authority or hold office in, or be an employee or appointee of, a Scottish public authority, or
   (c) hold any other office, employment or appointment or engage in any other occupation, being an office, employment, appointment or occupation which, by virtue of section 42(3B)(a), that person could not have held, or as the case may be, engaged in when Commissioner.
   (2) The restriction in sub-paragraph (1) –
   (a) starts when the person ceases to be the Commissioner, and
   (b) ends on the expiry of the financial year next following the one in which it started.

SCHEDULE 3

POWERS OF ENTRY AND INSPECTION

Grant of warrants

1(1) If a sheriff is satisfied by evidence on oath supplied by the Commissioner that there are reasonable grounds for suspecting –   1.598

(a) that a Scottish public authority has failed or is failing to comply with –
  (i) any of the requirements of Part 1 of this Act;
  (ii) so much of a notice given to it by the Commissioner under subsection (5) of section 49 as, by virtue of subsection (6)(b) of that section, requires steps to be taken; or
  (iii) an information notice or an enforcement notice; or
(b) that an offence under section 65(1) has been or is being committed,

and that evidence of such a failure to comply or of the commission of the offence is to be found on any premises specified as part of that evidence, the sheriff, subject to paragraph 2, may grant to the Commissioner such warrant as is mentioned in sub-paragraph (2).

The Commissioner may seek a warrant where there are "reasonable grounds" for suspecting that certain failures of compliance have occurred or are still occurring or that an offence of altering records with the intent to prevent disclosure has taken place. The grounds might come from a variety of sources: from the Commissioner's own direct knowledge and experience arising from investigations; practice assessments or responses to notices issued; a whistleblower from within the authority; or a third party, for example an investigative journalist.

1.599   The compliance failure may relate to any of the requirements of Pt 1 of FOISA. The nature of such failings is not obvious, but could relate to improper charging of fees, or improper issuing of notices that information is not held etc. The following are also grounds for application for a warrant:

- failure by an authority to comply with the steps required of it within a decision notice;
- failure by an authority to comply with an information or enforcement notice;
- where a request for information has been made to an authority and a person is suspected of altering defacing, blocking, erasing, destroying or concealing a record to prevent disclosure of information to which the applicant is entitled.

1.600   The evidence of failure of compliance, or the commission of offence, may be found not only on the premises of the authority which received the request or to which a notice applies. A warrant can be sought in respect of any premises. These could include the offices of another authority, a private company or an individual's home. The warrant can even extend to evidence which may be found in vehicles.[322]

At the time of writing, the Commissioner has given notice to only one authority[323] demanding access to information held by it (on behalf of another authority).   **1.601**

Grant of warrants (cont'd)

1(2) **The warrant is one which authorises the Commissioner, or any member of the Commissioner's staff, at any time within seven days after the date of the warrant-**

    (a) **to enter and search the premises;**

    (b) **to inspect and seize any documents or other material found there which may constitute the evidence in question; and**

    (c) **to inspect, examine, operate and test any equipment found there in which information held by the authority may be recorded.**

The actions which can be taken under warrant are considerable: **1.602**

- a search of the premises can be conducted;
- any documents or material which may constitute the evidence in question can be seized and taken away. This could include paper files, electronic storage devices, CCTV film;
- equipment can be inspected to establish, for example, whether evidence is held on back-up tapes; system servers, personal computers, mobile phones etc;
- equipment can be operated, which might include confirming whether information is automatically updated, is readily generated or is scheduled for deletion after a certain time;
- tests can be carried out which might establish, for example, whether equipment has been re-programmed.

Grant of warrants (cont'd)

2(1) **A sheriff must not grant the warrant unless satisfied –**

    (a) **that the Commissioner has given seven days' notice in writing to the occupier of the premises demanding access to them; and**

---

322 Paragraph 11 of this Schedule.
323 As required by para 2(1)(a) of this schedule.

(b) that either –
(i) access was demanded at a reasonable hour and was unreasonably refused; or
(ii) although entry to the premises was granted, the occupier unreasonably refused to comply with a request by the Commissioner, or any member of the Commissioner's staff, to permit the Commissioner or any such member of staff to do any of the things referred to in paragraph 1(2); and
(c) that the occupier has, after the refusal, been notified by the Commissioner of the application for the warrant and has had an opportunity of being heard by the sheriff on the question of whether or not it should be granted.
(2) Sub-paragraph (1) does not apply if the sheriff is satisfied that the case is one of urgency or that compliance with the provisions of that sub-paragraph would defeat the object of the entry.

1.603   Usually a warrant will be sought only where the Commissioner, having given adequate notice, has attempted to gain access to the premises and either has been unreasonably denied entry or has not been permitted to carry out searches, inspect documents or examine equipment.

1.604   Also, the warrant will usually be granted only after the occupier of the premises has been told that a warrant has been sought and has been given the opportunity to make representations to the sheriff.

1.605   However, clearly there is a danger that having to give notice of an intention to search (and also notice of a warrant being sought) provides the opportunity for steps to be taken to conceal or destroy evidence, or to disable or to remove equipment, thus defeating the object of the entry. It could also materially hinder an investigation on a matter of urgency. In such circumstances the sheriff can grant the warrant without the steps above being taken.

Execution of warrants

3   A person executing the warrant may use such reasonable force as may be necessary.

4   The warrant must be executed at a reasonable hour, unless it appears to the person executing it that there are grounds for suspecting that the evidence in question would not be found if it were so executed.

5(1)   If the premises in respect of which the warrant is granted are occupied by a Scottish public authority and any officer or employee of the authority is present when the warrant is executed, that officer or employee must be shown the warrant and supplied with a copy of it; and if no such officer or employee is present a copy of the warrant must be left in a prominent place on the premises.

(2)   If the premises in respect of which the warrant is granted are occupied by a person other than a Scottish public authority and that person is present when the warrant is executed, the person must be shown the warrant and supplied with a copy of it; and if the person is not present a copy of the warrant must be left in a prominent place on the premises.

6(1)   A person seizing anything in pursuance of the warrant must give a receipt for it if asked to do so.

(2)   Anything so seized may be retained for so long as is necessary in all the circumstances; but the person in occupation of the premises must be given a copy of anything that is seized if that person so requests and the person executing the warrant considers that it can be done without undue delay.

A warrant for entry, search and seizure under FOISA can apply only   1.606
to the Commissioner and his staff and not to the police who will be responsible for reporting a case to the procurator fiscal. The MoU between the Commissioner, the COPFS and the police[324] explains the arrangements for the Commissioner and the police to work together to gather the evidence and investigate the case. The Commissioner is responsible for obtaining and executing any warrants, but the police force concerned will provide any appropriate assistance in the process (without prejudice to police officers' powers at common law). In practice, where a warrant is granted to the Commissioner his investigating officer will arrange for a police officer to be in attendance for the execution of the warrant to prevent disorder and to advise the Commissioner's officer on search procedures.

Section 6(2) provides that anything seized (documents or other   1.607
materials) can be retained for as long as necessary, but that copies

---

324 Memorandum of Understanding with the Crown Office and Procurator Fiscal Service and Scottish Police Forces in relation to the investigation of criminal offences: http://www. itspublicknowledge.info/home/AboutSIC/StrategicAgreements.asp.

must be provided to the person occupying the premises if they request it.

Matters exempt from inspection and seizure (cont'd)

7   The powers of inspection and seizure conferred by the warrant are not exercisable in respect of information which is exempt information by virtue of section 31(1).
     If the information is exempt for the purposes of safeguarding national security then the warrant cannot be used to inspect or seize the documents or other material containing such exempt information.

8(1) Subject to the provisions of this paragraph, the powers of inspection and seizure conferred by the warrant are not exercisable in respect of –
     (a) a communication between professional legal adviser and client in connection with the giving of legal advice to the client with respect to the client's obligations, liabilities or rights under this Act; or
     (b) a communication between professional legal adviser and client, or between such adviser or client and another person, made in connection with or in contemplation of proceedings under or arising out of this Act and for the purpose of such proceedings.

(2) Sub-paragraph (1) applies also to –
     (a) a copy or other record of such communication as is there mentioned; and
     (b) a document or article enclosed with or referred to in such communication if made in connection with the giving of any advice or, as the case may be, in connection with or in contemplation of and for the purpose of such proceedings as are there mentioned.

(3) This paragraph does not apply to anything in the possession of a person other than the professional legal adviser or client or to anything held with the intention of furthering a criminal purpose.

(4) In this paragraph references to the client of a professional legal adviser include references to a person representing such a client.

1.608   The powers of entry and inspection cannot be used to inspect or seize certain material which is subject to legal professional privilege.

This is the case, however, only if the material is in the possession   **1.609**
of a professional legal adviser or client – if the warrant is being
executed on the premises of a third party, then such material is not
excluded.

The exclusion does not apply if anything is held with the intention   **1.610**
of furthering a criminal purpose, even if otherwise the information
would be legally privileged (such as a communication between a
professional legal adviser and a client providing legal advice as to
obligations, liabilities or rights under FOISA).

Matters exempt from inspection and seizure (cont'd)

9   **If the person in occupation of premises in respect of which
the warrant is granted objects to the inspection or seizure
under it of any material on the grounds that the material
consists partly of matters in respect of which those
powers are not exercisable, that person must, if requested,
provide in response to the warrant a copy of so much of the
material as is material in relation to which the powers are
exercisable.**

The evidence as to non-compliance or an offence may be found in   **1.611**
documents or other material which contains information unrelated
to the exercise of the warrant. The person in occupation of the
premises (but not any other) may object to this extraneous material
being inspected or seized (which may be the case if this could disrupt
activities). If so the onus is upon them, and not the Commissioner or
any person exercising the warrant, to make and provide a copy of the
material which does come within the scope of the warrant.

Offences

10(1)   **A person who –
(a) intentionally obstructs a person who is executing the
warrant; or
(b) fails, without reasonable excuse, to give the person
who is executing the warrant such assistance as that
person may reasonably require for executing it,
is guilty of an offence.**

Assistance may be required to locate documents or to operate   **1.612**
equipment if evidence is to be found. The execution of the warrant
cannot be thwarted by intentionally obstructive behaviour or by any

person unreasonably withholding assistance in response to a request for such help from those exercising the warrant. This applies not only to the person occupying the premises, but to anyone who is obstructive or is required to provide assistance.

Offences (cont'd)

10(2) A person guilty of an offence under sub-paragraph (1) is liable, on summary conviction, to a fine not exceeding level 5 on the standard scale.

If summarily convicted of an offence, the maximum penalty is a fine of £5000 (Level 5 on the standard scale).

Vessels, vehicles, etc.

11   In this schedule, "premises" includes vessel, vehicle, aircraft or hovercraft, and references to the occupier of premises include references to the person in charge of a vessel, vehicle, aircraft or hovercraft.

SCHEDULE 4

CONSEQUENTIAL AMENDMENTS TO SCOTTISH PUBLIC SERVICES OMBUDSMAN ACT 2002

1.613   1   In section 19(8) of the Scottish Public Services Ombudsman Act 2002 (asp 11) (which restricts the purposes for which information obtained by the Ombudsman from the Information Commissioner may be disclosed) –

(a) the words from "the Information Commissioner" to "Freedom of Information Act 2000 (c.36)" become paragraph (a); and

(b) after that paragraph, there is inserted the word "or" and the following paragraph –

"(b) the Scottish Information Commissioner by virtue of section 63 of the Freedom of Information (Scotland) Act 2002 (asp 13)".

2   In schedule 5 to that Act (which specifies persons or bodies to whom the Ombudsman in certain circumstances may disclose information in relation to certain matters), after the entry relating to the Information Commissioner, there is inserted –

"The Scottish Information Commissioner

1. A matter in respect of which the Commissioner could exercise any power conferred by –

(a) section 44 (recommendations as to good practice) of the Freedom of Information (Scotland) Act 2002 (asp 13); or

(b) Part 4 (enforcement) of that Act

2. The commission of an offence under section 65 (offence of altering etc. records

with intent to prevent disclosure) of that Act".

Chapter 2

ENVIRONMENTAL INFORMATION

Long before the introduction of the Freedom of Information (Scotland)   **2.01**
Act 2002 ("FOISA"), people already had certain statutory entitlements
to environmental information. Comprehensive rights were delivered
by the Environmental Information Regulations first introduced in
1992[1] and amended in 1998[2] which gave the public the right to ask for
information which "relates to the environment" and which was held
by a "relevant person", such as central and local government and other
bodies with responsibilities in relation to the environment.

The access to environmental regime advanced still further   **2.02**
when the UK signed the Convention on Access to Information,
Public Participation in Decision-Making and Access to Justice in
Environmental Matters (the "Aarhus Convention") in 1998. There
are three "pillars" which form the key principles behind the Aarhus
Convention – the rights of access to information, public participation
in decision-making and access to justice in environmental matters.
The purpose of access to environmental information, according to
the Aarhus Convention Implementation Guide,[3] is so "that members
of the public can understand what is happening in the environment
around them. It also ensures that the public is able to participate in
an informed manner". This Convention in turn gave rise to European
Directive 2003/4/EC (the "Directive").[4] Our most recent Environmental
Information (Scotland) Regulations 2004 (the "EIRs") implement in
Scotland the obligations arising from this Directive. FOISA, by contrast,
is a purely domestic law.

The EIRs give the public rights of access to environmental   **2.03**
information held by Scottish public authorities. They came into force

---

1 Environmental Information Regulations 1992 (SI 1992/3240).
2 Environmental Information (Amendment) Regulations 1998 (SI 1998/1447).
3 http://www.unece.org/env/pp/acig.pdf.
4 Directive 2003/4/EC of the European Parliament and of the Council of 28 January 2003 on
   public access to environmental information and repealing Council Directive 90/313/EC.

on 1 January 2005, along with FOISA, and cover any information that is considered to be "environmental information" as defined by the EIRs.

2.04   Despite this long pedigree and wide scope of application, public authorities often appear unsure of their obligations under the EIRs and unaware of the distinct differences between the EIRs and FOISA. This has caused requests to be mishandled, resulting in adverse decisions by the Commissioner.

2.05   From the outset, three fundamental issues need to be acknowledged:

- environmental information is much wider in scope than is often appreciated – information contained in planning applications, contracts, financial projections or even press releases may be environmental information;
- all requests for environmental information must be dealt with under the EIRs. Authorities cannot opt to deal with requests for environmental information under FOISA alone;
- there are important differences between the EIRs and FOISA, such that guidance and systems put in place to deal with FOISA requests may be inadequate or misleading when it comes to dealing with requests for environmental information (see Appendix 1: EIRs and FOISA – The Key Differences).

WHAT IS ENVIRONMENTAL INFORMATION?

2.06   In the EIRs at reg 2(1) "environmental information" has the same meaning as in Art 2(1) of the Directive, namely *any* information in written, visual, aural, electronic or any other material form on:

(a) the state of the elements of the environment, such as air and atmosphere, water, soil, land, landscape and natural sites including wetlands, coastal and marine areas, biological diversity and its components, including genetically modified organisms, and the interaction among these elements;

(b) factors, such as substances, energy, noise, radiation or waste, including radioactive waste, emissions, discharges and other releases into the environment, affecting or likely to affect the elements of the environment referred to in para (a);

(c) measures (including administrative measures), such as policies, legislation, plans, programmes, environmental agreements, and activities affecting or likely to affect the elements and factors referred to in paras (a) and (b) as well as measures or activities designed to protect those elements;

(d) reports on the implementation of environmental legislation;

(e) costs–benefit and other economic analyses and assumptions used within the framework of the measures and activities referred to in para (c); and

(f) the state of human health and safety, including the contamination of the food chain, where relevant, conditions of human life, cultural sites and built structures inasmuch as they are or may be affected by the state of the elements of the environment referred to in para (a) or, through those elements, by any of the matters referred to in paras (b) and (c).

The use of the word "any" qualifying the word "information" indicates a legislative intention that environmental information should be interpreted widely. 2.07

No types of information are excluded from the potential ambit of environmental information. It is important to appreciate that environmental information may be used, or found in, or extend beyond what is not specifically an environmental topic. Court cases have confirmed that environmental information, and the scope of the Directive, should be interpreted broadly.[5] 2.08

The Commissioner's decisions have shown that information must be read in context to establish whether it is or is not environmental. When information was sought on the construction of a six-lane motorway into Glasgow, which would clearly impact on the environment, it was determined that documents which ostensibly had no environmental content should be dealt with under the EIRs as they formed part of the administrative process by which a costly and controversial scheme was given approval. As such, it was information relating to measures (including administrative measures), such as policies, legislation, plans and programmes affecting or likely to affect the environment.[6] 2.09

5 For example, *Mecklenburg v Kreis Pinneberg* (C–321/96) [1998] ECR 3809; *Glawischnig v Bundesminister* (C–316/01) [2003] ECR I-5995, 12 June 2003 (these decisions concerned Dir 90/313/EEC and not Dir 2003/4/EC); *Office of Communications v Information Commissioner* [2009] EWCA Civ 90; *BERR v Information Commissioner and Friends of the Earth* (EA/2007/0072) Information Tribunal, 2008; *Network Rail Ltd v Information Commissioner and Others* (EA/2006/0061/0062), Information Tribunal, 2007; *Port of London Authority v Information Commissioner and Hibbert* (EA/2006/0083), Information Tribunal, 2007.

6 Decision 056/2008: Mr Rob Edwards and the Scottish Ministers.

2.10   Similarly, a name on its own may not be environmental. However, where that name was of a fish farm from which farmed salmon escaped into the marine environment then it was found to be environmental.[7]

2.11   There is also no geographical restriction to the information, as the EIRs are not confined to information about the Scottish environment. So, for example, information on overseas aid programme grants for schemes that impact upon the environment in Africa may come within the definition of "environmental information" for the purposes of the EIRs, if that information is held by a Scottish public authority.

REGULATION 2(1) DEFINITION (a): ELEMENTS

> "(a) the state of the elements of the environment, such as air and atmosphere, water, soil, land, landscape and natural sites including wetlands, coastal and marine areas, biological diversity and its components, including genetically modified organisms, and the interaction among these elements".

2.12   There are two aspects to this definition; first, the *state* of the elements of the environment and, second, the *interaction* among the elements of the environment. The state of the elements, or components, of the environment covers both quality and quantity. It will include physical, biological and chemical characteristics. It is not limited to current conditions, but includes past and predicted future conditions.

2.13   *Air and atmosphere*: the atmosphere is the collection of gases that surround the Earth which are retained by the Earth's gravitation, forming its gaseous envelope. The distinction between air and atmosphere suggests that "air" refers to that which we breathe, which would include air found within buildings and structures.

Water: will mean water in all its forms (vapour, ice, liquid) and is not limited by scale (from oceans to the smallest droplet). It includes water under ground or on the surface and water in natural settings (rivers and lakes) and man-made (reservoirs, canals).

Soil: can be taken to mean the unconsolidated mineral or organic material top layer of the Earth's surface in which plants grow.

Land: is the solid parts making up the Earth's surface, but may also include land under the surface. "Land" has been described as all land

---

7   Decision 182/2006: Mr Bruce Sandison and the Fisheries Research Services.

surfaces, buildings, land covered by water, and underground strata.[8] By including underground strata, the implication is that land also includes natural minerals and deposits such as salt, coal, limestone, slate, iron etc.

Landscape: this is defined by the European Landscape Convention 2000 as "an area, as perceived by people, whose character is the result of the action and interaction of natural and/or human factors". Scottish Natural Heritage, the statutory adviser on landscape in Scotland, has identified many different landscapes - woodland, farmland, croftland, urban, coastal, mountainous - and within these there are many variations.

Natural sites, including wetlands, coastal and marine areas: "natural sites" recognises the importance of protected areas such as World Heritage Sites; "Natura 2000" nature conservation sites under European Directives; Sites of Special Scientific Interest ("SSSIs"); National Nature Reserves ("NNRs") and any other similar sites. However, a site will not need to have been designated to qualify as a "natural site". All natural sites that possess a specific value, local significance or special natural or historic value can be taken to be a natural site. "Natural" does not necessarily mean devoid of human interference, and the protection and/or management of a site will not preclude it from being classified as natural.

Biological diversity and its components: Article 2 of the Convention on Biological Diversity 1992 defines the term "biological diversity" as the variability among living organisms from all sources, including, for example, terrestrial, marine and other aquatic ecosystems and the ecological complexes of which they are part. This includes diversity within species, between species and of ecosystems. The components of biodiversity must be taken to include: genetic diversity - the genetic composition of a species (genes, DNA, RNA etc); species diversity - every living thing, every single species (plant, animal, bacteria, viruses etc); and ecosystem diversity - all habitats whether natural or man-made (from arctic wilderness to urban sprawl). In addition, biological diversity and its components should not be limited in time - for instance, it will include dead and extinct individual organisms and species.

---

8 See the Guidance on the Environmental Information Regulations 1992. "Land" includes building and other structures, land covered with water, and any estate, interest, easement, servitude or right in or over land": Interpretation Act 1978, Sch 1.

- When a request was made for the results of badger surveys, the Commissioner concluded that these related to "biological diversity and all its components", and so the information within them fell within the definition of environmental information.[9]
- The Commissioner concluded that details of discussions between the UK and Chinese Governments about the prospect of Giant Pandas coming to Edinburgh Zoo related to the potential transfer of an endangered wild species from one part of the world to another, and must count as a measure likely to affect biological diversity and its components.[10]

"Genetically modified organism" ("GMO"): according to the EU Directive on the deliberate release into the environment of genetically modified organisms, "an organism, with the exception of human beings, in which the genetic material has been altered in a way that does not occur naturally by mating and/or natural recombination" is a GMO.[11]

"The interaction among these elements": this recognises that no one aspect of the environment can be fully understood in isolation and that the interaction between the elements is just as important as the elements themselves.

- The fact that a loss adjuster's report related to the interaction of water (as rainwater) with an infrastructure (the drain or gully) potentially causing damage (flood and erosion) to further built structures brought the contents of a report within the definition of environmental information.[12]

REGULATION 2(1) DEFINITION (b): FACTORS

2.14   "(b) factors, such as substances, energy, noise, radiation or waste, including radioactive waste, emissions, discharges and other releases into the environment, affecting or likely to affect the elements of the environment referred to in (a);"

2.15   *Factor:* "factor" in this sense should be taken to mean simply something that has an effect on an element of the environment. It is important to note at this stage that it is possible for an "element" to be a "factor":

---

9   Decision 044/2007: Mr G Crole and Transport Scotland.
10 Decision 051/2009: Advocates for Animals and the Scottish Ministers.
11 Article 2(1) of Directive 2001/18/EC of the European Parliament and of the Council on the deliberate release into the environment of genetically modified organisms and repealing Council Dir 90/220/EEC.
12 Decision 096/2006: Mr George Waddell and South Lanarkshire Council.

for instance, water will become a "factor" in an incidence of flooding. Equally, a "factor" may also be an "element" – for example, radon gas is emitted naturally, and in certain areas it can build up in people's homes and become a health risk, but the radon gas (the factor in this instance) is still also an "element".

Substances: includes all material/matter, natural or synthetic – for example, chemicals, pharmaceuticals, hormones, antibiotics, oil, particulates, gases and liquids.

Energy: can be expressed in traditional scientific language – thermal, chemical, electrical, kinetic, quantum, electromagnetic, laser, potential, light, sound etc. Common usage for the term centres on power generation – oil-fired, coal-fired, gas-fired, nuclear energy and renewable energy (wind power, hydro power, wave/tidal energy, solar energy etc). However, "energy" is not restricted to large-scale power plants and electricity generation. It also includes heat (heat, in the form of hot water emitted into a river, for example, can have a drastic effect on the plants, animals and fish living in the vicinity), combined heat and power, renewables (including micro-renewables), biomass, fuel cells etc. "Energy" will also include sunlight, geothermal, radio waves, microwaves, radar waves etc.

Noise: although noise is itself energy, it is included here separately. It was also specifically mentioned in the original European Directive on Environmental Information in 1990[13] and in the original UK EIRs in 1992. Noise may be subjective, localised and transient. A simple dictionary definition of "noise" is "a sound, especially one that is loud, unpleasant, or disturbing". Noise also includes vibrations.[14]

Radiation or waste, including radioactive waste: radiation can be natural (sun, cosmic rays, radioactive chemicals and elements, minerals, liquids and gases) or man made (including mobile phone and wi-fi radiation emissions). A wide variety of materials in regular use in industry, medicine, science and research are radioactive.

Waste: "waste" has been broadly interpreted under the European Waste Framework Directive[15] and also the Waste Framework Directive 2008,[16] to mean any substance or object which its holder intends to, or is required to, or does, discard. So it is not confined to that material which

---

13 1990/313/EEC.
14 See Environmental Protection Act 1990, s 79(7).
15 2006/12/EC.
16 2008/98/EC.

has already been disposed of, but waste material still held on site. This covers a wide range of possibilities, including household waste; industrial waste and commercial waste; municipal waste; clinical waste; landfill and construction and demolition wastes; mining and agricultural wastes; sewage sludge and dredged spoils; and Special Waste; hazardous waste; toxic waste; and others.

Radioactive waste: radioactive materials are used in many situations, settings and industries and are far more widespread than commonly thought. Radioactive materials are used in common products, ranging from the luminous dials on watches to smoke detectors.

Emissions, discharges and other releases: Directive 2003/4/EC does not offer a definition of "emission" or "discharge". A widely quoted definition of "emission" comes from the European Integrated Pollution Prevention and Control (IPPC) Directive:[17] "emission shall mean the direct or indirect release of substances, vibrations, heat or noise from individual or diffuse sources ... into the air, water or land". "Discharges" is not expressly defined in the IPPC Directive; however, common usage of the term in this context suggests that it may generally be reserved (although not exclusively) for liquid releases into water.[18]

- Fish Legal argued that data about sea lice released from fish farm cages into the marine environment related to information on "emissions". Scottish Natural Heritage countered that sea lice are a naturally occurring part of the marine ecosystem and are not emitted, discharged or released. The Commissioner did not require to come to a view on this.[19]

2.16   "... affecting or likely to affect the elements of the environment referred to in (a)".

2.17   Information about the factor would not be environmental information unless the factor is "affecting or likely to affect" the elements of the environment. Authorities, understandably, assume that the effect must be detrimental or large scale. However, the consequence of affecting the elements could also involve a beneficial effect, for example certain changes to aquatic habitats may improve

---

17   Council Directive 96/61/EC of 24 September 1996 concerning integrated pollution prevention and control [1996] OJ L257/26.
18   This approach to interpretation is also supported by the common usage of the term "discharge" in current water pollution legislation and regulation, for example the Water Environment (Controlled Activities) (Scotland) Regulations 2005.
19   Decision 046/2010: Fish Legal and Scottish Natural Heritage.

biodiversity by attracting or sustaining additional fish or bird populations. The use of the words "likely to" indicates a higher threshold than is found in reg 2(1)(f) below ("may be affected by …") and suggests that there must be a degree of evidence to suggest that likelihood of the factor having the supposed effect is more than hypothetical. "Likely to" can be interpreted by way of reference to the balance of probabilities.[20]

> "Where information of the kind referred to in paragraph (b) of the definition of 'environmental information' in reg 2(1) is made available, the authority shall, if the applicant so requests, provide such information as is available to it of the place where information can be found on the measurement procedures, including methods of analysis, sampling and pre-treatment of samples, used in compiling the information, or refer the applicant to the standardised procedure used."

2.18

Regulation 5(5) requires a Scottish public authority to supply further information on the place where information can be found about the measurement, analysis and sampling methods used in compiling the information. Alternatively, authorities can refer the applicant to the standardised procedure which was used. This regulation only applies when a request is made for that information and only to the extent it is available to it. This allows scrutiny not only of the outcome of tests but also the basis on which conclusions were arrived at.

2.19

REGULATION 2(1) DEFINITION (c): MEASURES AND ACTIVITIES

> "(c) measures (including administrative measures), such as policies, legislation, plans, programmes, environmental agreements, and activities affecting or likely to affect the elements and factors referred to in paragraphs (a) and (b) as well as measures or activities designed to protect those elements".

2.20

This section of the definition deals with two aspects – measures and activities. Information about a measure or activity is environmental information if the measure or activity:

2.21

- affects or is likely to affect the elements of the environment;
- affects or is likely to affect a factor which itself affects or is likely to affect an element of the environment; or
- is designed to protect the elements of the environment.

---

20   The interpretation of "likely " is also discussed in relation to FOISA, s 2 in Chapter 1.

2.22   Again, the effect need not be detrimental or large scale. Depending on the circumstances, it may be small and/or beneficial. There must, however, be a link between the measure/activity and an element/factor.

2.23   *Measures*: "measures" will comprise steps taken to secure an effect (past, present or future) and the methods, processes or instruments used. Administrative measures are specifically mentioned, but the interpretation of "measures" is not restricted to those of an administrative nature. Measures will also encompass regulatory, economic and voluntary tools, such as Acts of Parliament, local by-laws, taxes, fines, charges and voluntary agreements. It should be assumed that "policies" refers specifically to "environmental policies", but will also takes into account development policies, economic policies, transport policies, health and safety policies etc, if they satisfy the definition. This category will include certain planning tools, including development (local and structure) plans by local authorities and other plans or documents, such as environmental impact assessments[21] and strategic environmental assessments[22] under the relevant legislation.

Where a measure is being proposed or being carried into effect, then the EIRs provide that *any* information on those measures is environmental information. As a consequence, this can capture information not only about what the measure is, but also about who was involved in the decision, when it was taken and what process led to the decision. However, the extent to which the information relates to the measure is a matter of judgement.[23]

- The Commissioner took the view that the publication by Scottish Ministers of bathing water pollution testing results formed part of a programme of measures designed to monitor and improve Scotland's bathing water standards in line with European law, and the monitoring and reporting of bathing water quality, and was therefore environmental information, However, an applicant's request for information went further than the actual results and included the process by which they were published. This encompassed documents containing information planning the announcement of the test results and information about water quality at various sites, progress on sampling and analysis, discussion and interpretation of the results. While some of

---

21   Environmental Impact Assessment (Scotland) Regulations 1999 (SI 1999/1).
22   Environmental Assessment of Plans and Programmes (Scotland) Regulations 2004 (SSI 2004/258) and Environmental Assessment (Scotland) Act 2005 (asp 15).
23   Decision 102/2009: Councillor David Alexander and Falkirk Council.

the information might have been narrowly viewed as simply containing information relating to the publication of data, the Commissioner concluded that the clearly environmental nature of the data meant that the information relating to its publication should also be viewed as environmental information.[24]

Activities: activities are not described in the definition, but the Aarhus Implementation Guide[25] refers to "... decisions on specific activities, such as permits, licences, permissions ...". Therefore, if the permit (or equivalent authorisation) can be viewed as the decision to allow the activity to proceed, then the activity must be the process, operation, actions or procedure for which the permit is required. However, it should not be assumed that a permit or authorisation is required in order for an action to be considered an activity. Some activities which bear upon the environment may not require authorisation, or be conducted under general binding rules which may arguably fall short of being a permit or authorisation. The interpretation of activities is likely to be broad and ranges, for example, from the construction of roads to agricultural practices.   2.24

> " ... affecting or likely to affect the elements and factors referred to in (a) and (b) as well as measures or activities designed to protect those elements".

As with the previous section, there is a qualifying statement associated with measures and activities. The measure or activity must affect, or be likely to affect, either the *elements* of the environment or the *factors*; or alternatively, in this case, be specifically designed to protect them.

A number of the Commissioner's decisions have shown that, broadly interpreted, these provisions bring far more information within the scope of the EIRs than authorities have perhaps appreciated. In particular, it has meant that detailed legal, contractual and financial information which may contain no specific reference to the environment or even the activity are still within scope if they relate to that activity.

- So, for example, information about the cost and financing of road building programmes is environmental information as

---

24 Decision 094/2008: Mr Rob Edwards and the Scottish Ministers.
25 *The Aarhus Convention: An Implementation Guide*, prepared by Stephen Stec and Susan Casey-Lefkowitz in collaboration with Jerzy Jendroska (UNECE, United Nations Economic Commission for Europe, New York and Geneva, 2000).

it relates to measures likely to affect the state of the elements of the environment, principally air and landscape. The fact that such information is not about earth moving or projecting carbon emissions does not matter. The details of how much the project will cost and how it will be paid for fall within the scope of any information relating to that activity.[26]

- Similarly, in a case involving a contract for the remediation for a disused quarry site, the information consisted largely of contractual legal clauses relating to the relationship of the parties, and various obligations, agreements and financial provisions appropriate to the proposals. The local authority did not agree that such complex legal documentation fell within the definition of "environmental information". The Commissioner's view was that the withheld information related to proposed measures, the ultimate intention of which was to bring about changes to the land in question, which constituted "environmental remediation", and so was within the scope of the EIRs.[27]

2.25   Information relating to planning applications will commonly fall under the definition of "environmental information" contained in the EIRs, as that information will, in most circumstances, explicitly relate to plans and developments which will have a direct impact on the land use and landscape of a particular area.[28]

This is primarily because the built environment and changes to it, by definition, will impact substantially on the environment in many ways, both directly and indirectly. Further, buildings are increasingly subject to audits and surveys of environmental performance, including energy consumption. Environmentally relevant aspects will extend to design, performance, construction, contamination, demolition, waste disposal and almost all other aspects of the life-cycle of a building. Planning matters will also go beyond buildings to include other infrastructure, such as roads, bridges, transport, and mobile phone masts.

Planning matters, that include planning policies, development plans, environ-mental assessments and similar information, are likely to be considered "measures". Reasons for or against planning

---

26 Decision 218/2007: Professor A D Hawkins and Transport Scotland; Decision 014/2008: Mr John McIntosh and Transport Scotland; Decision 056/2008: Mr Rob Edwards and the Scottish Ministers.
27 Decision 033/2009: Mr Paul Drury and East Renfrewshire Council.
28 Decision 045/2008: Dr Alex Morrow and the City of Edinburgh Council.

decisions, and conditions attached to grants of permission are also likely to be covered by this part of the definition. Discussions on proposed developments even before formal planning applications have been submitted could be included, as these can involve consideration of their potential effects on the elements of the environment, for example regarding landscape and flooding.[29] A local plan (including maps) is environmental information and so too is any information held by a local authority on objections to or comments on the plan.[30]

REGULATION 2(1) DEFINITION (d): REPORTS ON THE IMPLEMENTATION OF ENVIRONMENTAL LEGISLATION

These constitute, for instance, any reports reviewing or monitoring the operation, performance, success or failure of environmental legislation. Information in this category may also fall within the definition in para (c). **2.26**

Specifically, Member States were obliged to report by 14 August 2009 to the European Commission on the experience gained in the application of the European Directive 2003/4/EC. **2.27**

The Department for Environment, Food and Rural Affairs responded on behalf of the UK Government,[31] but confined its report to the legislation as it related to England, Wales and Northern Ireland, noting that experience derived from the application of the Scottish Regulations was the subject of a separate report produced by the Scottish Government.[32] **2.28**

REGULATION 2(1) DEFINITION (e): COSTS-BENEFIT AND OTHER ECONOMIC ANALYSES

"(e) costs benefit and other economic analyses and assumptions used within the framework of the measures and activities referred to in (c)". **2.29**

---

29 Decision 101/2008: Mr Alistair Johnson and East Renfrewshire Council.
30 Decision 102/2009: Councillor David Alexander and Falkirk Council.
31 Public access to environmental information – Experience gained in the application of Directive 2003/4/EC DEFRA 2009: http://www.defra.gov.uk/corporate/policy/opengov/eir/pdf/commission-report-uk.pdf.
32 Reporting about the experience gained in Scotland in the application of Directive 2003/4/EC concerning on public access to environmental information http://www.scotland.gov.uk/Resource/Doc/921/0085214.pdf.

2.30   The desire to include economic and financial information in the definition stems from the recognition that it is important to integrate environmental and economic considerations in decision-making. This section is qualified by referring back to para (c) "measures and activities", and therefore to the economic and financial aspects taken into account during the framing of measures or activities.

- A business plan for a Highland housing fair was environmental information, wrongly withheld by a local authority.[33]

REGULATION 2(1) DEFINITION (f): THE STATE OF HUMAN HEALTH

2.31   "(f) the state of human health and safety, including the contamination of the food chain, where relevant, conditions of human life, cultural sites and built structures inasmuch as they are or may be affected by the state of the elements of the environment referred to in (a) or, through those elements, by any of the matters referred to in (b) and (c)".

2.32   In contrast to the definitions in (a), (b) and (c), this definition refers to specific fields. It can be broken down into two main areas:

- the state of human health and safety (including the contamination of the food chain where relevant to the state of human health and safety) and conditions of human life; and
- the state of cultural sites and built structures.

2.33   However, these specific fields fall within the definition of "environmental information" only to the extent that:

- they are or may be affected by the state of the elements of the environment; or
- through those elements, they are or may be affected by factors, measures or activities affecting or likely to affect the elements of the environment.

2.34   "*the state of human health and safety, including contamination of the food chain*": this could include information about public health affected or endangered by, for example, air, water and soil pollution. It could include information on respiratory conditions caused by particulate matter, or the endangerment to human health from land contaminated

---

33   Decision 094/2009: Mr Brian MacGregor and Highland Council.

by toxic metals. Special mention is made of the contamination of the food chain, and this follows concerns over BSE and other health issues.

"conditions of human life": this aspect acknowledges the connection **2.35** between social and environmental factors. As with human health and safety, this appears to be intended to apply to large-scale factors, for example information on housing, poverty, employment, social welfare, heating, access to clean water, sanitation, healthcare, education and justice, rather than information on an individual scale.

- A request was made for papers relating to the development of the Scottish Executive's environmental justice strategy. The Commissioner considered that environmental justice is concerned with the effects of the environment on people and communities, and seeks particularly to identify and eliminate injustices where certain groups bear a disproportionate burden of environmental risk. As such, the information concerned the state of human health and conditions for human life.[34]

- A firm of lawyers asked for copies of notices pursuant to s 80 of the Environmental Protection Act 1990 ("EPA"). An abatement notice under s 80 of the EPA will be served in circumstances where the local authority considers that the by-products of human activity, such as fumes, odour, smoke, dust, effluvia, insects, light or noise, may be prejudicial to health or a nuisance. The notices were composed substantially of information relating to noise and odour emissions, factors which will affect the elements of the environment, and as such fall within the definition contained in reg 2(1)(h). The Commissioner noted that the very fact that these were having an effect on the surrounding environment, and in turn affected others, led to the Council issuing the notice in the first place. The Commissioner concluded that the nuisances concerned were specifically of an environmental nature and that the notices fell under the definition of "environmental information" in reg 2(1)(f).[35]

Cultural sites: cultural sites will constitute places which are recognised **2.36** to have a particular literary, educational, artistic, anthropological or historical value, or have religious, ethnic, or social significance – for example, World Heritage Sites (such as St Kilda), scheduled monuments, listed buildings, archaeological sites, castles, parks,

34 Decision 120/2008: Mr Rob Edwards and the Scottish Ministers.
35 Decision 129/2007: MacRoberts Solicitors and Aberdeenshire Council.

gardens and buildings. These sites can be modern or historical, and urban as well as rural locations.

2.37   *Built structures*: as indicated above, buildings in a general sense are included as part of the definition of "land" as an element; the specific mention of "built structures" allows a specific focus on particular buildings, as well as other infrastructure. According to the Aarhus Implementation Guide, "built structures" refers to man-made constructions. It is not limited to large buildings and objects such as dams, bridges, highways, etc but can also cover small constructions and even landscaping or other transformation of the natural environment.

> "... inasmuch as they are or may be affected by the state of the elements of the environment referred to in (a) or, through those elements, by any of the matters referred to in (b) and (c) –".

2.38   This paragraph is also subject to qualifications, in order to place boundaries on what is considered environmental information as opposed to (for example) social or economic information. However, this qualification is not the same as those in earlier parts of reg 2. The earlier qualification in para (c) refers to "affecting or likely to affect", whereas para (f) refers to "as they are or may be affected by". The term "affecting" indicates an actual, tangible effect, and "likely to affect" implies a distinct probability of doing so in future.

2.39   By contrast, the wording "as they are [affected] or may be affected by" is a much more hypothetical and thus less definite element in the test. This is understandable – to require a more definite causal relationship could exclude information which had been or was being compiled in respect of human health concerns from environmental factors, but for which no effect had yet been established.

THE INTERPRETATION OF "ENVIRONMENTAL INFORMATION"

2.40   It is clear that the definition of what constitutes "environmental information" should not be viewed too narrowly, but that the interpretation must be in line with the definition in the EIRs. Authorities should not restrict the application of the EIRs to instances where the information relevant to the request is observably environmental; for example, it is for "data derived from the monitoring of activities that affect or are likely to affect the environment".[36] Authorities appear to have difficulty where:

---

36   Reg 4(2)(e).

- the request itself does not specifically make reference to the environment;
- the request itself does not specifically make reference to the EIRs (or makes reference to FOISA instead);
- the information found to be relevant to that request is not exclusively environmental;
- the information is found to be environmental by virtue of being "policies, plans and programmes relating to the environment".

Authorities should not assume that they will be alerted by the nature of the request as to whether it is for environmental information. There is certainly no obligation upon applicants to cite the EIRs when making a request and many will not make any ostensible reference to the environment. Indeed, the applicant may be unaware that the information within the scope of their request is environmental. The onus is upon the authority to recognise that the information held is environmental and that it should be dealt with under the EIRs. 2.41

The scope of the EIRs is clear from the Commissioner's decisions which have concluded that the EIRs apply to the following wide range of information: 2.42

- Information about the process of ministerial decision-making on the M74 completion scheme. This included documentation on the legal and administrative as well as the more ostensibly environmental aspects of the project, given that all were integral to bringing such an environmentally significant scheme to fruition.[37]
- The projected cost of a pest control programme in Dundee. The cost was integral to the extent of the measures being taken to protect built structures and human health from the effects of gulls. Additionally, it represented an integral part of the information on measures or activities which affect biological diversity, given the impact on the gull population.[38]
- The presentation and communications strategy relating to the conservation of the red squirrel in Scotland.[39]
- Diplomatic issues surrounding the introduction of Giant Pandas to Edinburgh Zoo. The Commissioner recognised the importance of the political context, but concluded that the underlying issue to which the withheld information related was the potential

---

37 Decision 056/2008: Mr Rob Edwards and the Scottish Ministers.
38 Decision 119/2008: Mr James Paul Kelly and Dundee City Council.
39 Decision 063/2008: Mr Rob Edwards and the Scottish Ministers.

transfer of endangered wild species from one part of the world to another, which counted as a measure likely to affect biological diversity and its components.[40]

2.43   There are cases where it was accepted that the information was not environmental and that FOISA was therefore the correct regime:

- The minor alteration of an existing building. Although it involved planning matters (which might usually suggest that the information was environmental), the information did not relate to a measure affecting, or likely to affect, the elements and factors referred to in the definition of "environmental information". Nor did it relate to the state of a built structure in so far as it is or may be affected by the state of the elements of the environment.[41]

- The ministerial consideration of the application by the Forth Estuary Transport Authority ("FETA") to initiate Road User Charges ("RUCs") on the Forth Road Bridge. Although the underlying reasons behind the application to introduce RUCs included a desire to encourage car sharing as a method of limiting emissions and congestion, and also as a method of reducing the load on the bridge following the discovery of corrosion and broken wires in the bridge's main cables, the information sought in this case was limited in scope to documents relating to the Ministers' decision to reject FETA's application in principle for road user charging, the content of which did not relate or refer to the wider environmental issues.[42]

WHICH BODIES ARE COVERED BY THE EIRs?

2.44   Regulation 5(1) of the EIRs (the duty to make environmental information available on request) applies to a "Scottish public authority".

2.45   Regulation 2 (interpretation) sets out the definition of a "Scottish public authority" (reg 2(1)):

> "Scottish public authority" means –
>
> (a) any body which, any other person who, or the holder of any office which is –

---

40   Decision 051/2009: Advocates for Animals and the Scottish Ministers.
41   Decision 073/2008: Mr Pritam Chita and Dundee City Council.
42   Decision 098/2008: Mr Rob Edwards of *The Sunday Herald* and the Scottish Ministers.

      (i) listed in schedule 1 to [FOISA] (but subject to any qualification in that schedule), or

      (ii) designated by order under section 5(1) of [FOISA];

(b) a publicly-owned company as defined by section 6 of [FOISA];

(c) any other Scottish public authority with mixed functions or no reserved functions (within the meaning of the Scotland Act 1998); and

(d) any other person who is neither a public body nor the holder of a public office and who is under the control of a person or body falling within paragraphs (a), (b), or (c) of this definition and –

      (i) has public responsibilities relating to the environment;

      (ii) exercises functions of a public nature relating to the environment; or

      (iii) provides public services relating to the environment

2.46 The definition of a "Scottish public authority" is wider than that under FOISA, as it encompasses any Scottish public authority with mixed functions or no reserved functions which is not included in Sch 1 to FOISA and any person "who is neither a public body nor the holder of a public office" who is under the control of a person or body falling within parts (a)–(c) of the definition and has public responsibilities, functions or provides public services relating to the environment. This means that private companies may also, in limited circumstances, be covered by the EIRs.

2.47 There is no definitive list of bodies that fall under this part of the definition, but a number of factors may be taken into consideration by the Commissioner when determining whether an organisation falls within the scope of the EIRs. These are set out below.

Listed in Sch 1, designated under s 5 of FOISA, or a publicly owned company

2.48 Any authority already listed as a public authority for the purposes of FOISA is automatically subject to the EIRs. Bodies which are designated by the Scottish Ministers under s 5 of FOISA are also automatically subject to the EIRs.

2.49 The provisions of FOISA can be extended to bodies that appear to the Scottish Ministers to exercise functions of a public nature or who are providing, under contract with a Scottish public authority, any services whose provision is a function of that public authority (s 5(1)).

A publicly-owned company as defined by section 6 of the Act

2.50   Publicly owned companies, as defined by s 6 of FOISA, are also covered by the EIRs under definition (b). However, s 6 of FOISA only covers companies which are *wholly* publicly owned. This provision therefore covers companies that are wholly owned by one or more public authorities. These include, for example, companies set up by local authorities to explore new economic and transport initiatives and companies set up by universities to develop the products of their research commercially. The Clyde and Western Isles ferry operator, Caledonian MacBrayne, is an example of a body covered by this provision.

Scottish public authority with mixed functions or no reserved functions

2.51   The Scotland Act 1998 ("Scotland Act") defines the scope of the legal competence of the Scottish Parliament and Scottish Ministers and defines the powers which are reserved to the UK Government and Westminster Parliament. Bodies with no reserved functions within the meaning of the Scotland Act are those which operate exclusively in Scotland and their function is within the legislative competence of the Scottish Parliament and Scottish Government.

2.52   Bodies with mixed functions are those which conduct public functions assigned to them by both governments. Local authorities, for example, have mixed functions. They, however, are already designated through Sch 1 to FOISA and so fall into the first category of Scottish public authorities. To date, no public authority has been identified as being subject to the EIRs purely on this basis.

Certain bodies controlled by Scottish public authorities or publicly owned companies

> Any person who is neither a public body nor the holder of a public office and who is:
> - under the control of a Scottish public authority subject to FOISA;
> - a publicly-owned company; or
> - a Scottish publicly-owned company of mixed or no reserved functions will itself be subject to the EIRs if it:
>   - has public responsibilities relating to the environment;
>   - exercises functions of a public nature relating to the environment; or
>   - provides public services relating to the environment.

This is a complex provision which has no equivalent under FOISA   2.53
and derives from European Directive 2003/4/EC. There has been only
one instance of the Commissioner finding that a body was within the
scope of EIRs on this basis (see Box below). However, there is case law
and precedent from elsewhere which may also help when considering
whether a body falls within the scope of the EIRs.[43]

For instance, the UK Information Commissioner found that a con-   2.54
sultancy, Environmental Resource Management Ltd ("ERM")[44] which
had been contracted to carry out and prepare an environmental assessment and report at the request of the Regional Assembly for the
North East of England ("RANE"), was covered by the Environmental
Information Regulations 2004 ("UK EIRs"). The circumstances of
this case are worth examining. The assessment was a statutory
requirement of the Strategic Environmental Assessment Regulations.
The authority had the choice of conducting the assessment itself or
contracting it out to a third party. By entering into the contract, not
only was ERM held to be under the control of the authority (by virtue
of the contractual relationship), but it was also held to have directly
assumed public functions relating to the environment while carrying
out the assessment.

The UK Information Commissioner has also concluded that   2.55
two Northern Irish housing associations are public authorities for
the purposes of the UK EIRs. One of these cases involved the Belfast
Improvement Housing Association,[45] which was registered under a
Government Department's list of housing associations and which was
eligible for a certain type of grant. These grants contribute about 70 per
cent toward the capital cost of developing general-purpose housing for
rent and a higher percentage of the cost of developing accommodation
for people in need of specialist accommodation, for instance elderly
and disabled people. Grants had environmentally related conditions
attached. Although an independent entity, the association had to
account to the Government Department for its use of these grant
monies, and the Department had the power to intervene if dissatisfied,
for example as a result of mismanagement. The UK Information
Commissioner decided that the housing association was covered by
the Environmental Information Regulations 2004, as it was under

---

43   Eg *Foster v British Gas* [1991] 2 AC 306; *Griffin v South West Water Services Ltd* [1995] IRLR 15;
     Poplar Housing and Regeneration Community Housing Association Ltd v Donoghue [2002] QB 48;
     R v Leonard Cheshire Foundation [2002] EWCA Civ 366.
44   ICO case reference FER0090259.
45   UK ICO case ref FER0152607 [Belfast Improvement Housing Association].

the control of the Government Department which had "the power to direct, manage, oversee and/or restrict the affairs, business or assets of a person or entity".[46]

2.56   An oddity of the situation is that the powers to define bodies as public authorities may appear to be greater in the rest of the UK than it is in Scotland because of the manner in which the Directive has been transposed into law north and south of the Border.

2.57   Recital (11) of the European Directive states:

> "... the definition of public authorities should be expanded so as to encompass government or other public administration at national, regional or local level whether or not they have specific responsibilities for the environment. The definition should likewise be expanded to include other persons or bodies performing public administrative functions in relation to the environment under national law, as well as other persons or bodies acting under their control and having public responsibilities or functions in relation to the environment".

2.58   Article 2 of the Directive provides the definition:

> "'Public authority' shall mean: (a) government or other public administration, including public advisory bodies, at national, regional or local level; (b) any natural or legal person performing public administrative functions under national law, including specific duties, activities or services in relation to the environment; and (c) any natural or legal person having public responsibilities, or providing public services, relating to the environment under the control of a body or person falling within (a) or (b)."

In Scotland, the Directive's reference to "public administrative functions under national law, including specific duties, activities, or services in relation to the environment" is not directly transposed into the EIRs. (Even so, the EIRs are likely to have to be read in the light of the Directive.) By contrast, the UK EIRs do include this specific reference and this has been material in decisions taken by the UK Information Commissioner. For instance, he concluded that the Port of London Authority was subject to the UK EIRs by virtue of the fact that the Port of London Act 1968, which created the Port of London Authority, places a duty on the authority to carry out functions of public administration.[47]

---

46   UK ICO case ref FER0152607, para 33: http://www.ico.gov.uk/upload/documents/decision notices/2008/fer_0152607.pdf.

47   UK ICO case ref FER0086096: http://www.ico.gov.uk/upload/documents/decisionnotices/2006/fer0086096_dn001.pdf.

The provisions of the Directive have given rise to expectations that **2.59** the functions of bodies such as public utility companies providing water and energy services might fall within the definition along with private contractors involved in PPP/PFI or similar contracts with environmental functions, for example functions relating to waste disposal, energy production, drainage, transport or environmental consultancy. (The more the body is fulfilling statutory responsibilities of a public authority, the more it might be thought to exercise functions of a public nature relating to the environment; or provide public services relating to the environment.) In practice, this has not proven to be the case. The UK Information Commissioner found that Network Rail was a public authority for the purposes of the UK EIRs, taking into account the key national strategic role played by Network Rail and the fact that it is subject to regulation by the Office of Rail Regulation, which exists to ensure the accountability of Network Rail to the public interest.[48]

However, this decision was overturned on appeal by the Infor- **2.60** mation Tribunal which disagreed that Network Rail had "functions of public administration", saying that the company "runs a railway system … It does not administer anything, save in the sense that it runs its own business" and concluded that it was not within the scope of UK EIRs, observing that "Whatever the position in 1947, running a railway is not seen nowadays in the United Kingdom as a function normally performed by a government authority".[49]

The privatised water companies were also found not to be public **2.61** authorities. The Upper Tier Tribunal accepted that the supply of water was once a function of public administration but held that in an era of privatisation this was no longer the case. The fact that the companies were subject to regulation was not enough for the purposes of the UK EIRs. The issue was one of control.

> "Regulation involves the regulator formulating policy and strategy, determining outcomes, setting standards, making and enforcing rules and issuing guidance for those bodies it regulates. Regulation may be 'light touch' or 'heavy-handed'. Control must go further than the functions associated with regulation … it connotes command or compulsion, and the power to determine not just ends but the means to achieve those ends."[50]

---

48 UK ICO case ref FER0071801, paras 5.1–5.6: http://www.ico.gov.uk/upload/documents/decisionnotices/ 2006/decision_notice_fer0071801.pdf.

49 *Network Rail v Information Commissioner* (Appeal Number: EA/2006/0061 and 0062), paras 28 and 29.

50 *Smartsource Drainage & Water Reports Ltd v Information Commissioner* [2010] UKUT 415 (AAC), para 95.

2.62   A similar determination involving private companies has yet to arise in Scotland but that thinking may be pertinent as it would have to be demonstrated that the body was "under the control" of a public authority (and that authority would have to be Scottish) for the EIRs to apply.

2.63   Surprisingly, perhaps, the Commissioner has dealt with very few cases concerning bodies which the applicant believed was within the scope of the EIRs. He has, however, determined that the Solway Shellfish Management Association is a public authority under the EIRs, even though it is not within the scope of FOISA.

Under whose control? – Solway Shellfish Management Association ("SSMA")

The SSMA was formed in order to apply for and manage a Regulating Order for the maintenance and regulation of a shellfish fishery on the Scottish Solway Firth. The Company's Board of Directors included representatives from Dumfries and Galloway Council and Scottish Natural Heritage, which are public authorities, and also the Royal Society for the Protection of Birds and local fishermen's associations, which are not. Consequently, the SSMA was not a wholly publicly owned company and was not within the scope of FOISA.

The Commissioner concluded that, by virtue of statute, the SSMA has public responsibilities relating to the environment, for regulating fishing of cockle beds and protecting fisheries.[51] It exercised those responsibilities largely by virtue of a Regulating Order made by Ministers in 2006,[52] which provided that the SSMA:

- could with the *consent of Scottish Ministers* impose restriction on the dredging, fishing for and taking of cockles;
- subject to any *directions given by the Scottish Ministers* may issue licences;
- set tolls and royalties to be paid by licence holder, *with the consent of Scottish Ministers*.

The Commissioner concluded that the nature of the relationship was such that the association was under the control of Scottish Ministers for the purposes of the EIRs (which was accepted by the Association in the course of the investigation).[53]

---

51   Sea Fisheries (Shellfish) Act 1967, as amended by Marine (Scotland) Act 2010.
52   Solway Firth Regulated Fishing (Scotland) Order 2006 (SSI 2006/57).
53   Decision 085/2011: Mr Thomas Clark and the Solway Shellfish Management Association.

WHAT DO THE EIRs REQUIRE PUBLIC AUTHORITIES TO DO?

Taken as a whole, the EIRs require more of Scottish public authorities than FOISA. Authorities must: 2.64

- actively disseminate information, particularly by electronic means (reg 4(1));
- make environmental information available to any person who requests it within 20 working days or, in exceptional cases where the request is both voluminous and complex, within 40 working days (regs 5(1) and 7(1));
- publish a schedule of charges and information on the circumstances in which a fee may be charged, waived or required to be paid in advance (reg 8(8));
- provide advice and assistance to someone who has made, or wishes to make, a request for environmental information (reg 9);
- refuse requests for environmental information only in accordance with the limited exceptions available, giving reasons and details of the mechanisms for review and appeal (regs 10, 11 and 13);
- transfer requests for environmental information if they do not hold the information but believe another authority does (reg 14);
- where requested, carry out a review of a decision not to make environmental information available (reg 16).

ACTIVE DISSEMINATION OF ENVIRONMENTAL INFORMATION

The EIRs oblige authorities to be active in providing environmental information rather than simply passively waiting to respond to any requests. 2.65

In part, this can be done by publishing material and making it available under the terms of the authority's publication scheme. (There is no explicit requirement under the EIRs for a publication scheme, but all bodies which are Scottish public authorities for the purposes of s 3 of FOISA are also Scottish public authorities covered by the EIRs. Section 73 of FOISA simply defines information as "information recorded in any form" and s 23 of FOISA makes no distinction between environmental and non-environmental information in publication schemes. Therefore, to the extent that Scottish public authorities hold environmental information, it should feature in the content of publication schemes.) 2.66

2.67   Where this is done, the provisions of reg 6(1)(b) of the EIRs may well apply, which allows an authority to refuse to provide information if the information is already publicly available and easily accessible to the applicant in another form or format.

2.68   However, the EIRs are predicated on information being readily and widely available and "active dissemination" by means of websites, telecommunications and electronic technology is expected. Regulation 4(2) refers to specific types of information which are to be made available in this way:

(a) texts of international treaties, Conventions or agreements, and of Community, national, regional or local legislation, on the environment or relating to it;

(b) policies, plans and programmes relating to the environment;

(c) progress reports on the implementation of the items referred to in sub-paras (a) and (b) when prepared or held by a Scottish public authority in electronic form;

(d) reports on the state of the environment;

(e) data or summaries of data derived from the monitoring of activities that affect or likely to affect the environment;

(f) authorisations with a significant impact on the environment and environmental agreements or a reference to the place where such information can be requested or found;

(g) environmental impact studies and risk assessments concerning those elements of the environment referred to in para (a) of the definition of "environmental information" in reg 2(1); and

(h) facts and analyses of the facts which the authority considers relevant and important in framing major environmental policy proposals.

2.69   The EIRs do not require information to be made available in electronic format if it is dated prior to 14 February 2003 (unless it was already available in that form), although making information available electronically would be good practice where this is reasonable.

2.70   Regulation 4(1) also states that authorities shall make that information "progressively" available to the public by electronic means. Developments in information technology are constantly changing the way in which information is created, stored and transferred, and the use of this term takes account of these possible changes in technology.

Where there is a requirement under any other legislation for a   2.71
Scottish public authority to maintain an accessible register containing
environmental information, these registers must be kept up to date
and accurate and "comparable" (reg 5(4)). Access to such registers must
be free (reg 8(2)(a)).

Under the EIRs (reg 6(1)(b)) a public authority must comply   2.72
with a request unless the information is already available and easily
accessible to *the applicant* in another form or format. Public authorities
should also be aware that providing the environmental information by
electronic means only may limit its accessibility to those members of
the public who do not have access to the internet and the appropriate
technology. So, authorities should make arrangements for providing
information in hard copy to anyone who cannot access it by electronic
means.

It is worth noting here that the EIRs are not the only regulations   2.73
which impose duties on public authorities to provide access to public
data proactively. The Directive on which the EIRs are based is part of a
suite of European Directives, including the INSPIRE Directive 2007/2/EC
and Directive 2003/98/EC on the re-use of public sector information,[54]
which are intended to standardise and ensure access to public data
across Europe. There is, it has to be said, a certain amount of overlap
among the Directives.

INSPIRE, which is short for "Infrastructure for Spatial Information   2.74
in Europe", requires Member States to provide public access to location
based data (for example, map data) held by public authorities.

The INSPIRE (Scotland) Regulations 2009, which came into force   2.75
on 31 December 2009, give effect to the Directive. They apply to bodies
which are Scottish public authorities for the purposes of FOISA or
which, in line with the definition of "Scottish public authority" in the
EIRs, have public responsibilities relating to the environment, exercise
functions of a public nature relating to the environment or provide
public services relating to the environment, provided they are under
the control of a body listed in s 3(1) of FOISA.

The duties under the 2009 Regulations are wide ranging. Both the   2.76
Scottish Ministers and the Commissioner are responsible for enforcing
the Regulations (the Commissioner is responsible for enforcing only
the parts which deal with public access to data). The right of access is
subject to a number of "limitations" which are based on the exceptions
in the UK EIRs as opposed to the Scottish EIRs and allow public
authorities to refuse to allow access where access would, for example,

---

54 See Chapter 11 (Publication Schemes).

adversely affect national security, intellectual property rights or the protection of the environment to which a spatial data set or spatial data service in question relates.

2.77   The Scottish Ministers issued a guide to the INSPIRE (Scotland) Regulations 2009 in March 2011.[55]

SCHEDULE OF CHARGES

2.78   Where a Scottish public authority is under a duty to make environmental information available (under the EIRs, reg 5(1)), it *may* charge a reasonable fee for doing so (reg 8(1)). However, the authority cannot charge a fee for allowing an applicant to access any public register or lists of environmental information held by it (reg 8(2)(a)). Equally, the authority cannot charge an applicant to examine the information requested at a place which the authority makes available for that purpose (reg 8(2)(b)). There is no definition of what is considered to be "reasonable" or of what charges can be taken into account, although reg 8(3) provides that where an authority charges a fee, it shall not exceed a reasonable amount and must not exceed the costs to the authority of producing the information requested. (However, under Recital (18) of the Directive, where public authorities make available environmental information on a commercial basis, and where this is necessary in order to guarantee the continuation of collecting and publishing such information, a market-based charge is considered to be reasonable.)

2.79   There is a specific requirement for the authority to publish and make available to applicants a schedule of its fees (reg 8(8)(a)) and information on the circumstances in which a fee may be charged, waived or required to be paid in advance (reg 8(8)(b)). (Recognising in so doing that under Recital (18) instances where advance payment will be required should be limited.)

2.80   Public authorities often fail in respect of this provision. It is often assumed that they can simply rely upon the FOISA Fees Regulations applying to general FOI requests. This is not sufficient, and as is discussed in Chapter 8: Charging for Information, if an authority has not published its schedule of charges then it may not be able to charge for environmental information. If authorities wish to harmonise charges applying to FOISA and EIRs requests, then they can do so.

---

55 http://www.scotland.gov.uk/Topics/Government/PublicServiceReform/efficient government/OneScotland/INSPIRE.

Bodies such as the Scottish Environment Protection Agency   2.81
("SEPA") have shown that it is possible to publish a simple charging
policy which combines FOI and EIRs (see Box).

Combined EIRs/FOISA Charging Policy – The SEPA Example[56]

You do not have to pay for:

- any information downloaded from our website;
- a single copy of any document;*
- multiple copies of any publication (for example advisory leaflet or annual report) which is already printed and available for free.

You may have to pay for:

- printing or photocopying costs of 10p per page (unless your request is for fewer than 50 pages or if it is a single document*);
- postage or other delivery.

You will have to pay for:

- any information that has a charge specifically indicated in the "classes of information".

*"Document" means anything listed in the publication scheme that SEPA considers to be a single, distinct item. For example, a work procedure or an edition of SEPA View is a document. The quality management system or the SEPA View series are not documents.

If we need to make a charge, we will contact you before sending any material.

Non-publication scheme information

If your enquiry takes more than seven hours of staff time to answer, you will have to pay

- £25 per hour of staff time for environmental information;
- £15 per hour of staff time for non-environmental information (but you only pay for 10% of the total cost).

NB for both types of information, there is no charge for the first 7 hours' work. If we need to make a charge, we will contact you before sending any material.

---

56 http://www.sepa.org.uk/about_us/access_to_information/charging_policy.aspx.

DUTY TO PROVIDE ADVICE AND ASSISTANCE

2.82   Under reg 9(1), a Scottish public authority shall provide advice and assistance, so far as it would be reasonable to expect the authority to do so, to applicants and prospective applicants.

2.83   Appropriate assistance might include:

- assisting in defining the information required;
- providing the outline of the different types of information that meet the terms of the request (noting, however, that the applicant is under no obligation to state why they want the information);
- providing access to detailed catalogues and indexes, where these are available, to help the applicant ascertain the nature and extent of the information held by the authority.

HANDLING REQUESTS FOR ENVIRONMENTAL INFORMATION

THE REQUEST

Regulation 5(1)

> **Subject to paragraph (2), a Scottish public authority that holds environmental information shall make it available when requested to do so by the applicant.**

2.84   Unlike under FOISA, which requires a request for information to be in writing or in another form capable of being used for subsequent reference,[57] the definition of a "request" under the EIRs is completely unqualified.

2.85   This means that any request, in any form, whether it is oral, written or recorded, will be a valid request under the EIRs.

2.86   Although public authorities would probably prefer requests to be in writing (particularly if the request is complex), they cannot insist that an applicant makes the request in writing. In cases such as this, it will often be a good idea for the authority receiving an oral request to write it down, date it and confirm with the applicant whether this is an accurate record of their request. However, it is the date on which the authority receives the oral request, and not the date of confirmation, that will count as the date of receipt.

---

57   FOISA, s 8(1)(a).

(In practice, hardly any applications are made to the Commissioner   2.87
concerning cases where environmental information has been verbally
requested. One rare case was when an MSP orally asked the Chief
Executive of tie Ltd, the company responsible for Edinburgh's tram
project, for its business plan.[58] This was recognised and responded to
as an EIR request.)

Authorities should be aware that a request left on voicemail or a   2.88
telephone answering machine is a valid request and the date of receipt
is the date when the message was left.

Also, as with FOISA, anyone or any organisation, irrespective of   2.89
geographical location, can ask for environmental information and
applicants are not required to state their interest in the information
sought.

Applicants can ask for copies of documents. As indicated in   2.90
Chapter 1, the Court of Session has determined that under FOISA "What
a person can request, in terms of section 1(1), is the information which
has been recorded, rather than the record itself. The right conferred
by section 1, where it applies, is therefore to be given the information,
rather than a particular record (or a copy of the record) that contains
it. Put shortly, the Act provides a right of access to information, not
documentation".[59] However, this judgment did not address requests
made under the EIRs and does not appear to apply to them.

The EIRs implement Directive 2003/4/EC, which also needs to be   2.91
taken into account in interpreting them. Recital (5) of the Directive
refers to the need for provisions of Community law to be consistent
with the Aarhus Convention. Article 4(3) of that Convention obliges
public authorities to make environmental information available when
requested, including "copies of the actual documentation containing
or comprising such information". Consequently, an applicant may
make a request under the EIRs formulated in terms of "copies of
documents" rather than "information", without asking for (or it
having to be understood as being for) the information contained in
the document.

A Scottish public authority "holds" information for the purposes of   2.92
the EIRs if it is:

(a) in its possession and has been produced or received by that
     authority; or
(b) held by another person on that authority's behalf,

---

58   Decision 048/2011: Shirley-Anne Somerville, MSP and tie Ltd.
59   *Glasgow City Council and Dundee City Council v SIC* [2009] CSIH 73, para 43.

and, in either case, it has not been supplied by a Minister of the Crown or Department of the Government of the United Kingdom and held in confidence (reg 2(2)).

2.93   Consequently, the EIRs apply to any information held by or on behalf of a Scottish public authority whether or not it was obtained as a direct consequence of that body's environmental, or other, responsibilities. It therefore includes information held by:

- a Scottish public authority on its own behalf (within the authority's buildings or elsewhere);
- others on behalf of the Scottish public authority (for example by consultants, private companies or in archives)

except where the information is held in confidence, having been supplied by a UK Minister or Government Department.

2.94   This regulation differs from the provision in FOISA, which defines information as being "held" by a Scottish public authority if it is held by the authority *otherwise* than on behalf of another person. The absence of such a specific exclusion in the Regulations does not necessarily mean that any environmental information held by the authority on behalf of others or simply to be found on its premises means that the EIRs apply to that information. The Regulations require, that, for the information to be "held" by an authority, it must be "in its possession" having "been produced or received by that authority". Information stored on the authority's premises solely on behalf of another body, and of which the authority makes no use, may not be in its possession. Similarly, information which is found on the authority's premises only in the personal belongings of staff (eg personal diaries or mobile phones) may not be said to be in its possession or received by it.

INFORMATION HELD IN CONFIDENCE

2.95   In terms of reg 2(2) of the EIRs, information is not considered to be held by a Scottish public authority if it holds that information in confidence, having been supplied it by a Minister of the Crown or by a Department of the Government of the United Kingdom.

2.96   For it to be held in confidence, the Commissioner has taken the view that the information in question must not only have been supplied under an obligation of confidentiality, but still be confidential at the time the request was received.[60]

---

60   Decision 036/2009: Mr Rob Edwards and the Scottish Ministers.

Even if it is held in confidence, this does not mean, however, that   2.97
the information is necessarily inaccessible under FOI legislation,
because a request for that information can still be made to the relevant
Minister of the Crown or UK Government Department under the
Freedom of Information Act 2000 (FOIA) or the (UK) Environmental
Information Regulations 2004. Therefore, authorities using this
provision should (under reg 9(1)) provide applicants with reasonable
advice and assistance on making a request for the information to the
relevant UK Minister or Department.

Where the authority claims that the information has been supplied   2.98
by a Minister of the Crown or Department of the Government of the
United Kingdom and held in confidence (and therefore is not held
in terms of reg 2(2)), the exception contained in reg 10(4)(a) (which
allows a public authority to refuse to make information available if it
does not hold the information when the request is received), should
be applied. This exception is subject to the "public interest" test and,
in line with the other exceptions in the EIRs, it must be interpreted
in a restrictive way and there should be a presumption in favour of
disclosure (reg 10(1) and (2)).

CLARIFYING THE REQUEST

Regulation 9(2)

> "Where a request has been formulated in too general a
> manner, the authority shall –
> (a) ask the applicant as soon as possible, and in any event
>   no later than 20 working days after the date of receipt
>   of request, to provide more particulars in relation to
>   the request; and
> (b) assist the applicant in providing those particulars.

Where a request is unclear, for example where the applicant has not   2.99
described the information sought in a way which would enable a
Scottish public authority to identify or locate it, or if the request
is ambiguous, the authority should, as far as practicable, provide
assistance to the applicant to enable the information required to be
described more clearly. Authorities should also bear in mind that
applicants cannot reasonably be expected to possess identifiers such
as file reference numbers or descriptions of particular records. It is
important that the applicant is contacted as soon as possible, preferably
by telephone, fax or e-mail, in cases where more information is needed,
to clarify what is sought.

2.100   In seeking to clarify what is sought, authorities should bear in mind that applicants are not required to disclose their aims or motivation for seeking the information.

2.101   Scottish public authorities have a maximum of 20 working days from receipt of the clarified request to provide the applicant with a response (reg 9(4)).

Regulation 10(4)(c)

> **A Scottish public authority may refuse to make environmental information available to the extent that –**
>
> ...
>
> **(c) the request for information is formulated in too general a manner and the authority has complied with its duty under regulation 9.**

2.102   Once a Scottish public authority has provided advice and assistance to an applicant whose request is unclear, and where the request continues to be formulated in too general a manner to enable an authority to identify any relevant information, the authority is not expected to seek further clarification and the request may be refused. However, the Scottish public authority must explain to the applicant why it cannot take the request any further and provide details of the authority's review procedure. Scottish public authorities should also note that reg 10(4)(c) is subject to the "public interest" test and that, in line with the other exceptions in the EIRs, it must be interpreted in a restrictive way and there should be a presumption in favour of disclosure (reg 10(1) and (2)).

2.103   A Scottish public authority must also, under reg 5(1), disclose any information it has been able to find relating to the request and to which no exception applies.

FORM AND FORMAT OF INFORMATION
Regulation 6

> **(1) Where an applicant requests that environmental information be made available in a particular form or format, a Scottish public authority shall comply with that request unless –**
>
> **(a) it is reasonable for it to make the information available in another form or format; or**
>
> **(b) the information is already publicly available and easily accessible to the applicant in another form or format.**

Regulation 6(1)(a) requires the Scottish public authority to give the applicant information in the form or format they have requested, unless there is another reasonable approach to supplying the information. A Scottish public authority should be helpful, as far as reasonable, taking into account that, for example, some IT users may not be able to read attachments in certain formats and that some members of the public may prefer paper to electronic copies. Authorities should also bear in mind their obligations under the Equality Act 2010 to provide information in accessible formats. **2.104**

Regulation 6(1)(b) is similar to s 25 of FOISA, which allows a Scottish public authority to refuse a request for environmental information where that information is otherwise accessible to the applicant in another form or format (bearing in mind that what may be accessible to one applicant may not be to another). **2.105**

TRANSFER OF REQUEST

Regulation 14

(1) **Where a Scottish public authority has received a request to make environmental information available and does not hold that information but believes that another public authority holds the information requested then it shall either –**

   (a) **transfer the request to the other authority; or**
   (b) **supply the applicant with the name and address of that other authority,**

   and inform the applicant accordingly with the refusal sent in accordance with regulation 13.

Unlike FOISA, the EIRs make provision for the transfer of a request from one authority to another. This regulation applies only if the authority does not hold the information in its own right and it is not held on its behalf by another body. **2.106**

If the Scottish public authority to which the initial request was made knows that it does not hold the information but believes that some or all of the information requested is held by another Scottish public authority, the authority should consider what would be the most helpful and prompt way of assisting the applicant with his request. The EIRs set out two options. **2.107**

- The original request can be transferred to the other authority. Before doing this, the authority which originally received the request should consult with the other authority to check that it does hold the information. A request or part of a request should not be transferred if there is any reason to doubt that the second authority holds the information or the applicant has not given their consent.[61]

• Alternatively, the public authority may give the applicant the name and address of the other authority to allow the applicant to make the request to that authority. If the authority is minded to transfer a request it should consult the person who made the request.

2.108   If an authority decides to transfer a request (reg 14(1)(a)) or provide the applicant with the name and address of that other authority (reg 14(1)(b)), it must still issue a refusal letter within 20 working days of receipt of the request to explain that it does not hold the information. That refusal notice must contain details about the review procedure and the applicant's right of appeal.

RECORDS TRANSFERRED TO THE KEEPER

Regulation 15

2.109   The EIRs make special provisions in relation to environmental information contained in a record which a Scottish public authority has transferred to the Keeper of the Records of Scotland at the National Archives of Scotland ("NAS"). Such information is deemed to be held by the Keeper on behalf of the authority.

2.110   Where a request is made to the Keeper for such a record and the record has not been designated as open for public access, the Keeper must send a copy of the request to the authority as soon as possible after receiving it. It is then for the authority to decide whether the information is subject to an exception (under reg 10(1)(a)), to apply the "public interest" test (under reg 10(1)(b)) and to notify the Keeper whether he can make the information available. (While FOISA extends the period for making information available in these circumstances to 30 days,[62] the EIRs make no such special provision.) If the record has already been designated as "open", the Keeper may make it available without reference to the authority which transferred the record.

---

61 Scottish Ministers' Code of Practice on the Discharge of Functions by Scottish Public Authorities under the Freedom of Information (Scotland) Act 2002 and the Environmental Information (Scotland) Regulations 2004 (December 2010), para 2.2. (At Appendix 3.)

62 FOISA, ss 21 and 22.

EXTENSION OF TIME

Regulation 7

Unlike FOISA, the EIRs (reg 7(1)) allow public authorities to extend   2.111
the time for complying with any request by up to 20 working days if
the request is both voluminous and complex and it is impracticable
for it to respond within the original 20 working days. The Scottish
public authority should inform the applicant as soon as possible, and
no later than 20 working days after the date of receipt of the request,
that an extension is considered necessary (reg 7(2)). This notice must
be in writing and must give the authority's reasons for considering
the information to be both voluminous and complex. The notice
must also tell the applicant of their rights to require the authority
to review its decision to extend the time period, and of their rights
to appeal to the Scottish Information Commissioner to investigate
whether the authority was entitled to extend the time limit to 40
working days (reg 7(3)).

There is little evidence of authorities formally informing applicants   2.112
of their intended use of this provision or of their rights to review and
appeal if the applicant wishes to challenge the extension of time taken
to respond to a request.[63]

CHARGING FEES FOR INFORMATION

The EIRs provide that no fee should be charged for: 2.113

- accessing public registers or lists of environmental information
  held by public authorities (reg 8(2)(a)); or
- examining information which has been requested at a place that
  the authority makes available for that purpose (reg 8(2)(b)).

Article 3(5) of the Directive introduces the requirement for arrange-   2.114
ments to be made which ensure that the right of accessing information
"can be effectively exercised, such as , the establishment and
maintenance of facilities for the examination of the information
required".

More often, an applicant will not want to examine or inspect   2.115
information, but to be provided with it. Where this happens, the
charging regime under reg 8 will apply.

---

63   The only decisions of the Commissioner which make reference to reg 7(1) being used are
     103/2008: Rob Edwards and the Scottish Ministers; and 095/2007: Mr John B Mackintosh
     and Renfrewshire Council.

Regulation 8

> 8 (1) Subject to paragraphs (2) to (8), where a Scottish public authority is under a duty to make environmental information available under regulation 5(1), it may charge a fee for so doing.
>
> ...
>
> (3) Fees charged under paragraph (1) shall not exceed a reasonable amount and in any event shall not exceed the costs to the authority of producing the information requested.

2.116   Regulation 8 of the EIRs therefore permits public authorities to charge a "reasonable amount" for making environmental information available. The EIRs specifically say that the fee charged must not exceed the costs to the authority of producing the information requested[64] and so indirect costs must not be passed on to the applicant. It is not entirely clear what *producing* entails, and therefore what costs can be taken into account. The Commissioner has come to the view that, as with FOISA, public authorities can charge for the staff time taken in the location and/or retrieval of that information (this will include staff time redacting information so that it can be provided in response to a request, but *will not* include time spent determining whether information is subject to one or more of the exceptions), as well as the actual costs of supplying the information such as the cost of photocopying the documents and postage.

2.117   However, if the applicant wants copies of documents which are already available for inspection, then fees cannot be charged for staff costs which have been incurred in locating and retrieving that information. In the leading case to date on charging for environmental information in such circumstances under the UK EIRs,[65] the UK Information Tribunal indicated that a reasonable charge would comprise the costs of producing copies of the information requested. The Tribunal concluded that:

- an authority must satisfy itself that a charge is reasonable. It must do this by only taking into account relevant considerations and ignoring any irrelevant ones;

---

64 Recital (18) of the Directive states that where public authorities make environmental information available on a commercial basis, and where this is necessary in order to guarantee the continuation of collecting and publishing such information, a market-based charge is considered to be reasonable.

65 *David Markinson v Information Commissioner* (EA/2005/0014).

- for example, the cost of paper and printing is a relevant factor and can be included in the charge. However, the cost of staff time in identifying, locating and retrieving the information (because the information is already available for inspection) is an irrelevant factor and cannot be included. As these staff costs must be disregarded when the information is inspected by the applicant (in accordance with reg 8(2)(b)), it is unreasonable to include them when calculating the cost of copying the same information.

There is no upper fees limit for responses to requests for environmental information and where the applicant is willing to pay a reasonable amount then the information should be provided.   2.118

As with FOISA, when a public authority issues a fees notice, the 20-working-day clock (this can be extended to 40 working days under the EIRs in limited circumstances) stops until the fees notice has been paid. Applicants have up to 60 working days to pay the fees notice under the EIRs.[66]   2.119

As noted above, the EIRs impose a duty on public authorities to publish and make the following available to applicants: 2.120

- a schedule of the fees charged for accessing environmental information; and
- information on the circumstances in which a fee may be charged, waived or required to be paid in advance (reg 8(8)).

Given that the power to make a charge is subject to reg 8(8), the Commissioner takes the view that unless a public authority has published and made available its schedule of fees, the public authority will not be entitled to make any charge under reg 8(1).   2.121

REFUSAL OF REQUEST

The EIRs work on the presumption that environmental information will be made available on request. However, an authority can refuse to provide environmental information if an exception applies under reg 10 and if, in all the circumstances, the public interest in disclosing the information is outweighed by the public interest in maintaining the exception.[67]   2.122

---

66 Interestingly, although reg 8(4) of the EIRs states that a public authority may require payment of whole or part of the fee in advance, Recital (18) of the Directive states that instances where advance payment will be required should be limited.

2.123   The exceptions must be interpreted in a restrictive way and with a presumption in favour of disclosure.[68]

2.124   (Although not described as an exception, an authority may also refuse to provide information if it includes personal data and certain conditions apply.[69])

2.125   It is important to note that environmental information which relates to information on emissions is given a special status under the EIRs as the exceptions contained in reg 10(5)(d)–(g) cannot be used to withhold information on emissions.[70]

2.126   Where a request for environmental information covers some information which can be released and other information which the authority believes is subject to one or more exceptions, the public authority must disclose the information which is not subject to any exceptions, unless the authority is not able to separate that information out.[71] As the Commissioner has noted, whether information can be separated out is a practical test but in many – if not indeed most – cases this will be possible.[72]

2.127   Where the public authority intends to refuse all or part of a request, or refuses to make the information available in a particular format, the refusal notice must:

- be in writing (reg 13(a));
- state clearly the reasons for refusal, citing the relevant exception(s) (including reg 11) (reg 13(b));
- where appropriate, specify how the public authority reached its conclusion with respect to the "public interest" test contained in reg 10(1)(b) (reg 13(b));
- state the basis for applying any exception (including reg 11), if it would not otherwise be apparent (reg 13(c));
- where environmental information is incomplete and the exception in reg 10(4)(d) is relied on, state the time by which the Scottish public authority considers that the information will be complete (reg 13(d));
- provide details of the provisions for a review by the authority and subsequent appeal to the Commissioner and the Court of Session (reg 13(e)).

---

67   Reg 10(2).
68   *Ibid.*
69   Reg 11.
70   Reg 10(6).
71   Reg 10(7).
72   Decision 141/2007: Integra Compliance Ltd and the Scottish Environment Protection Agency.

The purpose of providing full and clear reasons to applicants is to   2.128
enable them to determine whether the refusal is well founded in fact
and law, and whether to challenge the decision for refusal.[73]

THE EXCEPTIONS

The EIRs permit Scottish public authorities to refuse a request if an   2.129
exception under reg 10(4) or (5) applies and the public interest in
making the information available is outweighed by that in maintaining the exception. (Regulation 11, although not an exception as
such, permits a public authority to withhold personal data in certain
circumstances.)

Unlike the exemptions in FOISA, all of the exceptions in reg 10 are   2.130
subject to the "public interest" test. In addition, public authorities
must interpret all of the exceptions in a restrictive way and must apply
a presumption in favour of disclosure.[74]

There are two categories of exception from the duty to provide   2.131
information on request. The first category is "class" exceptions. The
second category can be applied only if disclosure of the information
would, or would be likely to, cause substantial prejudice to a particular
interest.

CLASS EXCEPTIONS

The first category is contained in reg 10(4), which provides a number   2.132
of exceptions from the duty to provide information on request based
upon the *type* of information held or the *nature of the request* rather than
upon the *content* of the information. Content, however, may still be
relevant in considering the "public interest" test.

Information not held (reg 10(4)(a))

When considering the application of this exception, public authorities   2.133
should bear in mind the differing definitions of what is "held" under
FOISA and the EIRs.

This exception applies *only* if the public authority receiving the   2.134
request does not hold the information, and does not make use of
the services of another body or person to hold the information on its
behalf. Where the exception does apply, the public authority would
have to provide advice and assistance to the applicant and, if the likely

---

73 Decision 141/2007: Integra Compliance Ltd and the Scottish Environment Protection
    Agency.
74 Reg 10(2).

holder of the information is known, ask the applicant whether the request should be transferred.

2.135   Note that this exception is subject to the "public interest" test, although if the Scottish public authority can evidence that it does not in fact hold the information in question, the application of the public interest would appear to be somewhat superfluous. However, there may be instances, for example where the information requested is in the physical possession of the public authority but the authority determines that it is not held on the basis that it was supplied by a Minister of the Crown or Department of the Government of the United Kingdom and held in confidence.[75] Here, the application of the "public interest" test will be more than simply academic (although in such cases the public interest in maintaining confidentiality will always be strong – see, for example, *Decision 036/2009: Mr Rob Edwards and the Scottish Ministers*).

Manifestly unreasonable requests (reg 10(4)(b))

2.136   A "manifestly unreasonable" request could include a request for information which places a substantial and arduous burden on a Scottish public authority. "Manifestly unreasonable" is not defined in the EIRs. However, the Aarhus Implementation Guide makes it clear that simply because a request is voluminous and complex does not make it manifestly unreasonable. The Commissioner has indicated that he is likely to take into account the same kinds of considerations as he would in reaching a decision as to whether a request is vexatious under s 14(1) of FOISA.[76] There may also be instances where it is appropriate for the Commissioner to consider the proportionality of the burden on the public authority in terms of the costs and resources involved in dealing with a request when considering the application of this exception.

> • Applying the equivalent exception under the UK EIRs, the Department for Environment, Food and Rural Affairs argued that compiling a list of 133 pieces of correspondence (including date, type of correspondence, sender, recipient and title) would be so time consuming that the request for the information was manifestly unreasonable.[77] The UK Information Commissioner

---

75   Reg 2(2).
76   Decision 024/2010: Mr N and the Scottish Ministers, para 22.
77   FS50078600: Department for Environment, Food and Rural Affairs: http://www.ico.gov. uk/upload/documents/decisionnotices/2007/decision_notice_fs50078600.pdf.

estimated that it would take approximately 10 hours to produce the list requested. While he agreed that the time involved in complying with the request was not negligible, he did not believe that the request could be regarded as manifestly unreasonable on the basis of the time required to comply with it.

- The Scottish Government argued that it was manifestly unreasonable for an applicant to request information contained within seven letters in support of a grant application while that application was still being processed, because of the potential for undue interference with the process should the information be released. The Commissioner considered the test of what is manifestly unreasonable to be a high one. It had not been met in this case, where clearly the application did not place a significant burden on the authority. What was being requested was not manifestly unreasonable, even though the authority may believe there were reasons why the information should not be disclosed (which were capable of being advanced through other exceptions, but which the authority had chosen not to do).[78]

Formulated in too general a manner (reg 10(4)(c))

A Scottish public authority may refuse a request for information if it is formulated in too general a manner and the authority has complied with its duty under reg 9. Therefore, before refusing a request under reg 10(4)(c), a Scottish public authority is obliged to communicate with the applicant to offer advice and assistance to find out if the request can be more closely defined before refusal is considered.

2.137

Material which is still in the course of completion, unfinished documents or incomplete data (reg 10(4)(d))

This regulation reflects the provisions of Art 4 of Directive 2003/4/EC, by which Member States may provide for a request for environmental information to be refused if (among other things) the request concerns material in the course of completion or *unfinished documents* or data. (However, the Directive is worded differently from the Aarhus Convention which makes reference only to materials in the course of completion and is silent on unfinished documents.)

2.138

The wording of the EIRs suggests that there is a distinction between the two, although neither is further defined.

2.139

---

78   Decision 024/2010: Mr N and the Scottish Ministers.

Material which is still in the course of completion

2.140   The Aarhus Implementation Guidance says that "in the course of completion" suggests "individual documents that are actively being worked on by the public authority" and that furthermore it is a document which "will have more work done on it within some reasonable time-frame".[79]

2.141   It could therefore apply to a current draft of a yet-to-be-completed report or it may involve a document which is about to be published which is currently being checked for errors.

Unfinished documents

2.142   This wording suggests that unfinished documents are distinct from material in the course of completion. It might therefore apply to incomplete drafts of a report on which work has been discontinued.

2.143   However, the status of drafts of a completed document is not immediately obvious.

2.144   The UK Commissioner held that the draft of a report jointly commissioned by the Chancellor of the Exchequer and the Secretary of State for Transport to examine the long-term links between transport and the UK's economic productivity, growth and stability could not be regarded as either unfinished or incomplete if by the time the request was made the final report had been completed.

2.145   The UK Tribunal disagreed, saying "If the Commissioner's argument is correct, no draft of any document could ever fall within the exception in Regulation 12(4)(d) once there was a final version. In our opinion this would be an unfortunate conclusion as it would mean that such drafts could not be subjected to the public interest balancing exercise".[80]

2.146   In Scotland, the Commissioner accepted that drafts of documents held by Scottish Ministers, such as letters which had been sent to the Prime Minister, relating to the Copenhagen Climate Change Summit, did fall within the scope of this exception (However, he went on the conclude that the public interest favoured the disclosure of much of the information.[81])

2.147   Some documents may be preliminary to later developments but may not be regarded as unfinished. For instance, a local authority argued that concept drawings of a proposed building submitted as

79   Aarhus Implementation Guidance, p 58.
80   *Secretary of State for Transport v Information Commissioner* (EA/2008/0052), para 80.
81   Decision 064/2011: Mr David Rule and the Scottish Ministers.

part of pre-planning discussion were unfinished, as the complete information would be evident only when a formal planning application was made. However, this was not accepted by the Commissioner, who took the view that the concept drawings were finished and complete information in their own right.[82]

Incomplete data

Whether or not material can be categorised as incomplete data will depend on the circumstances and needs to be considered on a case-by-case basis. Data which is part of routine monitoring over a prolonged period need not be regarded as incomplete simply because the final results have not been compiled. As an example, the Scottish Environment Protection Agency publishes details of its bathing water pollution monitoring after each sample has been analysed, rather than withholding the results until a complete data set of the bathing water season has been compiled.

2.148

A Scottish public authority relying upon the exception in reg 10(4)(d) must (under reg 13(d)) state the time by which the authority considers that the information will be finished or completed, when issuing its refusal. This allows the applicant to make a new request for the information once the information is finished or completed.

2.149

Internal communications (reg 10(4)(e))

Regulation 10(4)(e) provides that a Scottish public authority may refuse to make environmental information available to the extent that the request involves making available internal communications.

2.150

The exception in reg 10(4)(e) is simply a matter of fact: it covers all internal communications, regardless of their content or the level of harm that disclosure would be likely to cause. This is similar to s 29 of FOISA dealing with ministerial communications, but differs from the exemptions at s 30 dealing with free and frank provision of advice etc which are subject to a "harm" test and only apply to information if its disclosure would, or would be likely to, have substantially prejudicial consequences.

2.151

However, internal communications cannot be withheld under reg 10(4)(e) unless there is a greater public interest in keeping the information secret than in disclosing it.[83] In assessing the public interest, both the harmful and beneficial consequences of disclosure need to be considered.

2.152

---

82 Decision 101/2008: Mr Alistair Johnson and East Renfrewshire Council.
83 Reg 10(1)(b).

Nature of "internal communications"

2.153   The Commissioner has accepted that "internal communications" could include internal e-mail exchanges, draft letters to an external organisation, and a file note prepared for internal use. The Commissioner reached this view after satisfying himself that the documents had been exchanged between officials in an authority, rather than being created and used by one person.[84]

2.154   Unlike the equivalent provision in the UK EIRs,[85] reg 10(4)(e) does not specifically state that internal communications includes communications between Government Departments (in the case of the UK EIRs, UK Government Departments are treated as separate public authorities).

2.155   On rare occasions, the Commissioner has accepted that it is possible for communications between two or more separate public authorities to be treated as "internal communications" for the purposes of reg 10(4)(e). For example, certain communications between the UK Government and the Radioactive Waste Advisory Committee, (established by the Government in 1978 to provide independent advice to Ministers on matters concerning the management of radioactive waste) were customarily treated by the parties as internal communications. The Commissioner accepted that this was the case in the 1990s when such information was being exchanged and that the exception applied.[86]

2.156   However, any public authority applying the exception in these circumstances must be able to demonstrate particular aspects of the administrative and legal relationship between the two bodies to show why communications between them should be considered to be internal. This will include consideration of matters such as the nature and context of the particular relationship and the nature of the communication itself.

2.157   The Scottish Ministers argued that an exchange of correspondence between the Scottish and UK Governments were "internal communications" for the purposes of the exception because of the need for the Scottish Government to work closely with the UK Government Departments on environmental and European matters. The Ministers stated that there is nothing in the EIRs or related guidance to indicate that authorities need to be part of the same UK administration for this exception to apply.

---

84   Decision 141/2007: Integra Compliance Ltd (trading as Compliance Link) and the Scottish Environment Protection Agency.

85   Regulations 12(4)(e) and (8) of the Environmental Information Regulations 2004.

86   Decision 044/2009 : Mr Rob Edwards of *The Sunday Herald* and the Scottish Ministers.

The Commissioner disagreed, saying that there was nothing 2.158 particular in the administrative or legal relationship between the Ministers and the UK Government, or in the particular communications under consideration, that meant they should be regarded as internal, rather than as communications between two distinct public authorities with an interest in matters of mutual concern.[87]

"SUBSTANTIAL PREJUDICE" EXCEPTIONS

The second category of exceptions is contained in reg 10(5), and is based 2.159 upon the *content* of the information requested. These are all subject to a "harm" test of substantial prejudice to certain issues, processes or persons and, as mentioned already, to the "public interest" test. In practice, there may be a number of overlaps between exceptions, for instance between different categories of information for which confidentiality is provided by law.

International relations, defence, national security or public safety (reg 10(5)(a))

International relations

Information may be withheld under this exception if, for example, 2.160 it contains confidential information obtained from (or which relates to) a foreign state, an international organisation or overseas territory, where disclosure might compromise any future co-operation with the UK in areas of vital interests to the UK.

Defence

This may include information regarding military establishments, 2.161 military exercises or the nature of military assets. To the extent that these affect or are likely to affect the elements of the environment, then this would be environmental information.

National security or public safety

The environmental information covered by this exception may 2.162 include, for example, information on the protection of critical national infrastructures, such as water supply.

This exception applied when a request was made for details of the 2.163 operational response plan to tackle a major fuel fire at a Kirkwall fuel depot in Orkney. A balance had to be struck between reassuring the

---

87 Decision 064/2011: Mr David Rule and the Scottish Ministers.

public that adequate measures were in place to deal with potentially catastrophic adverse events, and ensuring that the tactical and detailed contingency plans contained within such measures were safeguarded against potential threats which could undermine or disrupt such plans. The Commissioner decided that the public interest in the effective conduct of the Fire and Rescue Service in relation to the health and safety of its staff and other emergency services, the safety of members of the community, as well as the need to consider the current terrorist threat assessment, clearly outweighed the public interest in disclosing the Site Specific Fire/Incident Plan.[88]

2.164   A certificate by Scottish Ministers under reg 12(1), stating that disclosure of the information would, or would be likely to, prejudice substantially national security, would be sufficient to conclude that this exception applies. However, such a certificate is not conclusive in relation to the "public interest" test, so the applicant can ask for a review of the application of the "public interest" test and could subsequently make an application to the Scottish Information Commissioner.

The course of justice (reg 10(5)(b))

2.165   A request for environmental information may be refused where the disclosure of the information would, or would be likely to, substantially prejudice:

- the course of justice, including law enforcement;
- the ability of a person to receive a fair trial;
- the ability of any public authority to conduct an inquiry of a criminal or disciplinary nature.

2.166   *The Aarhus Convention: An Implementation Guide* says:

"Public authorities also can refuse to release information if it would adversely affect the ability of a public authority to conduct a criminal or disciplinary investigation. In some countries, public prosecutors are not allowed to reveal information to the public pertaining to their cases. The Convention clearly does not include all investigations in this exception, but limits it to criminal or disciplinary ones only. Thus, information about a civil or administrative investigation would not necessarily be covered". (p 59)

This exception applies to investigations or inquiries conducted by any level of government, and to any institution or public authority (local,

---

88   Decision 108/2008: Mr Simon Brogan and Highland & Islands Fire Board.

regional, national or international), and may relate to proceedings which are ongoing or proceedings likely to take place in the future. It could include any information which, if disclosed, could prejudice the enforcement or appropriate administration of law, which includes the prevention, investigation or detection of a crime, or the apprehension or prosecution of offenders. Every effort should, however, be made to make information available once the proceedings have been completed.

Unlike s 36(1) of FOISA, neither the wording of reg 10(5)(b) nor the 2.167 definition in the Implementation Guide to the Aarhus Convention explicitly excepts documents to which a claim to confidentiality of communications in legal proceedings could be maintained (subject to the "public interest" test). However, the Commissioner has taken the view that this particular exception may cover information which is covered by legal professional privilege, particularly where a public authority is or is likely to be involved in litigation.[89] (Information may also be excepted by virtue of legal professional privilege under the provisions of reg 10(5)(d).)

Intellectual property rights (reg 10(5)(c))

This exception will protect information that forms the basis of 2.168 registered rights – such as patents, trademarks and designs – and unregistered rights – such as copyright, and unregistered design rights. It does not cover confidential information that does not benefit from such legal protection. The exception should be applied only where there is a real risk that the disclosure (or further dissemination after disclosure) would, or would be likely to, seriously undermine the rights concerned. If the information would enjoy protection, even after disclosure, from the Copyright, Designs and Patents Act 1988, the case against disclosure would be considerably weaker

The confidentiality of the proceedings of any public authority where such confidentiality is provided by law (reg 10(5)(d))

This exception may apply to information relating to certain proceed- 2.169 ings of any public authority where such proceedings are considered to be confidential. Confidential information need not be released, but this exception should not cover transactions or business activities of an administrative or routine nature.

---

89 Decision 096/2006: Mr George Waddell and South Lanarkshire Council.

2.170   The proceedings in question may be those of the public authority receiving the request, or those of any other public authority. The meaning of the term "proceedings" is not entirely clear, but will include a range of investigative, regulatory and administrative/governance processes and other activities carried out according to a statutory scheme.

2.171   In most cases where this exception will apply, there will be a specific statutory provision prohibiting the release of the information. However, there may also be cases where the common law of confidence will protect the confidentiality of the proceedings. In particular, the Commissioner has accepted the application of the exception to information protected by legal professional privilege, for example when SEPA was asked to provide legal advice on the extent of certain of its powers.[90]

Confidentiality of commercial or industrial information where such confidentiality is provided by law to protect a legitimate economic interest (reg 10(5)(e))

2.172   Again, confidentiality may be provided either by explicit statutory restrictions on disclosure or by the common law of confidentiality. The information covered by the exception will include a range of commercially sensitive information such as trade secrets, information supplied by contractors, information supplied as part of a tendering or procurement process and information held by regulators.

2.173   It can also cover requests for information such as costs–benefit or other financial analysis, if disclosure would, or would be likely to, substantially prejudice the confidentiality of matters to which any commercial or industrial confidentiality applies.[91]

2.174   In applying this exception, an authority may have regard to provisions such as s 22 of the Environmental Protection Act 1990, which excludes information from a public register about the affairs of any individual or business where that information is commercially confidential. Where information is kept off the public register, this may provide an indication as to whether that information is commercially sensitive, and therefore whether the exception in reg 10(5)(e) is applicable.

2.175   Confidentiality may also be based on the common law of confidence. This may be acknowledged in a contract, although merely

---

90 Decision 069/2008: Robin Thompson and the Scottish Environment Protection Agency.
91 Decisions 141/2007: Integra Compliance Ltd and the Scottish Environment Protection Agency; and 119/2008: Mr James Paul Kelly and Dundee City Council.

stating that certain information is confidential within a contract does
not necessarily make it so.

Generally, the protection of information under this exception   2.176
should be limited to the minimum time necessary to safeguard the
commercial or industrial interest in question.

Information relating to the lease of a site in Glenrothes by   2.177
Intelligent Energy (Europe) Ltd (such as the company's Business Case
and the draft Head of Terms between the Council and the company)
was properly withheld, taking into account all of the circumstances
surrounding the negotiations between the partie at the time of the
request.[92]

Interests of the individual providing the information (reg 10(5)(f))

This exception applies in situations where the information was   2.178
supplied on a voluntary basis in the expectation that it would not be
disclosed to a third party and where the supplier has not consented to
disclosure.

In that context, the purpose of this exception is, for example,   2.179
to ensure the continuation of the flow of voluntary information
between companies and their regulators when collecting statistical
data and conducting sample surveys. Making such information
available to the public could possibly inhibit open and construc-
tive discussions between environmental control authorities and
industry.

This exception applies only where: 2.180

- the environmental information was provided voluntarily, ie the
  supplier was not under, and could not have been under, any legal
  obligation to supply it to the Scottish public authority;
- there are no other circumstances that entitle the Scottish public
  authority to disclose it; and
- the supplier has not consented to its disclosure.

Because the "harm" test also applies to this exception, it applies only   2.181
where disclosure of the information would, or would be likely to,
substantially prejudice the interests of the person who provided the
information.

If a Scottish public authority is able to require the information to be   2.182
provided under statutory obligation (whether used or not) then that
information will not fall within this exception (see Box).

---

92   Decision 071/2011: Mr Craig Mitchell and Fife Council.

The extent of a statutory obligation to provide information

After Scottish Natural Heritage ("SNH") refused to provide certain information about fish farming in Loch Ewe and its environmental impact, Fish Legal argued in its application for a decision from the Commissioner, that the fish farming industry could be compelled to provide the information following the introduction of the Aquaculture and Fisheries (Scotland) Act 2007 (the "Fisheries Act").

The Commissioner agreed that the Fisheries Act gives Scottish Ministers the power to compel fish farming businesses to provide certain information about their operations. However, in this case the information in question was provided voluntarily to SNH by a third-party organisation, the Area Management Group. As the legal obligation created by the Fisheries Act did not apply to that group as a body (even though it applied to the fish farming businesses represented among its membership), the application of the exception at reg 10(5)(f) was not excluded.

Decision 046/2010: Fish Legal and Scottish Natural Heritage

Protection of the environment (reg 10(5)(g))

2.183   A Scottish public authority may refuse to supply information in order to protect the environment to which it relates, for example the nesting location of rare birds. The ultimate aim of the EIRs is to increase the protection of the environment by ensuring greater access to environmental information. It would clearly be inconsistent with the purpose of the EIRs if disclosure of information would lead to damage to the environment.

2.184   So the Commissioner accepted that information contained in badger surveys, carried out as part of an assessment of road building plans, could be withheld, as disclosure of the detailed information would diminish the current level of protection for the badgers' habitat.[93]

2.185   However, in a case which related to information voluntarily provided by fish farm operators about the escape of farmed fish, Scottish Ministers argued that disclosing the information would result in a chain of events ending in damage to the environment. Disclosure, it was said, would harm their relationship with the aquaculture industry, leading to a reduction in co-operation and the flow of information as a result of which the research necessary to improve fish

---

93 Decision 044/2007: Mr G Crole and Transport Scotland.

farming procedures would be adversely affected and as a consequence the environment would be harmed. The Commissioner found that, although the withheld information had indeed been provided voluntarily, the Ministers had the power, under existing legislation, to require the operator to provide them with such information. Furthermore, the Commissioner did not accept that the regulation, which has to be interpreted in a restrictive way, could be applied with such a broad hypothesis of a sequence of events or that the Ministers had adequately demonstrated that disclosure of the information would, or would be likely to, substantially prejudice the environment to which the information relates.[94]

EMISSIONS (REG 10(6))

Information relating to emissions is given special status under the EIRs. Regulation 10(6) provides that, to the extent that the environmental information to be made available relates to information on emissions, a Scottish public authority cannot rely on the following exceptions:

2.186

- reg 10(5)(d) – the confidentiality of proceedings;
- reg 10(5)(e) – the confidentiality of commercial or industrial information;
- reg 10(5)(f) – the interests of the person who provided the information;
- reg 10(5)(g) – the protection of the environment.

As previously noted, "emissions" are not explicitly defined in the EIRs, or in the Directive, but a commonly cited definition is the "direct or indirect release of substances, vibrations, heat or noise from individual or diffuse sources (…) into the air, water or land".[95] This very broad definition captures a great deal of information. In addition, reg 10(6) applies in relation to any information on emissions which suggests that information need not necessarily be measurements of volume or direct impact, but could be about or related to emissions.

2.187

The breadth of this can be seen from a decision of the UK Information Commissioner which ruled that information on electromagnetic emissions from technology generally used to interconnect computers and other IT apparatus around the home

2.188

---

94 Decision 071/2009: Fish Legal and the Scottish Ministers.
95 Council Directive 96/61/EC of 24 September 1996 concerning integrated pollution and prevention control, Art 2(5).

is environmental information. In that case the authority, OFCOM, argued that the emissions were too low to have an impact upon the environment and therefore did not fall within the UK EIRs. The Commissioner rejected this argument on the grounds that (a) where there is uncertainty or scientific dispute about the level of emissions it would be "unrealistic to expect the Commissioner to resolve such scientific issues"; (b) "information explicitly confirming an absence or low level of emissions would still seem to be information about emissions"; (c) "the fact that home networking devices produce a certain level of electromagnetic emissions does not have to record or reflect a direct effect on the elements of the environment. What is relevant is that the information is on a factor (ie electromagnetic emission) which does".[96]

THE "PUBLIC INTEREST" TEST

2.189   All of the exceptions under the EIRs are qualified by being subject to a "public interest" test. The same considerations as set out in Chapter 1 for qualified exemptions under FOISA apply.

2.190   Where information falls within the exception by class this should not be taken to mean that there is an inherent public interest in withholding all of that information from the applicant. In respect of internal communications, for example, there is a general public interest in making environmental information held by public authorities accessible, to enhance scrutiny of decision making and thereby improve accountability and participation. In weighing up the adverse and beneficial effects of disclosure in terms of the public interest the authorities should have regard to the content of that information. There does not have to be a demonstrably marked public interest in disclosing the information; if the public interest arguments for withholding the information (for example, by reference to harm) are lacking, then the information should be disclosed.

2.191   In a case concerned with the calling in of the planning application by Trump International Golf Links Scotland, on examining "the actual content of the information under consideration, the Commissioner ... found little that would significantly inform the ongoing public debate on any aspect of the Ministers' involvement in the calling in of the planning application", particularly in light of information which the Government had already released. However, there appeared to be nothing within the withheld information which persuaded the

---

96   Decision FS50301488: Office of Communications.

Commissioner that its release would have (or would have had) any of the detrimental effects claimed by Ministers. In which case, and with the presumption in favour of disclosure in reg 10(2)(b) of the EIRs in mind, disclosure was ordered.[97]

As mentioned in the previous chapter, the European Court of Justice has considered the correct approach to considering the balance of the public interest so far as environmental information is concerned.[98]   2.192

The judgment relates to an information request made to OFCOM under the UK EIRs for the precise location of mobile telephone base stations. OFCOM withheld the information under two separate exceptions in the UK EIRs, but the UK Information Commissioner ordered OFCOM to disclose the information. While he was satisfied that the exceptions applied, he considered that, in each case, the public interest lay in disclosing the information. His decision was eventually appealed to the Supreme Court, which referred the matter to the ECJ.[99]   2.193

The ECJ took the view that, when a public authority applies more than one exception to the same piece of information, a *two-stage* "public interest" test should be carried out by the authority. The first step is to consider whether, in relation to each exception cited, the public interest in making the information available is outweighed by that in maintaining the exception. Where more than once exception is considered to apply, the second step is then cumulatively to weigh all the grounds for refusing to disclose the information against all of the public interests served by disclosure and to come to a conclusion as to whether the information should be disclosed. The ECJ was clear that this could lead to information being disclosed which might otherwise have been withheld, and not just to information being withheld which might otherwise have been disclosed.   2.194

The manner and consequence of giving effect to this dual test are not yet obvious. However, given that the ECJ's judgment is based on the wording of the EU Directive on which the EIRs are based,[100] the "public interest" test in FOISA will continue to be carried out on an exemption-by-exemption basis. It is also possible that the effects of the ECJ judgment will be felt less in Scotland than in the rest of the UK; in the EIRs, the "harm" test is one of "substantial prejudice",   2.195

---

97 Decision 139/2008: Mr Rob Edwards and the Scottish Ministers.
98 *Office of Communications v Information Commissioner* (C-71/10) [2011] EUECJ.
99 *Office of Communications v Information Commissioner* [2010] UKSC 3.
100 Directive 2003/4/EC on public access to environmental information, Art 4(2).

while, in the remainder of the UK, the test is one of "adversely affect". In practice, this means that exceptions are less likely to be found to apply when considering the Scottish EIRs, with the consequence that there is no need to go on to consider the "public interest" test.

PERSONAL DATA (REG 11)

2.196   Regulation 11(1), concerning personal data, is sometimes described as a "quasi-exception" as it provides that, to the extent that the environmental information requested includes personal data *about the applicant*, then the duty under reg 5(1) to make that environmental information available will not apply.(However, in line with the duty to advise and assist under reg 9, the applicant should be advised how to make a subject access request for their personal data under s 7 of the DPA.)

2.197   To the extent that the environmental information requested includes personal data about an individual *other than the applicant* (third-party personal data), the data does not have to be made available if any of the following circumstances applies:

- disclosure would breach any of the data protection principles contained in the DPA (this is an absolute exemption);
- disclosure would contravene a s 10 notice under the DPA (right to prevent processing likely to cause damage or distress) and, in all the circumstances of the case, the public interest in making the information available is outweighed by the public interest in not making the information available;
- the information is exempt from disclosure under s 7(1) of the DPA (ie where the data subject would not be entitled to be given the information through a subject access request) and, in all the circumstances of the case, the public interest in making the information available is outweighed by the public interest in not making the information available.

2.198   Regulation 11 of the EIRs is very similar to the personal data exemptions contained in s 38(1)(a) and (b) of FOISA. However, unlike FOISA, reg 11(6) specifically allows a public authority to respond to an information request by neither confirming nor denying whether it holds personal data, if doing so would involve disclosing personal data in breach of reg 11. (The "neither confirm nor deny" provisions in s 18 of FOISA do not allow a public authority to refuse to confirm or deny whether it holds personal data.) The application of this provision has been considered by the Commissioner in *Decision 039/2011: Mr Dominic Kennedy of* The Times *and Scottish Ministers.*

In that case Ministers had been asked for copies of corres-   2.199
pondence between Prince Charles and the First Ministers, as well
as the Government's Chief Planner concerning particular planning
developments in the north-east of Scotland, and also any about
red squirrels. The Ministers replied by citing reg 11(2) and (6) and
refusing to confirm whether any correspondence had taken place.
But the Commissioner came to the conclusion that confirming
whether the correspondence did in fact exist would not breach
reg 11.[101]

As noted in Chapter 1 where this case is also referred to,[102]   2.200
Ministers were concerned not to allow disclosure under the EIRs
to undermine the reliance that the heir to the throne can place on
the confidentiality and privacy of his communications with the
Government which are subject to an expectation of confidence
analogous to the Convention of confidentiality that exists between
the Sovereign and the Government:

> "The Ministers maintained that removal of this protection would
> restrain the Prince of Wales from raising some matters for fear that
> his views, or even the knowledge that he had expressed his views
> to a member of the Government, would ignite controversy. They
> suggested that he would be prevented from discharging his duties
> as Heir to the Throne by the threat that publicity would undermine
> the perception of political neutrality which is a foundation of the
> constitution."

In the Commissioner's view, had the topics not been ones on which   2.201
the Prince of Wales has spoken publicly, or if they related to his
family life, there would be considerably less weight to the legitimate
interest in establishing whether correspondence had been exchanged
on this subject. However the developments in places such as Ellon
and Ballater were those in which he had taken an active interest (for
example, organising local workshops through his Foundation) and he
was a high-profile patron of the charity which was set up to protect
red squirrels. These were issues on which he had not only spoken
openly but had done so in a manner which urged specific action and
outcomes. While acknowledging the constitutional Convention cited
by Ministers, the Commissioner found the legitimate interests of the

---

101 Decision 039/2011: Mr Dominic Kennedy of *The Times* and the Scottish Ministers.
102 Pt 1, Ch 1, ss 18 and 41.

Prince of Wales regarding communications between the Sovereign or heir to the throne and Government to be outweighed by the "competing legitimate and public interest in understanding the role of the Prince of Wales, and topics on which he corresponds with government Ministers on matters of environmental policy, at least on those matters of public advocacy and expressed views".

2.202   (The Ministers subsequently advised the applicant that they held no correspondence between the Prince of Wales and the First Minister or the Chief Planner on the subjects listed in his request.)

NO PROHIBITION ON DISCLOSURE (REG 5(3))

2.203   Regulation 5(3) provides that any enactment or rule of law which would prevent information from being made available in accordance with the EIRs shall not apply. In other words, there is no prohibition on disclosure. This provision stands in stark contrast to s 26(a) of FOISA, which provides that information is exempt information if its disclosure by a Scottish public authority (otherwise than under FOISA) is prohibited by or under an enactment.

2.204   This important distinction is illustrated in the case where the name of a fish farm, from which escapes of farmed salmon had occurred, was requested. The Fisheries Research Service (the "FRS") argued that details collected under the Diseases of Fish Act 1983 can be disclosed only "with the written consent of the person by whom the information was provided" and that any person who discloses any such information in contravention "shall be guilty of an offence and liable on summary conviction to a fine …". As the company operating the fish farm had refused to provide consent this represented a prohibition on disclosure such that the information was exempt under s 26(a) of FOISA. However, the Commissioner held that the name of the farm, which was the site or location of the incident which had caused an impact on the environment, and in the context of the overall request about information regarding the escapes, was environmental information and was therefore subject to the EIRs rather than to FOISA. As a result, the Commissioner found that no statutory bar applied and ordered the FRS to disclose the information.[103]

2.205   Subsequently, the names of all Scottish fish farms from which, in total, over one million fish had escaped or died in a single year, was published following an EIR request.[104]

---

103 Decision 182/2006: Mr Bruce Sandison and the Fisheries Research Services.
104 http://www.fishfarmer-magazine.com/news/fullstory.php/aid/829/Protest_group_%93names_and_shames%94_salmon_farmers.html.

REQUESTS UNDER FOISA AND THE EIRs – USE OF S 39(2) OF FOISA

The interplay between the obligations of the EIRs and FOISA has often caused authorities difficulty when it comes to complying with requests for environmental information. The EIRs place a duty on Scottish public authorities to make available environmental information on request – consequently, all requests for environmental information must be responded to under the EIRs.[105] However, at the same time, FOISA imposes a duty on all Scottish public authorities to respond to requests for any information they hold, and as the definition of "information" in FOISA simply means "information recorded in any form"[106] – this does not exclude environmental information.

2.206

Accordingly, when a request is made for environmental information, regardless of whether it is expressly made under either EIRs or FOISA, a Scottish public authority must consider the request under both FOISA and the EIRs.

2.207

But, to avoid dealing with the same information under two access to information regimes, s 39(2) of FOISA allows an authority to exempt information from disclosure under FOISA if it is environmental information which Scottish public authorities are obliged, under the EIRs, to make available to the public (or be so obliged if an exception did not apply).

2.208

So, an aware authority should recognise that some or all of a request is for environmental information, apply the appropriate provisions of the EIRs to the information which is environmental and claim the exemption at s 39(2) in respect of it.

2.209

However, this course of action has not been taken where the authority:

2.210

- fails to recognise that the information is within the scope of request is environmental;
- maintains that the information is not environmental;
- believes that even if some information within scope is environmental it can choose to deal with the request entirely under FOISA.

IS IT ENVIRONMENTAL INFORMATION?

The onus lies on the authority to recognise correctly that information within the scope of a request is environmental, even if the applicant

2.211

---

105 EIRs, reg 5(1).
106 FOISA, s 73.

fails to specify that they are seeking environmental information or mistakenly cites FOISA in the request, as was the case when the campaigning group Advocates for Animals sought correspondence relating to the proposed introduction of Giant Pandas to Edinburgh Zoo.

2.212   As the Commissioner said in his decision: "Advocates for Animals made their information requests under FOISA, at least to the extent that they referred to 'Freedom of Information' and 'FOI' rather than making any explicit reference to the EIRs. This is hardly unusual, however, and does not absolve the public authority of responsibility for considering whether the information requested is in fact environmental."[107]

2.213   In an earlier case, the Scottish Ministers had also argued that they need not consider the EIRs because the applicant had specified FOISA. The Commissioner had this to say: "A reference to one law within an information request should not be interpreted as indicating that applicants have (or even could have) waived their rights under another access regime, or that the law they cite is the most appropriate route for their request. Applicants may be unaware of their rights or be unaware that the information identified as falling within the scope of their request contains environmental (or, as the case may be, non-environmental) information."[108]

2.214   Authorities regularly fail to appreciate that the information is environmental. Often this is because there is nothing in the terms of the request or the type of information asked for appears to be self-evidently environmental. Furthermore the request may be directed at an authority which does not think of itself as primarily addressing environmental issues. In terms of immediately recognising that a request is for environmental information there is a considerable difference between, say, the Scottish Environment Pollution Agency being asked about specified pollution incidents and a request to a local authority for a business plan for a housing fair. Even so the obligation lies with the authority to consider the information which it holds within the terms of the request and distinguish between that which is, and is not, environmental. As has been made clear earlier, the definition of what is "environmental" is broad.

MUST THE EIRs ALWAYS BE APPLIED?

2.215   Even where the authority acknowledges that the information may be environmental it is sometimes argued that a pragmatic approach

---

107 Decision 051/2009: Advocates for Animals and the Scottish Ministers.
108 Decision 218/2007: Professor A D Hawkins and Transport Scotland.

should be taken to confine consideration to FOISA – often reflecting the fact that such an acknowledgement comes only after the authority has dealt with the request and requirement for the review under FOISA and made its comments to the Commissioner in defence of that position. Authorities sometimes point to the limited amount of the information in dispute which is environmental compared with the majority of information which has to be dealt with under FOISA. Or they will suggest that as it concerns matters which do not have a significant environmental impact there is no need to invoke the EIRs. Some argue that, in any case, authorities have a choice as to the statutory regime under which a request for environmental information is considered. So long as there is no detriment to the applicant, it is argued, the authority is entitled to confine itself to FOISA.

The Commissioner set out his understanding of the relationship between FOISA and the EIRs in some detail in *Decision 218/2007: Professor A D Hawkins and Transport Scotland*. This involved a request for a range of information on the route which had been approved by the Transport Minister for a new major road – the Aberdeen Western Peripheral Route ("AWPR").

2.216

To the extent that Ministers accepted that any of the information fell within the scope of the EIRs, they maintained that the clear majority would be covered by FOISA. Consequently, as the decision in this case notes, Ministers "believed that the most practical way forward was to handle the request under FOISA" on the basis that "the limited amount of environmental information being withheld under FOISA exemptions would also have been withheld under the equivalent EIR exceptions and, given that the public interest considerations were the same, their approach caused no detriment to Professor Hawkins and was probably easier to understand".

2.217

The Ministers went on to claim that where a request straddles both FOISA and the EIRs, an authority is entitled to make a judgment as to which regime it would be most appropriate to apply. They submitted that this judgment can be questioned by the Commissioner only if it is likely to be detrimental to the applicant. The "no detriment" argument was therefore taken beyond a pragmatic approach to be turned into a "legal litmus test". The Commissioner disagreed with the Ministers on all counts.

2.218

First, he was of the view that all, not some, of the information was environmental. It comprised "information about measures and activities, in respect of a road building programme, which is likely to affect the state of the elements of the environment, principally the air and landscape, and information about factors such as emissions

2.219

likely to affect the elements of the environment. This information also includes cost benefit and other economic analyses and assumptions within the road building plans".

2.220   Second, even if only some the information was environmental, the Ministers' approach of considering the request only and entirely under FOISA was not lawful: "for any information that is environmental, even if it is considered under FOISA, the information must be considered under regulation 5 of the EIRs. Regulation 5 clearly provides that 'a Scottish public authority that holds environmental information shall make it available when asked to do so by any applicant'. This right is not diminished by the fact that non-environmental information may also have been requested". The primacy of the EIRs, is such that "… if the information falls within the definition of environmental information, authorities have both an obligation and an option. They have the *obligation* of dealing with the request under the EIRs and they have the *option* of claiming the exemption at section 39(2) of FOISA, which means they do not, at the same time, have to respond to the request under FOISA".

Dealing with requests for environmental information – a summary

The Commissioner's position in *Decision 218/2007: Professor A D Hawkins and Transport Scotland* has been summarised in many other cases as follows:

a. The definition of what constitutes environmental information should not be viewed narrowly.

b. There are two separate statutory frameworks for access to environmental information and an authority is required to consider any request for environmental information under both FOISA and the EIRs.

c. Any request for environmental information therefore *must* be dealt with under the EIRs.

d. In responding to a request for environmental information under FOISA, an authority may claim the exemption in s 39(2).

e. If the authority does not choose to claim the s 39(2) exemption, it must, in addition to dealing with the request under the EIRs, also deal with the request fully under FOISA, by: providing the information; withholding it under another exemption in Pt 2; or claiming that it is not obliged to comply with the request by

> virtue of another provision in Pt 1 (or a combination of these).
> f. The Commissioner is entitled (and indeed obliged), where he considers a request for environmental information has not been dealt with under the EIRs, to consider how it should have been dealt with under that regime.

CLAIMING THE S 39(2) EXEMPTION – THE "PUBLIC INTEREST" TEST

If a Scottish public authority claims the exemption under s 39(2), it also needs to consider the "public interest" test under s 2. It is perhaps surprising that the exemption in s 39(2) is not absolute, but is instead subject to the public interest test. Despite this, s 39(2) has largely been treated as a technical provision to allow authorities to manage the complex relationship between the EIRs and FOISA, both of which give individuals rights to request environmental information.   2.221

As there is a separate statutory right of access to environmental information, the Commissioner has considered that the public interest in maintaining this exemption and allowing access in line with the requirements of the EIRs will generally outweigh the public interest in requiring the disclosure of information under FOISA.[109]   2.222

This is predicated on an understanding that the information would not be more capable of being disclosed under FOISA than if it was considered under the EIRs alone. If, however, that was not the case then it may be that the public interest would favour not maintaining the exemption and require the request to be responded to under both FOISA and the EIRs.   2.223

IF S 39(2) IS NOT CLAIMED

There is no obligation on a Scottish public authority to claim the s 39(2) exemption when responding to a request for environmental information. If s 39(2) is not claimed, a Scottish public authority must consider the application under FOISA. However, as should now be clear, this does not detract from the Scottish public authority's obligation to also consider the request under the EIRs, to the extent that the information requested is environmental information. Accordingly, in such circumstances, the Scottish public authority is required to consider the request under both regimes.   2.224

---

109 Decision 120/2008: Mr Rob Edwards and the Scottish Ministers.

2.225   Applications made to the Commissioner under s 47 of FOISA
require a decision on whether a request for information has been
dealt with in accordance with Pt 1 of FOISA *and* the EIRs.[110] Where a
public authority has not claimed the exemption under s 39(2), the
Commissioner is therefore also obliged to consider the application
under both regimes.

2.226   As the comparative table in Appendix 1 makes clear, FOISA and
the EIRs are not identical and so it is possible for different results to
be reached when considering the same request under each regime.
However, if the information is capable of being disclosed under
one regime but not the other it is likely that the Commissioner will
require disclosure. There is no obvious advantage to be gained by
authorities choosing not to claim s 39(2) in the hope of relying on the
provisions of FOISA.

2.227   Where, during the course of an investigation, it is the Commissioner's view that a request encompasses environmental information,
which has until then only been considered under FOISA, this is raised
with the public authority and an opportunity is offered to apply s 39(2)
of FOISA. Often authorities have failed to claim s 39(2) by oversight or
because they have not recognised that all or some of information is
environmental and redress this on being alerted by the Commissioner.

2.228   Sometimes, however, an authority disagrees that the request
is for environmental information and declines to apply s 39(2) of
FOISA. In such cases the Commissioner requests full submissions
from that authority with its reasons for withholding information
under both regimes. In *Decision 102/2009: Councillor David Alexander and
Falkirk Council* the local authority was not persuaded that information
relating to the Falkirk Local Plan was environmental and declined to
claim the exemption at s 39(2), thereby requiring the Commissioner
to deal with the application under both FOISA and the EIRs (since
it was the Commissioner's view that most of the information was
environmental). In that case, however, the authority did make
supplementary submissions on exceptions which it claimed would
apply if the information was environmental. A similar stance was taken
by Dundee City Council when dealing with a request for a contractors
quote for providing a gull egg removal service.[111]

2.229   Clearly, where the request encompasses both environmental and
non-environmental information, the EIRs will apply only to the extent

---

110 Under reg 17(1) of the EIRs, s 47 – and, indeed, the whole of Pt 4 of FOISA – applies to
    appeals made under the EIRs, subject to limited modifications.
111 Decision 119/2008: Mr James Paul Kelly and Dundee City Council.

that the information is environmental and the provisions of FOISA will apply to the remainder.

CONCLUSION

The proportion of applications to the Commissioner which involve environmental information has increased from 4 per cent in 2008 to 9 per cent in 2010, in part reflecting a gradual awareness on the part of authorities of the scope of the EIRs. 2.230

Generally, however, the extent to which requests concern information and the degree to which the Environmental Information Regulations differ from the general rights under FOISA has been under-appreciated. This could mean that applicants have been incorrectly refused information under FOISA which should have been disclosed under the EIRs. 2.231

APPENDIX 1

EIRs AND FOISA – THE KEY DIFFERENCES

	EIRs	FOISA
Format of request	There is no requirement under the EIRs that requests should be made in a format capable of having some permanency. Oral requests are valid requests for environmental information, although Scottish public authorities are encouraged to record any oral requests for reference.	FOISA requires requests to be in writing or any other format capable of having some permanency (s 8(1)(a)).
Copies of documents	The duty on public authorities to make environmental information available includes the duty to provide copies of documentation.	FOISA provides a right of access to information, not to documentation.
The definition of a "Scottish public authority"	The definition of a "Scottish public authority" is wider under the EIRs than under FOISA.	Only those bodies listed in Sch 1 to FOISA, designated by order under s 5 of FOISA, or publicly owned companies as defined by s 6 of FOISA (s 3(1)).
Charging	Scottish public authorities may charge for producing the information requested (reg 8(3)), but may not charge for inspecting information (reg 8(2)). Charges may be made only in accordance with a published schedule of charges (reg 8(8)), but which may be at variance with the FOISA Fees Regulations.	Scottish public authorities may charge for locating, retrieving and providing the information only in terms allowed by Fees Regulations other than for information published through a publication scheme (for which separate charging may apply).[1]

---

1   Freedom of Information (Fees for Required Disclosure) (Scotland) Regulations 2004 and Freedom of Information (Fees for Disclosure under Section 13) (Scotland) Regulations 2004.

Cost limit	The EIRs do not have an upper cost limit, effectively meaning that a request cannot be refused on cost grounds. (However, excessive cost may mean that the request is manifestly unreasonable (reg 10(4)(b)). With no lower cost threshold, a Scottish public authority may make a charge for the provision of any information under the EIRs.	Section 12(1) of FOISA provides that a Scottish public authority is not obliged to respond to a request if it estimates that the cost of complying with the request would exceed a prescribed amount (currently £600). A Scottish public authority may make a charge for information between specified limits (Fees Regulations made under s 9(4)) but cannot charge for the first £100 of costs.
What information is "held"	Environmental information is "held" by a Scottish public authority if it is in its possession and it has been produced or received by that authority (reg 2(2)(a)). Unlike FOISA. the EIRs do not specifically exclude information held on behalf of another person.	Under FOISA, information is not "held" if it is held on behalf of another person (s 3(2)(a)(i)).
Transfer of request	Unlike FOISA, the EIRs make provision for the transfer of a request from one body to another (reg 14) (but only if the body does not hold the information or make use of the services of another body to hold this information on its behalf (reg 2(2))).	FOISA does not allow for the transfer of requests between Scottish public authorities. A refusal notice must be served. The applicant should be advised of which body does hold the information if it is reasonable to expect an authority to do so (s 15(1)).

Extension of 20-working-day period	A Scottish public authority may extend the 20-working-day period for making the information available by up to a further 20 working days, but only if the volume *and* complexity of the information requested make it impractical for the authority to comply with the request or to make a decision to refuse to do so (reg 7(1)).	There is no extension to the 20-working-day period in which a Scottish public authority must respond to a request under FOISA.
Active dissemination	A Scottish public authority must organise and keep up to date environmental information with a view to active and systematic dissemination of that information (reg 4(1)).	There is no direct equivalent under FOISA, although Scottish public authorities are required to adopt and maintain a publication scheme (s 23(1)).
Prohibitions on disclosure	The EIRs specifically provide that any enactment or rule of law which would prevent the making available of information in accordance with the EIRs shall *not* apply (reg 5(3)).	FOISA specifically provides that information is exempt information if its disclosure is prohibited by or under an enactment (s 26(a)).
Discretion to accept representa-tions or requests for review	There is no discretion afforded to Scottish public authorities under the EIRs to accept representations for review where they fall outwith the timescales set out in the EIRs.	A Scottish public authority may comply with a requirement for review made after the expiry of the time allowed if it considers it appropriate to do so (s 20(6)). Unlike under the EIRs, any subsequent application to the Commissioner will be valid where this provision is invoked.

Public interest and restrictive interpretation	All of the EIRs exceptions are subject to the "public interest" test (reg 10(1)(b)); should be read in a restrictive way (reg 10(2)(a)) and a presumption in favour of disclosure should be applied (reg 10(2)(b)). (Regulation 11, which deals with personal data, is a quasi-exception to which the "public interest" test applies only in parts.)	The "public interest" test only applies to certain exemptions under FOISA (as set out in s 2).
Historical records	The exceptions in the EIRs do not fall away after a set period.	Certain exemptions cannot be applied to a "historical record" as defined by s 57 of FOISA.

Part II

KEY ISSUES OF INTERPRETATION

Chapter 3

KEY ISSUE 1: NOT A CLASS APART – WHY A CLASS-BASED APPROACH CANNOT BE TAKEN TO CONTENTS-BASED EXEMPTIONS

The express purpose of freedom of information was to bring an end   **3.01**
to a culture of secrecy in public administration. That much was made
clear by the Minister for Justice in bringing forward the legislation.
So it was always likely to be the case that tensions would become
apparent between the new presumption in favour of disclosure and
an engrained culture which was founded upon guarding against
unauthorised disclosure and preserving certain traditions of public
administration.

The notion that an intrusive press and other inquisitive parties   **3.02**
might be able to gain access to the process of deliberation and the
giving of advice to Ministers was challenging. Matters may have moved
on since England's official censor under Charles II expressed his
distaste for public newspapers "because I think it makes the Multitude
too Familiar with the Actions and Counsels of their Superiours".[1] Over
300 years later, however, Sir Norman Brook, the "formidable" Secretary
to the Cabinet, did not hesitate to march into the office of the Editor
of *The Times* to confront him over an article which had revealed the
membership of certain ministerial committees. Brook let him know
that "we, as officials serving the Cabinet, thought that the publication
in the Press of such details of Cabinet organisation were a hindrance
to the efficient discharge of public business".[2] A further 60 years later,
one of his successors as Cabinet Secretary, Lord Turnbull, warned an
Information Tribunal against "the effects of exposure of the internal
workings of the executive" if the exemptions against disclosure were
not rigorously applied.[3]

---

1   Roger L'Estrange, quoted in Andrew Marr, *My Trade* (Macmillan, London, 2004), p 7.
2   Sir Norman Brook, quoted in Peter Hennessy, "The Long March" in *Open Government* (ed
    Stephen Platten) (Canterbury Press, Norwich, 2003), p 22.
3   Department for Education and Skills and Information Commissioner and the *Evening
    Standard* (EA/2006/0006), para 28.

3.03   Lord Turnbull's evidence was subsequently called upon by Scottish Ministers during one of the most fundamental disagreements between the Commissioner and any authority. This concerned the approach which could properly be taken to the exemptions protecting the free and frank provision of advice and exchange of information at s 30(b)(i) and (ii). At issue was whether this contents-based exemption could be claimed in respect of all advice given by officials, almost irrespective of content. Scottish Ministers held that that the Commissioner should simply accept that it was "more practical to recognise that releasing advice or views is likely to have a substantially inhibiting effect", arguing that officials would be inhibited substantially in the giving of advice in the future if they were aware that any information of that type (ie advice) could be disclosed. The Commissioner took the view that this quasi-class-based approach to a contents-based exemption was contrary to statute.

THE *ALEXANDER* CASE

3.04   The key decision which brought this issue to a head was *Mr William Alexander and the Scottish Executive*.[4] Mr Alexander had made a request for information relating to the commencement of certain statutory reforms in ss 25–29 of the Law Reform (Miscellaneous Provisions) (Scotland) Act 1990 (the "1990 Act") which would extend the right to conduct litigation and the rights of audience to members of a professional or other body, opening up competition in the provision of legal services.

3.05   It has been said that these were among the most controversial provisions in the Law Reform Bill, and that "to secure their passage, Ministers at the time gave undertakings that the provisions would not be implemented until other reforms contained in the 1990 Act, such as the introduction of solicitor advocates, had had time to bed down".[5]

3.06   Although the Secretary of State for Scotland reached agreement with the Lord President that work on the commencement of ss 25–29 should start in June 1996, this decision was subsequently reversed.

3.07   Within days of the Freedom of Information Scotland Act coming into force on 1 January 2005, Mr Alexander made his request to the Scottish Executive for "any information it holds regarding the commencement of sections 25 to 29" (these being the relevant sections of the 1990 Act).

---

4   Decision 057/2005: Mr William Alexander and the Scottish Executive.
5   http://www.scotland.gov.uk/Topics/Justice/legal/Rights-of-Audience-1-1/Background.

When the matter eventually came to the Commissioner, the   **3.08**
Executive argued that "disclosure of *any* advice or opinion is likely
to constrain officials and other stakeholders from providing candid
advice in future, which will substantially prejudice the conduct of
public affairs by jeopardising the effectiveness of government". The
Commissioner rejected this premise, saying: "The Executive appears
to have treated the exemptions in section 30(b)(i) and (ii) as class
exemptions, rather than assessing whether the release of the particular
advice or opinion contained within each document would be capable
of having an inhibiting effect."[6]

Ministers challenged this view and, in the first case arising   **3.09**
from FOISA to be heard by the Court of Session, argued that the
Commissioner had "erred in law in concluding that the engagement of
these exemptions must necessarily involve a document by document
assessment".[7]

Counsel for the Ministers submitted that it was not necessarily the   **3.10**
content of individual documents which could give rise to substantial
inhibition, claiming that "a class of documents, irrespective of
individual content, might equally engage this exemption".[8] As an
example, it was suggested that the exemption would apply to any
information as a class, which might show that such advice was being
given by officials to Ministers about the building of a nuclear power
station quite apart from the content of any advice given.

In response, it was submitted that Ministers could not exclude   **3.11**
the Commissioner's jurisdiction "by stamping a file with 'Advice to
Ministers' or the like. Each case in which information was sought
required to be considered in its own circumstances. 'Private space'
for Ministers [to consider advice and exchange views] was not to be
protected by the comfort of a class approach".[9]

In its opinion the court noted that certain of the exemptions apply   **3.12**
by reason of the information in question being of a specified type or
class – for example, s 29(1)(a) (formulation or development of Scottish
Administration policy). Others, including s 30, apply by reason of the
prejudicial effect which disclosure would have or would be likely to
have. The court made clear that the approach to class- and content-
based exemptions is different:

---

6 *Mr William Alexander and the Scottish Executive*, para 66.
7 *Scottish Ministers v Scottish Information Commissioner (William Alexander's application)* [2006]
   CSIH 8 at [9].
8 *Ibid.*
9 *Ibid* at [10].

"In the former case one will begin with the defined class and then ascertain whether relevant information falls within it. Thus, it may be possible to conclude, without scrutiny of the content of each particular document, that a group of documents (for example, all the documents in a particular file) falls, as a group, within the scope of the exemption in question. In the latter case one will necessarily begin with the scrutiny of relevant individual documents and the ascertainment of whether they contain particular information which, read in the context of related information, has or is likely to have the specified prejudicial effect. That is because it is only after such scrutiny that it will be possible to say whether such information will have or is likely to have such an effect."[10]

3.13   Although this exercise might identify, and separate out, the kind of information which would have a prejudicial effect if disclosed, the court made it clear that "The circumstance that one ends up with a 'class', namely, with pieces of information of that particular kind, does not mean that a class-based approach to the exercise is ever legitimate".[11]

RESPONDING TO THE MINISTERS' GENERAL ARGUMENTS ON S 30

3.14   Although the court found in favour of the Commissioner,[12] Ministers continued to take issue with the Commissioner's interpretation. In May 2007 officials submitted an "Annex of general arguments on application of the section 30(b)(i) and (ii) exemptions", setting out their disagreement with the way in which the Commissioner had considered application of these exemptions and the "public interest" test.

3.15   The Ministers disagreed, for example, with the view that matters such as the subject, content, context, manner of expression and timing of the advice should be taken into account when considering whether disclosure would inhibit substantially the free and frank provision of advice, saying that these considerations seemed more appropriate to the application of the "public interest" test.

3.16   These considerations had already been set out in an even earlier decision, *Mr Reiner Luyken and the Scottish Executive*,[13] in which the Commissioner required Ministers to disclose the full report that served

---

10 *Scottish Ministers v Scottish Information Commissioner (William Alexander's application)* [2006] CSIH 8 at [13].

11 *Ibid.*

12 As a postscript, ss 25–29 of the Law Reform (Miscellaneous Provisions) (Scotland) Act 1990 were finally brought into force in 2007.

13 Decision 041/2005: Mr Reiner Luyken and the Scottish Executive.

as the basis for their decision not to give consent to a community company to proceed with buying a forest estate under land reform legislation.[14] In that case, in rejecting the Ministers' arguments for exempting the information under s 30(b)(i), the Commissioner said:

> "... to insist that the release of any advice to Ministers, regardless of its substance, would substantially inhibit officials from providing any candid advice negates any sensible application of the harm test. As I have consistently stated I expect requests for information to be assessed on an individual basis, taking into account the effects anticipated from the release of the particular information involved. This would have to consider:
>
> • the subject-matter of the advice or opinion,
> • the content of the advice and opinion itself,
> • the manner in which the advice or opinion is expressed, and
> • whether the timing of release would have any bearing (releasing advice or opinion while a decision was being considered, and for which further views were still being sought, might be more substantially inhibiting than once a decision has been taken)."

The *Luyken* decision had been referred to in the *Alexander* case at the Court of Session, with counsel on behalf of Ministers submitting that it was wrong to "list in bullet points, elements which turned upon individual content without having due regard to class effect". 3.17

The court, however, having rejected the class approach to the exemption, found nothing wrong with the approach adopted by the Commissioner, "namely, (1) that each case was to be assessed on the facts and circumstances of that case and (2) that the proper approach was to assess whether the release of the advice or opinion contained within each document would be capable of having an inhibiting effect". The court recognised that "Clearly such information may be sensitive in a number of respects" and held that if the expression is read by reference to the *Luyken* decision "it is clear that it embraces sensitivity in relation to issues such as timing, content and subject matter".[15] 3.18

Nevertheless the Executive still maintained that these were matters to be disregarded when considering harm from disclosure, and in their Annex to the Commissioner had set out how, in their view, consideration of the exemption should be approached. 3.19

---

14 Coigeach Community Company Ltd had wished to purchase Drumrunie Forest Estate under the Land Reform (Scotland) Act 2003.

15 *Scottish Ministers v Scottish Information Commissioner (William Alexander's application)* [2006] CSIH 8 at para 14.

16 Decision 089/2007: Mr James Cannell and Historic Scotland.

3.20   These views were subsequently addressed in *Mr James Cannell and Historic Scotland*.[16] In that case, solicitors (on behalf of Mr Cannell) had requested the material which was available to the Secretary of State which had enabled him to decide that a public inquiry should be held in relation to the removal of eight decorative panels from Mr Cannell's category B listed property without the necessary listed building consent having been applied for or granted.

3.21   In response, Historic Scotland (an agency of the Scottish Executive) confirmed that it held a single document containing advice to the relevant Minister but which it withheld, citing the exemptions under s 30(b)(i) and (ii) of FOISA.

3.22   It was argued that officials regularly advised Ministers on similar cases and they could feel constrained from offering full and frank advice on future occasions if they were concerned that their comments would be made public in such circumstances.

3.23   The Executive's views on the application of the exemption as conveyed in the Annex to the Commissioner were laid out:

- consideration of the nature, subject, content, context, manner of expression and timing of the information is more appropriate to the application of the "public interest" test than a determination of whether substantial inhibition is occurring or is likely to occur;
- substantial inhibition is likely to be the cumulative effect of a number of separate releases of information rather than the result of one release, or perhaps even several releases;
- future events being impossible to predict with any degree of certainty, it should be recognised that releasing advice or views is, by definition, likely to have a substantially inhibiting effect;
- it is reasonable to expect a degree of consistency in decisions about what information should be released and therefore, where internal communications are released in one or more cases, it is inevitable the officials will conclude that there is a high probability that other internal communications will also require to be disclosed, leading to inhibition of the way in which advice or views are given in the future. The Executive did not believe officials in an organisation as large as itself will generally be familiar with the detailed circumstances which have led to information being released in one case but not in another and will simply note that internal communications are likely to be released.

3.24   It was difficult to see how these arguments amounted to anything other than the class-based approach to the s 30(b) exemption which the courts had already rejected. The effect and perhaps the purpose of this approach would mean that there would be little distinction in practice between information which related to the formulation of policy and that which was advice to Ministers. In the Commissioner's view, the Executive was "effectively claiming that the prospect of harm should be readily accepted, with the possibility of disclosure still provided for by the public interest test, which can then be used to consider the nature and degree of harm and whether this outweighs the benefits of release, and that real consideration of whether the information could be disclosed or not would take place when balancing the public interest".

The Commissioner rejected this reasoning, saying: 3.25

"It is clear that the public interest test is only engaged if the authority can show that without the application of the exemption, the disclosure of the information would, or would be likely to, inhibit substantially the free and frank provision of advice. If this cannot be shown, the public interest in release or in withholding does not require to be considered. The factors which could give rise to harm by way of substantial inhibition therefore have to be considered when determining whether the exemption applies."

(In the *Cannell* case it was found that disclosure of the report by Historic   3.26
Scotland would not inhibit substantially the provision of advice in the future and it was ordered to be given to the applicant.)

A CASE-BY-CASE APPROACH TO THE "HARM" TEST: WHY IT MATTERS

At the time of this prolonged dispute was, first, ensuring that the   3.27
threshold of harm established by Parliament in passing the legislation was crossed *before* moving on to consider the "public interest" test and, second, that, in doing so, the "harm" test was applied to the content of the information — "document by document" – rather than to a class or type of information.

Attention has been paid to the construction of the "harm" test in the   3.28
Scottish legislation which requires an authority to demonstrate that *substantial* prejudice or inhibition would occur from disclosure. It can be debated as to what extent this is different in effect from the simple test of prejudice in the equivalent UK FOIA exemptions but there can be little doubt that it is meant to convey that even if some harm results from disclosure, that is not sufficient to engage the exemption. In *An Open Scotland*, the Executive's consultation document on freedom of

information, Scottish Ministers said: "We propose that the harm test is demanding ... our use of substantial prejudice is intended to make it clear that information covered by a content based exemption should be disclosed unless the prejudice caused by disclosure would be real, actual and of significant substance."[17]

3.29   This aspiration appears at odds with the Executive's subsequent approach which would have, in essence, considered the sensitivity of the *subject-matter* of the advice or exchange and then exempted all information related to it, irrespective of content. (As indicated above, it was suggested, as an example, that this would be appropriate where Ministers were discussing the building of a nuclear power station.) In their view the safety net against unjustified non-disclosure would be that the "public interest" test would then apply as to whether the information should be disclosed.

3.30   However, the consequence of this line of thinking is that officials would be able routinely to rely on knowing that their advice and opinion would be withheld, however innocuous or sensitive, however blandly or trenchantly expressed, unless some specific public interest overwhelmed the normal practice of doing so. As the Commissioner starkly observed in the *Luyken* decision: "That is not how FOISA works."[18]

3.31   The reason why it cannot work in the way the Executive advanced is that, not only is it contrary to statute but it is also likely improperly to disadvantage the applicant. For instance, the public interest in Mr Cannell getting access to a report about the removal of his decorative panels might have been slight. However, as he would have been entitled to point out, no view of the public interest needed to be taken, because the *harm* in giving him the information was also slight or at least not sufficient to pass the substantial inhibition threshold. In the absence of the necessary degree of harm, it was unnecessary and indeed contrary to statute to consider the public interest.

3.32   Where *class-based* exemptions are concerned, no judgment needs to be made of the harm from disclosure before applying the exemption. All that needs to be established is whether the information falls within the category of exemption by type or class. It is when balancing the public interest that account can be taken of the harm from disclosure. The harm to the public interest, for example in making officials more guarded in commenting on certain policy options, might be slight but if it is greater than the minimal public interest in disclosure then it

17   Scottish Ministers, *An Open Scotland – Freedom of Information: A Consultation* (1999 SE/1999/51).
18   Decision 041/2005: Mr Reiner Luyken and the Scottish Executive at para 16.

may warrant the information being withheld; equally, the harm may be significant but not sufficient to warrant the exemption being maintained where the public interest in disclosure is considerable.

Matters are quite different when dealing with *contents-based* **3.33** exemptions such as those contained in s 30. If it is accepted that the exemption applies then it can never be said that harm is slight, as a threshold "harm" test must have been passed before the public interest can considered. When it comes to balancing the public interest in disclosure with that in maintaining the exemption, the scales are heavily weighted by the acceptance that disclosure would or would be likely to cause substantial prejudice (which the authority will nearly always argue it is not in the public interest to allow to happen).

It is because of this distinction that the focus of examination, for **3.34** s 30 as with any other contents-based exemption, is on whether the harm claimed by authorities stands up to scrutiny; if it is does not, the exemption does not apply and the public interest arguments are set aside. The key question, then, which has to be answered when claiming any contents-based exemption, is: "Where is the harm?".

Chapter 4

KEY ISSUE 2: WHERE IS THE HARM? – APPLYING CONTENTS-BASED EXEMPTIONS AND EXCEPTIONS

Many of the provisions in FOISA and the EIRs which allow information to be withheld require authorities to demonstrate not only that the consequences of information being released into the public domain would be harmful but that the nature and extent of the harm would be substantial. The question "Where is the harm in disclosure?" has been at the core of many decisions.   **4.01**

The following contents-based FOISA exemptions apply only where disclosure "would or would be likely to prejudice substantially":   **4.02**

- a programme of research or the interests of certain individuals or authorities, if information obtained in the course of, or derived from, a programme of research which is continuing with a view to a report of the research being published, was disclosed before the date of publication (see s 27(2));
- relations between any administration in the United Kingdom and any other such administration (s 28);
- the maintenance of the convention of the collective responsibility of the Scottish Ministers; or the effective conduct of public affairs (s 30(a) and (c));
- the defence of the British Islands or of any colony; or the capability, effectiveness or security of any relevant forces (s 31(4));
- relations between the United Kingdom and any other state; relations between the United Kingdom and any international organisation or international court; the interests of the United Kingdom abroad; or the promotion or protection by the United Kingdom of its interests abroad (s 32(1)(a));
- the commercial interests of any person (s 33(1)(b)); the economic interests of the whole or part of the United Kingdom or the financial interests of an administration in the United Kingdom (s 33(2));

- the prevention or detection of crime; the apprehension or prosecution of offenders, the administration of justice etc (s 35(1)(a)–(h));
- the exercise of a Scottish public authority's functions in relation to the audit of the accounts of other Scottish public authorities; or the examination of the economy, efficiency and effectiveness with which such authorities use their resources in discharging their functions (s 40(a) and (b)).

4.03   The "harm" test is worded differently in two exemptions such that information is exempt if disclosure "would or would be likely to":

- inhibit substantially the free and frank provision of advice; or the free and frank exchange of views for the purposes of deliberation (s 30(b));
- endanger the physical or mental health or safety of an individual. (s 39(1)).

4.04   Similarly, the EIRs permit authorities to refuse to make environmental information available if its disclosure "would, or would be likely to, prejudice substantially":

(a) international relations, defence, national security or public safety (reg 10(5)(a));
(b) the course of justice, the ability of a person to receive a fair trial or the ability of any public authority to conduct an inquiry of a criminal or disciplinary nature (reg 10(5)(b));
(c) intellectual property rights (reg 10(5)(c));
(d) the confidentiality of the proceedings of any public authority where such confidentiality is provided for by law (reg 10(5)(d));
(e) the confidentiality of commercial or industrial information where such confidentiality is provided for by law to protect a legitimate economic interest (reg 10(5)(e));
(f) the interests of the person who provided the information where that person:
  - was not under, and could not have been put under, any legal obligation to supply the information;
  - did not supply it in circumstances such that it could, apart from the EIRs, be made available; and
  - has not consented to its disclosure (reg 10(5)(f)); or
(g) the protection of the environment to which the information relates (reg 10(5)(g)).

MEANING OF "PREJUDICE SUBSTANTIALLY"

There is no statutory definition in the legislation as to what constitutes **4.05**
substantial prejudice or inhibition. However, the Code of Practice
introduced by Scottish Ministers alongside FOISA indicated that
"authorities should consider disclosing the information unless the
prejudice caused would be real, actual and of significant substance".[1]

This has been reflected in the Commissioner's view that the **4.06**
emphasis afforded in statute by requiring the harm to be "substantial",
as compared with the simple and unqualified test of prejudice in the
equivalent UK FOIA exemptions, means that a high hurdle needs to be
cleared. The damage caused by disclosing the information must be of
some real and demonstrable significance, as opposed to hypothetical
or marginal; and such damage would need to occur in the near or at
least foreseeable future, and not at some distant time.

The meaning of the word "likely" is open to interpretation. The **4.07**
general legal principle was explained by Chadwick LJ[2] when he said that
"likely" does not carry any necessary connotation of "more probable
than not". It is a word which takes its meaning from the context.

In a data protection case[3] judicial guidance was given as to the **4.08**
meaning of "likely" in the following terms: "the degree of risk must be
such that there may very well be prejudice ... even if the risk falls short
of being more probable than not".

However, Scottish Ministers were at pains to point out that the **4.09**
"harm" test in the legislation was greater than under a previous
voluntary Code of Practice on Access to Scottish Executive Information,
saying "the Code refers to the *possibility* of harm being caused and the
test is the 'reasonable expectation of harm or prejudice'. Under our
proposals the test of 'would or would be likely to cause substantial
prejudice' is the more stringent one of the *probability* of substantial
prejudice".[4]

THE "HARM" TEST

It is worth considering the effect of having such a high hurdle. The first, **4.10**
as discussed in the previous chapter, is that these exemptions cannot

---

1   Scottish Ministers' Code of Practice on the discharge of functions by public authorities
    under the Freedom of Information (Scotland) Act 2002, para 72. This Code has been
    superseded by a later version.
2   *Three Rivers District Council v Governor and Company of the Bank of England (No 4)* [2002] EWCA
    Civ 1182, [2003] 1 WLR 210.
3   *R (on the appl'n of Lord) v Secretary of State for the Home Department* [2003] EWHC 2073 (Admin).
4   "An Open Scotland – Freedom of Information: A Consultation", laid before the Scottish
    Parliament by Scottish Ministers November 1999 (S/199/51), 4.12 (original emphasis
    retained).

be regarded as effectively class exemptions whereby, if information falls broadly within their scope (for example, being concerned with commercial transactions or the provision of advice by officials), an assertion of some potential harm from disclosure would be sufficient to cause the exemption to apply. Authorities have to show why *in all the circumstances of that particular case,* the harmful consequences of disclosure warrant the exemption being claimed.

4.11   Second, it is the *plausibility* of that claim which is tested when the matter is referred to the Commissioner. Unless the prospect of harm, as disputed between authority and applicant, is completely baseless or entirely self-evident, a judgement has to be formed as to whether the degree of concern and caution expressed by the authority is justified.

4.12   Authorities *have* been able to argue successfully that if information was disclosed then harm would occur – this much is clear from the Commissioner's decisions. In particular, cases which involve law enforcement are treated with caution to ensure that criminal investigations are not impeded or that a fair trial is not jeopardised. Disclosure is not likely to be required if information may be used to commit crime or avoid detection. Variously, the Commissioner has determined that information should be withheld concerning:

- a witness protection programme;[5]
- unmarked police vehicles;[6]
- an NHS Counter Fraud investigation;[7]
- a police file concerning a missing person.[8]

4.13   Indeed, the police are particularly successful in arguing that the information they hold should not be disclosed, often because it would harm law enforcement. In the period January 2005 to December 2010, 60 per cent of decisions taken by the Commissioner concerning Scottish police forces found wholly in their favour. By comparison, only 40 per cent of all decisions in the same period wholly favoured the authority.

4.14   Yet even the police can overstate their case – asserting harm where it appears unlikely to happen. Strathclyde Police argued that releasing details of the number of policemen on duty at a particular football match would have profound consequences for law enforcement

---

5   Decision 084/2010: Ms Sarah Beech of *The Digger* and the Chief Constable of Strathclyde Police.

6   Decision 079/2010: Mr Joe Hands and the Chief Constable of Strathclyde Police.

7   Decision 084/2008 Mr John Falconer and the Common Services Agency for the Scottish Health Service.

8   Decision 069/2007: Mr Leslie Brown and the Chief Constable of Strathclyde Police.

and public safety. They argued that "public dissemination of these numbers would compromise any advantage held by the police over individuals or groups intent on disrupting the match in question or future matches, causing serious public disorder with the likelihood of serious injury".[9] But how likely was it that hooligan groups would use this information either to confront the police or to avoid the police presence to attack each other? In the Commissioner's view it was highly unlikely that the events envisaged by the police would come about. The match in question was a Kilmarnock v Falkirk cup semi-final. Given the modest size of the expected attendance, the teams had gained special permission from the Scottish Football Association to hold the game at a much smaller stadium than would normally be used for such matches. (The game was played in front of 10,000 fans.) The Commissioner concluded that knowledge of the number of officers used to police this particular match could not be used to build up a pattern of information which could then be used against Strathclyde Police in future. Despite the fears expressed by the police, it has not been subsequently suggested that the information, once disclosed, has been used to cause public disorder and violence.

In many other instances authorities have been unable to make a convincing case for withholding the information requested. This is either because the harm as described by the authorities has not been felt to be significant or because it has not been accepted that disclosure would result in the dire consequences which it was claimed would be likely to happen.   4.15

CLAIMED HARM – DID IT HAPPEN?

Where, subsequently, information has been disclosed contrary to the significant fears of the authority, the most obvious question, as in the policing case above, is: "Did the harm happen?"   4.16

SURGICAL MORTALITY RATES – WHAT HARM FROM DISCLOSURE?

Perhaps the most prominent Scottish case where the degree of harm had to be weighed against the likelihood of its occurrence came about as a result of a request for the complete list of clinical outcomes (mortality rates) of all surgeons in Scotland. The detail requested included the name of each surgeon in each clinical speciality. The Common Services Agency, which held the information, was concerned   4.17

---

9   Decision 071/2008: Mr S and the Chief Constable of Strathclyde Police.

that some of the data may not be accurate (for example, by attributing outcomes to the wrong surgeon) and feared in particular that the information could be misinterpreted as it did not take account of what is called "case mix". (As the decision notice in this case explains: "Case-mix adjustment attempts to remove confounding factors (e.g. age, deprivation category, other morbid conditions such as diabetes or asthma) to allow meaningful comparisons to be made between surgeons and hospitals. The differences in outcome between hospitals are likely to reflect to some extent differences in the case-mix of patients admitted."[10])

4.18   The CSA set out a scenario for substantial prejudice which, in the Commissioner's view, depended on:

> "the following presumed causal chain of events: information is released which is inaccurate and is not adjusted for case mix; this is published by a media which fails to acknowledge the inadequacies of the information and draws up league tables of performance or draws unwarranted conclusions from the information; this in turn leads to criticism or concern over the performance of individual clinicians, who, in response, withdraw their cooperation from processes which have been established to gather data on, and audit, clinical performance. As a consequence, there would be an impact on the quality of healthcare".[11]

4.19   This was a challenging request, asking for information which, so far as could be ascertained, had not been disclosed so comprehensively anywhere in the world, and particularly not in a raw form. The concerns of the CSA were understandable. Nevertheless, some information of this type, regarding individual surgeons who carried out coronary artery bypass grafts at a number of hospitals across the UK, had previously been disclosed. Some of this data, including that from Scotland, was not risk adjusted to take account of case mix, and no evidence had been presented or found from here or elsewhere of surgeons withdrawing co-operation from audits of surgical performance as a result.

4.20   After the Commissioner ordered disclosure, the information was published by the CSA, attaching a disclaimer as to how the figures could be interpreted and declaring that "surgeons may be reluctant to operate on high-risk cases of this kind if information is to be made public and judgments of performance made or implied".[12]

---

10   Decision 066/2005: Mr Peter MacMahon of *The Scotsman* and the Common Services Agency for the Scottish Health Service.

11   *Ibid*, para 68.

12   http://www.indicators.scot.nhs.uk/Surgical/Main.html.

However, press coverage of the data was reported soberly and 4.21
presented in context and did not, as feared by the CSA, result in league
tables or identify any clinician as "the worst in Scotland".

Did the anticipated harm actually occur? The specific harm to the 4.22
effective conduct of public affairs claimed by the CSA in this case
was that surgeons would stop voluntarily reporting to the Scottish
Audit of Surgical Mortality ("SASM"). Almost every consultant
surgeon and anaesthetist in Scotland participates in this peer review
process which is initiated following the death of a patient within 30
days of an operation or during the patient's last admission. Whether
surgeons turned their back on the SASM process in protest is testable
by establishing whether an appreciable and otherwise unattributable
change occurred subsequent to the disclosure of information. The
Commissioner's decision was published in December 2005 and the
mortality data was disclosed by the CSA in February 2006. The SASM
annual reports, however, show virtually no change in the level of
co-operation, with 88 per cent compliance in 2004; 90 per cent in 2005;
89 per cent in 2006; and 88 per cent in 2007.[13] Furthermore, no evidence
has been presented that surgeons declined to carry out high-risk
procedures following disclosure. Whatever view is taken as to the
value of the data or the interpretation of it, the harm claimed did not
come about.

WHAT HARM TO COMMERCIAL INTERESTS?

Another area where harm is often argued concerns commercial 4.23
interests. In the circumstances of specific cases the Commissioner
has agreed that the commercial interests of contractors and suppliers
would be harmed if details of their tender for an IT contract[14] or
schedule of charges for building work were disclosed.[15]

However, requests for commercial contracts have also prompted 4.24
trenchant claims of harm that neither were plausible nor came to
pass. Northern Constabulary argued that if the purchase price of
vehicles bought from Land Rover UK, under an arrangement with
the Police Information Technology Organisation ("PITO"), was
disclosed to a journalist, serious consequences would follow. After
pointing out that UK police forces had saved over £20 million due
to this PITO contract, the force argued that "If we are now required

13 Scottish Audit of Surgical Mortality Summary Reports: http://www.sasm.org.uk/
   Reports/main.html.
14 Decision 131/2008: Mr N and East Ayrshire Council.
15 Decision 021/2008: Mr Conor McNally and Glasgow City Council.

to release details of the prices negotiated under this contract, it may cause all the manufacturers to reconsider their position and potentially withdraw. The cost to UK police forces would be in the millions".[16]

4.25   Undoubtedly, then, such harm, if it did occur, would be substantial; but the question for the Commissioner was whether it was plausible that a major national procurement contract would collapse if, in this case, the purchase prices of two company cars for the Chief Constable and his deputy were disclosed.

4.26   Clearly, the concern on the part of Land Rover was that the vehicles had been supplied at a substantial discount compared with the price shown on a dealer's forecourt. The company maintained that the basis of fleet sales pricing was too complex to explain to the public and so it would come under pressure to match that discounted price. However, the Commissioner took the view that the public could readily understand the fundamental basis of the price differential, which came from fleet sales volume and the marketing benefits to Land Rover of its vehicles being seen to be used by the emergency services, and ordered disclosure.

4.27   What about the harm which it was said would ensue? There is no evidence of police forces subsequently being unable to enter into contracts with vehicle suppliers, or of having to pay inflated prices as a result. When, in the following year, the same newspaper asked for the cost of the replacement vehicle for the Range Rover, this was provided promptly by the force without demur.

4.28   These two cases involve very different considerations of harm: the potential for patient care to suffer and the possible jeopardy to advantageous contracts. What they have in common, however, is that they are based upon what is effectively a worst-case scenario, which depends upon a series of events culminating in a significantly harmful outcome. This is not an unusual line of argument for public authorities to take. Other such cases are mentioned elsewhere in this book – including one where the Scottish Prison Service argued that disclosing the performance statistics of its prisoner escort service contractor would cause that company's share price to fall[17] and another where the City of Edinburgh Council argued that if it disclosed how much it paid to a consultancy it would undermine its ability to secure best value from future contracts, thereby harming

---

16   Decision 066/2006: Mr John Robertson, Aberdeen Journals Ltd, and the Chief Constable of Northern Constabulary.

17   Decision 053/2006: Professor Sheila Bird and the Scottish Prison Service.

the financial interests of the Scottish or UK Governments which might have to make good any shortfall.[18]

What the passage of time has shown is that where arguments made against disclosure were regarded as over-stated, empirically it can be seen that the claimed harm has not come about. This lends itself to the likelihood that a merely speculative possibility of prejudice, based upon a prospect of harm which is conceivable, but unlikely, will not pass the "harm" test.   **4.29**

The above cases all involve judgement calls on the likelihood of harm which, if it came about, would have serious consequences for healthcare, law and order, and commercial transactions, which the public authority had limited means to avoid. However, these are not typical of most cases where an exemption based on harm is claimed – usually the focus of concern is the potential impact on the business of public administration.   **4.30**

WHAT HARM TO THE EFFECTIVE CONDUCT OF PUBLIC AFFAIRS?

No other harm-based exemption is invoked as often as s 30 regarding "prejudice to the effective conduct of public affairs". Of all of the Commissioner's decisions (harm based or not), 10 per cent involve claims that the free and frank provision of advice would be inhibited substantially; a similar percentage applies to those decisions – often involving the same cases – where the effect of disclosure on the free and frank exchange of views for the purposes of deliberation is at issue.   **4.31**

Regularly, authorities withhold information found in: formal minutes; letters to external organisations; official advice to Ministers; internal briefing notes; and informal e-mails between officials on a wide range of public affairs. Just as regularly, some of this information is ordered to be disclosed. The Commissioner's decisions reflect a range of issues – for example, the development of the free personal care policy in Scotland; ship-to-ship oil transfer in the Firth of Forth; the closure of Caithness Blood Bank; financial support to voluntary organisations in Edinburgh; the funding arrangements for the passenger terminal at Inverness Airport.   **4.32**

What binds these various issues and forms of information is that authorities have painted a picture of seriously adverse consequences from disclosure which will not just affect the quality of deliberation and advice on a particular matter but, much more widely, would strike at the heart of the process of the conduct of public affairs.   **4.33**

---

18   Decision 074/2011: Ms Caroline Gerard and City of Edinburgh Council.

4.34   Yet the Commissioner has often rejected such arguments by concluding that the claimed consequence is out of all proportion to the content and nature of the information in question. The reasons, as listed in one case, have much in common with what has been found in many others, in that the information:

- was routine and administrative in nature;
- simply related to the process of informing persons of outcomes, or of what is happening in a process, without any apparent controversy;
- contained advice or information of a factual nature only;
- included material which was already in the public domain; or
- represented the normal exchange of officials in the course of their work, expressed in a manner which was not likely to be affected significantly by disclosure.[19]

4.35   The question again arises as to what effect, if any, disclosing this type of information has had. According to the arguments made on behalf of Ministers and others, there should by now be widespread, and harmful, changes to previous practice as a result of freedom of information putting official advice and exchange of views into the public domain. Even where the information was routine or factual, it has been argued that officials would not have regard to the content of specific disclosures, but would simply be aware that what might have been previously regarded as information for internal circulation only was being disclosed and that this would inhibit the manner in which advice was given or views exchanged in the future. Primarily this would be evidenced by a so-called "chilling" effect – where Ministers and officials would at the very least avoid recording their views and instead rely upon oral briefings and discussion; while this might not inhibit the free and frank nature of advice, it might limit the number and location of those who could be involved in the exchange and also make it difficult to maintain the public record as to how decisions were arrived at. If information did have to be written down then it might be less informative, and more guarded. In particular, officials may fear that proffering controversial proposals may create hostages to fortune which, if disclosed, might foment political and press attacks focused on an option which Ministers had no intention of pursuing.

4.36   These kinds of concerns have been expressed in many other countries following the passage of freedom of information laws. Yet,

---

19   Decision 208/2007: Coupers Seafoods Ltd and Scottish Enterprise Grampian, para 23.

a study of Canada, Australia and New Zealand regarding such fears concluded: "it is impossible to find any evidence to substantiate them".[20]

When asked for evidence of a "chilling" effect as result of FOI, Scottish Ministers have argued that it is difficult to attribute change to any specific disclosure but that "they knew from their intimate knowledge of the Government and from conversations with staff that they often felt much more inhibited in what they wrote down and that sometimes they had been asked for oral rather than written advice or views on sensitive topics. They admitted that this was not concrete evidence, but argued that it was impossible to provide evidence of advice or views being inhibited, or the provision of oral advice where written advice would have been provided before, i.e. to prove a negative".[21]   4.37

The prevalence of an FOI-induced "chilling" effect in UK central government was the subject of the academic research conducted by the Constitution Unit at UCL led by Professor Robert Hazell. Interviews were conducted with 56 civil servants officials from eight different Whitehall Government Departments, encompassing FOI officers, policy and press officers, and officials working in records management and procurement.   4.38

Whitehall had real concerns that FOI would prejudice the proper working of government, by undermining collective Cabinet responsibility, making civil servants less willing to give free and frank advice and threatening Civil Service neutrality if such advice was exposed. The study concludes bluntly: "in practice none of these fears have been realised".[22]   4.39

It found that "despite an abundance of anecdote about the chilling effect, substantive evidence is hard to find"[23] and concluded that "it is a powerful myth associated with FOI, which is hard to eradicate despite the lack of evidence".[24]   4.40

However, that is not to say that disclosure could not have a prejudicial effect, especially when the information relates to current matters. Among many decisions upholding the use of the exemption, the Commissioner has accepted that release of ongoing exchanges between the First Minister's office and a government   4.41

---

20 R Hazell, B Worthy and M Glover, *The Impact of the Freedom of Information Act on Central Government in the UK* (Palgrave Macmillan, London 2010), p 180.

21 Decision 105/2008: Mr Rob Edwards and the Scottish Ministers, para 51.

22 Note 20 above, p 256

23 *Ibid*, p 161

24 *Ibid*, p 256.

agency regarding planning permission for a listed building would be substantially inhibiting,[25] as would details of ongoing internal discussion between members of a Board prior to a meeting with Ministers.[26]

4.42   Nor is it right to be complacent about the possibility that certain information is not being recorded or retained. There are cases where applicants have queried the paucity of information relating to their request and the Commissioner has been told that although meetings may have taken place, no record was kept by any of those attending, or at the every least no further information within the scope of the request has been located despite extensive searches.[27] As noted in Chapter 1, the ostensible culture of the Water Industry Commission for Scotland of not recording or retaining written information derived from meetings or discussions was regarded by the Commissioner as "highly unusual practice which appears to have the consequence that it would be very difficult for it to evidence and document its work or decision making, for either internal purposes or external scrutiny".[28]

CONCLUSION

4.43   If it is the case that some authorities have overstated the harm which they say would result from disclosure, what lessons can be learned?

4.44   First, authorities faced with requests for similar information in the future should be less cautious and disclose the information (unless the circumstances of a particular case justify withholding). There is evidence of this happening on matters of commercial interest. The revised Code of Practice issued by Scottish Ministers has extensive guidance on the disclosure of information relating to contracts or procurement processes, indicating not only that contractors should be informed that information about the contract may be disclosed but also that authorities should consider inserting into contracts a requirement upon the contractor to disclose certain information.[29]

---

25   Decision 130/2009: David Rule and the Scottish Ministers.

26   Decision 021/2011: Mr Peter Cherbi and the Scottish Legal Complaints Commission.

27   See, for example, Decision 025/2011: Mr Simon Johnson of *The Daily Telegraph* and the Scottish Ministers; Decision 127/2009: West Highland Free Press and the Scottish Ministers.

28   Decision 084/2011: Mr Tommy Kane and the Water Industry Commission for Scotland.

29   Scottish Ministers' Code of Practice 2010, para 4.1.2: Inclusion of disclosure provisions in contracts.

The Scottish schools standard contract contains such a clause   4.45
requiring the contractor to assist the authority in complying with
FOISA:[30]

> "The Contractor shall co-operate, facilitate, support and assist the
> Authority to comply with the Freedom of Information (Scotland) Act
> 2002 and any codes of practice applicable from time to time relating
> to access to public authorities' information. In the event that the
> Authority is required to provide information to any person as a result
> of a request made to it under such Act and/or codes, the Authority
> shall adhere to the requirements of such Act and/or codes in disclosing
> information relating to this Agreement, the Project Documents and
> the Contractor."

Second, if authorities wish to maintain that harm will come about,   4.46
they should expect those claims to be tested by the Commissioner if
the case is appealed. Bald assertions, weak hypotheses and generalised
claims with no specific reference to the circumstances of the case
are not likely to be persuasive. Furthermore, full and convincing
arguments need to be contained in the submission made to the
Commissioner, in response to the invitation to authorities to make
comments when given notice of an application. Such submissions
should not be used as an opening gambit, to be expanded or built
upon in response to questions in the course of investigation. Instead,
they need to be made in the expectation that the Commissioner will
come to a decision wholly based upon the strength of the arguments
made in a submission.

Third, claims of harm tend to be more accepted where the issue is   4.47
one of sensitivity and discussion is ongoing at the time of the request.
This is on the ground that it is more likely that an official may be
inhibited from proffering controversial options or advice if previous
such exchanges of views on the same issue have been disclosed before
a formal submission has been made to a Minister or an agreed position
on behalf of an authority has been taken. Even then, once such
discussions have ended and decisions have been made or meetings
have taken place, the degree of harm may decline.

Fourth, if FOI is provoking a reaction, that is only to be expected,   4.48
given that the stated aim of FOI was to bring about a change of culture
within public authorities. So far as the effective conduct of public
affairs is concerned, measures can be taken by authorities to improve

30 Scottish schools standard PPP contract Version 3 June 2004: http://www.scotland.gov.uk/
    Topics/Government/Finance/18232/19138.

the capacity to disclose information while mitigating concerns about inhibition, for example:

- official advice and formal exchanges can be written with potential disclosure in mind;
- instructions can be issued, requiring a record to be maintained of decision-making processes.

4.49   A more professional approach can be taken to internal exchanges between officials. Often, some of the information in dispute is expressed in a colloquial, informal manner. Opinion and anecdote may be exchanged between colleagues which may be all too free and frank, the disclosure of which would simply embarrass the official and their authority. If so, that is not a reason for exempting information under FOISA, but it may be a reason for adopting a more professional standard of exchange.

Chapter 5

KEY ISSUE 3: GOVERNMENT INFORMATION – THE EXTENT OF SPECIAL PROTECTION

The information and interests of the Government are afforded greater   5.01
protection from disclosure than those of any other authority. There
are a number of specific exemptions in FOISA which apply only
to information held by or concerning the interests of the Scottish
Administration. There are also provisions in FOISA which apply to
other authorities but not to the Scottish Administration or which can
be overridden by powers available only to Ministers.

For instance, the maintenance of the convention of the collective   5.02
responsibility of the Scottish Ministers is given specific protection;[1] so
too are relations between the Scottish Administration and any other
administration in the United Kingdom.[2]

When it comes to deciding whether an exemption is required to   5.03
be applied to certain information, for the purpose of safeguarding
national security, a Minister can take the decision out of the hands of
any public authority, and of the Commissioner, by signing a certificate
which is conclusive of that fact.[3]

Greater powers of intervention also allow the First Minister, in   5.04
certain circumstances, to exercise a veto over the Commissioner's
decisions. By signing a certificate, the First Minister causes a decision
notice or enforcement notice given to the Scottish Administration by
the Commissioner to cease to have effect.[4]

And the Scottish Administration cannot be prosecuted for the   5.05
offence of preventing the disclosure of information by altering,
destroying, concealing etc a record; only its staff face this sanction.[5]
If the same offence is committed other than within Government (and
Parliament), the prospect of conviction applies to "the authority and

---

1 FOISA, s 30(a).
2 *Ibid*, s 28(1).
3 *Ibid*, s 31(2).
4 *Ibid*, s 52. This veto has not yet been used.
5 *Ibid*, s 68.

to any person who is employed by, is an officer of, or is subject to the direction of, the authority".[6]

5.06   However, the privileged provision in FOISA which is most commonly used by Ministers is that concerning "the formulation of Scottish Administration policy etc" at s 29. By the wide-ranging nature of the exemption, if it can be demonstrated that the *content* of the information relates to:

(a) the formulation or development of government policy;
(b) ministerial communications;
(c) the provision of advice by any of the Law Officers or any request for the provision of such advice; or
(d) the operation of any ministerial private office

then the exemption applies. There is no "harm" test.

5.07   (By contrast, other authorities seeking to withhold information regarding the making of policy need to look to other provisions such as prejudice to the effective conduct of public affairs (s 30), in which case, however, a sufficient degree of harm from disclosure needs to be demonstrable before the exemption applies.)

5.08   Such class-based exemptions are, in the eyes of some legal commentators, "outrageously broad".[7] Even so, it cannot be taken to mean that any matter which is within the sphere of responsibility of government decision-making is covered. Drawing directly upon meanings put forward for the equivalent provisions in the UK legislation,[8] the Commissioner has taken the view that:

> "The formulation of government policy suggests the early stages of the policy process where options are considered, risks are identified, consultation takes place and recommendations and submissions are presented to Scottish Ministers. The development of government policy suggests the processes involved in improving upon or amending already existing policy and could involve the piloting, monitoring, reviewing, analysing or recording the effects of existing policy."[9]

5.09   Although the scope can, consequently, be wide ranging, there is an important distinction to be made between the *drawing up of* or *expanding*

---

6   FOISA, s 65(1).

7   P Birkenshaw, *Freedom of Information – The Law, the Practice and the Ideal* (3rd edn, Butterworths, London, 2001), p 296.

8   M Turle, *Freedom of Information Manual* (Sweet & Maxwell, London, 2005), p 123, regarding FOIA, s 35.

9   Decision 130/2006: Mr Paul Hutcheon of *The Sunday Herald* and the Scottish Executive, para 17.

upon a policy, which attracts the exemption, and the *implementation* or *administration* of that policy, which may not. Insufficient recognition may be given to this difference.

For instance, when the Minister for Health called a meeting   5.10
between a health authority and elected members of Parliament to help resolve a local dispute concerning service provision at a hospital in West Lothian, that might have been regarded as providing problem-solving leadership. However, he was not by that process formulating or developing government policy. The Commissioner concluded that:

> "The issue at hand was a policy or operational decision of the other public authority" (namely NHS Lothian)

and

> "The involvement of the Minister does not automatically transform this process into one which is now the formulation or development of Scottish Administration policy."[10]

In that case, the Ministers argued that the information needed simply   5.11
to *relate* to the formulation or development of Scottish Executive policy. That is so, but, as the decision makes clear, "relate to" must mean more than simply having some association with activity in a thematic policy area, such as health, for which responsibility is devolved to the Executive. Otherwise, virtually any information regarding deliberation or decisions relating to a policy area would come within the scope of the exemption.

However, it should be acknowledged that carving out policy   5.12
making from the broad responsibilities of government may not reflect the way in which Ministers and officials view or go about their work. This was pointed out in a paper produced by former civil servants for the UK Commissioner which said that in "day-to-day activity, there is simply no operational need to define at any given point whether what people are doing is formulating, developing, promoting or delivering government policy".[11]

The report suggests that the broad contexts in which officials might   5.13
say they are engaged in "policy" include:

- the setting out by Government of a coherent overview approach to a key area or sector of society;
- a set of initiatives or interventions aimed at bringing about specific goals;

---

10   Decision 130/2006, para 21.
11   P Waller, R M Morris and D Simpson, "Understanding the Formulation and Development of Government Policy in the context of FOI" (The Constitution Unit), p 68, para 3.6.

- one-off initiatives in the normal course of events;
- continuing political debate;
- reaction to external events;
- operational issues requiring political judgement;
- what does the Government think about … ?

5.14   To a greater or lesser extent, the formulation or development of policy might be taking place while, at the same time, and engaging those same officials, current policy is being articulated or implemented. The nature of policy making is also subject to change, with more emphasis at the outset perhaps in delivering outcomes. It has been argued that while late 20th-century policy making in Britain was characterised by "a stark separation between policy-making and service delivery",[12] it was replaced by a "pragmatism … so deeply held that it will implement any solution that seems to work",[13] reflected in the pithy view that "what matters is what works". As a result, while

> "Distinctions can certainly be drawn between 'policy development and formulation' and delivery – and such distinctions may well be drawn in practice … a strong trend in recent years has been to regard attention to delivery issues as an integral part of policy making and not something to be managed separately. This blurs further a boundary which was never well defined."[14]

5.15   In coming to a view, then, as to what is within the scope of the exemption, regard must be paid to the content of the information, the nature and substance of which may readily identify whether it concerns policy making or day-to-day operational activity. For instance, in a case which involved the Scottish Government's sexual health strategy, the Commissioner observed that "the information sought is policy formulation at its purest; that is, the actual drafts of the strategy".[15]

5.16   Once it has been established that information is within the scope of the exemption, then the issue is whether it is in the public interest to disclose or withhold all or some of the information.

BALANCING THE PUBLIC INTEREST

5.17   The clear intent of s 29 is to afford special protection to the deliberative process of government when formulating or developing its policies.

---

12   N Flynn, "Modernising British Government" in *Parliamentary Affairs*, vol 52 no 4, October 1999, p 590.
13   *Ibid*, p 591.
14   Waller *et al*, note 11 above, p 15.
15   Decision 075/2006: Mr Paul Hutcheon and the Scottish Executive, para 92.

This was made clear by the Justice Minister, who said this exemption was "required to ensure that matters can be candidly and frankly discussed in Government and a full record can be kept without at every turn taking into account the possibility of publication".[16]

However, this does not obviate the need to consider the public interest in disclosure and does not create a presumption against disclosure when doing so. This exemption is subject to the same test at s 2(1)(b) as all other qualified exemptions, which is whether "in all the circumstances of the case, the public interest in disclosing the information is not outweighed by that in maintaining the exemption".   **5.18**

The courts have acknowledged: **5.19**

> "That the statute creates or at least acknowledges a public interest in the disclosure of requested information is confirmed by the terms of section 2(1) which requires, in the case of non-absolute exemptions, the weighing of 'the public interest in disclosing information' against the public interest in maintaining the exemption."[17]

In England, the same position has been taken by the Information Tribunal: **5.20**

> "It can be said … that there is an assumption built into FOIA, that the disclosure of information by public authorities on request is in itself of value and in the public interest, in order to promote transparency and accountability in relation to the activities of public authorities."[18]

Despite this, there has been a quasi-absolute exemption flavour to some of the submissions which have been made to the Commissioner, suggesting broadly that in most circumstances any information to do with policy making should be withheld as not being in the public interest.   **5.21**

Variously, it has been argued that.   **5.22**

- the public interest weighs against disclosure as policy making on an issue continues over lengthy periods;
- the sensitivity of a subject requires all information related to it to be withheld;
- disclosure prior to the policy being decided or policy outcome achieved would affect the quality of advice or deliberation;

---

16 Jim Wallace, MSP, Justice 1 Committee, February 26 2002, col 2346.
17 *Scottish Ministers v Scottish Information Commissioner (William Alexander's Application)* [2006] CSIH 8.
18 *Department for Work and Pensions v Information Commission* (EA/2006/0040), para 29.

- disclosure once the policy outcome had been achieved would unhelpfully re-open debate;
- information will be taken out of context or misinterpreted, therefore adversely affecting the capacity to deliver policy objectives.

5.23 In the circumstances of a case, some of these may well justify information being withheld (although the Ministers' original code of practice did not permit misinterpretation to be taken into account when considering the public interest in whether to disclose information).[19]

5.24 However, in many cases these arguments have been enveloped within a blanket approach which appears to maintain that the public interest weighs heavily in favour of protecting the policy-making process in principle (not just the formulation of a particular policy or the sensitivity of the information in question), to the extent of creating a strong presumption of non-disclosure in general.

5.25 However, this approach has been resisted by the Commissioner in favour of one which discerns factors which influence whether information on policy making should be disclosed in the public interest or not .

TIMING OF THE REQUEST

5.26 An obvious factor is the timing of the request and the stage at which policy formulations has reached. Section 29 of FOISA clearly contains an acknowledgement that the degree to which protection needs to be given shifts after a policy has been determined, by stipulating that statistical information which is used to provide an informed background to the taking of a decision is not to be regarded as relating to the formulation or development of policy *once* that decision has been taken.[20] More generally, it may be found that the balance of the public interest may shift in favour of disclosure following a decision, meaning that information which it may have been premature to disclose before a policy decision was taken may warrant being put into the public domain subsequently.

5.27 However, on issues of timing, it is not necessary for the policy to be carried fully into effect or wholly discarded before the information can be disclosed. Delays and changes in policy thinking may warrant disclosure on the ground of public accountability.

5.28 In the prominent *Alexander* case cited previously, the Scottish Executive (as it then was) was asked in 2005 for any information it held

---

19 Scottish Ministers' Code of Practice on the discharge of functions by public authorities under the Freedom of Information (Scotland) Act 2002, para 75.
20 FOISA, s 29(2).

regarding the commencement of certain sections of the Law Reform (Miscellaneous Provisions) (Scotland) Act 1990.

Ministers claimed, in refusing to provide the information, that **5.29** a decision not to introduce these provisions had been taken in early 1997 but, since then, it had remained a matter of ongoing policy formulation. On the face of it, this meant that a policy decision had been taken in 1997, but policy formulation on the matter which had begun in 1997 within the Scottish Office under the Conservative administration was continued by the Scottish Office under the Labour Government elected later that year before being carried on under the devolved Labour/Liberal Democrat Scottish Executive following the Scottish Parliament election in 1999, and was still being formulated by the new administration, following a further election in 2003.

The Commissioner did not accept that it was a seamless process of **5.30** policy formulation and found that a distinct and active phase of policy development had started in the relatively recent past. Information pre-dating this was less sensitive because it belonged to a superseded phase of policy formulation and the public interest warranted it being disclosed.[21]

In another high-profile case, the Commissioner determined that **5.31** information prepared by the Office of the Chief Economic Adviser setting out revised revenue projections from a local income tax (and the assumptions upon which they were founded) should be disclosed after the Government had announced that it would delay bringing forward any legislation to introduce such a tax until the next Parliament.[22]

These are matters of judgement turning on the facts and circum- **5.32** stances of the case. On a policy issue of some political sensitivity, Ministers may be justified in seeking to preserve a "private space" for discussion, and to ensure that not only they but those they are engaging in policy discussion (including civil servants, expert advisers and representatives of stakeholder organisations) are fully able to consider options and consequences without inhibition.

In such a case involving a "summit" on sectarianism in Scotland, **5.33** the Commissioner said: "on a matter of sensitivity such as sectarianism in Scotland, it is in the public interest to allow officials and Ministers the space to float ideas, to argue amongst themselves and to come to

21 Decision 057/2005: Mr William Alexander and the Scottish Executive. This case was appealed by the Ministers to the Court of Session which upheld the Commissioner's decision in January 2007.

22 Decision 025/2011: Mr Simon Johnson of *The Daily Telegraph* and the Scottish Ministers. This case was appealed by Ministers to the Court of Session in March 2011 but the appeal was withdrawn in July 2011 and the information released to Mr Johnson.

conclusions about what the policy should be".[23] Even so, he went on to point out that this was particularly the case where the information is of recent origin and involves issues, people and activities which are still currently engaged on the policy issue. Where the content is of a greater vintage it may still retain the quality of being drafts, options etc, but may have lost any capacity to cause harm as a result of the passage of time, so the public interest balance may shift.

5.34   In general, it might be said that more weight is given to arguments for withholding information where policy discussions are at an early stage as compared with information regarding a policy which has been determined and made known and has been or is being carried into effect.

CONTENT OF THE INFORMATION

5.35   The second main factor to take into account is the *content* of the information. While this is a class-based exemption, meaning that all of the information related to the formulation or development of a policy comes within its scope, when it comes to the consideration of the balance of the public interest in disclosure, the content of the information can have a bearing. Even on a controversial issue which is currently being developed, there may be information which can be disclosed, either because it is already largely in the public domain or because it consists of routine or innocuous material.

5.36   These considerations were at the fore in a case concerning the policy of providing an additional 1,000 police officers in Scotland's communities. Political arguments ensued as to the extent to which this commitment was being met by government and whether the resources could be said to be "additional" capacity.

5.37   Ministers argued that if the withheld information were to be disclosed while the issue remained "live", there would be the inherent danger that certain arguments might be taken out of context, open to misrepresentation or perceived to be misleading and that the way the issue might appear in the press would have a stronger influence on officials' thinking than longer-term policy making. The consequence would be to inhibit Ministers, and the members of the Additional Policing Capacity Board set up to deliver on the policy objective, from proper consideration of relevant issues, which would be harmful as the programme of deployment was still under way.

5.38   The arguments made by Ministers against disclosure were largely being made generically and did not take sufficient account of the

---

23   Decision 166/2006: Mr Martin Williams of *The Herald* and the Scottish Executive, para 60.

specific circumstances of the case, with regard to the content of the information or the state of policy making at the time of the request.

As a consequence, the Commissioner noted: **5.39**

> "applying the Ministers' broad arguments means that they are of the view that it would not be in the public interest to release certain information even though it is already in the public domain … the Commissioner should conclude that, on balance, the public interest would be better served by withholding relatively innocuous, factual information, for example, a note of a visit having been taken by the Cabinet Secretary to Tulliallan Police College on 10 March 2008. Yet that visit was referred to in the Ministers' press release and was widely reported in the media at the time. The Commissioner cannot agree that release of such information could be contrary to the public interest".[24]

More importantly, the Commissioner found that the policy had largely   **5.40**
been determined and was being carried into effect at the time of the request. While it would be subject to further discussion and adjustment as the programme of additional resource was being rolled out, he did not believe that those involved in decision making (many of whom were high-ranking police officers) would be inhibited in contributing to further developments.

The *status* of the documents in which the information is contained   **5.41**
may have a bearing on the judgement as to what is in the public interest to disclose, but does not automatically determine the outcome. As an example, when an MSP asked for papers relating to the comparative costs of the procurement of a Public Private Partnership prison as opposed to one procured in the public sector, the relevant information was to be found in two Cabinet papers. The Scottish Prison Service (the "SPS") put forward some broadly applicable arguments regarding the nature of Cabinet discussions and why in general these should not be disclosed. However, there is no specific exemption for Cabinet minutes or papers in FOISA (as exists in some other countries). Rather than rely simply on the status of the documents, the SPS disclosed some material from those Cabinet papers in the public interest. Then with regard to the content, the authority candidly indicated that the withheld information set out a range of policy options for Ministers' consideration in respect of specific prisons and that, throughout the documents, consideration is given to the stated policy of the Government (the commitment to a publicly owned and run prison

---

24   Decision 077/2010: Mark Howarth and the Scottish Ministers, para 56.

service) and the realities of being able to move towards it legally, practically and financially.

5.42   It was the combination of the arguments specific to the circumstances of the request, and the fact that due regard had been given to putting information into the public domain, in the public interest, that persuaded the Commissioner that information had been justifiably withheld.[25]

CONCLUSION

5.43   It is readily evident from the Commissioner's decisions that the exemption at s 29 applying to the formulation of government policy has often been correctly applied and that the submissions made have justified why the information should be withheld in the public interest. Equally clearly, there is no basis for an approach which regards it as providing a quasi-absolute assurance that no information relating to policy making will be disclosed.

---

25   Decision 145/2008: Paul Martin, MSP and the Scottish Prison Service.

Chapter 6

KEY ISSUE 4: PERSONAL INFORMATION – DEALING WITH THIRD-PARTY DATA

Perhaps the most frequent and contentious disputes under FOISA   **6.01**
concern third-party data and whether the exemption at s 38(1)(b)
applies. Like tectonic plates, the right to information and the right to
privacy grind against each other, often sending out seismic shocks
which disrupt any settled notion of a *modus vivendi* between the two
regimes. The task is to reconcile the legal imperative to keep personal
data safe and to prevent it being misused by those who have collected it,
with the wide right to be given information held by public authorities,
some of which may include or be derived from personal data. In doing
so, the courts have made it clear that the general presumption in favour
of disclosure created by FOISA does not apply to personal data, taking
into account the powerful rights and obligations established by Council
Directive 95/46/EC on the protection of individuals with regard to the
processing of personal data and on the free movement of such data (the
"Directive") and, under Art 8 of the European Convention on Human
Rights, the right to respect for private life.

Lord Hope has put it plainly by saying "In my opinion there is   **6.02**
no presumption in favour of the release of personal data under the
general obligation that FOISA lays down" and that the references
which FOISA makes to provisions of the Data Protection Act 1998
must be understood in the light of the legislative purpose of the 1998
Act: "The guiding principle is the protection of the fundamental rights
and freedoms of persons, and in particular their right to privacy with
respect to the processing of personal data."[1]

Where disclosure of information would contravene the data   **6.03**
protection principles, the exemption in FOISA is absolute, and the
authority is not required to go on to consider where the balance of the
public interest lies in relation to the information.[2]

---

1   *Common Services Agency* v *SIC* [2008] UKHL 47, per Lord Hope at para 7.
2   There are a number of different exemptions in s 38 of FOISA, but only two are subject
    to the "public interest" test – s 38(1)(b) when read with s 38(2)(a)(ii) (where disclosure

6.04   In practice, the key issues to consider are: (a) whether the requested information constitutes personal data; and, if so, (b) whether disclosure would contravene any of the data protection principles.

(A) DOES THE REQUESTED INFORMATION CONSTITUTE PERSONAL DATA?

6.05   Clearly, if the information in question does not constitute personal data, the exemption under s 38(1)(b) of FOISA cannot be applied, and there is no need to consider further the complex tests which have to be satisfied before deciding whether the information request can be complied with.

6.06   The two main elements of personal data are that the information must "relate to" a living person, and that the person must be identifiable.[3] Information will "relate to" a person if it:

- is about them;
- is linked to them;
- has some biographical significance for them;
- is used to inform decisions affecting them;
- has them as its main focus or;
- impacts on them in any way.

6.07   It may appear obvious that the information is personal – and often it is: for example a statement to the police by the victim of an assault; the contents of a CV; or a performance appraisal of an employee.

6.08   However, even if a person is readily identifiable, it does not necessarily mean that the information *relates* to them.

6.09   In one case all information relating to the compassionate release of the Libyan national convicted of bombing the Pan Am plane which exploded over Lockerbie, Abdelbaset Ali Mohmed Al-Megrahi, from Greenock Prison was withheld by Strathclyde Police on the basis that it was the personal data of him or his family. However, the Commissioner found that it was not possible to take a blanket approach to the information which had been withheld, but that it was

---

would contravene s 10 of the DPA) and s 38(1)(b) when read with s 38(3) (where the data subject would have no right to access if the information if they made a subject access request for it).

3 The UK Information Commissioner, who is responsible for enforcing the DPA throughout the UK, has issued a technical guidance note entitled "Determining what is personal data": http://www.ico.gov.uk/upload/documents/library/data_protection/detailed_specialist_guides/personal_data_flowchart_v1_with_preface001.pdf.

necessary to consider the actual information, including the extent to which the focus of the information was on a third party and to what extent the information is biographical, has personal connotations or affects the data subject's privacy. The information which had been withheld concerned security arrangements to be put in place for Mr Al-Megrahi's relocation. While the Commissioner agreed that a small amount of the information withheld from the applicant was the personal data of Mr Al-Megrahi or his family, the focus of most of the information was the number of police officers to be involved, their roles, how long they would be working and how much the security arrangements might cost. Clearly, it could not be said that such information had no relevance at all to Mr Al-Megrahi or his family, but with reference to the "continuum of relevance or proximity to the data subject" envisaged by Auld LJ in *Durant v Financial Services Authority*,[4] the Commissioner came to the conclusion that the focus of such information was not on Mr Al-Megrahi or his family, and, further, that the information was not "biographical in a significant way", again as envisaged by Auld LJ.[5]

Such a conclusion may be arrived at even where the names of individuals are involved. The UK Information Tribunal, in considering a request for the names of individuals who had attended events or received corporate hospitality from a public authority under the UK Freedom of Information Act 2000, came to the conclusion that the names of the individuals were not personal data, on the basis that they were not the focus of the information.[6]

6.10

DO STATISTICS EFFECTIVELY ANONYMISE PERSONAL DATA?

In some cases, there is no doubt that if a person is identifiable, the information relates to them, but the question is whether they are actually identifiable. This has been a particularly fraught issue when dealing with requests for statistics, and fissures in the interpretation of the legislation continue to appear. Depending on the outcome, statistical data may become public at a level of detail which cautious public authorities would have previously sought to prevent, to guard against the possibility of inadvertent identification of an individual; or it could mean that currently accepted release of national data derived from sensitive personal data is cast into doubt.

6.11

---

4   [2003] EWCA Civ 1746.
5   Decision 007/2011: Mr Gordon Aikman and the Chief Constable of Strathclyde Police.
6   Tony Harcup and the Information Commissioner and Yorkshire Forward (EA/2007/0058).

6.12   The issue came to prominence following a request for information made less than 2 weeks after FOISA came into force. This became, in turn, the first application made to the Commissioner and the first freedom of information appeal in the UK to be considered by the House of Lords. It was also the first time that the House of Lords had ever been asked to consider the definition of "personal data".

6.13   In 2005, Mr Collie, a researcher for the Scottish Green Party, asked the Common Services Agency for the National Health Service (the CSA) to provide him with information about the numbers of cases of childhood leukaemia in Dumfries and Galloway, broken down by year and by census ward. The CSA refused to disclose the information, because it was concerned that the disclosure would run the risk of identifying the children involved.

6.14   Although leukaemia is the commonest of childhood cancers, only 40 cases are diagnosed for the whole of Scotland each year. Disclosure of the incidence for each of the 47 census wards in Dumfries and Galloway would show that the vast majority had no cases and pinpoint the specific small geographical areas where a diagnosis had occurred. Given that the total population of a census ward in that region ranges from 2,400 to 3,500, it would be possible for any person seeking to identify children with leukaemia to focus enquiries on the relatively small number of households where they lived. However, the Commissioner ordered the CSA to disclose the numbers either as a total for the whole of the health board area, or by census ward, using a statistical tool described as "barnardisation" (which had been brought to his attention by the CSA), designed to disclose numbers in a way which gives the flavour of the statistics without disclosing the actual numbers involved. However, subsequently, the CSA, worried that disclosing information even in this format would lead to the children being identified, appealed the decision to the Court of Session (which upheld the Commissioner's decision) and then to the House of Lords.

6.15   The House of Lords agreed that the Commissioner was entitled to require an authority to respond to an information request by considering what information could be provided even if the actual information which had been asked for proved to be exempt from disclosure under s 38; this could be done by barnardisation or broad aggregation into larger numbers over a wider area.

6.16   In coming to a decision, the Lords looked at Directive 95/46/EC and, in particular, at Recital (26) of the Preamble to this Directive.

Recital (26) says: **6.17**

"Whereas the principles of protection must apply to any information concerning an identified or identifiable person; whereas, to determine whether a person is identifiable, account should be taken of all the means likely reasonably to be used either by the controller or by any other person to identify the said person; whereas the principles of protection shall not apply to data rendered anonymous in such a way that the data subject is no longer identifiable; whereas codes of conduct within the meaning of Article 27 may be a useful instrument for providing guidance as to the ways in which data may be rendered anonymous and retained in a form in which identification of the data subject is no longer possible."

Recital (26) makes it clear that the data protection principles shall not   **6.18**
apply to data which has been rendered anonymous in such a way that the data subject is no longer identifiable. The Lords were therefore clear that the definition of "personal data" in s 1(1) of the DPA had to be taken to permit the release of information which had been rendered anonymous in such a way that individuals were no longer identifiable from it.

The question to be determined, however, was "identifiable by   **6.19**
whom?". Section 1(1) of the DPA defines "personal data" as data which relate to a living individual who can be identified:

(a) from those data; or
(b) from those data and other information which is in the possession of, or is likely to come into the possession of, the data controller.

In the leading opinion in the case, Lord Hope said, at para 24:   **6.20**

"The formula which this part of the definition uses indicates that each of these two components must have a contribution to make to the result. Clearly, if the 'other information' is incapable of adding anything and 'those data' by themselves cannot lead to identification, the definition will not be satisfied. The 'other information' will have no part to play in the identification. The same result would seem to follow if 'those data' have been put into a form from which the individual or individuals to whom they relate cannot be identified at all, even with the assistance of the other information from which they were derived. In that situation, a person who has access to both sets of information will find nothing in 'those data' that will enable him to make the identification. It will be the other information only, and not anything in 'those data', that will lead him to this result."

6.21   No argument was made in that case or in similar cases that individuals could be identified by the data alone, as the disputed information is simply numbers. The practical concern of bodies such as the CSA and indeed the Commissioner has been to guard against identification once the information left the control of the authority and came into the possession of the recipient by utilising that number with some other information to effect identification.

6.22   However, the court indicated that this may not be the sole consideration. Lord Hope took the view, at para 26, that "the question is whether the data controller, or anybody else who was in possession of the barnardised data, would be able to identify the living individual or individuals to whom the data in that form related". He acknowledged that if it was impossible for the recipient of such altered or disguised data to identify anyone, then the information would not constitute "personal data" in his hands. "But", he pointed out, "we are concerned in this case with its status while it is still in the hands of the data controller, as the question is whether it is or is not exempt from the duty of disclosure that FOISA says must be observed by him".

6.23   This issue has continued to be considered by the courts. In 2005, the Pro-Life Alliance made a request under the UK Freedom of Information Act 2000 for abortion statistics held by the Department of Health. Until 2003, statistics had been published detailing the number of abortions carried out where there was a substantial risk that, if the child were born, it would suffer from such physical or mental abnormalities as to be seriously handicapped ("ground (e) abortions"). The statistics gave the abnormality in question and stated whether the abortion had been carried out after 24 weeks. However, in 2003, the Department of Health significantly reduced the detail of the statistics released, removing any cell counts under 10, producing no figures for ground (e) abortions over 24 weeks and providing only total figures for congenital abnormalities (subdivided into two categories) and chromosomal abnormalities.

6.24   The Pro-Life Alliance asked the Department of Health to provide it with the figures for 2003, but in the same format as the information had been disclosed in 2002. The Department of Health refused to do this. The case was appealed to the Information Commissioner, who ordered the information to be disclosed. That decision was subsequently appealed to the Information Tribunal.

6.25   Before the Information Tribunal, the Information Commissioner and the Department of Health argued different interpretations of Lord

Hope's judgment. The Tribunal's decision[7] preferred the Department of Health's interpretation and came to the conclusion that what matters is whether the data, even if it is not identifiable to a third party, could be reconstituted to its original form by the data controller (here, the Department of Health). Only if it was not possible for the data controller to do this could the information be released without further reference to the DPA by virtue of being fully anonymised. On that basis, the Tribunal concluded that abortion statistics requested from the Department of Health constituted "personal data" as the authority could readily identify patients from the records it held.

The obvious problem with this conclusion is that for all practical purposes it is virtually impossible to come up with a formula or regime which would prevent a data controller, who holds the personal records, reconstituting the data. As a consequence, almost all statistics abstracted from personal data held by an authority would be likely to remain as personal data. Clearly this would be at odds with currently accepted practice, and could have implications for major national data-gathering exercises such as the Scottish Household Survey, given that each time the statistics were disclosed (regardless of whether this was in response to an FOI request), the data controller would be required to find a condition in Sch 2 to the DPA which would permit the data to be disclosed, even if it were accepted that the statistics, except in the hands of the data controller, were fully anonymised. This could cause particular problems where the statistics related to sensitive personal data (for example, racial or ethnic origin, religious beliefs, trade union membership, physical or mental health, sexual life and criminal offences). Such figures would never be capable of release, even at a national level, unless one of the very restrictive conditions in Sch 3 to the DPA could also be applied. **6.26**

The practical inability to anonymise information where the data controller has personal records from which statistical data is derived would effectively mean that Recital (26) has no purpose. As Baroness Hale in the CSA case observed at para 91: **6.27**

> "We would all like the legal position to be that, if the risk of identification can indeed be eliminated, the Agency is obliged to provide it. That reflects the expectation in Recital 26 of the European Directive 95/46/EC: that the principles of protection shall not apply to data rendered anonymous in such a way that the data subject is no longer identifiable. It would have been so much easier if this had been clearly stated in the Data Protection Act 1998."

---

7 *Department of Health v The Information Commissioner and Pro Life Alliance* (EA/2008/0074).

6.28   Baroness Hale, while agreeing with Lord Hope, therefore seemed to take a more pragmatic view, in expressing the route by which information could be disclosed into the public domain. In her opinion (para 92):

> "The Agency may well have the key which links those data back to the individual patients. The Agency therefore could identify them and remains bound by the data protection principles when processing the data internally. But the recipient of the information will not be able to identify the individuals either from the data themselves, or from the data plus any other information held by the Agency, because the recipient will not have access to that other information. For the purpose of this particular act of processing, therefore, which is disclosure of these data in this form to these people, no living individual to whom they relate is identifiable."[8]

6.29

The Information Tribunal's decision in the abortion statistics case was subsequently appealed to the High Court but, before that hearing took place, the House of Lords' judgment, and the means by which an individual might be identified from the disclosure of statistics, was the
6.30   subject of discussion in the Court of Session.

Three housing associations had asked the Chief Constable of Strathclyde Police for the numbers of registered sex offenders ("RSOs") in and around Glasgow, by postcode area. The Commissioner agreed with the Chief Constable that the disclosure of the statistics would identify individual RSOs and that they should be withheld. The housing associations subsequently appealed the decision to the Court
6.31   of Session.

The Court of Session did not find it necessary to choose between or reconcile what was described as the "hard-line" approach of Lord Hope with the "purposive, even adventurous" line taken by Baroness Hale. It elected to avoid commenting on the "hard-line" approach, under which, according to the Lord President, "on a strict interpretation of the domestic legislation, anonymised information could not be released unless the data controller at the same time destroyed the raw material from which the anonymisation was made (and any means of retrieving

---

8   However, there has been a move to follow Baroness Hale's reasoning in a decision of the Upper Tribunal which considered the disclosure of personal data in a request concerned with the treatment of persons detained in the conflicts in Iraq and Afghanistan: *All Party Parliamentary Group on Extraordinary Rendition and the Information Commissioner and the Ministry of Defence* [2011] UKUT 153 (AAC). The Upper Tribunal came to the view that there had not been a majority judgment in the CSA case and that it was therefore able to follow Baroness Hale's reasoning.

that material)", other than to observe that "it is hardly consistent with Recital (26) to the Directive".[9]

WOULD A PERSON BE IDENTIFIABLE IF STATISTICS WERE MADE PUBLIC?

That Glasgow housing associations case, however, focused attention on the extent to which a person could be said to be identifiable when the information was put into the public domain. The presence of sex offenders in certain areas has been the subject of several FOI requests in Scotland. Broadly, it can be said that the police have been extremely reluctant to reveal such information except at very large aggregations, fearing that vigilante action may be pursued or that high-risk offenders might go to ground. However, the Commissioner has considered this stance to be too cautious and has ordered the disclosure of statistics relating to the number of registered sex offenders of no fixed abode in the Northern Constabulary area[10] and of all RSOs for the much smaller area of Peterhead/Buchan area of Aberdeenshire.[11] In coming to the likelihood or possibility of identification, account was taken of the geographical size and the resident population of an area, the presence of any major population centres or conurbations and the number of registered sex offenders per head of population.

6.32

In the Glasgow housing associations case, the information requested was statistical information about the number of registered sex offenders living in specified postcode districts, within the Greater Glasgow area. The populations in each of these districts vary from around 4,000 to over 10,000 – with one exception where the population is under 1,000. Furthermore, the request required the data to be broken down by the risk categories. The Commissioner's decision focused on the Recital (26) requirement that, when considering whether a person is identifiable, "account should be taken of all the means likely reasonably to be used by the controller or by any other person to identify the said person". He concluded that the geographical and population size of the postcode districts meant it was unsafe to release the statistics and that there was a risk of identification where they were combined with other publicly

6.33

9 See the opinion of the Lord President at para 19: *Craigdale Housing Association and Others v Scottish Information Commissioner* [2010] CSIH 43.
10 Decision 222/2006: Mr Murdo McLeod of *Scotland on Sunday* and the Chief Constable of Northern Constabulary.
11 Decision 177/2007: Sam Coull and the Chief Constable of Grampian Police – note that Grampian Police had not relied on the exemption in s 38 of FOISA here.

available information, especially in light of evidence from the police of attempts to locate and identify sex offenders.

6.34   The court agreed that the effect of disclosure was to place the information in the public domain, not just into the hands of the recipients, in this case the housing associations,[12] saying: "A purposive approach therefore required a consideration of the information already available in that domain." But "It is not clear from the decision letter why the disclosure of a statistic that in a particular district the number of resident RSOs was four or fourteen or forty would lead to the identification of the individuals in question or what other information when taken with these statistics would reasonably allow for such identification".[13]

6.35   The effect of this opinion is to place the onus upon the authority to explain the route by which identification would be possible when dealing with statistics which do not ostensibly identify any individual. If it is not possible to evidence how individuals would be identified then the data is said to be anonymous.

6.36   As noted above, the Court of Session did not find it necessary to choose between the different approaches taken by Lord Hope or Baroness Hale in the CSA case. As a result, uncertainty over the definition of personal data remained.

6.37   The matter was, however, addressed by the High Court in the appeal by the Department of Health against the Information Tribunal's decision in the abortions statistics case.[14]

6.38   The High Court came to the conclusion that, although the Department of Health held both the statistics and other information which would identify the patients who had had the abortions, the information would not be personal data in the hands of the recipients, as individuals could not be identified from the statistics. As such, in the High Court's view, the statistics were not exempt from disclosure under the UK equivalent of s 38(1)(b).

6.39   The Department of Health subsequently disclosed the abortion statistics to the Pro-Life Alliance.

6.40   Shortly after, the Commissioner issued a revised decision in the Glasgow housing associations case.[15] Following further investigation, Strathclyde Police had been unable to satisfy the Commissioner that

---

12 See *Office of Government Commerce v Information Commissioner* [2008] EWHC 774 (Admin), [2009] 3 WLR 627, per Stanley Burnton J at para 72.

13 At para 29.

14 *Department of Health v Information Commissioner* [2011[EWHC 1430 (Admin).

15 Decision 014/2009: Dunbritton Housing Association, Craigdale Housing Association and Blochairn Housing Co-operative (dated 12 July 2011).

disclosure of the statistics would lead to the identification of one or more of the offenders or what other information, when taken together with these statistics, would enable identification. He therefore ordered the statistics to be disclosed, although not broken down into risk categories.[16]

(B) IF IDENTIFICATION WOULD OCCUR, WOULD DISCLOSURE CONTRAVENE THE DATA PROTECTION PRINCIPLES?

Schedule 1 to the DPA lists eight principles with which data controllers are required to comply.   6.41

Although regard has to be had to all the principles, in practice it is the first data protection principle which has to be satisfied when considering whether information can be released in response to a FOISA request. This principle states that personal data shall be processed *fairly* and *lawfully* and, in particular, shall not be processed unless at least one of the *conditions* in Sch 2 to the DPA is met and, in the case of *sensitive* personal data, at least one of the conditions in Sch 3 is also met.   6.42

There are therefore three separate aspects to the first data protection principle: (i) fairness; (ii) lawfulness; and (iii) the conditions in the Schedules. However, these three aspects are interlinked. If there is a specific condition which permits the personal data to be disclosed, the disclosure will probably also be fair and lawful.   6.43

THE SCHEDULE 2 CONDITIONS

Schedule 2 to the DPA lists six conditions relevant for the purposes of the first principle. These can be summarised as follows: 6.44

(1) the data subject has given his consent to the processing;

(2) the processing is necessary for the performance of a contract to which the data subject is a party or for the taking of steps at the request of the data subject with a view to entering into a contract;

(3) the processing is necessary for compliance with any legal obligation to which the data subject is subject;

---

16   He agreed with Strathclyde Police that the risk categories were exempt from disclosure under FOISA, ss 35(1)(a) and 39(1).

(4) the processing is necessary to protect the vital interests of the data subject;

(5) the processing is necessary for the administration of justice or for the exercise of certain functions, including those conferred on any person by or under an enactment;

(6) the processing is necessary for the purposes of legitimate interests pursued by the data controller or by the third party or parties to whom the data are disclosed, except where the processing is unwarranted in any particular case by reason of prejudice to the rights and freedoms or legitimate interests of the data subject.

6.45   (The Secretary of State may also specify particular circumstances in which Sch 2 is to be taken to be satisfied.)

6.46   Again, all relevant conditions should be considered by public authorities but, in dealing with requests under FOISA, conditions 1 and 6 are the only ones likely to be relevant.

6.47   The first condition requires that the data subject has consented to the processing. According to the Directive, consent must be freely given, specific and informed[17] While this condition is relatively easy to understand, condition 6 is more complex. In effect, there are three separate tests:

1. Does the applicant have a legitimate interest in obtaining this personal data?

6.48   There is no definition within the DPA of the term "legitimate interest". It is often possible to discern a wider public interest, such as scrutiny of the actions of public bodies or public safety, which can be said to be shared or expressed by the applicant. When a journalist asked for details of the number of police officers convicted of drink driving and whether they had been dismissed, disciplined etc, this had no bearing upon his own private interests. It was not felt necessary to enquire further as to why he, personally, wanted the information. Due to the serious nature of such convictions, and the fact that a police officer's duty is to maintain public order and prevent and detect crimes, there appeared to be a clear legitimate interest in knowing what had happened to the police officers convicted of the offences. How the police deal with such incidents is a matter of public confidence and disclosure into the public domain via the press was legitimate.[18]

---

17   Article 2(h) of the Directive.
18   Decision 065/2009: Mr Ian Cobain of *The Guardian* and the Chief Constable of Dumfries and Galloway Constabulary.

In some cases, however, the legitimate interest might be personal   6.49
to the applicant, concerning grievances which they are pursuing.
Notwithstanding that the legislation is generally "applicant blind",
when it comes to personal data, the legitimate interests of the
applicant are a consideration, and may have to be enquired into
by the authority before determining whether the information
should be disclosed. Even then, a wider public interest may be discerned.
For instance, a householder was not content with assurances given
by a local authority technical expert that developments on adjacent
land had not caused instability to his property. The Commissioner
found that the individual applicant had a legitimate personal interest
in knowing the qualifications of the employee on whom the Council
relied to make decisions affecting his personal property. In addition,
he also considered that a wider legitimate interest was shared with the
general public in knowing that those public authority employees who
have a significant role in making decisions on issues relating to public
safety are appropriately qualified to do so.[19]

However, there are cases where the lack of a perceived legitimate   6.50
interest in personal data is a sufficient basis for refusing a request.
In one case[20] the applicant did not have a demonstrable legitimate
interest in receiving the telephone numbers dialled by councillors on
mobile phones provided by the local authority.

2. If yes, is the disclosure necessary to achieve these legitimate interests?

In considering whether disclosure is necessary, the question to be   6.51
asked is whether the disclosure is proportionate as a means and fairly
balanced as to ends, or whether the legitimate interests could be met
by means which interfere less with the privacy of the data subjects.[21]

This test could be taken to allow judgemental questioning of the   6.52
purpose to which the information will be put (either by questioning
the applicant or simply by assuming what that purpose may be).

---

19 Decision 055/2007: Professor Ronald MacDonald and Highland Council.
20 Decision 043/2011: Mr Y and Aberdeen City Council,
21 The word "necessary" within condition 6 (and, indeed, within all of the conditions in
     Schs 2 and 3 to the DPA) should reflect the meaning attributed to it by the European Court
     of Human Rights when justifying an interference with a recognised right, namely that
     there should be a pressing social need and that the interference be both proportionate
     as to means and fairly balanced as to ends. The meaning of the word is, therefore, not
     synonymous with "indispensable", nor has it the flexibility of such expressions such as
     "admissible", "ordinary", "useful", "reasonable" or "desirable". See *Sunday Times v United
     Kingdom* (1979) 2 EHRR 245 and *Corporate Officer of the House of Commons and the Information
     Commissioner, Heather Brooke et al* [2008] EWHC 1084 (Admin).

The authority might be expected to come to a view as to whether a sought-after outcome may be served only by disclosing all of the information. If it judges that the same outcome could be achieved with less interference with the privacy of data subjects, then the condition would not be met. However, coming to such a judgement could be highly intrusive as to the personal circumstances of the applicant, for example where the information is wanted to pursue a complaint against the authority or a third party.

6.53   An activist with the environmental campaigning group "Plane Stupid" complained that she had been approached by a police officer to act as an informant. She claimed there was a lack of clarity about the officer's employment status at the time and asked for the date of his commission to confirm that he was a serving police officer when she was approached.

6.54   The Commissioner accepted that she had a legitimate interest in obtaining the requested information. However, he also found that a straightforward confirmation of the officer's employment status at the relevant time, which he would consider less intrusive in the circumstances, would suffice. As Strathclyde Police was prepared to confirm that it employed the officer, he concluded that disclosure of the officer's commission date was not necessary for the purposes of the applicant's legitimate interests.[22]

6.55   In practice, where applicants have established a legitimate interest, the test of necessity tends not to be the focus of argument. Although authorities do express doubts as to whether the information is capable of allowing certain conclusions to be drawn, that often forms part of the argument of unwarranted prejudice to the interests of the data subject.

3. Even if the processing is necessary for the legitimate interests of the applicant, would the disclosure nevertheless cause unwarranted prejudice to the rights and freedoms or legitimate interests of the data subjects?

6.56   Notwithstanding that the applicant, and the public more generally, have a legitimate interest in the information, disclosure may still not be justified if the loss of privacy may have an adverse effect on the data subject which is not warranted. Only if the legitimate interests of the applicant outweigh those of the data subjects can the personal data be disclosed. The circumstances of the case bear heavily upon the outcome.

---

22   Decision 177/2010: Ms Matilda Gifford and the Chief Constable of Strathclyde Police.

For instance, when Detective Constable Shirley McKie denied that a   **6.57**
fingerprint at a murder scene was hers, it led to a train of events which
saw her acquitted of perjury, given apologies by Ministers and on
behalf of the police, and awarded a substantial out-of-court financial
settlement. The affair threw Scotland's fingerprint service into turmoil
and an official inquiry was commissioned. Perhaps not surprisingly,
freedom of information requests were made in relation to the case,
including by members of Ms McKie's family. This included information
from or about officers of the then Scottish Criminal Records Office,
fingerprint experts and Parliamentarians. Given the nature of the case,
some of this was clearly highly charged opinion, and touched upon
matters of employment and discipline.

In coming to a decision, the Commissioner determined that   **6.58**
the names and addresses of members of the public who had made
representations on the matter should be withheld. But disclosure
was justified where representations purported to express expert
opinion, given that it was in a professional capacity that influence was
being brought to bear on Ministers. Certain representations made by
SCRO officers to their local MSP could properly be withheld but, in
the circumstances of that case, other information held by Ministers
regarding the employment of those officers could be disclosed. In the
decision it was noted: "While it is very unusual for him to order the
disclosure of information which relates to disciplinary action being
taken against an individual, the Commissioner has taken account of
the amount of information about the action taken against the officers
in the public domain and the high profile of this case."[23]

As the McKie case shows, in coming to a view on the balance of   **6.59**
legitimate interests, account needs to be taken of:

- whether the information relates to the individual's public life (ie
  their work as a public official or employee) or their private life
  (ie their home, family, social life or finances). Information about
  an individual's private life will deserve more protection than
  information about them acting in an official or work capacity. As
  an example, identifying Scotland's surgeons and their surgical
  mortality rate, even though clearly personal data, was seen as
  relating entirely to their professional life and disclosure did not
  breach the data protection principles;[24]

---

23 Decision 109/2010: Iain McKie and Mhairi McKie and the Scottish Ministers, para 110.
24 Decision 065/2005: Mr Camillo Fracassini and the Common Services Agency for the
    Scottish Health Service.

- the seniority of an individual's position, and whether they have a public-facing role. The more senior a person is, the less likely it is that disclosing information about their public duties will be unwarranted or unfair. This has often been the basis for disclosure, for example, disclosing the identity of senior fire officers named in a report;[25]
- the potential harm or distress that may be caused by the disclosure. For example, there may be particular distress caused by the release of private information about family life. Some disclosures could also risk the fraudulent use of the disclosed information (for example, details of bank accounts) or pose a security risk (for example, addresses, work locations or travel plans where there is a risk of harassment or other credible threat to the individual). This type of disclosure is unlikely to be warranted;
- whether the individual has objected to the disclosure. However, although such an objection would be a factor to take into account, it is not automatically enough to make the disclosure unwarranted or unfair;[26]
- the reasonable expectations of the individual as to whether their information would be disclosed. However, as with consent, in the absence of other factors disclosure will not be automatically unwarranted or unfair just because the person was not aware of the possibility of disclosure.

THE SCHEDULE 3 CONDITIONS – SENSITIVE PERSONAL DATA

6.60   Schedule 3 to the DPA lists nine conditions relevant for the purposes of processing "sensitive personal data". These can be summarised as follows:

(1) the data subject has given his explicit consent to the processing of the personal data;
(2) the processing is necessary for the purposes of exercising or performing any right or obligation conferred or imposed by law on the data controller in connection with employment;
(3) the processing is necessary to protect the vital interests of the data subject or another person;

---

25   Decision 161/2007: Mr Michael McParlane and the Strathclyde Fire Board.
26   Decision 033/2010: Mr Tom Gordon and the Scottish Ministers.

(4) the processing is carried out by a not-for-profit body which exists for political, philosophical, religious or trade union purposes with appropriate safeguards;

(5) the information contained in the personal data has been made public as a result of steps deliberately taken by the data subject;

(6) the processing is necessary for the purposes of, or in connection with, any legal proceedings, for obtaining legal advice or establishing, exercising or defending legal rights;

(7) the processing is necessary for the administration of justice or for the exercise of certain functions, including those conferred on any person by or under an enactment;

(8) the processing is necessary for medical purposes and is undertaken by a health professional or equivalent;

(9) the processing is of sensitive personal data consisting of information as to racial or ethnic origin and is necessary for identifying or keeping under review equality of opportunity or treatment between persons of different racial or ethnic origins.

As with Sch 2, the Secretary of State can also specify other circumstances in which sensitive personal data can be processed. For example, the Data Protection (Processing of Sensitive Data) Order 2000[27] sets out additional conditions which permit the processing of sensitive personal data.

However, for the purposes of s 38 of FOISA, it is likely that only **6.61** conditions 1 and 5 of Sch 3 will be relevant, given that the other conditions are very restrictive in nature. Conditions 1 and 5 in themselves are restrictive; for condition 1 to apply, consent must be *explicit*. With condition 5, inadvertent disclosure by the data subject or disclosure which was intended to be confidential would not meet this condition.

In practice, it is extremely rare for an FOI request for sensitive **6.62** personal data to succeed. The power of the protection afforded in law is evident in cases concerning Abdelbaset Ali Mohmed Al-Megrahi. Following his release from a Scottish prison on compassionate grounds in 2009, politicians and journalists were among those demanding to know which doctors had been responsible for making the diagnosis and prognosis of his terminal cancer,[28] and to have

---

27 SI 2000/417.
28 Decision 190/2010: Thomas Smith of the *Daily Mirror* and the Scottish Ministers.

access to the monthly reports on Mr Al-Megrahi's medical condition that he was required to provide to his supervising officer as a condition of the licence governing his release from prison.[29] In both cases, the Commissioner found that this was sensitive personal data and, although some medical information had been released with Mr Al-Megrahi's consent, the remainder of the medical information (without the benefit of consent) could not lawfully be disclosed as none of the Sch 3 conditions could be satisfied. The question of whether there was a legitimate public interest in the information could not be taken into account, no matter the notoriety of the case and the political and media clamour.

6.63   Given the unlikelihood of disclosure being ordered, it is clearly important to establish whether information identifying any person does constitute sensitive personal data. In responding to a complex request for the number of students who had graduated from the University of Glasgow and the names of the schools the students had attended, the University refused to disclose the numbers where the number was less than five, on the basis that disclosing the figures would lead to the identification of pupils, and that this would be contrary to the data protection principles. The University also took the view that the figures were sensitive personal data, on the basis that disclosure would identify an individual as having attended a denominational or faith school.

6.64   In his decision,[30] the Commissioner agreed that disclosing the information would involve the processing of personal data; he was satisfied that disclosure would lead to individuals being identified. However, he did not agree that disclosing the information would involve the processing of sensitive personal data.

6.65   He noted that Art 8 of the Directive prohibits the processing of personal data which *would* reveal a person's religious or philosophical beliefs, except in limited circumstances (ie unless a condition in each of Sch 2 and 3 applies). However, he took the view that confirming that a person had attended a denominational or faith school some years before graduating would not reveal a person's beliefs, given the many reasons why someone would attend a particular school.

6.66   The Commissioner also considered that the purpose of the processing was relevant. In this case, the applicant was not seeking the numbers of pupils of a particular religion or faith who had gone on to attend the University. There was, therefore, no targeting of a specific religion or faith. Therefore, even if disclosing the numbers did reveal a

---

29   Decision 098/2010: George Foulkes MSP and East Renfrewshire Council.
30   Decision 156/2011: Mr Ralph Lucas and the University of Glasgow.

person's religion or faith (which the Commissioner did not consider it would), that would be incidental to the purpose for which the data was being processed. As that would be incidental to the purpose for which the data was being processed. As such, the Commissioner concluded that it was not necessary for a condition in Sch 3 to be met before the information could be disclosed.

FAIRNESS

Usually, if a condition in Sch 2 to the DPA (and Sch 3, where relevant) permits data to be processed, the disclosure will also be fair, as the same types of considerations are taken into account, such as the role and seniority of an individual, expectations of privacy etc.   **6.67**

However, wider issues may come into play here, such as the extent of public knowledge of personal details, which in other circumstances might not warrant disclosure, as happened in the Shirley McKie case mentioned above. In another decision, it was similarly found that the names of various officers mentioned in the complaint investigation report could be released due to the fact that the names were already known, with some having been referenced in a publicly available fatal accident inquiry report relating to the case.[31]   **6.68**

The use to which the information is likely to be put, such that the data subject may be put in fear or distress, may make it unfair to disclose. Here again, the specific circumstances of the case will have a strong bearing on the outcome. In one case, a local authority was able to evidence a genuine risk of harm should full details of the expense claims submitted by a named councillor be released. The Commissioner accepted that, while such information would usually be released, the specific circumstances of this case meant that disclosure would be unfair to the data subject.[32]   **6.69**

LAWFULNESS

With regard to the first principle, unlawful disclosure might arise where disclosure would represent a breach of confidence, or where there is a law that prohibits disclosure (for example, the Official Secrets Act 1989). However, in such cases, public authorities would usually seek to rely upon the exemptions in s 26 (Prohibitions on disclosure) or s 36 (Confidentiality) of FOISA. It should also be noted that if there are no conditions in Sch 2 and/or 3 which would   **6.70**

---

31   Decision 003/2007: Mr Allan McLeod and the Northern Joint Police Board.
32   Decision 235/2006: Councillor William Buchanan and Falkirk Council.

permit the personal data to be disclosed, then the disclosure of the data would of itself be unlawful, on the basis that disclosure would breach the first data protection principle (s 4(4) of the DPA requires data controllers to comply with the data protection principles). Any breach of a data protection principle will render disclosure unlawful. Conversely, in most cases, where a condition in Sch 2 (and Sch 3 where relevant) permits the data to be processed, it is likely that the disclosure will be otherwise lawful.

CONCLUSION

6.71   Legal commentators have observed that "strikingly complex provisions" govern the interaction between freedom of information law and the Data Protection Act.[33]

6.72   Some expressed concern that authorities may be put "between a rock and a hard place" so far as personal data was concerned, facing enforcement action by the Scottish Information Commissioner under FOISA if they did not disclose and enforcement action by the UK Commissioner under the DPA if they did.[34] That has not been the case. If anything, it may be that authorities have been able to resist disclosing certain information in response to specific requests utilising the s 38 exemption but, if choosing to publish similar data of their own accord, face no sanction from the UK ICO, not least because nobody believes the information relates to them personally.

---

33   A White, "Relationship between freedom of information and data protection" in P Carey and M Turle (eds), *Freedom of Information Handbook* (2nd edn, The Law Society, London, 2008) at p 247.

34   J Munro, *Public Law* (2nd edn, W Green, Edinburgh, 2007), p 225.

Chapter 7

KEY ISSUE 5: WHO WANTS TO KNOW? – ISSUES CONCERNING THE IDENTITY OF THE APPLICANT

The freedom of information rights in Scotland can be used by anyone, anywhere in the world. A request for information simply has to state the name of the applicant and an address for correspondence. An applicant does not have to identify themselves further, for example by way of citizenship, residence or professional status. Nor, except in very limited circumstances, do they have to justify their request by providing reasons as to why they want or need the information.   **7.01**

The intention of such an "applicant and purpose blind" approach is clearly to prevent authorities from providing information to some individuals or organisations but denying it to others because of who they are or the presumed motive for their request. In the past, authorities might have disclosed certain information to academic researchers but not to campaigners; or been reluctant to provide information to a known troublesome individual which might otherwise be given to another member of the public. Such a discretionary, not to say discriminatory, approach which may have been possible under a voluntary disclosure regime is not tolerable where there is a statutory right of access to information.   **7.02**

This stance is consistent with international provision, as described by McDonagh and Paterson: **7.03**

> "Three well known and interconnected principles of FOI legislation militate against the taking into account of the circumstances of individual applicants. The first is that FOI should operate in a manner that is 'applicant blind'. The second is that disclosure under FOI should be treated as though it were disclosure to the world, while the third requires that the motives and identity of an applicant should be ignored when assessing whether or not disclosure is in the public interest in the context of claims for exemption which require public interest assessments."[1]

---

1   "Freedom of Information: taking account of the circumstances of individual applicants" in 2010 *Public Law* at p 506.

7.04   However, these principles are not iron rules and, perhaps more than is acknowledged, there are circumstances where the identity of the applicant or the purpose of their request is deemed to be relevant. For instance, under FOISA, the identity of the applicant can be taken into account when determining whether:

- the applicant is requesting their own personal data. If so, the authority does not need to comply under FOISA (on the basis that the applicant has subject access rights under the Data Protection Act);
- the applicant is making a repeated request (s 14(2));
- the information is already available to the applicant (s 25(1)). For instance, it may be the case that, although the information is not generally available, it is known to be available to a particular applicant: for example, it has already been provided to them by the authority or the applicant is the author of information held by the authority.

7.05   The purpose or motives of the applicant may be relevant where:

- the request is for a third party's personal information. Applicants may need to demonstrate that they have a legitimate interest in the information;
- the authority considers that the request is vexatious. Although the authority cannot determine that an applicant is vexatious, it may be that the purpose of the request is held to be so.

7.06   The circumstances of the applicant may have to be taken into account, for example where the applicant is disabled.

7.07   Nevertheless, authorities are not expected, or entitled, to require every applicant to confirm their identity, motive or circumstance where this can or should have no bearing on the handling of the request. Even where it could have a bearing, authorities may choose not to make any enquiry if it does not affect their intended course of action. For example, even where the authority believes that the information may be available to a particular applicant, it may decide that it is less burdensome simply to provide another copy than to establish whether the applicant is the same person to whom information was given some time in the past or still holds it.

7.08   In the limited circumstances in which the identity of the applicant is relevant, then, in practice, authorities are usually able to come to a view based on the information to hand – which is the name and address of the applicant and the terms of the request.

APPLICATIONS ON BEHALF OF OTHERS

On occasion, however, it may not be clear whether an individual is acting   7.09
on their own behalf or that of another person. For example, requests
are often received on behalf of researchers who work for members of
the Scottish Parliament or journalists working for newspapers. Usually
it makes little practical difference as to whether they are making the
request in their own right or in the name of their employer. However, it
could have a bearing. If circumstances change in the course of dealing
with the request, for example the journalist were to move to another
title or the MSP were to leave Parliament, then it would be important
to know to whom the response (or a decision if an application is made
to the Commissioner) should be made. In a number of cases the
Commissioner has confirmed with the researcher whether the request
is on their own behalf or that of an MSP.

Usually, where an agent is acting on behalf of a client that is made   7.10
known when submitting a request for information and in subsequent
correspondence. For example, in *Decision 103/2009: Barr Ltd and Argyll
and Bute Council* it is clear that although the information request
to the council about a schools building project was submitted by
the legal firm Pinsent Masons, it was on behalf of its client Barr Ltd.
In such cases it is the identity and the circumstances of the client
which need to be taken into account, as they are the applicants under
FOISA.

What happens, however, if the agent does not disclose that it   7.11
is acting on behalf of another or fails to identify its client? This rare
occurrence came to the fore as a result of a request made by MacRoberts,
a firm of solicitors, to Glasgow City Council and Dundee City Council
for detailed information regarding properties in both cities. Following
an application to the Commissioner, it became clear that the firm was
acting on behalf of an unnamed client. Nevertheless, the decision was
issued on the basis that MacRoberts had made a valid application
which satisfied the basic requirements of s 1(2) by stating its name
as the applicant and an address for correspondence, even if it was
believed that the request was being made for the purpose of assisting
its unnamed clients.

Subsequently, however, the Court of Session held that the Com-   7.12
missioner was in error in coming to that view. It found that, in this
circumstance:

> "Section 1(2) does not resolve the matter: it merely informs the reader
> that the term 'applicant' refers to the person who makes the request.
> In a case where the request is made by an agent acting on behalf of

his principal, the question is which of them should be regarded for the purposes of the Act as having made the request. It is necessary to look elsewhere in the Act to find pointers towards the answer to that question."

THE RELEVANCE OF THE IDENTITY OF THE APPLICANT

7.13   The court placed weight on the fact that the identity of the applicant is relevant to the application of a number of provisions of FOISA. In addition to consideration as to whether a request for personal information constitutes a subject access request or involves information readily available, as listed above, it also noted that "the identity of the person making the request is also relevant to the application of the provisions concerned with the aggregation of costs, in section 12(2) of the Act and the relevant regulations (the Freedom of Information (Fees for Required Disclosure) (Scotland) Regulations 2004, SSI 2004 No 467)".

7.14   The opinion points out that it may be necessary to know whether the applicant is a child and, if so, what age, given that:

> "It is also apparent from section 69 that questions may arise under the Act as to the legal capacity of a person who seeks to exercise the right of access under section 1(1): a question which has arisen in other jurisdictions with freedom of information legislation (as in *Wallace v Health Commissioner of Victoria* [1985] VR 403, a decision of the Supreme Court of Victoria)."

7.15   Warming to this theme, the court further observed:

> "It would seem absurd, in a case where a request was made by an agent acting on behalf of an *incapax*, to determine the question by assessing the capacity of the agent rather than that of the person on whose behalf he was acting. In short, several of the provisions of the Act can only operate sensibly and effectively, and as the Scottish Parliament must therefore be taken to have intended, if the applicant, in a case where the request is made by an agent acting on another person's behalf, is taken to be the person on whose behalf it is made."

7.16   The court concluded:

> "In our opinion, the true applicant in that situation was the client, who should therefore have been named in accordance with section 8(1)(b). In view of the potential importance of the identity of the applicant to the operation of the Act, as we have explained, compliance with section 8(1)(b) must, in our view, be regarded as an essential requirement of a valid request under the Act."

In short, therefore, following that judgment, the position in Scotland   7.17
is that where a public authority receives an information request from a
person who states that he or she is acting on behalf of another person,
but the request does not name that person, the information request is
invalid.[2]

CLARIFYING THE IDENTITY OF THE "TRUE APPLICANT"

However, a bald refusal of the application is not appropriate. The public   7.18
authority still has a duty to provide reasonable advice and assistance
to the person making the request, including providing advice to the
person acting on behalf of the unnamed applicant. The expressed view
of the court is that

> "we do not intend to suggest that purported requests which are
> technically deficient in such respects as these should be refused out of
> hand. It would ordinarily be reasonable in such circumstances, at least
> as a matter of good practice (and arguably as required by section 15), for
> a public authority which received such a request to advise the agent of
> the relevant requirements of the Act, so that the deficiency might be
> cured".[3]

The authority should therefore explain why the request is invalid, and
what needs to be done to make the request valid – which is usually
simply no more than to provide the name of the applicant.[4]

Clarifying the identity of the "true applicant" may not cause any   7.19
great difficulty in most cases. However, what should happen if an
application is made which does not indicate that it is made on behalf
of another, but the authority strongly suspects it to be so? The court
in *Glasgow City Council and Dundee City Council v Scottish Information
Commissioner* is silent on this point.

In these circumstances, if the identity of the applicant has a bearing   7.20
on the response to the request, then there is nothing to prevent an
authority from raising the issue with a purported applicant. However,
there is no obligation on applicants to answer any query about whether
requests have been made on behalf of another person (where the
applicant has made no claim to that effect) and the authority should
draw no inferences from an applicant refusing to do so. Where the

---

2 See "The Commissioner's Guidance on validity of requests following Court of Session
   Opinion", para 5.2.
3 At para 78.
4 *Ibid*, para 5.3.

applicant has confirmed that they are the true applicant or refused to respond and the matter is subsequently referred to the Commissioner, the authority must be able to demonstrate to the Commissioner that there are reasonable grounds for believing that the request was made on behalf of another person.

7.21   What advantage does it give to a potentially undeclared true applicant to go through an agent or a third party? The main benefit to such an individual is obscurity – seeking or securing information without displaying their interest. This may happen where an individual believes themselves to be in a vulnerable or adversarial relationship with the authority and fears that disclosing their identity may have adverse consequences. This could be done without an obvious agent–client relationship. One website[5] which specialises in "investigating UK universities through freedom of information" encourages the submission of topics which can form the basis of a request to a specific university or to all 145 higher education institutions. Among these so-called "round-robin" requests was an enquiry into how many staff had made employment tribunal claims and whether gagging agreements were signed. Similarly, the requirements for university staff to gain permission before they give television interviews about their work has also been enquired into.

7.22   Why would anyone feel the need to mask their interest in this way? Notwithstanding that the motive of the applicant should not be taken into account, the very fact that an information request has been pursued through the formal procedures of FOISA (for example, by requiring a review if no response is received or information is withheld) may be regarded by those in an authority as somehow changing the relationship with a known individual, for example between an employee and employer; a social worker and a client; or a third-sector partner and a funding authority. Research has shown that many working in voluntary organisations fear that an FOI request will be regarded as an aggressive form of engagement and may jeopardise relationships with officials in authorities and the prospect of future funding from authorities. In a survey, 49 per cent of respondents said that they would be discouraged from requesting information under FOI because of a fear that it might harm working or funding relationships.[6]

7.23   Some voluntary bodies "chose to make a request through a third party in order to ensure their organisation was not directly associated

5   AcademicFOI.com.
6   K Spence, *Volunteering Information? The Use of Civil Society Laws by the Third Sector in Scotland*, (University of Strathclyde), p 5, para 4.3: http://www.itspublicknowledge.info/home/ SICResources/ResourcesCivilResearch.asp.

with the request [28 per cent]. Indeed, one respondent commented, 'We strongly suspected the possibility of "backlash" if we asked directly.'[7]

If there is a potentially undeclared true applicant, would accepting the request as valid affect the capacity of an authority to withhold information or cause inappropriate disclosure? While accepting the court's view that there are a number of provisions in FOISA for which the identity of the applicant is relevant, in practice, failing to identify a true applicant is only rarely going to allow access to more information and could result in less. The most obvious instance concerns personal information. Knowing the identity of the true applicant is important in determining whether the information constitutes the "personal data of which the applicant is the data subject" and therefore is exempt from disclosure under s 38(1)(a). However, the purpose of this exemption is to allow the much *greater* access to an individual's own information under the Data Protection Act 1998.

7.24

This is illustrated by a somewhat confusing case in which a health board was asked for information about staff involved in prescribing and administering two injections to a named patient. The request came from an individual who had previously been authorised to act as the representative of the patient in relation to a complaint about the administration of the injections. The application to the Commissioner was initially believed to be invalid, on the ground that the request had been made on behalf of another, unnamed, person (being the patient) and was not made by the "true applicant". However, the applicant insisted that on this occasion he was not acting in this capacity. The application was therefore treated as a valid third-party request for personal information – but as a consequence the information could not be disclosed as it would contravene the data protection principles.[8]

7.25

Similarly, if an applicant obscured their true identity by making a request through a third party then the considerable restrictions on disclosure imposed by the requirements of s 38(1)(b) would come into play

7.26

CONCLUSION

Leaving aside personal information, in practice what matters most when determining what information should be provided is not the

7.27

7   K Spence, *Volunteering Information? The Use of Civil Society Laws by the Third Sector in Scotland*, (University of Strathclyde), p 6.
8   Decision 034/2011: Mr W Hunter Watson and Grampian NHS Board.

identity of the applicant but issues of whether information is held; how costly it would be to comply with the request; whether exemptions apply; and the public interest in disclosure.

7.28   The Court of Session was at pains to point out that "We do not suggest that the Commissioner is under a general obligation to make enquiries about applicants".[9] The same holds true for authorities.

---

9   *Glasgow City Council v Scottish Information Commissioner* at para 69.

Chapter 8

KEY ISSUE 6: CHARGING FOR INFORMATION – NOW AND IN FUTURE

CHARGING FOR INFORMATION UNDER FOISA

The fee regime attached to freedom of information legislation can be far more determinative of whether information is actually disclosed than the application of exemptions or any other consideration of the request. FOI laws and regulations which mandate up-front administrative fees or prohibitive charges for information can deter requests or exclude those with no capacity to pay.   **8.01**

In Scotland, our fee regime has been purposefully designed to allow most requests to be met without any financial impediment, while at the same time aiming to place a ceiling on the burden on authorities arising out of any single request.   **8.02**

Consequently, the FOISA fee-charging structure is strongly regulated, is reasonably generous to the applicant and the amount which may be charged for information is clearly not intended to allow for full cost recovery by the authority when responding to requests. As indicated in Part I, the Freedom of Information (Fees for Required Disclosure) (Scotland) Regulations 2004 (the "Fees Regulations") stipulate that: **8.03**

- the first £100 of costs are provided free of charge;
- for projected costs above £100, but below £600, authorities may make a charge of up to 10 per cent of these costs;
- authorities do not have to comply with a request where the estimated cost of doing so would exceed £600.

The Fees Regulations provide constraints on the nature of costs which can be charged for and a limit on the fee rate. An authority can charge for the costs it "reasonably estimates ... that it is likely to incur in locating, retrieving and providing such information in accordance with the Act". This is intended to cover staff costs in searching through electronic or paper files to locate specifically   **8.04** requested information as well as the cost of copying and dispatching the information to the applicant.[1] However, any estimate of the cost of staff time in locating, retrieving or providing the information shall not exceed £15 per hour per member of staff.

8.05   The Commissioner takes the view that the term "provision" includes the cost of redacting exempt information from a document to allow it to be provided to the applicant. However, the Fees Regulations make it clear that no account can be taken of staff or other costs incurred in determining whether an exemption applies or considering some other aspect of the case, such as whether the information request is valid; the Fees Regulations specifically exclude costs incurred in determining whether the person seeking the information is entitled to receive the requested information or, if they are not so entitled, whether they should nonetheless be provided with the information or should be refused it.

8.06   Similarly, no account can be taken of staff or other costs incurred in determining whether the authority holds the information specified in the request; or whether the person seeking the information is entitled to receive the requested information or, if not so entitled, should nevertheless be provided with it or should be refused it.[2]

8.07   Investigations have found charges which were not justified on the basis that:

- staff costs were overstated by claiming the maximum amount allowed for employees on junior grades who were paid less than £15 per hour;
- staff costs included an element for overtime;
- costs were included which should not have been, for example charging staff costs for the time taken to consider whether exemptions applied;
- charges for copying the material were excessive;
- charges for providing the information were based upon photocopying and postage when it could have been made available electronically at less cost;
- the authority had aggregated the costs of more than one request from an applicant. (At present there is no provision under FOISA for public authorities to do so.)

---

1   Freedom of Information (Fees for Required Disclosure) (Scotland) Regulations 2004 (SSI 2004/467), reg 3(1).
2   Ibid, reg 3(2)(a)(i) and (ii).

(A different approach has been taken in the UK, due to the difference **8.08** in the wording between the Scottish Fees Regulations and the Freedom of Information and Data Protection (Appropriate Limit and Fees) Regulations 2004. There, the High Court concluded that while a charge could be made to extract information which fell within the scope of a request from information which did not, no charge could be made for redacting information on the basis that it was subject to one or more exemptions under the Freedom of Information Act 2000.[3])

The authority has to secure the agreement of the applicant before **8.09** any charge is made, so, if it intends to levy a charge, it must issue a fees notice setting out the basis on which the costs have been calculated and secure the applicant's agreement to pay.[4] The applicant can be required to pay the fee in advance of being provided with the information.

In most cases, the maximum amount which will be charged under **8.10** FOISA is £50. (However, an authority can elect to provide information which would cost more than £600 and can charge £50 plus the amount by which the projected costs exceed £600.[5])

Given the modest amount which can be charged, it is perhaps not **8.11** surprising that few authorities appear to find it worthwhile to calculate and issue a fees notice. Most tend to concentrate instead on estimating whether complying with a request for information would exceed the £600 stipulated maximum. If it does, the information does not need to be provided, although in light of the obligation to provide advice and assistance in s 15 of FOISA, the authority is required to discuss with the applicant how the request could be narrowed to bring it within the upper cost limit and indicate what information could be provided for less than £600.[6]

CHARGING FOR ENVIRONMENTAL INFORMATION

There is scope for adopting a markedly different approach to charging **8.12** under EIRs, which could make the cost to applicants of being provided with environmental information much more significant than for a request made under FOISA.

---

3 *Chief Constable of South Yorkshire Police v Information Commissioner* [2011] EWHC 44 (Admin).
4 Freedom of Information (Fees for Required Disclosure) (Scotland) Regulations 2004, reg 4(4).
5 Freedom of Information (Fees for Disclosure under Section 13) (Scotland) Regulations 2004 (SSI 2004/376), reg 4.
6 See Decision 154/2007: Andrew Picken (*Evening News*) and Robert Seaton and the City of Edinburgh Council.

8.13   A Scottish public authority is entitled to charge a fee for making environmental information available,[7] but the charging regime is not stipulated in the manner of FOISA. Instead, authorities are required to publish their own schedules of fees[8] and in so doing are required to ensure that "Fees charged shall not exceed a reasonable amount and in any event shall not exceed the costs to the authority of producing the information requested".[9]

8.14   This approach to charging reflects the provisions in Directive 2003/4/EC on public access to environmental information and in particular Recital (18):

> "Public authorities should be able to make a charge for supplying environmental information but such a charge should be reasonable. This implies that, as a general rule, charges may not exceed actual costs of producing the material in question. Instances where advance payment will be required should be limited. In particular cases, where public authorities make available environmental information on a commercial basis, and where this is necessary in order to guarantee the continuation of collecting and publishing such information, a market-based charge is considered to be reasonable; an advance payment may be required. A schedule of charges should be published and made available to applicants together with information on the circumstances in which a charge may be levied or waived."

8.15   (It should be pointed out that the EIRs do not faithfully adopt the wording of the Directive. Recital (18) makes it clear that the requirement for applicants to make advance payments should be limited, but the EIRs simply stipulate, without caveat, that "A Scottish public authority may require that payment of the whole or part of a fee under paragraph (1) be made in advance of making information available",[10] perhaps in an attempt to bring it into line with the FOISA regime.)

8.16   Some authorities, such as the Scottish Environment Protection Agency (SEPA), have sought to harmonise the FOISA Fees Regulations and their schedule of charges for environmental information, ensuring, for example, that a similar amount of environmental information will be provided free of charge or at a discounted rate as would apply to non-environmental information (see Chapter 2).

---

7   Environmental Information (Scotland) Regulations 2004 (SSI 2004/520), reg 8(1).
8   *Ibid*, reg 8(8)(a).
9   *Ibid*, reg 8(3).
10   *Ibid*, reg 8(4).

However, some other authorities in Scotland and elsewhere in the UK have sought to take advantage of the scope provided by the EIRs to draw up a schedule of charges which: **8.17**

- calculates costs on an hourly staff rate or other measure which is higher than that permitted under the respective Fees Regulations;
- makes no provision for supplying any information free of charge; or
- does not restrict the fees notice to a proportion of costs.

As a consequence, the difference between a request which falls under FOISA and that which is dealt with under the EIRs could be considerable (see Box below) and charges under the EIRs could become a major disincentive to making or proceeding with requests. **8.18**

The potential cost difference between FOISA and EIRs

An authority estimates that it would take 8 hours of a senior member of staff's time to comply with a request. It is unsure whether the information is environmental, so it calculates the fee according to the Fees Regulations for FOISA and its schedule of charges under the EIRs

FOISA

The cost for staff time would be capped at £120 on the basis of the maximum chargeable rate of £15. The first £100 of this cost would be free of charge and for the amount above £100 the authority could charge only 10 per cent of the projected costs.

The fees notice, in the unlikely event of the authority being minded to issue one, would come to £2.

EIRs

The authority has set its chargeable staff costs at a higher maximum of £25. Applying this maximum rate gives a total of £200. While the authority may have made discretionary provision in its schedule to waive or limit some element of the allowable fee, it decides to issue a fee notice for the full amount if the EIRs apply.

The charge under the EIRs would be 100 times greater than under FOISA

So far, there have not been cases of significant fees being charged under the EIRs as, when it comes to charging for environmental information, most authorities have chosen to apply the same fee basis as for FOISA. **8.19**

This probably reflects the fact that very few authorities actually charge for information and that estimating costs by differentially charging where the information requested contains environmental and non-environmental information would be administratively onerous.

8.20   However, if this should change, then the Commissioner is likely to question the basis on which charges for environmental information is being made:

IS THE AUTHORITY ENTITLED TO CHARGE?

8.21   An authority is not permitted to:

> "charge a fee for allowing an applicant to –
>
> (a) access any public registers or lists of environmental information held by it; or (b) examine the information requested at a place which the authority makes available for that purpose."[11]

This reflects Article 5(1) of the Directive.

8.22   Public registers of environmental information have been held at national and local authority levels for many years, often to allow access to details in permits given for commercial or other activities. A current example is the Scottish Pollutant Release Inventory, a publicly accessible electronic database of releases of 215 pollutants to air, water, sewer and land, which is designed to comply with the requirements of a Community obligation on the implementation of a European Pollutant Release and Transfer Register. This is available to view on SEPA's website.[12]

8.23   If SEPA were to impose a charge to access the data on site (not that it wishes to do so), this would be contrary to reg 8(2).

8.24   Generally, reg 8(2) covers the familiar circumstance where a local authority provides for public inspection of planning applications during business hours at a specified Council office. The EIRs do not permit a charge to be made for inspecting such publicly available information.

8.25   This does not mean that anyone who asks for environmental information and indicates that they are willing to view it at a location of the authority's choosing can always expect to be allowed to do so without charge. If that request does not involve information which the authority has already compiled and makes available for inspection, then in effect the authority is entitled to consider whether there is a cost involved for the staff time taken in locating

---

11   Environmental Information (Scotland) Regulations 2004, reg 8(2).
12   http://www.sepa.org.uk/air/process_industry_regulation/pollutant_release_inventory. asp.

and retrieving the information (and reproducing it if access to the original material is not possible). Fees which would otherwise be incurred as a consequence of requiring the authority to comply with an environmental information request cannot be avoided simply by opting to examine the information *in situ*.

There are more readily acceptable circumstances where the applicant might take advantage of the free inspection provision. Certain information relating to an environmental matter might attract a very modest fee for locating and retrieving, but be held in a format which would be costly to reproduce. In such a situation, the applicant could opt to avoid this element of the cost by requesting to examine the information *in situ*. No charge could be made for the inspection aspect of supplying the information, although the authority would still be entitled – if it wished – to recover the marginal costs of locating and retrieving the information.

8.26

HAS THE AUTHORITY INFORMED THE PUBLIC OF ITS CHARGING REGIME?

A Scottish public authority shall publish and make available to applicants:

8.27

"(a) a schedule of its fees; and
(b) information on the circumstances in which a fee may be charged, waived or required to be paid in advance."[13]

Many Scottish authorities have not done so, mutely relying instead on the general provisions of FOISA Fees Regulations. While this may serve well enough, the lack of explicit provision is at variance with the requirements of the EIRs.[14]

8.28

The Commissioner's view is that in the absence of a published schedule of fees, an authority is not entitled subsequently to seek to impose a fee in response to a particular environmental information request, and claim in justification reg 8(1).

8.29

(In a case which came before the Irish Commissioner, concerning whether fees had been published, an authority argued that it was not a mandatory requirement that the list of fees, and information on

8.30

---

13   Environmental Information (Scotland) Regulations 2004, reg 8(8).
14   In a rare case, Decision 095/2007: Mr John B Mackintosh and Renfrewshire Council, it was found that an authority did not have a published schedule of charges under the EIRs and had acted unreasonably in charging for environmental information. However, the Commissioner accepted that if it issued a fees notice using the FOISA Fees Regulations as the basis for calculation, that would be reasonable. However, that case does not reflect the Commissioner's current view as to the effect of reg 8(1).

charges, should be available to the applicant *in advance* of a request. In her decision the Commissioner concluded: "The ordinary meaning of 'publish' is to make something generally known or to disseminate to the community in general. Clearly, what is provided for is the making available of charging information both to the public generally, including potential applicants for environmental information, as well as to actual applicants who have already made a request for access to environmental information." Accordingly, she took the view that a charge could not be made where no schedule of fees was published.[15])

IS THE CHARGE REASONABLE OR EXCESSIVE?

8.31   The fee to which an authority is entitled "shall not exceed a reasonable amount and in any event shall not exceed the costs to the authority of producing the information requested".[16]

8.32   One of the reasons for requiring the authority to publish a schedule of charges is no doubt to establish whether the charging regime is itself reasonable. If the amounts proposed would have the purpose or effect of dissuading requests and thereby obstructing the release of environmental information, then the basis of scheme itself may be unreasonable.[17]

8.33   Where an authority demands what appears to be an unreasonable amount, the basis for its charge is open to challenge. When a Mr Markinson inspected certain papers at his local Council offices, related to the original planning application for his house, he found them complex and difficult to follow. In response to his request for photocopies of some papers he was given the Council's printed leaflet of fees and charges, under which it charged £6 for each building control or planning decision notice and 50p for each other photocopied sheet contained in the planning file.

8.34   The UK Information Tribunal, in hearing an appeal on the proposed costs, was told that the Council had taken into account the officer time in locating and retrieving the documentation to produce the information in the first place. The Tribunal took issue with this, observing that the regulations provide that "the information in question should be made available for inspection free of charge

15   CEI/07/0006: Open Focus & Sligo County Council (26 May 2008).
16   Environmental Information (Scotland) Regulations 2004, reg 8(3).
17   The UK Commissioner has taken the view that "it is not reasonable for authorities to pass on their full costs of responding to a request to an applicant. Furthermore, in considering a charge, the authority should have regard for what is reasonable from the applicant's point of view as well as the authority's own point of view": David Markinson and the Information Commissioner (EA/2005/0014), para 9.

and we believe that, if the costs of locating and retrieving a piece of information should be disregarded for that purpose, it is not open to a public authority to regard it as reasonable to include them in calculating the cost of copying the same material".[18]

The Tribunal also rejected as irrelevant considerations such as whether a lower charge would affect the Council's revenue stream or increase staff workload (by encouraging more requests for copies). 8.35

The "reasonableness" test has not yet featured prominently in decisions of the Scottish Information Commissioner. However, if authorities move to a full cost charging regime then it is unlikely to be long before appeals are made. 8.36

THE FUTURE OF CHARGING UNDER FOISA?

Some Scottish authorities have pressed for an increase in fees which can be charged under FOISA. The purpose of such an increase would appear to be: to deter requesters; to avoid the burden of having to respond to requests; or to recover the costs of so doing. The arguments for doing so vary, relating to the burden caused by the volume of requests; the nature of the requesters (such as press or commercial applicants); or the lack of public as opposed to personal interest in the information requested by applicants who make a series of requests. Higher charges may provide a greater element of cost recovery. However, the overall effect of the range of changes suggested would appear to be to limit the amount of time which the authority would have to expend (and limit the amount of information which could be requested or be provided). It would also make it more likely that the cost ceiling would be breached, meaning that no information would have to be provided at all. Furthermore, if authorities can more readily make a charge and indicate a greater intention to do so, then this may deter requests from being made or pursued. 8.37

Some of the measures being canvassed are: 8.38

- increasing the maximum rate at which staff costs spent on locating, retrieving and providing information can be charged (currently £15 per hour);
- removing the right to the free provision of information costing less than £100;
- reducing the upper cost limit of £600 so that many demanding requests need not be complied with;

18 David Markinson and the Information Commissioner (EA/2005/0014), para 33(c).

- aggregating the costs of responding to more than one request from the same person for the purpose of charging a fee or establishing that the upper limit had been exceeded.

8.39   None of these proposals would require a change to primary legislation; all could be done by Order in Parliament.

8.40   Before any such amendments to the Fees Regulations were made, serious consideration would have to be given to the purpose, practicalities and consequences – unintended as well as intended – of change.

"DETERRENCE" CHARGING

8.41   Most authorities do not currently charge for information, even where they could, because the cost of issuing a fees notice and administering payment makes it uneconomic to do so. Increasing the amount which can be charged for staff time may still not offset the administrative costs to issue notices, far less raise significant net revenues to defray the burden of complying with requests. It would, however, allow more substantial fees notices to be issued in the expectation that this would discourage applicants from persisting with their requests. The deterrence value of charges is clearly not without its attractions.

8.42   However, is it acceptable to allow authorities to levy a charge, if the cost to the authority of issuing the notice and administering the fee is more than the income derived? In such an event it would appear more likely that the purpose of a charge is to deter a request or dissuade an applicant from pursuing their request rather than ostensibly to recover some of the costs of meeting a request. It is notable that the US Freedom of Information Act does not allow authorities to make a deterrence charge which would cost the authority more to administer than it would collect in return.[19]

BREACHING THE UPPER LIMIT

8.43   Higher charges for staff time would also increase the likelihood that the cost of responding to a request would breach the upper limit, particularly if this cost ceiling was reduced from the present £600. (So, for example, if the staff hourly rate was increased to, say, £25 and the upper limit was reduced to £400 then the maximum chargeable staff time which could be taken to deal with a request would fall to 16 hours compared with 40 hours currently.)

---

19   "No fee may be charged by any agency under this section – if the costs of routine collection and processing of the fee are likely to equal or exceed the amount of the fee" (Freedom of Information Act 5 USC 552, § 4A (iv)(I)).

INEQUITABLE AND DISCRIMINATORY CHARGING?

One consequence of universally applying increased levels of charging **8.44** (and in particular to remove or reduce the "first £100 free" provision) would be, for all practical purposes, to exclude those with low income or no income – such as those on benefits, the refugee community or young people – who simply could not afford to make payment or may not even have access to cash or bank accounts to do so. Authorities might argue that, in such cases, they have discretion over whether to require payment. However, it would be a major departure from the "applicant blind" nature of FOISA if applicants were asked to apply for a financial concession on the basis of their status.

Even if it was not thought generally equitable or cost effective **8.45** for the authority to issue fees notices, authorities might consider discretionary charging to be advantageous if the effect was to discourage demanding requests from the press, businesses or frequent requesters. However, it is certain to be controversial, and perhaps the basis of challenge, if the discretion to impose charges was thought to be used in a discriminatory fashion depending upon the authorities' attitude towards the requester or the nature of the information requested. (Authorities looking to other regimes for support for differential charging may be discomfited to find that in the US the major beneficiary of such a policy is the media – often the very category which Scottish authorities may wish to discourage by fees notices. US agencies can charge "representatives of the news media" only for the cost of reproduction of documents – around 20 cents per page – and not, as in the case of supplying members of the public, additionally being allowed to charge for the cost involved in searching for records.[20])

AGGREGATION

The capacity to aggregate requests might address the frustration felt **8.46** where an authority receives a letter with several specific questions on the same matter – each of which may have to be treated as separate requests under s 1. Section 12(2)(a) of FOISA permits the Scottish Ministers to make regulations to allow costs to be aggregated where two or more requests are made to an authority by one person. But such regulations have not yet been made, not least perhaps because of the practical consequences and in particular where aggregation applied to requests made on unrelated matters over a period well separated in time. For instance, if aggregation was permitted, an applicant might

---

20   Freedom of Information Act 5 USC 552, § 5(a)(4)(A)(II–III).

make a request and receive no response from an authority for, say, a month and, while waiting for response to a request for review, the applicant might make another request for information to the same authority on an entirely unrelated matter. Even though these requests were made 7 weeks apart, the authority could aggregate them and decline to comply with either of them if in total the costs of doing so exceeded the upper limit. Aggregation would reward the dilatory authority.

8.47   Conceivably, an aware requester could avoid aggregation by having a relative or friend make the subsequent request. However, such a cat-and-mouse game between an applicant and an authority is hardly consistent with a law which makes requests commonplace. Avoidance measures would be unlikely or impractical in the case of an elected representative or news journalist who makes several requests in the course of their normal activities. Yet again, it would be open to the discretion of the authority to decide whether to carry out such aggregation, but this too could lead to claims of discriminatory treatment from those who believed they have been singled out for such action.

8.48   Aggregation could also affect different persons who appear to the authority to be acting in concert or whose requests appear to have been instigated wholly or mainly for a purpose other than the obtaining of the information itself.[21] Certainly, FOISA should not reward those who wish to abuse it by overwhelming or tying up the resources of an authority. However, if this was felt to be the purpose of a request, then the authority may well be able to argue that, taken in context, it was vexatious.

8.49   The concern with combining requests from different persons appearing to act in concert is that it might permit an authority to refuse to respond to demands for information on a matter of significant local or national concern which had prompted requests for information from many individuals. Although the cost to comply with each might have been less than £100 (so that no fee could be charged by the authority) if by aggregation the cost of replying to any or all of them exceeded £600 then there would be no obligation upon the authority to comply with any of them.

CONCLUSION

8.50   It has been a commendable feature of the freedom of information regime in Scotland that it has rarely been the case that, where an

---

21   Under FOISA, s 12(2)(b).

applicant is entitled to receive information, the cost of being provided with it has proven to be at issue. This has been achieved by design, not accident. There was never any intention to make compliance cost-neutral for authorities through full cost recovery. Nor were people to be deterred from making or pursuing requests by the prospect of having to pay an appreciable amount for information (the substance of which may be unknown at the point of payment). Backstop provision has been made for regulations to counter abuse of the freedom of information rights. However, the effect – and perhaps the intention – of the demand in some quarters for increased costs and greater restrictions would simply be to inhibit use (not tackle abuse) of these rights. This is considered further in Part IV.

Part III

COMPLIANCE AND GOOD PRACTICE – THE COMMISSIONER'S ROLE

Chapter 9

THE CONDUCT OF INVESTIGATIONS

The primary function of the Commissioner is to decide whether   9.01
Scottish public authorities have dealt with requests for information
in accordance with the freedom of information laws. This process is
triggered when a person who is dissatisfied with a response (or lack of
response) from a public authority to a request makes an application to
the Commissioner for a decision (commonly these are also referred to
as "appeals").

When an application is received the Commissioner's purpose is   9.02
to come to a sound determination as quickly as possible. In doing
so, the aim is to provide an outcome which can be accepted by both
the applicant and the authority. Where it is not accepted, the decision
should be capable of withstanding judicial challenge.

The first issue the Commissioner needs to address, however, is   9.03
whether a decision is actually required.

VALIDATION OF APPLICATION

Not every application which is received requires to be investigated.   9.04
Around 30 per cent of applications are closed without investigation
largely because they are not valid or insufficient information has been
provided to allow investigation.

When validating an application the key considerations are: 9.05

DOES THE CASE INVOLVE A "SCOTTISH PUBLIC AUTHORITY"?

Applications sometimes involve requests for information made   9.06
to bodies based in Scotland but which are covered by the UK Act
or the request may involve a body which is not covered by FOI
legislation at all. Only a handful of mistaken applications are made
each year.

DOES IT INVOLVE A SCOTTISH PUBLIC AUTHORITY BUT THE COMMISSIONER IS NOT PERMITTED TO CONSIDER THE APPLICATION?

9.07   No decision is required where the application concerns a request for review made to the Commissioner, a procurator fiscal or the Lord Advocate (to the extent that the information requested is held by the Lord Advocate as head of the systems of criminal prosecution and investigation of deaths in Scotland).[1] (This applies to fewer than 10 applications annually.)

HAS A REQUIREMENT FOR REVIEW BEEN MADE TO THE AUTHORITY?

9.08   This is the single biggest reason for applications being rejected, affecting on average some 40 cases annually. Applicants cannot seek a decision from the Commissioner unless they have requested a review from the authority and either have received no response from the authority within 20 working days or are dissatisfied with the response received.

WAS THE REQUIREMENT FOR REVIEW MADE WITHIN THE TIMESCALES ALLOWED?

9.09   A requirement for review is *premature* if fewer than 20 days have elapsed since the initial request for information was submitted to the authority, unless a response was received from the authority before the request for review was made. A requirement for review is *late* if 40 working days have elapsed since the authority's response to the original request was given to the applicant (or since the authority should have responded to the original request). Although under FOISA (but not the EIRs) an authority may choose to respond to a late requirement for review, it is not obliged to do so, in which case the application may be invalid.

IS THE APPLICATION TO THE COMMISSIONER PREMATURE OR HAS IT BEEN MADE IN TIME?

9.10   The applicant must wait 20 working days after making a requirement for a review to a public authority before submitting an application to the Commissioner unless the review has been carried out (and the applicant notified of the outcome) before the application was made. If an application is premature the applicant will be asked to make an application at a later date if they remain dissatisfied.

---

1   FOISA, s 48.

An application to the Commissioner should be made within 6 months of receipt of the notice of review or, where no review was carried out, within 6 months of the date by which the review should have been undertaken. A late application may be accepted, however, if there are extenuating circumstances. In particular, applications have been accepted where the authority has not informed the applicant of their rights of appeal. The legislation places the onus upon authorities to make applicants aware of their rights, including the timescale within which applications should be made. Where they have not done so, the Commissioner's view tends to be that applicants should not be penalised for the failings of the authority. **9.11**

IS THE APPLICATION IN THE CORRECT FORMAT?

The application must be in writing (or some other recordable format), state the name and an address for correspondence and specify: **9.12**

- the request for information to which the requirement for review related;
- the matter which was the subject-matter of the requirement for review;
- the matter which gives rise to the application to the Commissioner.

HAS THE APPLICANT USED A PSEUDONYM OR IS THE APPLICATION ANONYMOUS?

The application to the Commissioner must state the name and address of the applicant. If the applicant has used a pseudonym or has remained anonymous, then it is not a valid application. **9.13**

HAS THE APPLICATION BEEN MADE BY A FIRM OF SOLICITORS ON BEHALF OF A CLIENT?

If a firm of solicitors has made an application on behalf of a client but refuses to name the client, the application is likely to be invalid. **9.14**

Coming to a view as to the validity of an application is helped considerably by having sight of the following documents: **9.15**

- the original request for information;
- the response from the authority (if a response was sent);
- the requirement for review by the applicant;
- the result of the review by the authority (if a response was sent).

If the applicant has not retained these documents, they will be asked to contact the public authority directly to ask for copies. **9.16**

9.17   If it is apparent that the request was for the applicant's personal data, then the Commissioner will alert the applicant to the issues involved (ie that even though the request is valid the information will be exempt under s 38(1)(a)) and that a better course of action would be to pursue the request as a subject access request under the Data Protection Act 1998). This often results in the application being withdrawn before the case proceeds to investigation.

CASE MANAGEMENT

9.18   Hundreds of applications are received by the Commissioner each year. The overarching aim is to come to a sound decision on all valid cases as quickly as possible. To do so, the caseload has to be managed.

9.19   A feature of the approach adopted by the Commissioner is that there are no "orphan cases"; that is, no applications sit in an unallocated queue or backlog. Immediately following validation, all valid cases are allocated to an investigator, who provides their direct contact details to the applicant and the authority. The investigator is the point of contact for applicants to submit further information or seek updates on progress and for authorities to make submissions. The relationship between the investigator, the applicant and the authority is important. It can lead to a better understanding of what the applicant wants, and what are the real concerns of the authority regarding disclosure. This is often vital in facilitating settlement. It also means that even where the outcome of a decision may not produce more information, nevertheless the applicant is more likely to be satisfied that their case has been thoroughly investigated.

9.20   Cases are not allocated on a "taxi rank" principle, with the first available investigator taking the next case. Instead, a process of case allocation seeks to ensure that the workload of each investigator is broadly similar by considering the nature of cases under investigation. A "weighting" system has been developed. When an application has been validated and is ready to be allocated to an investigator, a manager makes an assessment of the nature of the case. Cases will be weighted on a scale of 1 to 4, with cases weighted 3 or 4 considered to be the most difficult or time consuming. In weighting the case, the manager will take account of the following factors:

- the amount of information covered by the case (unless it is clear that the £600 "upper cost limit" rule will apply and the case can be dealt with relatively quickly);
- whether the decision will break new ground or whether the investigator will be able to rely on precedent;

- the number of relevant exemptions cited by the public authority;
- the profile and sensitivity of the case; and
- the complexity and volume of the arguments put forward by the applicant and/or public authority.

Each of these factors is separately ranked 1 to 4, with the average score then being used to give the weighting of the case.   **9.21**

An indicative timescale for each case is then agreed with the investigator, and regular case progress meetings are held. The organisational target is to close valid cases within 20 weeks on average. Clearly some cases will take longer, but even then the aim is to ensure that all cases are closed within 10 months   **9.22**

The Commissioner does not prioritise cases, on the basis of either subject-matter or an assessment that some are of greater public interest or value than others. Arguments have been made that priority should be given to cases thought to be of a wide public interest compared with those which matter only to individuals. An indicator of public interest could be the topicality and the degree of controversy regarding an issue. Indeed, it is recognised that there may be particular merit in accelerating the investigation of particular cases where a decision or outcome is due to be taken, upon which the information in dispute has a bearing.   **9.23**

However, a general system of case prioritisation has been decided against. First, it would make case management susceptible to lobbying by politicians, the media and interested parties for a decision to be made on a particular application by a certain time. Acceding to such pressure might undermine the independence of the Commissioner.   **9.24**

In any case the insistence that a matter of topicality or controversy be given priority does not mean that a speedy decision could be made. There is an irreducible time required to validate the case, notify the authority, obtain copies of any information which has been withheld, secure submissions, and consider the content of the information in dispute. The very fact that it is controversial suggests that careful investigation will be required to come to a decision capable of withstanding public and judicial scrutiny.   **9.25**

Second, while many applications concern issues of particular concern only to certain individuals, these are often on matters which affect them deeply. A case may relate to, for example: **9.26**

- the care received by a relative in hospital or a care home;
- issues concerning justice at the hands of the law enforcement bodies;

- decisions by an authority which affect someone's employment or livelihood.

9.27   An element of the applicant's dissatisfaction may be that their request or concerns has or have not been taken seriously. They rely upon the Commissioner dealing with their request fairly. To be told that their application is adjudged to be of lesser importance and a decision on it is to be delayed to allow the investigator to concentrate on higher-profile cases would undermine the chance of securing an outcome which is accepted by them.

9.28   The Commissioner's approach, then, is to improve the overall efficiency of the investigative process. The indicative timescales for each case are gauged on how readily the case can be closed, based upon: the consideration of the extent of dissatisfaction; the volume of information in dispute; the number of exemptions claimed; and the extent of precedent dealing with similar requests etc.

9.29   By this process certain cases can be closed relatively quickly, particularly those where the complaint is that the authority has failed procedurally. These are classified by the Commissioner as "technical investigations".

TECHNICAL INVESTIGATIONS

9.30   Where an applicant has complained about a public authority's failure to respond to an information request or a request for review, or a failure to respond within the timescales laid down in the legislation, this is treated as a technical investigation.

9.31   Technical investigations may also consider other procedural breaches, for example failure to include required content in certain notices such as the right to review or right to application to the Commissioner.[2] The decision notice issued in a technical case considers only the public authority's compliance on procedural matters – it does not consider whether the applicant should have received any or all of the information they asked for. If the Commissioner finds that the authority failed to respond to a request or a requirement for review, the decision notice will require the authority to issue a response to the applicant. Depending upon the response issued, the applicant may then wish to submit a fresh application for a decision from the Commissioner.

---

2   FOISA, s 2 (Content of certain notices); EIRs, for example reg 13 (Refusal to make information available), which contains the requirement to, eg, specify reasons for refusal in notices, and include details of the right to review of appeal.

Typically, a technical investigation will be completed in around   9.32
6 weeks.

FULL INVESTIGATIONS

Ideally, the Commissioner should be able to come to a decision by   9.33
considering the:

- grounds of dissatisfaction expressed by the applicant;
- responses given to the applicant by the authority following the
  initial request;
- responses given to the applicant by the authority following a
  requirement for review;
- submissions made by the authority to the Commissioner;
- content of the information withheld.

As Macdonald and Jones have pointed out: "the Act does not refer to   9.34
any other steps to be taken by the Commissioner before he reaches
his decision on the application. Hence it would seem that both the
applicant and the authority have only one opportunity to set out their
contentions: the applicant in the application and the authority in its
comments on the application".[3]

As will be seen, the Commissioner has indicated to authorities that   9.35
the onus lies on them to make a full submission, justifying their stance,
in the first instance. With more than 5 years of experience, authorities
should now be aware that muddled application of exemptions,
generalised assertions of harm, and inadequate consideration of the
"public interest" test make for an unconvincing basis for withholding
information. They should not be surprised if the Commissioner,
confronted by poor submissions, simply comes to an unfavourable
decision rather than providing repeated opportunities for the authority
to improve its case.

However, many investigations have required extensive com-   9.36
munication with the authority and applicant to understand better the
issues involved to come to a formal decision or to reach an informal
settlement. Supplementary submissions have often been needed from
the authority in justification of the application of exemptions and on
the "public interest" test.

Furthermore, in the course of coming to a decision, new elements   9.37
to be considered are often introduced, such as:

- authorities claim further exemptions not previously made
  known to the applicant;

---

3   Macdonald and Jones, p 721.

- more information is found to be within the scope of the request;
- the question of excessive costs is considered belatedly.

9.38   This entire process of obtaining relevant submissions, securing further explanation and researching the issues related to the application is referred to as an "investigation" in the Commissioner's decisions.

UNDERSTANDING THE APPLICATION

9.39   The investigation must focus on those aspects of the public authority's handling of the case with which the applicant is dissatisfied – see s 47(1) of FOISA. This does not exclude the possibility that other aspects of the way in which the request was handled will also be considered in the Commissioner's decision – for example, technical breaches such as a failure to meet deadlines for responses.

9.40   Applications are acknowledged within 2 working days. Once they have been validated, an investigation is opened. At this stage, if information has been withheld from the applicant, the public authority will usually be asked to provide a copy to the Commissioner for the purposes of his investigation. The case is then allocated to an investigator. The Commissioner's investigator will contact the applicant within 5 days of a case being allocated, and provide updates to the applicant as the investigation proceeds. Sometimes further comments are sought from the applicant in the light of submissions from the authority, especially if the authority submits new grounds for withholding information. It is particularly pertinent to receive comments where the circumstances of the applicant may have a bearing on the case, for example where legitimate interest needs to be established for the disclosure of third-party personal information.

9.41   The authority is contacted within 3 weeks of a case being allocated, and, in line with s 49(3)(a), is invited to provide "comments" on the application. This is the primary opportunity for the authority to set out its full response to the grounds of dissatisfaction raised by the applicant and to supply any additional information. The authority is explicitly told at this early stage that the Commissioner expects to reach a decision on the basis of the authority's response, and there may not be a further opportunity for comment. By this point the investigator:

- will be aware of the authority's initial response to the applicant and response to requirement for review; and
- will already have had sight of any information which has been withheld.

So the authority will be prompted to address specific points in its submissions relevant to the case. The authority will be given a limited amount of time (at least 15 working days) to reply.

CONTACTING A THIRD PARTY

On rare occasions a third party may be contacted regarding a case which   9.42
involves them. However, it is the authority's responsibility to make the case for withholding information, not any other party. So, for example, while it may be useful to get a contractor's explanation of why harm to its commercial interest may result from disclosure, the onus is on the authority to say why in its view such harm would be substantially prejudicial and also why the public interest does not favour disclosure.

Contact may also be made with third parties unconnected to the   9.43
case for the purposes of specialist advice, for example statisticians.

(The lack of standing for third parties under the FOI regimes in   9.44
the UK, as compared with the provision in many other countries has been described as "a notable (and in the eyes of many, lamentable) difference" in that "interested third parties have no statutory right to be notified about requests made for information which affects them, nor is there any procedure under FOIA by which they maintain an objection to its disclosure (known in the US as reverse FOI)".[4] Similarly, third parties have no standing to make an application to the Commissioner about a proposed or actual disclosure of information.)

CONSIDERING SUBMISSIONS

Once the authority has submitted its comments on the application,   9.45
the question is whether all of the information necessary to come to a decision has been gathered.

The most common deficiencies at this stage are:

- the information appears to be environmental but the authority   9.46
  has not claimed the exemption at s 39(2) of FOISA (in which circumstance the investigator will contact the authority to remind them to do so);
- the authority has raised new matters or exemptions which were not raised with the applicant;
- new information within the scope of the request (but not previously considered) has been uncovered and exemptions applied;

---

4   J Ison, "Enforcement and Appeals" in P Carey and M Turle (eds), *Freedom of Information Handbook* (2nd edn, 2008, Law Society, London), p 350.

- there are apparent technical breaches which the applicant has not commented upon (often because they are unaware of them), but which the Commissioner may wish to address in a decision notice – for example, delays, failure to inform the applicant of right to review or application to the Commissioner or inadequacy of search.

9.47   The investigator may have to enter into a further round of correspondence with the authority and, in certain circumstances, the applicant before completing the investigation.

9.48   On certain but rare occasions a meeting may be held with an authority simply to speed up the investigation, for example by avoiding a succession of e-mails asking for further elaboration on a complex or sensitive matter.

INFORMATION NOTICES

9.49   In the course of an investigation the Commissioner may choose to require the authority to provide information by issuing an information notice.[5] The Commissioner can also issue an information notice to determine whether an authority has complied or is complying with FOISA or whether the practice of an authority conforms to one of the codes of practice.

9.50   Information notices are sent to the Chief Executive (or equivalent) of the public authority and a copy is also usually sent to the public authority official dealing with the investigation.

9.51   Notices are not issued as a matter of course. They are usually issued where the investigator is having difficulty in obtaining information from the authority following an informal request for the information concerned.

9.52   On some occasions authorities have requested that a notice be issued so that they can be obliged to supply personal data to the Commissioner. However, the Commissioner's view is that authorities are legally entitled to provide him with such information without the need for this additional safeguard, as the Data Protection Act 1998 permits authorities to release personal data (including sensitive personal data) to the Commissioner for the purposes of his investigations.[6]

---

5   FOISA, s 5.

6   Condition 5(b) of Sch 2 to the Data Protection Act 1998 allows processing of personal data necessary for the exercise of any functions conferred on any person or under any enactment. There is a similar provision for sensitive personal data in Condition 7(1)(b) of Sch 3.

However, there are restrictions on some authorities providing information to the Commissioner. The Criminal Procedure (Scotland) Act 1995 restricts the capacity of the Scottish Criminal Cases Review Commission to provide the Commissioner with information for the purposes of investigation. 9.53

The Scottish Legal Aid Board cannot provide information "furnished" to it by a third party without their consent, unless the Commissioner has issued the Board with an information notice for that information.[7] This specified form of disclosure was made possible by an amendment to the Legal Aid (Scotland) Act 1986. 9.54

It might be thought that the purpose of an information notice is to avoid a prolonged delay in the coming to a decision caused by an authority failing to co-operate with an investigation. This happens where the authority simply does not respond to a request for information, is repeatedly late in responding or challenges the request for the information. 9.55

However, issuing an information notice can also introduce delay. Strangely, FOISA is silent on the period within which an authority must produce the information when the notice is used in respect of an application to the Commissioner. However, it is now accepted that the information need not be supplied before the expiry of the period of appeal to the Court of Session against the notice, which is 42 days. 9.56

Given this inbuilt delay, use is made of an information notice to secure comments from the authority in only limited circumstances (for example, where the Commissioner is of the view that a decision cannot reasonably be come to without further information). As has been made clear earlier, there is no requirement upon the Commissioner to prompt the authority to make better submissions, and there is a general injunction on authorities to make their case in full to the Commissioner at the first opportunity. Where submissions are lacking or inadequate, the Commissioner may still come to a decision even if additional information might have been desirable. 9.57

The notice can seek both recorded and unrecorded information. So an information notice has been used to secure information about what certain individuals in an authority knew, such as whether relevant information had ever been created, and to secure confirmation of certain actions, for example the extent of searches conducted by the authority. 9.58

The public authority does not have to provide certain information in respect of its communications, as a client, with its professional 9.59

7 Legal Aid (Scotland) Act 1986, s 34(2)(f).

legal adviser where the communications concern advice to the authority on its obligations under FOISA or related legal proceedings. The notice will make this clear. However, the authority can choose to provide such advice to the Commissioner and the notice will explain that it may be helpful in understanding the authority's position to do so.

9.60   As with a decision notice, failure to comply with an information notice can lead to action in the Court of Session, where the authority may be dealt with as if the authority had committed a contempt of court; however, unlike a decision notice, the Commissioner can withdraw an information notice at any time, for example if the notice has been complied with.

COMING TO CONCLUSION

9.61   In coming to a conclusion particular regard is had to:

- the terms of the request for information and response by the authority and the terms of the requirement for review and response by the authority;
- the basis of the applicant's dissatisfaction.

9.62   This ensures that the decision deals only with information within the scope of the request and does not take into account material or developments which have occurred since the response was made to the requirement for review.

9.63   The focus is on the applicant's express dissatisfaction, as some other aspects of the authority's dealing with the request may not be disputed: for example, the applicant may accept that personal information within the scope of the information requested is exempt while maintaining that other information should be disclosed.

9.64   Account will be taken of relevant comments made by the authority when notified of the application and any subsequent submissions.

9.65   However, where several exemptions are applied to the same information, not all of these may be considered in the decision notice. For example, if the Commissioner accepts that information has been properly withheld under s 29 as relating to the formulation of government policy, the same information may not be further considered under s 30 concerning the free and frank provision of advice.

9.66   The decision will be informed by:

- precedent established by previous decision notices on a similar matter;

- the Commissioner's own briefings and guidance on exemptions etc;
- Scottish Ministers' Codes of Practice;
- legal advice provided to the Commissioner;
- decisions of the UK Information Commissioner's Office, the Information Tribunal and other court decisions.

Information available from external sources may also help form **9.67** a conclusion. On a remarkable number of occasions, authorities have claimed that a matter is confidential or that disclosure would be harmful, only for it to be found that the same, or largely similar, information is already available.

Fox example, Tayside Police refused to release details of the **9.68** policing costs for three 2009 football fixtures, arguing that release would be detrimental to law enforcement by allowing those intent on causing harm to gauge the likely police presence at future games. However, similar information had been released by other forces, and was readily available online, with no evidence subsequently emerging of the adverse consequences predicted by Tayside Police.[8]

Sometimes the withheld information is even already published **9.69** on the authority's own website. For example, the Scottish Legal Complaints Commission withheld a range of information relating to a research study conducted on its behalf, including details of the available budget. The SLCC had argued that the release of this information might harm the commercial interests of the academic institution which had carried out the research. However, the Commissioner's investigation discovered that this information had previously been published by the SLCC, and was freely available from the SLCC website at the time the applicant made his information request. Similarly, other information relating to interviews undertaken as part of the study was deemed confidential, despite the fact that it had also previously been published by the SLCC.[9]

APPROVING A DECISION

For the first few years nearly all decisions were personally approved **9.70** and signed by the Commissioner. Nowadays a substantial proportion of all decisions are signed on the Commissioner's behalf by senior staff under delegated authority. These are usually the straightforward or

---

8 Decision 183/2010: Mr Ben Wood and the Chief Constable of Tayside Police.
9 Decision 089/2010: Mr Peter Cherbi and the Scottish Legal Complaints Commission.

technical cases where the outcomes are clear and where the precedent from previous decisions by the Commissioner is well established.

9.71   A decision is drafted by the investigator and then passed to a senior manager for scrutiny and, where appropriate, approval.

9.72   Cases passed to the Commissioner for approval are given an internal classification:

- "red" cases are those where the Commissioner requires to see the case file, documentary evidence and other background information, usually because the issue to be decided upon is sensitive, complex or raises new issues of interpretation. The Commissioner will consider in detail the information which has been withheld, the submissions made by the authority and the applicant and any relevant matters which the investigator has introduced as a result of the investigation. The Commissioner may vary the outcome from that drafted, although usually in "red" cases the Commissioner's guidance will have been sought in the course of the investigation;

- "white" cases are those where the issues are relatively straightforward and the draft decision speaks for itself. In those cases, only the draft is provided to the Commissioner in the first instance, without the accompanying file or other information.

THE DECISION NOTICE

9.73   The legislation says very little about what should be contained within a decision notice. It does not expressly require the notice to contain reasons for the decision, although it is to be expected that the Commissioner would explain to the authority and the applicant how he has reached his conclusions, there being a clear duty in common law for decision-making bodies to provide reasons for their decisions. (For example, in *Singh v Secretary of State for the Home Department* the court set out that:

> "The basic duty will be satisfied if the reasons given by the decision maker come within the ambit of what was said in *Wordie Property Co Ltd* i.e. that 'the decision must, in short, leave the informed reader and the court in no real and substantial doubt as to what the reason for it were and what the material considerations which were taken into account in reaching it'."[10])

9.74   However, there is no requirement under FOISA to make decisions publicly available. The Commissioner has chosen to publish his

---

10   *Singh v Secretary of State for the Home Department* 2000 SC 219, 2000 SLT 243 at 222.

decisions. (On very rare occasions, specific decisions may not be capable of being published or some details may be edited.) Publication is relatively common practice internationally – the Slovenian Commissioner helpfully even publishes her key decisions in English translation. Some Commissioners may on occasion publish a summary or withhold certain details, for example the name of the applicant. (The Western Australia Information Commissioner publishes some decisions only in note form, summarising the decision. The Irish Commissioner publishes her decisions but sometimes with sensitive sections deleted.) Other Commissioners or Ombudsmen do not choose, or are not allowed, to publish, for example in Canada and New Zealand. There are a variety of reasons for not publishing – to avoid "naming and shaming" authorities, or because the process is non-legalistic and the outcome is intended to be communicated to the authority and the applicant alone. The drawback, however, is that it means that there may be little in the way of precedent to allow authorities and applicants to understand how the law is being interpreted. This can mean that authorities continue to rely on lines of argument which have been repeatedly rejected by the Ombudsman or Commissioner.

The benefits of publication of decision notices are: 9.75

- making available to all the Commissioner's interpretation of the provisions of FOISA and the EIRs in precedent-setting decisions. These so-called "platform decisions" are referred to in the Commissioner's briefings on exemptions;
- restraining general assumptions as to the interpretation of exemptions etc if the decision turns on the specific details of the case;
- informing authorities as to how to respond to broadly similar requests;
- encouraging the press and public to be aware of the kind of information which is being requested and disclosed;
- exhibiting good practice by disclosure

Furthermore, even where the decision is communicated only to the 9.76 applicant and authority, no constraint can be placed upon them from further disseminating the decision in full or in part – and with the advent of websites specifically for the purpose of tracking FOI requests and outcomes this is highly likely to happen. Publishing ensures that the full decision is in the public domain and not just those elements which the authority or applicant may wish to circulate after receipt.

9.77   The decision notice always names the authority and usually names the applicant. However, in around 14 per cent of cases the application is anonymised to protect the identity of the applicant or to prevent the identification of an individual related to the applicant. When an applicant is contacted at the outset of an investigation they are informed that decisions will be published and asked whether they wish their name to be anonymised.

Applications from prisoners

A number of applications dealt with by the Commissioner come from prisoners.

Arrangements have been made so that correspondence between the Commissioner and prisoners is treated as "privileged". Correspondence from the Commissioner is not to be opened by the Scottish Prison Service but may instead be opened by the prisoner him- or herself. This is particularly important as applications may concern a refusal by the Scottish Prison Service to provide information in response to a request. Communication with prisoner applicants relies heavily on letters as they have limited access to telephones and none to the internet.

The Commissioner's decision notices in such cases are usually anonymised, as it may be obvious that the applicant is a prisoner, which is, in itself, sensitive personal data.

9.78   Sometimes a single decision notice will be issued, covering more than one application. This occurs where cases, usually from the same applicant on the same subject-matter and to the same authority, have been conjoined. However, where an MSP submitted an equivalent request to separate Scottish police forces on Special Branch files, a conjoined decision was issued.[11] A conjoined decision may involve requests from more than one individual, as in the case of two virtually identical requests to the Scottish Government for information on a decision not to "call in" a planning application.[12]

---

11   Decision 128/2006: Christine Grahame, MSP and the Chief Constables of Central Scotland Police, Dumfries and Galloway Constabulary, Grampian Police, Lothian and Borders Police, Northern Constabulary, Strathclyde Police and Tayside Police.
12   Decision 060/2005: Mr David Elstone and the Scottish Executive; Mr Martin Williams of *The Sunday Herald* and the Scottish Executive.

GIVING REASONS

The courts have recognised that there are constraints upon what can   9.79
be said by way of explanation in a decision notice, and in particular
the need to avoid falling foul of the safeguards in FOISA against
disclosing information gathered in the course of investigation. Judges,
in coming to a view as to the adequacy of the reasons for disclosure in
a case, concluded that the Commissioner had complied with the duties
imposed on him (by s 49(6) of FOISA), saying:

> "To the extent that there was an obligation on him at common law to
> give proper and adequate reasons for his decision, the respondent had
> done so. The standard was not an exacting one (*South Bucks DC v Porter
> (No 2)*, per Lord Brown at p 1964). The appellants had ready access to all
> the documents in question and could, and should, read the decision
> in light of the treatment of each document. Had the respondent
> endeavoured to give further particularisation, he would have been at
> risk of disclosing the contents of the documents. To do so would have
> risked the commission of a criminal offence under section 45 of the
> Act".[13]

Nevertheless they have also made it clear that where the Commis-   9.80
sioner does give reasons, these must be intelligible. In *Craigdale Housing
Association and Others v Scottish Information Commissioner*, for example,
the court acknowledged that while there is no statutory duty for the
Commissioner to give reasons for his decisions, where reasons are
given voluntarily, the court is entitled to review them. The court went
on:

> "We recognise that the respondent must be circumspect not to disclose
> information which ought not to be disclosed (and that the ability
> of the court to supervise the exercise by him of his powers may be
> circumscribed accordingly) ... But a need for such circumspection does
> not absolve the respondent from giving intelligible reasons for his
> decision. A failure to do so will amount to an error in law."[14]

The challenge, then, is to give sufficient reasons to make the decision   9.81
intelligible but not reasons so detailed as to reveal either the actual
information in dispute or sensitive submissions made by the authority
(or applicant) to the Commissioner.

The legislation specifies that the decision must be issued to the   9.82
applicant and the authority (s 49(5)). This does not appear to allow

---

13   *Scottish Ministers v Scottish Information Commissioner* [2006] CSIH 8 at para 10.
14   *Craigdale Housing Association and Others v Scottish Information Commissioner* [2010] CSIH 43
     (XA51/09) at para 28.

for one version of the decision notice to be issued to the authority, indicating, with direct reference to the content of documents, why arguments were accepted or rejected and another version to the applicant which summarises the outcomes but without giving away the content of the withheld information.

9.83   However, mindful of the Court of Session's opinion, on some rare occasions decisions have been sent to the authority with a covering letter, expanding on the decision notice by making more explicit the reasons for ordering disclosure in a manner which might have to be more obliquely expressed in the decision notice itself. (The UK ICO has used confidential annexes to decision notices, to the same effect.)

9.84   This was evident in a decision, cryptically published as being about "Correspondence between the First Minister and a named individual".[15] The case exhibits the problem in adequately explaining the reasoning behind a decision (in that case ordering disclosure) without compromising the duty not to disclose the substance of the information which the authority had made available to the Commissioner in the course of the investigation. As noted in the decision:

> "Given the nature of the withheld information, the Commissioner does not consider it possible to set out his consideration of the relevant public interest arguments adequately in a public document without giving at least a strong indication of the substance of what has been withheld and thus potentially breaching section 45 of FOISA. He will therefore record that consideration in a covering letter to the Ministers to accompany this decision."

9.85   The decision established that "the subject matter of the correspondence is of significant public interest, and a matter on which subsequent public statements have been made by the First Minister. It is a matter of considerable public interest that Ministers' earlier actions and views on this matter should be known".

9.86   In fact, as subsequently became known when Ministers complied with the decision and disclosed the information, the correspondence was with Sir Fred Goodwin, then Chief Executive of the Royal Bank of Scotland. In it the First Minister offered his support for the takeover bid for the Dutch Bank ABN-AMRO and wrote: "It is in Scottish interests for RBS to be successful, and I would like to offer any assistance my office can provide. Good luck with the bid."[16]

---

15 Decision 106/2010: Mr Tom Gordon and the Scottish Ministers.
16 *The Herald*, 8 August 2010: http://www.heraldscotland.com/news/politics/revealed-salmond-s-support-for-goodwin-over-disastrous-rbs-deal-1.1046662.

However, the First Minister was subsequently critical of the takeover   9.87
which had led in part to the collapse of RBS and the need for public bail-
out. These were the "specific circumstances of the case" which caused
the Commissioner to say it was in the public interest to disclose the
letter – which could not be detailed in the decision but instead were
made plain in the covering letter.

The need for caution has not dissuaded the Commissioner, in the   9.88
majority of cases, from providing detailed decision notices.

"TECHNICAL AND LEGALISTIC" DECISION NOTICES

It is important to recognise that a decision notice comes at the end of a   9.89
process during which neither the applicant nor the authority has been
prepared to accede to the view of the other and where no settlement
has taken place. It is often the case that information is released in
response to an application or during an investigation. What then
remains in dispute is information which the authority is determined to
withhold and about which the applicant insists on a decision from the
Commissioner. Relationships between the parties can be adversarial,
with entrenched positions. Both parties deserve a full account of why
the outcome in a disputed case has not favoured them if acceptance is
to be secured.

The intent is to write the decision notice in an informative   9.90
way such that applicants and authorities can accept the outcome.
Nevertheless they tend to be phrased formally so as to provide a
sound basis to defend the decision in the courts if they are not
accepted. Notices can also be long, as it is important to make clear to
authorities what is required of them to comply fully. This sometimes
means that detailed appendices accompany decisions, involving the
interplay between many documents and exemptions, identifying
specific paragraphs or lines from which information can be withheld
or must be disclosed. As a result, some decision notices can extend
to over 100 pages.[17]

Although in Scotland the vast majority of decisions are accepted   9.91
by authorities and applicants, with very few being appealed to the
courts, the need for the decision notice to be capable of judicial
scrutiny can mean that the applicant receives a document phrased in
a manner which does not venture far from the expressed wording in
the legislation. Former Deputy First Minister Lord Wallace, who was

---

17   See, eg, the notice in Decision 109/2010: Iain McKie and Mhairi McKie and the Scottish
     Ministers, which runs to 119 pages (http://www.itspublicknowledge.info/UploadedFiles/
     Decision 109-2010.pdf).

responsible for navigating the FOI Bill through Parliament, has raised concerns about this:

> "Reading through the Commissioner's decisions, let alone the judicial judgements, I was struck by just how technical and legalistic much of this has become. I suspect that this was always an inevitability, but I didn't see it as detailed at the time and it makes it more important to be conscious of engaging the public and not giving the impression that this is a topic only for lawyers and anoraks."[18]

9.92   Perhaps there was an expectation that an appeal to a Commissioner, rather than to a court, would provide a more informal process. The hope may have been that authorities and applicants, in acknowledgement that a fair and impartial consideration of the dispute had taken place, would be prepared to accept decisions expressed in summary rather than legally detailed terms (which might explain the expectation in FOISA that decisions would usually be issued within 4 months of receipt of an application).

9.93   This approach may work where the dispute is dealt with by an Ombudsman who does not issue legally enforceable decisions. However, it is less well suited to a situation where, in order to establish an error in law, counsel for the authority or for the applicant will challenge loose wording in a decision to suggest that the reasoning is unintelligible or irrational or shows that irrelevant matters have been considered and relevant issues have been excluded.

9.94   In any event, where the decision is that a public authority has not dealt with a request for information in accordance with Pt 1 of FOISA, or in accordance with the EIRs, the decision notice must formally specify:

- the fact that there has been a breach of Pt 1, or the fact that the public authority has not complied with the requirements of the EIRs;
- the provision of Pt 1 or the EIRs with which the authority failed to comply, and why;
- the steps which the authority must take to comply with the provision or regulation;
- the time within which those steps must be taken; and
- details about the right to appeal to the Court of Session under s 56.

---

18   Lord James Wallace, "Freedom of Information: Hope and Experience", inaugural lecture at the Centre for Freedom of Information, 29 January 2009: http://www.centrefoi.org.uk/portal/images/lordwallacesspeech.pdf.

In general, decision notices will require information to be disclosed   9.95
to the applicant immediately after the expiry of the period for appeal
(42 days). The Commissioner takes steps to ensure that the decision
notice has been complied with, and asks the public authority to
provide evidence of compliance.

FOLLOWING THE DECISION

The Commissioner will contact both the authority and the applicant   9.96
to confirm compliance with the notice. When compliance has been
established a letter will be sent to the authority to record this.

The Commissioner cannot simply withdraw or revise a decision   9.97
notice once issued, although certain errors can be simply remedied.
The Court of Session has made it clear that administrative changes can
be made, observing that: "where errors of an administrative nature ...
are noticed, it should not ordinarily be necessary to bring an appeal
to remedy them. The respondent has, in our view, an implicit power
to correct administrative errors drawn to his attention".[19] An error
might be that the text of a decision orders disclosure of a particular
document but the appendix indicates that the same document should
be withheld. In such circumstances a clarifying amendment can be
made.

Similarly, if an authority is not clear about what it is required to   9.98
disclose and a clarifying amendment to the notice is required, then the
authority should seek clarification from the Commissioner within the
time period for appeal.

The applicant or the authority will occasionally ask for further   9.99
clarification of the reasons for the decision, and within circumspect
bounds this may be provided. However, where such a request is clearly
in effect challenging the decision, the applicant or authority will be
reminded of their right to appeal the decision on a point of law.

The Commissioner has only rarely decided not to require full   9.100
compliance with a decision. One such occasion was when Scottish
Natural Heritage was allowed to withhold information which might
reveal the sites of freshwater pearl mussels but the Commissioner
ordered the authority to release other information. Only at the point
of preparing the information for release did SNH realise that it had
not properly identified to the Commissioner all instances where
this information was recorded, and so compliance with the decision
notice would have inadvertently resulted in the required disclosure of

---

19 Opinion of the Court of Session in *Scottish Ministers v Scottish Information Commissioner*:
    http://www.scotcourts.gov.uk/opinions/2007CSIH08.html.

some of the very information the Commissioner had agreed could be withheld. The Commissioner recognised that this was contrary to the intention of the decision notice. Having accepted that the release of the site of a protected species would occasion the harm (which he had agreed should be avoided), he therefore informed the authority (and the applicant) that he would not enforce the terms of the notice for that specific information.[20]

NO DECISION REQUIRED

9.101   Not all investigations lead to a decision. No decision is required if the application is:

- withdrawn;
- settled;
- abandoned;
- frivolous or vexatious.

WITHDRAWN APPLICATIONS

9.102   An applicant is entitled to withdraw an application. Reasons for withdrawing an application may include:

- the authority belatedly provides an acceptable response, for example releasing all the information requested;
- the applicant has received the information from another source;
- the applicant is no longer interested in the information.

9.103   It may become apparent during an investigation that no useful purpose would be served by the issue of a decision notice, perhaps because:

- the applicant has received all the information requested;
- the request was for the applicant's own personal data (and therefore exempt under FOISA); or
- the cost of complying with the request would exceed the s 12 limit.

9.104   In such cases the option of withdrawing the application may be raised with the applicant.

9.105   Applicants may choose to withdraw an application when it becomes apparent in the course of investigation that a decision is not

20   Decision 073/2010: Dr A D Hawkins and Scottish Natural Heritage.

likely to result in information being disclosed to them, for example if it is clear that the public authority does not hold the information, or that the Commissioner will almost certainly regard the information as absolutely exempt, given the precedent of previous decisions

SETTLEMENT

Many cases are withdrawn because settlement has taken place in the course of an investigation.   9.106

FOISA (s 49(4)) provides that the Commissioner may "endeavour to effect a settlement". Settlement is a process by which both parties agree to a course of action as a result of which the applicant withdraws their application to the Commissioner for a decision. It may involve a compromise by one or both parties. Settlement will generally result in a positive outcome for the applicant, although not necessarily in the release of all or any of the information originally requested. In some settled cases, the outcome may be that the applicant is satisfied to receive quite different information from that which he or she originally requested. Or an authority can undertake to resolve a problem for the applicant and therefore the applicant no longer wishes to obtain information related to the matter.   9.107

Where settlement is explored neither the authority nor the applicant forfeits their option to maintain their original position. The applicant's right to a decision is safeguarded. However, the aim of the Commissioner in effecting settlement is to secure terms which are more advantageous to the applicant than continuing with the application. If settlement is achieved it is done in the expectation that the authority may require withdrawal of the application to the Commissioner as the basis for settlement.   9.108

At any stage in the investigation it may become apparent that the parties may be willing to settle on the basis that: 9.109

- the applicant wants to try to resolve the case without waiting for a formal decision to be issued; or
- the applicant needs information more quickly than might be achieved if a formal decision were to be issued; or
- the authority recognises that the information should have been released when it received the initial request for the information and indicates that it would like to settle; or
- the applicant, or the public authority, or both parties, has or have not understood the other party's position, which, if explained, would allow the matter to be resolved; or

- limited disclosure, or arranging access to the information for the applicant without disclosure under FOISA, is likely to meet the applicant's needs.

9.110   By their nature, settlements are informal agreements, often individual to the circumstances of the applicant. The Commissioner does not publish determinations in these cases, so there is generally lower awareness of the nature of settled cases and their impact.

9.111   But a flavour of what has taken place comes from the following examples:

- a solicitor wanted information on behalf of his client from an authority which claimed not to hold it. During the investigation the authority offered to provide the solicitors with an explanation of informal discussions which had taken place, on matters covered by the request. The offer was accepted and the case settled;
- the bereaved parents of a son who had died in an accident wanted to be given a copy of pages from a police officer's notebook (containing witness details) and a sudden death report. Given the circumstances, the police force (with the agreement of the procurator fiscal) responded to a proposal from the Commissioner to show the parents the information, on which basis the case was settled. The information in this case was not released under FOISA and therefore would not necessarily be provided to other people who asked to see it;
- following a complaint about unhygienic standards in a public authority's staff canteen, the applicant wanted to know what action had been taken against a member of the catering staff. The authority refused, on the ground that this was personal information. The investigator established that a more general explanation of what had happened as a result of the complaint would satisfy the applicant. The authority agreed to provide this and the case was settled.

9.112   There is no obligation on the Commissioner to pursue settlement and it is not appropriate to do so in many cases. For example:

- the authority may raise the prospect of settlement at a very late stage in the investigation, perhaps recognising that an adverse decision from the Commissioner was likely. Pursuing settlement would simply further delay the issue of a decision and the disclosure of information as a consequence;

- where the case may be better determined by a decision notice, for example where the reasoning or outcome would set an important precedent and would assist in other similar cases;
- where information is going to be disclosed, there may be a greater public interest in having the information disclosed under FOISA or EIRs (and entering the public domain) than in seeing it provided only to the applicant by informal agreement;
- attempting settlement may not be appropriate in cases where public authorities have: withheld information for a long period of time; been generally unco-operative; or where the manner in which the public authority dealt with the application is so poor that this should be recorded within a decision.

ABANDONED CASES

On occasion, the applicant does not notify the Commissioner of their wish to withdraw an application; rather, they simply abandon it. This usually becomes evident from the failure of the applicant to respond to enquiries from the investigator. In these circumstances the applicant will be notified by letter that the case will be treated as abandoned and no decision issued if no response is received within 10 days. In addition, the investigator will attempt to seek a response by e-mail or phone where such contact details are held.   9.113

If no response is received then a formal notification will be sent by recorded delivery: 9.114

- advising the applicant that the Commissioner has determined that no decision falls to be made as the application has been abandoned;
- giving reasons for the determination;
- advising of the right of appeal the determination to the Court of Session.

FRIVOLOUS OR VEXATIOUS APPLICATIONS

Section 49(1) allows the Commissioner to determine that the application to him is frivolous or vexatious, in which case no decision is required to be made. This is independent of any claim by the authority that the request to it was vexatious under s 14. It is notable that authorities cannot claim that the request to them was frivolous.   9.115

The terminology (which also features in the equivalent Irish FOI laws) is not particularly helpful and can cause resentment.   9.116

Notwithstanding that it applies to the application, the applicant may feel that they are judged to be frivolous or vexatious.

9.117   It is very rare for the Commissioner to use this provision (there have been only 19 cases in 5 years). However, it has been thought appropriate to do so where, for example, an applicant made repeated applications for his own personal data and the Commissioner had issued a number of decisions determining that this information could not be provided under FOISA; when he made yet another application on the same basis, it was held to be vexatious. In such cases the applicant will be formally notified of this outcome, the reasons and the right of appeal to the courts.

Chapter 10

PRACTICE ASSESSMENTS

In the course of dealing with applicants' complaints that they have not   **10.01**
received all the information they have requested, the Commissioner
has also regularly found that the authorities have failed to comply
with other provisions in FOISA, such as not responding on time, or
failing to inform the applicant of the right of appeal etc. Such failures
to comply are often recorded and commented upon in the decision
notice, even if the authority is not required to take any action in
respect of that specific failure.

However, these deficiencies may form the focus of the applicant's   **10.02**
complaint, especially where they have not received any response to
their request for information. Investigations into these cases are
termed "technical investigations" and will often lead to the authority
being required to remedy the failing by complying with the request,
by providing the information or specifying the exemptions under
which it is being withheld.

Over a period of time, it may become apparent whether these are   **10.03**
isolated departures from good practice or are indicative of systemic
poor practice by the authority.

The Commissioner has a statutory role to promote the follow-   **10.04**
ing of good practice by Scottish public authorities.[1] In particular,
he may assess whether a Scottish public authority is following
good practice,[2] and where it does not conform with the codes
of practice,[3] then he may give the authority a practice recommendation.

---

1 FOISA, s 43(1).
2 *Ibid*, s 43(3).
3 FOISA specifically refers to the Codes of Practice issued under s 60 (general good practice)
   and s 61(records management) of FOISA, but reg 17(2)(d) of the EIRs makes it clear that
   the Commissioner's powers under s 43 also extend to the Code of Practice issued under
   s 62 of FOISA (environmental information).

10.05   The Section 60 Code of Practice, first issued in 2004, was substantially revised in 2010 following consultation. The revised code,[4] which is a joint Section 60/62 Code and therefore includes good practice guidance on both FOISA and the EIRs, is shorter than its predecessor, in recognition of the "considerable body of guidance" developed by the Scottish Information Commissioner. It also reflects developments since FOISA and the EIRs came into force; for example the need for more guidance on advising and assisting requesters and a new chapter on disclosure of information relating to contracts or procurement processes.

10.06   If FOISA and the EIRs can be said to be the letter of the law, the Codes of Practice embody the spirit and it is necessary for both to be observed if freedom of information is to work.

10.07   Good practice should be focused on ensuring that applicants are given a proper response and the information to which they are entitled at the first time of asking. It is an important safeguard that they have an opportunity to have the response to their request reviewed by the authority and even more to have an independent Commissioner deal with any continuing dissatisfaction. However, it is far preferable for the applicant to be given a prompt and satisfactory reply, which contains the information requested or adequate reasons why it cannot be provided. This reduces the likelihood of the applicant making use of the appeal processes which can be time consuming and resource intensive.

10.08   (An internal analysis of the time and staff costs to the Scottish Government of processing freedom of information requests estimated that:

- the average staff cost of responding to an FOI request was £189 and average staff time taken was 7 hours and 22 minutes;
- the average staff cost of responding to a review was £292 and the average staff time taken was 8 hours and 35 minutes;
- the average staff cost of responding to an appeal to the Commissioner was £720 and the average staff time taken was 21 hours and 25 minutes.[5])

10.09   Good practice can also reduce the impact of FOI on the resources of authorities by having systems in place which anticipate requests for

4   Scottish Ministers' Code of Practice on the Discharge of Functions by Scottish Public Authorities under the Freedom of Information (Scotland) Act 2002 and the Environmental Information (Scotland) Regulations.
5   Scottish Government Freedom of Information Costing Exercise 2009–2010 Final Report (November 2010): http://www.scotland.gov.uk/Resource/Doc/933/0107309.pdf.

information. These include sound records management systems; tracking systems to deal with requests for information; and clear, adequately resourced allocation of responsibility across the authority for dealing with information requests and requests for review.

In the course of investigations, the Commissioner has recorded   **10.10**
many instances where authorities get the basic requirements wrong. In addition to failing to respond to requests, breaching timescales or failing to inform applicants of their rights, as mentioned above, there are other common deficiencies, such as not recognising that a request is for environmental information.

To address deficiencies and to identify good practice the Commis-   **10.11**
sioner instituted a programme of practice assessments of authorities, which are, in effect, audits of authorities' performance and systems.

PRACTICE ASSESSMENTS

An assessment of a Scottish public authority's compliance with   **10.12**
legislation and the relevant codes of practice is carried out[6] where the Commissioner has evidence or intelligence which suggests that the authority concerned is not fulfilling its responsibilities under FOISA, the EIRs and/or the codes of practice, either systemically or in significant respects.[7]

Around 15 authorities are included in an annual programme of   **10.13**
assessment and their voluntary co-operation is sought. So far, no authority has refused to co-operate with the assessment programme.

PRE-ASSESSMENT

At least 2 months prior to the on-site visit, the authority is told in   **10.14**
more detail of the issues of concern which are to be addressed by the assessment and is invited to complete a pre-assessment questionnaire.

The information gathered in response provides the assessors   **10.15**
with details of the authority's organisational structure (in particular, highlighting who deals with FOI requests), relevant policies, procedures, systems and examples of standard documents. Furthermore, the authority is asked to provide a log of requests received over a specified period (which might vary depending on the size of the

6   Practice assessments are carried out under FOISA, s 43(3).
7   Some initial assessments were carried out of authorities which were thought to be performing well, to provide a performance benchmark and to identify what could be regarded as good practice.

organisation) and a sample of requests and requirements for a review dealt with by the authority. These items are used by the assessors to inform the development of the assessment plan and to prepare for the on-site assessment.

10.16   Other sources of information available to the Commissioner may be used to inform the preparation of the assessment plan. The assessors may:

- review enquiries and cases relating to the authority that have been dealt with by the Commissioner for evidence of the authority's practices, including cases currently under investigation;
- consider the current approved publication scheme and any issues which have arisen regarding the provision of information under it;
- check the authority's website to see how prominently details of FOI rights are displayed and how easy it is for an FOI request to be made;
- review the authority's policies and procedures;
- undertake research to understand the nature of the authority, its stakeholders and likely sources and destinations of FOI requests, and to gain a sense of the extent to which the information it holds is likely to be environmental information;
- undertake an analysis of the sample of requests that have been provided and request further samples, if required;
- consider the authority's co-operation with the Commissioner's investigations, taking account of such matters as timeliness of responses, need to use information notices etc.

10.17   The assessment plan is shared with the authority so that it can comment on the plan and to ensure, by discussion, that the staff and facilities required are available for the on-site visit.

ON-SITE ASSESSMENT

10.18   An opening meeting is held with the Chief Executive (or designated representative) and designated FOI officer of the authority to explain the purpose and scope of the assessment, how the assessors plan to proceed during their on-site visit, what information will be examined (and why), how long the assessment is scheduled to take, and what action may be taken in relation to poor or unacceptable practice. The opening meeting provides the authority's representatives with the opportunity to ask questions.

Once the assessment is under way, the assessors gather information   **10.19**
which will allow them to come to a view as to the adequacy, appro-
priateness and overall quality of the authority's:

- awareness of its obligations under FOISA and the EIRs;
- responses and other communications with applicants (ensuring,
  in particular, that applicants are advised of their right to request
  a review and to make an application to the Commissioner, where
  relevant);
- review arrangements and their implementation in practice;
- ability to search for and locate relevant information on receipt of
  a request;
- ability to recognise FOI requests where they are not clearly
  marked as such, and to deal with requests as "business as usual"
  only where appropriate;
- ability to recognise and appropriately respond to requests for
  environmental information.

Business as usual

Many authorities adopt what has been termed a "business as usual"
policy to routine information requests. This usually means that the
authority responds without reference to FOISA or the EIRs.

The Commissioner considers that an authority should only deal
with a request for information as a "business as usual" request in
order to facilitate the routine provision of all information requested
by the applicant. If the public authority is unable or unwilling promptly
to provide all or some of the information requested, or has other
grounds for suspecting that the applicant may not be completely
satisfied by the response, the request should be dealt with under
FOISA/EIRs, and in particular by informing the applicant of their right
of review etc.

Where a "business as usual" approach is evident, assessors will
recommend that the authority develop an explicit statement of
practice, reflecting the provisions expressed by the Commissioner.

Although the assessment is underpinned by a checklist to ensure   **10.20**
rigour and consistency,[8] the assessors will omit elements where they

---

8 The assessments are carried out in line with the guidelines set down in BS EN ISO
   19011:2002, which is the British Standard providing guidance on carrying out a quality
   audit.

already have sufficient information or where it is clear that there is no evidence of practice (for example, where no fee notices have been issued).

10.21   At the conclusion of the assessment, a meeting is held with the authority's representatives at which the assessors identify key issues and any immediate response by the authority is discussed and noted.

ASSESSMENT REPORT

10.22   Throughout, the approach taken to the assessment process is to secure the co-operation of the authority. The intention is to produce an analysis of the authority's practice, identifying what it does well and what needs to be improved.

10.23   To this end, a draft of the assessment report will be shared with the authority (unlike a draft decision on an application to the Commissioner, which is not shared with an authority). The authority will be asked for comments and will be given the opportunity to propose a voluntary action plan to address any deficiencies.

10.24   An assessment report is detailed, running to 20–40 pages, depending upon the scale of the authority's responsibilities and volume of FOI traffic it receives. It contains an executive summary at the front so that senior executives in the authority can quickly grasp what has been found.

10.25   The final report will contain the agreed action plan. This prioritises the steps which need to be taken to improve compliance and to improve practice, on a scale of 1–3. Priority 1 requires immediate action; priority 2 requires action within 3 months; and priority 3 action should be completed within 6 months. Where there are fundamental failings which are given a high priority, the authority often takes action to rectify these soon after the final de-briefing meeting, even before the report is issued. Action on other issues may be desirable, but not urgent, or will require a longer time frame, for example refresher training of frontline staff.

FOLLOW-UP

10.26   After all timescales for compliance specified in the final assessment report have expired, follow-up checks are made to establish the extent to which the agreed action plan has been implemented.

GOOD PRACTICE

10.27   A practice assessment does not just highlight areas for improvement; it also identifies good practice which can be shared with other authorities.

The types of practice which attract positive comments are: 10.28

- *organisational culture*:
  - a culture of openness and transparency which extends beyond those who are primarily tasked with handling FOI requests;
  - senior members of the organisation demonstrate clear knowledge of FOI, along with commitment, support and positive attitude towards FOI;

- *internal systems*
  - robust FOI monitoring and logging systems, which are accessible to all relevant staff and assist in compliance with the statutory timescales;
  - consistency in FOI responses;
  - monitoring of internal performance;

- *structure and processes*
  - the establishment of flexible structures to deal with FOI requests, reflecting the requirements of the organisation;
  - a robust and independent review procedure;

- *knowledge*
  - an organisation-wide minimum level of knowledge of FOI;
  - rolling training programmes;
  - a willingness to improve continually in light of internal experience and external developments;

- *communications*
  - effective internal communication channels within the organisation;
  - a willingness to assist requesters as far as reasonably possible in order to provide them with the information sought.

Individual assessments point to specific examples of good practice, 10.29
acknowledging the authority's achievements, but also serving to draw these to the attention of other authorities.

An early assessment of Perth and Kinross Council identified a 10.30
number of instances which drew favourable comment:

- the local authority has a dedicated FOI e-mail address which can be used to make requests directly. As a result, approximately two-thirds of all FOI requests submitted to the Council are received directly by its FOI Team (and requests received by other departments are redirected to it);

- the authority has designated Service Co-ordinators in each of its Services who are key contacts for assisting in the processing of FOI requests. Some Services also have designated Information Providers with responsibility for retrieving all possible information within their specific area at the request of the FOI Team and providing it to the Service Co-ordinator;
- where an applicant is dissatisfied with a response, the review process is independent of the original decision process and the senior official appears to be unfettered in applying his judgement and discretion in coming to a conclusion on review;
- the Council encloses a leaflet with all of its decision letters which provides information to requesters on their right to review and the process for requesting a decision from the Commissioner;
- these systems help the authority to cope with a year-on-year increase in FOI requests, which, in 2010, were 25 per cent higher than the number received in the previous year.

10.31   The assessments also highlight examples of specific initiatives intended by the authority to boost performance.

10.32   For instance, the University of Glasgow improved its compliance response times from 79 per cent to 96 per cent of replies being made within 20 working days by putting in place an electronic monitoring system. Each request was given a unique identifier, and specialist FOI staff were given access to the system to check progress, even where the responsibility for replying lay elsewhere.

CONCLUSION

10.33   Assessments are an important, although less high-profile, function of the Commissioner. Already, they appear to have resulted in individual authorities appreciably improving their practice, thereby providing a better response to applicants and, by focusing on "getting it right first time", reducing the burden on authorities.

Chapter 11

PUBLICATION SCHEMES

The purpose of a freedom of information regime is not just to wait until information is requested before publishing it, but also to anticipate the type of information which should be put into the public domain and to publish this as a matter of course. Pro-active publication of information by public authorities is not just a matter of good practice, but a statutory obligation under FOISA. Each authority is required to publish information in accordance with a publication scheme which it has the responsibility to adopt and maintain; and that scheme has to be approved by the Commissioner.

11.01

This requirement for approved publication schemes was described by the Justice Minister as "a novel concept to us in the United Kingdom and Scottish FOI regimes"[1] as it is not a feature of comparable legislation. The task of preparing and approving these was given as one reason why FOISA might not come into effect until several years after the legislation was passed.

11.02

It would have been impossible had not the Commissioner been able to approve some model publication schemes to cover all of the general practitioners, general dental practitioners, optometrists and community pharmacists which come under the scope of FOISA. These schemes, drawn up in conjunction with the relevant professional bodies, such as the British Medical Association, were then deemed to be adopted by the individual practitioners. (Approval of these schemes has been extended to 2014.)

11.03

However, several hundred so-called bespoke schemes had to be approved for all of the other authorities. Tranches of approval for local government, police, the National Health Service, educational institutions, etc were timetabled in the course of 2003 and 2004 and completed in time to allow the legislation to come fully into force by the desired date of 1 January 2005.

11.04

---

1   Mr Jim Wallace, Scottish Parliament Official Report, 24 April 2002, col 11196.

11.05   Although the legislation had placed a statutory obligation upon the authorities to adopt and maintain etc a publication scheme, it had taken a somewhat laissez-faire approach as to how the duties might be met. Authorities are directed by s 23 of FOISA to have regard to the public interest in allowing public access to information held by them and in particular to information which:

> "(i) relates to the provision of services by it, the cost to it of providing them or the standards attained by the services so provided; or
> (ii) consists of facts, or analyses, on the basis of which decisions of importance to the public have been made".[2]

11.06   Beyond that, authorities are free to publish as they see fit, tailored to their own circumstances, in recognition of their varying size and public-facing functions.

11.07   Whatever they choose to do, the law requires that their publication scheme must specify:

> (a) classes of information which the authority publishes or intends to publish;
> (b) the manner in which information of each class is, or is intended to be, published; and
> (c) whether the published information is, or is intended to be, available to the public free of charge or on payment.[3]

11.08   This has resulted in some confusion as to the purpose and, therefore, the appropriate content of such schemes. Some authorities believed it had to cover all of the published material which they held, so sought to include the contents of their libraries in their scheme. Others believed that it should be a virtual catalogue or publications list of the material which they made publicly available, free or for a charge, and submitted schemes running to up to 150 pages detailing titles.

11.09   The extent to which publication schemes were fit for purpose was to be a matter for the Commissioner and again the legislation is not prescriptive about how matters should be resolved in the event that schemes could not readily be approved. The Justice Committee was simply told: "A publication scheme will have to go to the commissioner anyway, and if the commissioner is unhappy with anything about it,

---

2   FOISA, s 23(3)(i). The UK FOIA, s 19 does not make an equivalent specific provision.
3   FOISA, s 23(2)(a)–(c).

that can be swept up in dialogue or discussion – or whatever process the commissioner invents – with the public authority."[4]

After the first round of approval was completed, it was clear that 11.10 renewing the schemes in a similarly tight timescale would dislocate investigative work by the Commissioner on applications and so an annual rolling programme of approval was instituted, with new schemes for Scottish Government and Parliament approved in 2008; local government, educational institutions and the police in 2009; and the NHS in 2010. The number of model schemes developed in conjunction with authorities rose to 14, which reduced some of the burden. However, it was still open to authorities to submit entirely bespoke schemes or to adapt the model scheme for their own purposes, in which case detailed checking for approval was still required.

To try to ensure high-quality and comprehensive submissions, 11.11 the guidance from the Commissioner's office on drawing up a scheme ran to 30 pages, and included standard statements on practical matters such as a charging policy and copyright. The process for the authorities and the Commissioner was still too bureaucratic and critical issues needed to be addressed. In particular there was often:

(i) a lack of clarity about what information was actually being published;

(ii) doubts as to whether information should be in a publication scheme if the authority still needed to consider exemptions following a request; and

(iii) the extent to which some charges levied could be said to be reasonable (compounded by variable charging practices between departments of large authorities).

CLARITY AS TO WHAT INFORMATION IS PUBLISHED

Section 23 of FOISA requires that publication schemes describe 11.12 the information published at the *class* level only. Detailed lists of information are not required for approval.

Publication Scheme – A Class of Information

An example of a class-level description in a publication is:

- Class of Information: Human Resources

---

4   Scottish Parliament Justice 1 Committee Official Report, 12 February 2002, col 3224.

> - Purpose of Publication: To explain how appointments are made, and to demonstrate staff training and development.
> - Description of information: Policies, procedures and other documents for recruiting, managing and developing staff. Details of jobs, responsibilities, rewards and benefits.[5]

11.13   The lack of specific detail, however, may not provide the public with an adequate explanation of what information is actually available; and sometimes it is not even clear to the public authority staff that certain information should be readily disclosed. Yet is important to have clarity about what is within the scope of a publication scheme as this can assume significance when it comes to a dispute about whether or not an authority has to comply with an information request made under s 1. As the Court of Session confirmed in 2009, where information is provided in accordance with an approved publication scheme, the s 25(3) exemption in FOISA (information otherwise accessible) may be claimed by an authority and it emphasised: "No further evaluation of whether the information is reasonably obtainable is necessary or appropriate."[6]

11.14   This is an absolute exemption – if the authority already makes the information publicly available through its publication scheme, it does not have to provide it in response to a request for it. Clear descriptions of published information are therefore essential for both the Commissioner (whose approval ensures that the s 25(3) exemption applies) and for the authority (which needs to be certain that it actually publishes the information before it claims the exemption).

THE USE OF EXEMPTION STATEMENTS

11.15   Publication schemes commonly contain an exemptions statement. This explains that information in a class will generally be published, but that occasionally some information may be withheld in terms of an exemption. (In the example given in the box above; there is a class-specific exemption statement which indicates that personal information may be withheld.) Experience has shown, however, that the effect of broad class descriptions, combined with wide-ranging

---

5   Taken from the Scottish Environment Protection Agency's Publication Scheme: http://www.sepa.org.uk/about_us/access_to_information/classes_of_information.aspx.

6   Opinion of the Court of Session in *Glasgow City Council v Scottish Information Commissioner*: http://www.scotcourts.gov.uk/opinions/2009CSIH73.html.

exemptions statements, can leave what is actually published open to too much interpretation. For example, an authority may undertake to publish its board papers in its publication scheme, but in practice when these are requested make available redacted documents, applying broad exemptions relating to commercial interests, conduct of public affairs etc.

Where there are concerns about potentially inappropriate disclosure, it may be better practice proactively to publish an edited form of the information, while indicating that certain details have been withheld, for example because of concerns over commercial interests. If an applicant wished to see that particular information they could still make a specific s 1 request and the authority would have to consider, in all the circumstances of the case, whether an exemption applied. (It may be that at the time of publication the information had a certain sensitivity, but that by the time of a request the substantial prejudice would not occur.) **11.16**

CHARGING FOR PUBLISHED INFORMATION

Section 23 of FOISA requires that publication schemes must specify only whether the information contained is free of charge or available on payment. The actual amount that authorities may charge, however, is not prescribed. The FOISA Fees Regulations do not apply to information published through a publication scheme. **11.17**

It is open to the authority to charge for information within the scope of the publication scheme which would otherwise be provided free of charge or for a lesser amount if the request was dealt with under s 1 of FOISA. **11.18**

Charging issues have proven to be one of the most challenging aspects of publication scheme approval. In order to provide certainty about what has been approved, the Commissioner has required authorities to set out the charges for their publication scheme information and he has then scrutinised how those charges have been calculated. A charge must be reasonable before the Commissioner will approve it. Charges which would exceed the cost to the authority of providing the information, for example photocopying and postage, have been questioned, and the inclusion of the costs of creating information or of delivering a function or service in the price of published information have been challenged. This approach has been particularly resource intensive for both the authority and the Commissioner as it often involves scrutiny at the document level (as a different charging basis may be applied to individual publications). **11.19**

A NEW APPROACH – THE SINGLE MODEL
PUBLICATION SCHEME

11.20   In 2010, the Commissioner proposed a significant change in approach.
The key features are:

- a single Model Publication Scheme is being made available by the
  Commissioner, suitable for adoption by all Scottish public
  authorities. The experience with sectoral model schemes had
  shown that they were of a better quality than many bespoke
  schemes as they tended to adopt a "high common denominator"
  approach. A single scheme is intended to provide consistency of
  provision across Scotland's public services;

- a generic set of classes of information describes the information which
  should be published by all public authorities. Authorities would
  not be able to depart from or vary the classes of information,
  but could publish more information if they wished to do so,
  which could still attract the exemption at s 25(3) as being readily
  accessible. The generic classes address the problems many
  authorities have had with class definition which made it difficult
  to establish what was being published and whether similar
  authorities were really providing the same type of information.

- a standard charging policy for published information. The charging
  policy is intended to cover most published information. If
  an authority charges for specific information at an amount
  which is incompatible with the policy, then its charges will be
  regarded as unreasonable. Authorities are able to propose to
  the Commissioner exceptional charges for individual items of
  information (for example where the information is provided on
  a commercial basis);

- a notification procedure. Authorities simply notify the Commissioner
  that they have adopted the model scheme and advise where their
  guide to information is published (see below). If an authority
  fails to notify the Commissioner of adoption, the Commissioner
  may consider enforcement action. This should significantly
  reduce the burden on authorities and the Commissioner's office
  of formally approving a scheme for each authority;

- a guide to information. Each authority has to publish its own
  guide setting out what information the authority publishes in
  accordance with the Model Publication Scheme and, importantly,
  how the public may access it. This allows the guidance to the
  public to be tailored to the provisions of each authority while

still adopting the model scheme. By preparing and prominently promoting a guide to publicly available information and, especially, where it may be found this should reduce the number of unnecessary requests under FOISA to the authority. (This addresses concerns by authorities that the public do not consult the publication scheme before making a request);

- *revised publication scheme guidance from the Commissioner*, setting out the requirements of the new approach and explaining key concepts. The guidance includes advice about charging for information, formats and accessibility;[7]

- *scrutiny of compliance*. A new monitoring procedure to ensure that authorities are publishing information in compliance with the scheme. This includes checking on the claimed online availability of information, to ensure links are functioning and that the content is up to date.

The Guidance issued by the Commissioner addresses two issues which have given rise to questions and disputes.

11.21

AVAILABILITY AND FORMATS

The Model Publication Scheme does not include information that is available only by inspection at the authority's premises or from a website. Where access is restricted in this way, it is not regarded as appropriate to approve the inclusion of such information in a publication scheme as it would attract an absolute exemption (by virtue of s 25(3)).

11.22

A requirement physically to inspect material would disadvantage those with mobility problems and may make it practicably inaccessible to anyone living at a distance from the location where the information can be viewed. That much appears to be acknowledged for material which an authority is *obliged* by or under an enactment to make information available for inspection. In such circumstances FOISA provides that it is not to be regarded as reasonably obtainable to an applicant.[8] The same should be true of information which the authority is not obliged to make available but which it chooses to make available by inspection. Yet if such material was permitted to be included in its approved publication scheme it would attract an absolute exemption

11.23

---

7 http://www.itspublicknowledge.info/ScottishPublicAuthorities/PublicationSchemes/PublicationSchemeGuidance.asp.

8 FOISA, s 25(1) and (2)(b)(i).

for being reasonably obtainable other than by making a request under FOISA[9] It is to prevent this that inspection-only information is not included in the Model Publication Scheme.

11.24   Similarly, information which is "web-only" available is not reasonably accessible to those who do not have access to the internet through issues of either cost, competency, or connection. It needs to be recalled that the right to information applies to anyone, anywhere and (virtually) of any age, and "web-only" fails to deliver that right to many.

Although internet access in the UK is widespread there are still significant disparities related to age and income. It is reported that 33 per cent of UK citizens over the age of 65 have an internet connection at home, as opposed to the UK-wide average of 71 per cent. Only 48 per cent of the DE social category have an internet connection at home.[10] Worldwide internet penetration is said to be less than 30 per cent.[11]

11.25   This is not to discourage authorities from primarily publishing information on the web – so doing significantly improves the capacity of those with internet capability to search for and access material. (Although a recurring problem where information is said to be online is that it is not available because of broken links and missing content.)

11.26   However, an alternative arrangement needs to be provided for people who do not want to, or cannot, access the internet. An authority may, for example, arrange to send out information in paper copy on request (although the authority may impose a charge for doing so, in line with its published charging schedule). Where a member of the public requires information in an alternative format, authorities should also be alert to their duties to comply with equality legislation. (Across the UK, broadband use by people with visual impairments (42 per cent), a hearing impairment (32 per cent) or a mobility impairment (36 per cent) was significantly below the UK average of 70 per cent, according to a Scottish Government report.[12])

CHARGING FOR INFORMATION AVAILABLE THROUGH THE SCHEME

11.27   The Commissioner's Guidance applies the following principles to charges for information made available through the publication scheme:

---

9   By virtue of FOISA, s 25(1) and (3).
10 "Scotland's Digital Future: A Strategy for Scotland" (Scottish Government, Edinburgh, 2011), p 21.
11 Internet World Stats 2011: http://www.internetworldstats.com/stats4.htm.
12 "Scotland's Digital Future", n 10 above, p 21.

- The Model Publication Scheme requires authorities to publish a charging schedule in the guide to information. If they have not done so, authorities cannot charge for information under this scheme. The charging schedule must clearly set out the circumstances in which a charge will be levied and the charges which will be applied.
- Material published on the authority's website or available to view at its premises must be provided free of charge, unless there is a statutory fee , for example to access registers. (In which case, a list of statutory fees must also be published.)
- Charges for providing information through the scheme should be reasonable and set at a level which does not exceed the actual costs to the authority of the consumables and postage costs.
- Staff time involved in creating the information should not be factored into charges for providing published information. An authority should not seek to recoup the costs of creating the information.

However, clearly, some authorities publish material for sale in a retail market, such as local history publications available for sale in museums or guidebooks for sale in art galleries etc. These commercial publications fall within Class 8 of the Model Publication Scheme and the charge applied is "market value" which can include the cost of production.   11.28

CHARGING FOR RE-USE OF INFORMATION

FOISA and the EIRs provide legal rights to access information held by a public authority. Access to the information does not mean that copyright has been waived, nor does it give the recipient the right to re-use the information.   11.29

The supply of documents under FOISA or the EIRs does not give the recipient the right to re-use the documents in a way that would infringe copyright, for example by making multiple copies or by publishing and issuing copies to the public. (However, in that regard, the "fair dealing" provisions of the Copyright, Designs and Patents Act 1988, ss 29 and 30 (for the purposes of research for non-commercial purposes, private study, criticism, review and news reporting) need to be borne in mind, where a authority wishes to place restrictions on the use to which its information may be put.)   11.30

11.31   The terms on which information produced by the authority can be re-used[13] by a third party are regulated by the Re-use of Public Sector Information Regulations 2005 (the "Re-use Regulations").[14]

11.32   The Re-use Regulations came into force in July 2005 and "set the standard licensing structure for re-use of public sector information for a purpose other than the one the information was originally created or gathered for. The Re-use Regulations are separate from information access legislation and they do not affect access to information".[15]

The Re-use Regulations specify that:

"the total income from any charge shall not exceed the sum of –

(a) the cost of collection, production, reproduction and dissemination of documents; and

(b) a reasonable return on investment".[16]

11.33   The purpose of a publication scheme is to tell the public what information the authority publishes, how to access it and whether any charges are applied to that access. In that regard the issue of re-use is not relevant to a publication scheme. Authorities may elect, in the spirit of helpfulness, to set out charges for both access and re-use of particular information contained in their schemes. The Commissioner's approval process does not take account of any charges for re-use that might be applied to information in a scheme.

CONCLUSION

11.34   Authorities are being encouraged to adopt the new model scheme in preference to submitting bespoke schemes. The new single publication scheme was made available to bodies listed in Pt 7 of the Freedom of Information (Scotland) Act 2002 and publicly owned companies, as their schemes expired in 2011, and is progressively being made available to other authorities whose schemes are due for renewal.

---

13   In this context, "re-use" means "the use by a person of a document held by a public sector body for a purpose other than the initial purpose within that public sector body's public task for which the document was produced": Re-use of Public Sector Information Regulations 2005 (SI 2005/1515), reg 4(1).

14   Directive 2003/98/EC on the Re-use of Public Sector Information.

15   National Archives, "Guide to applying the Re-use of Public Sector Information Regulations 2005" (July 2010).

16   Re-use Regulations, reg 15(2).

MODEL PUBLICATION SCHEME 2011

INTRODUCTION

The Freedom of Information (Scotland) Act 2002 (the Act) requires   A2.01
Scottish public authorities to produce and maintain a publication
scheme. Authorities are under a legal obligation to:

- publish the classes of information that they make routinely
  available
- tell the public how to access the information and whether
  information is available free of charge or on payment.

The Act also allows for the development of model publication schemes   A2.02
which can be adopted by more than one authority.

ABOUT THIS SCHEME

This model publication scheme was produced by the Scottish   A2.03
Information Commissioner and has his approval until 31 May 2015.
    It is suitable for adoption by: A2.04

- any authority listed in Part 7 of Schedule 1 of the Freedom of
  Information (Scotland) Act 2002
- any publicly-owned company, as defined by section 6 of the
  Freedom of Information (Scotland) Act 2002

The scheme may also be suitable for adoption by other Scottish public   A2.05
authorities. Any other authority who wishes to adopt the scheme
should apply to the Commissioner for approval to do so.
    This scheme must be adopted in its entirety, **without amendment**.   A2.06
It commits an authority to:

- publishing the information, including environmental information, that it holds and which falls within the classes of information below.
- producing a guide for the public to that information

A2.07   The Commissioner has issued guidance to accompany this scheme www.itspublicknowledge.info/ScottishPublicAuthorities/Publication Schemes/PublicationSchemeGuidance. The guidance explains these requirements in further detail, including listing the types of information the Commissioner expects authorities will publish under each class of information.

GUIDE TO INFORMATION

A2.08   An authority adopting this model publication scheme must produce a guide to the information it publishes through the scheme. The authority can decide the format of its guide.

A2.09   The guide must:

- allow the public to see what information is available (and what is not available) in relation to each class,
- state what charges may be applied
- explain how to find the information easily
- provide contact details for enquiries and to get help with accessing the information
- explain how to request information that has not been published

AVAILABILITY AND FORMATS

A2.10   The information published through this scheme should, wherever possible, be available on the authority's website. There must be an alternative arrangement for people who do not want to, or cannot, access the information either online or by inspection at the authority's premises. An authority may, for example, arrange to send out information in paper copy on request (although there may be a charge for this).

EXEMPT INFORMATION

A2.11   An authority must publish the information it holds that falls within the classes of information below. If a document contains information that is exempt under Scotland's freedom of information laws (for example sensitive personal data or a trade secret), the authority should remove or redact the information before publication and explain why.

COPYRIGHT

A2.12   Where an authority holds the copyright in the information made available in accordance with this scheme, that information may be copied or reproduced without formal permission, provided that:

- it is copied or reproduced accurately
- it is not used in a misleading context, and
- the source of the material is identified

Where the authority does not hold the copyright in information it publishes, this should be made clear.   A2.13

CHARGES

The authority must publish a charging schedule which explains when there is a charge for publications available through the scheme and how any charge will be calculated. There should be no charge to view information on the authority's website or at its premises, except where there is a statutory fee, for example, for access to registers.   A2.14

The authority may charge for computer discs, photocopying or postage and packing associated with supplying the information, but the charge must be no more than these elements actually cost the authority. The authority may not pass on any other costs for information in Classes 1–7 below. An exception is made for commercial publications (see Class 8 below) where pricing is on a retail basis.   A2.15

The authority must give the recipient advance notice of any charges to be applied.   A2.16

CONTACT

The authority must provide contact details for enquiries about any aspect of this publication scheme or to ask for copies of the authority's published information.   A2.17

The authority is under a duty to provide advice and assistance to anyone who wants to request information which is not published and the authority's guide to information must provide contact details for this purpose.   A2.18

THE CLASSES OF INFORMATION

The authority must publish information that it holds which falls within the following classes. Once published, information should be available for the current and previous two financial years. Where information has been updated or superseded, only the current version need be available (previous versions may be requested from the authority).   A2.19

The Commissioner's Guidance which accompanies this scheme provides lists of the types of information he expects authorities to   A2.20

publish under each class. The authority's guide to information should make clear what is available under each class.

CLASS 1: ABOUT THE AUTHORITY

Class description:
Information about the authority, who we are, where to find us, how to contact us, how we are managed and our external relations

---

CLASS 2: HOW WE DELIVER OUR FUNCTIONS AND SERVICES

Class description:
Information about our work, our strategy and policies for delivering functions and services and information for our service users.

CLASS 3: HOW THE AUTHORITY TAKES DECISIONS AND WHAT IT HAS DECIDED

Class description:
Information about the decisions we take, how we make decisions and how we involve others

---

CLASS 4: WHAT THE AUTHORITY SPENDS AND HOW IT SPENDS IT

Class description:
Information about our strategy for, and management of, financial resources (in sufficient detail to explain how we plan to spend public money and what has actually been spent).

CLASS 5: HOW THE AUTHORITY MANAGES ITS HUMAN, PHYSICAL AND INFORMATION RESOURCES

Class description:
Information about how we manage the human, physical and information resources of the authority

CLASS 6: HOW THE AUTHORITY PROCURES GOODS AND SERVICES FROM EXTERNAL PROVIDERS

Class description:
Information about how we procure goods and services, and our contracts with external providers

CLASS 7: HOW OUR AUTHORITY IS PERFORMING

Class description:
Information about how the authority performs as an organisation, and how well it delivers its functions and services

CLASS 8: OUR COMMERCIAL PUBLICATIONS

Class description:
Information packaged and made available for sale on a commercial basis and sold at market value through a retail outlet e.g, bookshop, museum or research journal.

Part IV

AFTERWORD

Chapter 12

THE STATE OF FREEDOM OF INFORMATION IN SCOTLAND

A decade after the passage of freedom of information laws in Scotland   **12.01**
is a suitable milestone to take stock, to consider our experience,
perhaps to reflect on how far we have come compared with others and
to anticipate the challenges that lie ahead.

COMPARISONS WITH THE UK

When considering where Scotland stands in the world of freedom   **12.02**
of information all too often the yardstick that seems to matter most
is how FOI in Scotland compares with that in the rest of the UK. It is
perhaps inevitable (however inadequate) that such an evaluation is
made and, from that perspective, there is evidence of a marked contrast
which reflects favourably on Scotland, not just in legislative provision
but in political reaction to the new rights.

The most commented upon distinction is that the Scottish law   **12.03**
has a stronger "harm" test, requiring authorities to demonstrate that
relevant interests would be "prejudiced substantially" before certain
exemptions apply. Scottish legislators pointedly persisted with
this test even after the UK Government dropped the requirement to
demonstrate "substantial harm" (which had been in the White Paper
Your Right to Know) in favour of a simple harm test of "prejudice".

However, there are many other notable – perhaps more significant –   **12.04**
differences between the UK and Scottish regimes. For instance:

- The time limit of 20 working days to respond to a request is
  extended under the UK FOIA for "such time as is reasonable in
  the circumstances" in order to decide where the public interest
  lies in cases where a qualified exemption may apply to the
  information.[1] Scottish authorities cannot extend the time taken
  for this reason and must respond within 20 working days.

---

1   UK FOIA, s 17(2)(b) and (3).

- Scottish authorities also have to respond to a requirement for review within 20 working days. The UK FOIA is silent on this as there is no provision in that Act for internal review by the authority. Instead, in its notice of refusal to disclose information the authority need only inform the applicant of any internal complaints procedure which it might have (or state that does not have one).[2]
- Under the UK legislation it is left to "the reasonable opinion of a qualified person ..." to decide whether disclosure of the information would prejudice the "effective conduct of public affairs".[3] The subjective opinion of an individual is irrelevant in Scottish law, which applies an objective test on comparable matters.[4]
- The UK FOIA contains special certificate provisions for the House of Commons (and the House of Lords). A certificate signed by the Speaker of the House of Commons is conclusive evidence that exemption from disclosure is required to avoid an infringement of the privileges of the House. (A certificate signed by the Clerk of the Parliaments provides a similar exemption for the House of Lords.[5]) The Speaker may also issue a certificate if he judges it necessary to avoid prejudice to the effective conduct of public affairs.[6] The UK Commissioner cannot challenge the application of this exemption where it is supported by an appropriate certificate. The Scottish legislation contains no corresponding provision, not least because there is no concept of "parliamentary privilege" in relation to the Scottish Parliament or its members in the sense understood by Westminster.[7]
- FOISA explicitly allows that "the Commissioner may endeavour to effect a settlement between the applicant and the authority".[8] FOIA is silent on this point.

12.05   These and other differences do not necessarily mean, in practice, that outcomes are significantly different north and south of the Border. Clearly, for example, the UK Commissioner is able to bring cases to an acceptable conclusion without the need for a decision, even

---

2   UK FOIA, s 17(7).

3   *Ibid*, s 36.

4   FOISA, s 30.

5   FOIA, s 34.

6   *Ibid*, s 36.

7   The Scotland Act 1998 has a number of provisions designed to give protection to Parliament so that it can conduct its business.

8   FOISA, s 49(4).

without the explicit powers of settlement which exist in the Scottish law. Even the benefits of the "stronger" "harm" test in Scotland may be somewhat overstated given that the UK Commissioner can still determine that information should be disclosed in the public interest despite the "lower" "harm" hurdle having been cleared. Certainly the UK legislation has proven capable of causing information to be disclosed which otherwise would be withheld.

However, it is well documented that some of the features of FOIA have hampered disclosure. There have been significant delays caused by UK authorities deliberating on the balance of the public interest. The Campaign for Freedom of Information has complained that "Government departments took extensions of more than 40 working days ... in 267 cases in 2008, that is in 21.5 per cent of all completed cases involving a public interest extension".[9]   **12.06**

In a similar vein the failure in UK legislation to specify a time-limit within which an internal complaints process should be completed is a significant deficiency compared with the review process in Scotland. Despite the UK Commissioner issuing guidance recommending that 20 days should be the norm and none should take longer than 40 days, government departments took longer than 60 days in 19 per cent of all internal reviews in 2008.[10]   **12.07**

(The UK Commissioner responded by establishing a fixed-term monitoring programme for bodies which had demonstrated poor practice in compliance with timescales, including those exceeding the 40-day extension by 15 days, where public interest arguments were being considered. In one such period in 2011 19 public bodies were being monitored, including 11 local authorities, two NHS trusts and two police forces, as well as the Equalities and Human Rights Commission, the UK Department of Education and the Welsh Assembly Government.[11])   **12.08**

However, it is not just the provisions of statute which point up differences. Once the UK legislation was in force there were signs of retrenchment as "a series of prominent actions without parallel in Scotland"[12] rolled out of Whitehall and Westminster.   **12.09**

9   Letter to UK Statistics Authority, 26 January 2010 (www.cFOI.org.uk).
10 *Ibid.*
11 http://www.ico.gov.uk/what_we_cover/promoting_openness/~/media/documents/
    library/Freedom_of_Information/Notices/list_of_ico_monitored_bodies_1april-30june.
    ashx.
12 K Dunion, "Freedom of Information in Scotland and the UK: Time to Notice the
    Difference" in R Chapman and M Hunt (eds), *Freedom of Information – Local Government and
    Accountability* (Ashgate, 2010), p 70.

SIGNS OF RETRENCHMENT IN THE UK

12.10   Almost from the outset there were moves to curb the use of FOI rights. Alarm bells rang when the UK Government commissioned a review of the impact of FOI which recommended that a flat fee should be imposed for all requests and the cost threshold should be reduced to £400. Although the Government indicated it did not support these particular measures, it did signal that it was minded to include reading time, consideration time and consultation time in the calculation of charges[13] – making it far more likely that requests would be refused on costs grounds alone. (However, subsequently it was decided that no such changes to the fees regulations would be made.)

12.11   Another attempt to clip the wings of FOI did make it through the House of Commons in 2007, in the form of a Freedom of Information (Amendment) Bill (all the more unusual for it being a Private Member's Bill). This would have amended the Freedom of Information Act 2000 "to exempt from its provisions the House of Commons and House of Lords and correspondence between Members of Parliament and public authorities".

12.12   It was particularly controversial for being pushed through when FOI requests were being submitted for MPs' expenses. The measure was only halted when it was defeated in the House of Lords.

12.13   By that time in Scotland I had already ordered the disclosure of certain travel expenses of the Leader of the Conservative Party in the Scottish Parliament (the consequences of which led ultimately to his resignation from his post).[14] Rather than resist further disclosure, the Presiding Officer of the Scottish Parliament agreed to the extensive publication of all expense claims, which occasioned no further scandal. Favourable attention was drawn to this Scottish regime by Jo Swinson, MP, in the course of a Commons debate on the Amendment Bill:

> "The freedom of information legislation in Scotland is seen as an exemplar both in the time allowed – information must be disclosed far more promptly – and in the level of scrutiny. Some Members of the House might be uncomfortable with the level of scrutiny that Members of the Scottish Parliament undertake. Every expense receipt is published online within a month of being submitted. That has led to an increased feeling among people in Scotland that they can see what their parliamentarians are doing, and that can only help to build

---

13 Freedom of Information – one year on: Government Response to the Constitutional Affairs Select Committee Report, October 2006 (Cm 6937).

14 Decision 033/2005: Paul Hutcheon, *The Sunday Herald* and the Scottish Parliamentary Corporate Body.

trust in politics. Unfortunately, this Bill will help to diminish trust in politics."[15]

EXERCISING THE VETO ON DISCLOSURE IN THE UK

Both in Scotland and the rest of the UK there is statutory provision for the decisions of the Commissioner to be overridden by Ministers. While this has not yet occurred in Scotland, the ministerial veto has twice been deployed in the UK. The ministerial certificate was first used on 23 February 2009 by the Lord Chancellor, Jack Straw, to prevent the release of Cabinet minutes relating to the war in Iraq.[16]   12.14

In doing so he overruled a decision of the Information Tribunal ordering disclosure. Later that year the veto was used again, to prevent the disclosure of the minutes of the 1998 meetings of the Cabinet sub-committee on devolution in Scotland, Wales and the English regions.[17]   12.15

In that instance the Lord Chancellor pre-emptively exercised the veto before the outcome of the Government's appeal to the Tribunal against the UK Information Commissioner's decision ordering disclosure. Christopher Graham, the UK Information Commissioner, submitted a report to Parliament which was critical both of the use of the veto before the Tribunal had been allowed to hear the appeal and also of the blanket nature of the exercise of the veto to withhold any information in Cabinet papers no matter the content. He was concerned that what should be the exceptional use could become the routine.[18] Since then the Coalition Government has issued a Statement of Policy[19] that the veto should be used only in exceptional circumstances and only following a collective decision of the Cabinet, in respect of information that relates to the operation of the principle of collective Cabinet responsibility, and setting out the criteria for its use.   12.16

The Speaker has also made use of his powers to issue a certificate to protect parliamentary privilege. A 2010 briefing paper from the House of Commons Library noted that "Since the implementation of   12.17

15   Jo Swinson, MP, *Hansard*, 18 May 2007, col 925.
16   Certificate of the Secretary of State for Justice, made in accordance with s 53(2) of the Freedom of Information Act 2000, 23 February 2009: http://www.justice.gov.uk/news/docs/FOI-certificate-section53-FOI-act-2000.pdf.
17   Certificate of the Secretary of State for Justice, made in accordance with s 53(2) of the Freedom of Information Act 2000, 10 December 2009: http://www.justice.gov.uk/news/docs/section53-certificate.pdf.
18   *Ministerial veto on disclosure of the minutes of the Cabinet Sub-Committee on Devolution for Scotland, Wales and the Regions* – Information Commissioner's Report to Parliament, HC 218, 5 January 2010.
19   http://www.justice.gov.uk/downloads/publications/policy/moj/foi-veto-policy.pdf.

the Act, the House has issued 12 certificates under Section 34 and four under Section 36. The Section 34 exemption has most commonly been used in relation to requests for Select Committee papers. The Section 36 exemption has been applied to different types of information, including one request for a copy of a briefing given to a Member by the House of Commons Library."[20] As indicated earlier, there is no equivalent provision in the Scottish legislation for the Presiding Officer of the Scottish Parliament to issue such certificates.

SIGNS OF PROGRESS IN UK COMPARED WITH SCOTLAND?

12.18   Overall, while there is good reason to take the view that FOI in Scotland stands up well in comparison with the equivalent UK regime, it would be misguided to assume that this will always be so or that Scottish law and practice is without its deficiencies. There are some interesting initiatives at the UK level, proactively to provide information, which appear to be more advanced than Scottish equivalent practice. The Cabinet Office has launched two consultations to support the Government's transparency strategy. The first of these, *Making Open Data Real*,[21] proposes the introduction of a "right to data" and a "presumption of publication" for information produced by public services. The second is the creation of a Public Data Corporation[22] to bring bodies such as the Met Office and Ordnance Survey together and impose a consistent set of principles around data collection, maintenance, production and charging. Raw data is being published which allows the public, press, and academics greater access to the basis on which conclusions on performance, spending or social trends can be drawn. There is active encouragement for those with technical skills to present the information in a way that is of greater use to the public and authorities are urged to make databases available in a manner which allows the data to be machine readable for that purpose.[23] A Government website provides links to "apps" constructed by such third parties which variously allow the public to compare care homes, check air quality or find out where roadworks are scheduled

---

20   House of Commons Library Standard Note SN/PC/05666 "Freedom of Information: the first five years", 28 July 2010.
21   http://www.cabinetoffice.gov.uk/resource-library/making-open-data-real-public-consultation.
22   http://www.cabinetoffice.gov.uk/content/consultation-data-policy-public-data-corporation.
23   http://www.nationalarchives.gov.uk/information-management/government-licensing/about-the-ogl.htm.

across the country.[24] Greater entrepreneurial third-party use of free public information is under discussion.

The UK Government has moved to extend the scope of bodies covered by UK FOIA. In September 2011 a Draft Order[25] was laid before the UK Parliament to designate the Association of Chief Police Officers, the Financial Ombudsman Service and the Universities and Colleges Admission Service as public authorities. More broadly, the UK Ministry of Justice has consulted with a range of bodies being considered for designation, including the Advertising Standards Authority and the Local Government Association, as well as approved regulators such as the Law Society and the Bar Council.   **12.19**

In Scotland there has been faltering progress to expand the scope of access to information. The focus of activity had been on the potential designation of bodies (under s 5 of FOISA) which appear to the Minister "to be carrying out functions of a public nature". The presumption was that periodic designation would ensure that access to information kept pace with the change in delivery of public services, especially where these were being delivered through long-term contractual partnerships between public authorities and the private sector or through arm's-length organisations such as trusts created by public authorities to deliver services on their behalf. The Policy Memorandum accompanying the Bill made it clear that "it is intended that this provision [s 5] will be used to bring within the scope of FOI private companies involved in significant work of a public nature, for example private companies involved in major PFI contracts".[26]   **12.20**

However, successive Governments have declined to make any such designation orders.   **12.21**

In November 2008, the Scottish Government did issue a discussion paper seeking views on the extension of the Freedom of Information (Scotland) Act 2002 to certain new bodies, principally registered social landlords, local authority trusts and contractors   **12.22**

But it indicated an uncertainty as to the legality of bringing any particular activity within the scope of a s 5 order, on two grounds. First, the absence of a definition of what constitutes a function of a public nature for the purposes of the Act (either in formal legal terms or what is commonly understood), and second the paucity of case law.   **12.23**

While having some prior consideration would have been of assistance, as I submitted at the time, the decision "does not appear   **12.24**

---

24   http://data.gov.uk/.
25   Freedom of Information (Designation as Public Authorities) Order 2011.
26   Scottish Parliament Corporate Body (2001) Freedom of Information (Scotland) Bill Policy Memorandum (SP Bill-36 PM) Edinburgh.

to depend upon satisfying some existing or otherwise externally determined criteria of functions of a public nature".[27] In the opinion of Professor Janet McLean, then Professor of Law and Governance at the University of Dundee: "This is primarily a political test. The statute confers a power on the Scottish Ministers to make a political judgement about what is a public function or a service. That decision represents a conclusion about whether the FOI accountability regime ought to apply to a particular service or activity. Public function will be in the eye of the beholder."[28]

12.25   Such hesitancy was in marked contrast to the confident assurances given while s 5 was being debated in the Scottish Parliament that these powers would be used sooner rather than later. As noted in Chapter 1, Jim Wallace, the Justice Minister, said: "Provisions allow providers of services to the public to be added to the Bill case by case, and I reassure the Parliament that that power will be exercised."[29]

12.26   It was not until July 2010 that Scottish Ministers published a formal consultation indicating that they were minded to extend the coverage of the Freedom of Information (Scotland) Act 2002 to leisure, sport and cultural trusts and other such bodies established by local authorities as well as to private contractors which run privately managed prisons and prison escort services; build and maintain schools; build and maintain hospitals; and build, manage and maintain trunk roads under PFI contracts. The Association of Chief Police Officers in Scotland and Glasgow Housing Association were also scheduled for designation.

12.27   But in January 2011 the Government announced that none of these bodies would after all be designated, saying that "any extension of legislation is not favoured by the majority of those bodies proposed for coverage at the present time".

12.28   This was a disappointing conclusion to a protracted process. As a consequence, it means that no additional bodies have been designated since FOISA come into force. On this issue at least, it cannot be said that Scotland is leading the way. However, even with the new-found enthusiasm in the UK Government for disclosure of data and the initiatives it is now taking on designation, there are still concerns over loss of FOI rights as a consequence of public

---

27 "Extending FOISA? The Commissioner's view" – response to Scottish Government discussion paper, 12 January 2010, para 12.
28 Janet McLean, Professor of Law and Governance, University of Dundee, Holyrood Conference speech, 10 December 2008, quoted in "Extending FOISA?", para 14.
29 Scottish Parliament Official Report, 24 April 2002, col 1112.

service changes. The effect of the proposed transfer of functions from NHS bodies to independent providers under the Health and Social Care Bill is particularly interesting. The UK Government proposes to make contractual provision requiring the independent providers to supply certain information to the clinical commissioning bodies (which will be covered by FOIA). This includes matters such as the numbers of patients treated; time taken to treat them; and performance quality reports against a range of specific indicators; figures on MRSA and *Clostridium difficile* infections; and reports on complaints.

The prospect of using contractual obligation, rather than desig-   12.29
nation, to safeguard access to information has been aired in Scotland but no so far taken forward. However, the Campaign for Freedom of Information has expressed concern that such an arrangement does not guarantee access to information which can be requested under FOIA.[30] The type of information, currently disclosed under FOIA, but not specified to be provided under the new contracts, includes the numbers of serious untoward and adverse incidents including foreign-trained locums; infection prevention reports; policy on the use of restraint to prevent patients from harming themselves; and arrangements for inspecting surgical instruments. Furthermore, no matter how well specified the contract, the providers will not be required to respond to FOI requests directly; only if they were designated would that be the case, which is still the preferred option of the Campaign where the providers' work consists primarily of treating NHS patients.

There is a lack of coherence when it comes to protecting the right   12.30
to information and keeping pace with the change in delivery of public service and in particular whether those expending public funds can be held to account at an operation or local level. The experience in Scotland is that rights to information are being lost as functions are being transferred from traditional and recognisable public bodies such as local authorities to bodies such as housing associations, arm's length companies and charities. Designation was intended at least in part to address this but Governments have shown a marked reluctance to use their powers. While contractual obligations, as are being proposed in England and Wales, may provide some access to information, these would be enforced in the first instance by the contracting body, not the Commissioner.

---

30   Letter from Maurice Frankel to the Secretary of State for Health, 6 September 2011: http://cfoi.org.uk/pdf/Lansleyletter.pdf.

AMENDING FOISA

12.31   The Scottish Government also surprisingly suggested that designation would be premature until certain "deficiencies" in the law were remedied by way of an Amendment Bill. One of these sought-after changes would address the need to extend the time within which prosecutions can be brought for the destruction of information after it has been requested and the other would reduce the 30-year lifespan of a "historical record". These are, by turn, necessary and desirable amendments but they appear to have very little bearing on the designation of additional bodies.

12.32   The Government has announced a Freedom of Information (Amendment) (Scotland) Bill. This will propose amendments to FOISA to "add strangeth and clarity" to the Act. If the Amendment Bill is brought forward to address these deficiencies it will provide a test of where Scotland is headed. Legislative review is not to be restricted to the two matters of historical records and prosecution. There will be a welcome opportunity to make a number of improvements to current provision where weaknesses have come to light since the Act came into effect

12.33   There is also scope to go beyond tidying up the current legislation to reshape the statutory framework. For example, the provisions of FOISA and the EIRs could be harmonised so that almost all exemptions are subject to a "public interest" test, and the other appreciable differences between them reduced. But it also opens up the prospect that those who would wish to rein back on the extent of FOI, constrain the take- up of such rights or relax the demands on authorities will come forward with more fundamental changes. It is not difficult to imagine certain authorities seeking to be taken outside the scope of the law altogether, by pressing to be removed from the Sch 1 list of public bodies. Potentially, proposals could limit the scope for the Commissioner to interpret certain provisions by introducing definitions and varying the terms of exemptions, as has
12.34   happened elsewhere.

Ireland's well-respected Freedom of Information Act of 1997 was barely out of its infancy when the Government made substantive changes to the regime with an Amendment Act. The thrust of many of these was restrictive. Wide-ranging limits were placed on the disclosure of information about the business of Government. For example, a new mandatory exemption was introduced for records which "consists of a communication between two or more members of the Government relating to matter which is under consideration by the

Government or is proposed to be submitted to the Government"[31] and furthermore extended the time-limit applying to such information from 5 years to 10 years.[32] To a much lesser extent, some changes have been made to the UK primary legislation to rein back on the extent of permitted disclosure. The Constitutional Reform and Governance Act 2010 amended s 37 of the FOIA to create a new absolute exemption for communications with the Monarch, the heir to the throne and the second in line.[33] The equivalent Scottish provisions at s 41(a) of FOISA are unaffected, but it remains to be seen whether the Scottish Government considers following suit.

CHARGING FOR INFORMATION

One area of contention which is likely to be raised is over the costs of FOI to authorities in complying with requests and the charges which they should be allowed to make. Even among those authorities with a positive attitude towards FOI there are notions of FOI "not being used by those for whom is it intended", and "abuse of FOI" by journalists, lawyers and elected representatives. Add to this an impatience at the demands of persistent if not vexatious requesters and there can be little doubt that the discourse around legislative review is likely to feature some pressure for the perceived burden of FOI on authorities to be addressed. Proposed measures may entail restrictive changes to statute, but the primary means are likely be financial, making use of existing regulatory powers.   12.35

Over the years, a whole range of financial impediments to limit the impact of FOISA have been proposed: 12.36

- increasing the maximum rate at which staff costs spent on locating, retrieving and providing information can be charged (currently £15 per hour);
- removing the right to the free provision of information costing less than £100;
- reducing the upper cost limit of £600 so that many demanding requests need not be complied with;
- aggregating the costs of responding to more than one request from the same person for the purpose of charging a fee or establishing that the upper limit has been exceeded;
- charging a fee for making a request.

---

31 Freedom of Information (Amendment) Act 2003, s 14(a)(i) and (ii).
32 *Ibid*, s 14(c).
33 This came into force on 19 January 2011 via the Constitutional Reform and Governance Act 2010 (Commencement No 4 and Saving Provision) Order 2011 (SI 2011/46).

12.37   Of these, only introducing a fee for making a request would require a change to the primary legislation – the rest could be done by Order in Parliament.

12.38   The likelihood is that any changes will have only a marginal impact on recouping some of the costs of administering FOI. As discussed in Chapter 8, the more likely effect, and perhaps intent, of increasing charges would be to deter requests and, by reducing the upper cost limit, to make it easier for authorities to avoid having to comply with requests.

12.39   The issue of charging to accommodate FOI requests is particularly sensitive in Scotland given the terms of our right to information laws. Unlike in many other countries (for example, the US; Ireland; South Africa) it is not necessary to invoke FOISA when making a request. Our system is designed so that even those who are unaware of their rights nevertheless have their requests complied with in line with statute. The corollary of this, however, is that all requests for recorded information are FOI requests – applicants cannot require the authority to deal with them on an informal basis. So if a fee was required when making an FOI application (as is the case in Ireland or Ontario), even requests which a Scottish authority would deal with routinely and in full would nevertheless require to be accompanied by payment. The concept of charging a fee for making a request is contrary to the whole basis of freedom of information in Scotland.

12.40   We need not look far from our shores to see what can happen when the fee regime changes. The Irish Amendment Act, referred to previously, controversially paved the way for fees to be paid simply for making a request. (If, as a consequence of the request, the applicant was entitled to receive any information, an additional payment could be required.) It stipulated that the fee must be "paid at the time of the making of the request or application concerned and, if it is not so paid, the head concerned or, as the case may be, the Commissioner shall refuse to accept the request or application, and it shall be deemed, for the purposes of this Act, not to have been made".[34]

12.41   The Irish Finance Minister justified the changes as being necessary to deter abuses of the Act and also "to reflect to some degree the work involved in processing a request". The fee was set at a "nominal" 15 euros, said by the Minister to be "pitched at a level which would not deter serious requesters but which would make less serious requesters hesitate".[35]

---

34   Freedom of Information (Amendment) Act 2003, s 30.
35   B Lenihan, TD, in a speech to the 10th Anniversary Conference – "Freedom of Information: The First Decade", Dublin, 15 May 2008.

In 2009 the total amount raised by all authorities in Ireland from   **12.42**
such fees and related charges was 115,000 euros, with one commentator
saying it was "highly probable" that the fee regime cost more to operate
than it generates in income.[36] However, not surprisingly – and indeed
as intended – FOI requests to Irish public authorities fell by 50 per cent
within the first year of upfront fees being charged.[37]

While there can be little doubt that an upfront fee would deter   **12.43**
requests and reduce the amount of information disclosed, it would
not necessarily reduce the burden of FOI on Scottish authorities, which
would be engaged in an inefficient administrative task of seeking
payment from the unsuspecting members of the public who had
simply asked a question, unaware that their requests fell within FOI or
required payment.

Given the basis of the Scottish FOI rights, before any measures are   **12.44**
taken which affect the capacity to charge, serious consideration would
have to be given to the purpose, practicalities and consequences –
unintended as well as intended. Deterring requests from the many,
even if the intent is to diminish demands made by the few, would
confound the purpose of the primary statute.

FOISA IN THE WORLD

More broadly, any review of the Scottish legislation should not only   **12.45**
take into account international experience but have regard to emerging
international norms and principles.

At the last count[38] there were more than 80 national FOI laws. The   **12.46**
accolade for the earliest of these is always accorded to Sweden's 1766
Freedom of the Press Act. The first truly modern law was the US Freedom
of Information Act which came into force in 1967. The international
move towards adopting FOI legislation has gathered momentum,
with 66 per cent of all national laws being passed in the last 10 years.
(Recent additions include Russia's "Federal law on providing access
to information" that came into effect in June 2010. Still to be added to
the growing list is Mongolia, following parligamentary approval for a
"Law on Information Transparency and Right and Freedom to Access
Information" in June 2011.)

---

36 Dr N O'Connor, *An Economic Argument for Stronger Freedom of Information Laws in Ireland*,
    TASC 2010, p 7: http://issuu.com/tascpublications/docs/an_economic_argument.
37 *Ibid*, p 7. Requests for non-personal information fell from 7,216 in 2003 to 3,191 in 2004.
    The new fees did not apply to requests for personal information.
38 R Vleugels, Overview of all FOIA laws – Sept 20 2010 http://right2info.org/resources/
    publications/ Fringe Special – Overview FOIA -sep 20 2010.pdf/view.

12.47   But in addition that list includes many "sub-national laws" which provide access to information held by state or provincial bodies – of which there are over 180 – encompassing the US, Australian, Mexican and Indian states, Canadian provinces, and German Bundesländer. Scotland is counted among these.

12.48   Yet, as UNESCO has observed:

> "Regardless of a remarkable trend toward adoption of FOI laws worldwide, international experience has shown this does not automatically translate into fulfilment of people's right to information. Among other obstacles, freedom of information is undermined by weak mechanisms for access and enforcement, the bad state of record-keeping and archive management systems and poor monitoring of FOI implementation. Those requesting information, who are actually a minority in every country, often face excessively formal requirements to present requests, significant delays or high fees, burdensome systems for disputing FOI requests' responses and thus often give up their quests."[39]

12.49   Over the years, to counter these deficiencies, there have been initiatives to set down the fundamental principles of FOI, against which countries can be gauged and to guide new laws. The Commonwealth Freedom of Information Principles were approved in 1999.[40] In the same year Article 19 published "The Public's Right to Know – Principles on Freedom of Information" which were endorsed by the UN Special Rapporteur on Freedom of Opinion and Expression, and by the Organisation of American States Special Rapporteur on Freedom of Expression.[41] More recent such initiatives include the 2008 Atlanta Declaration and Plan of Action for the advancement of the right of access to information.[42]

12.50   By reference to these international yardsticks it can reasonably be said that Scottish law and performance stand up reasonably well to scrutiny and comparison.

- FOISA is founded on a principle of maximum disclosure, giving a right to any recorded information held by an authority. The

39   UNESCO, Freedom of information: current status, challenges and implications for news media (2010): http://portal.unesco.org/ci/en//ev.php URL_ID=29474&URL_DO=DO_TOPIC &URL_SECTION=201.html.

40   Communiqué Meeting of Commonwealth Law Ministers, Port of Spain, Trinidad, 10 May 1999.

41   Article 19, *The Public's Right to Know: Principles on Freedom of Information Legislation* (London, 1999).

42   www.cartercenter.org/.../Atlanta%20Declaration%20and%20Plan%20of%20Action.pdf.

applicant does not have to demonstrate their interest in the information to justify being given it; rather the onus is on the authority to justify why, by reference to stated exemptions, non-disclosure is warranted.[43]

- The timescales for providing information are specified and reasonable.[44]
- The appeal process meets the preferred model of: first, internal review, then free right of appeal to an independent administrative body capable of ordering disclosure, and then to the courts.[45]
- Individuals are not deterred from making requests by excessive costs – information is normally provided free or at low cost.[46]
- Authorities are obliged proactively publication acheme).[47]

However, in several respects FOISA could be stronger. Not all exemptions are subject to a "harm" and "public interest" test.[48] **12.51**
There remain certain statutory prohibitions on disclosure, which is contrary to the principles that the right to information should take precedence.[49]

The failure to use the provisions in FOISA to designate bodies carrying out public functions is contrary to the international principle **12.52**
that FOI needs to apply to "non-state actors". The Atlanta Declaration describes these as those bodies which receive "public funds or benefits (directly or indirectly); carry out public functions, including the provision of public services; and exploit public resources, including natural resources".[50]

And some recommendations which have emerged from practice in more recent FOI regimes have not been considered in Scotland. **12.53**
These include "clear penalties and sanctions for non-compliance by public officials",[51] reflected perhaps in the powers available to the Commissioners in India to fine officials and order compensation for applicants.

---

43 See Art 19, Principle 1; Atlanta 4(a) and 4(e)(4).
44 See Atlanta 4(f).
45 See Art 19, Principle 5; Atlanta 4(k).
46 See Art 19, Principle 6; Atlanta 4(f).
47 See Art 19, Principle 2; Atlanta 4(d).
48 See Art 19, Principle 4; Atlanta 4(g).
49 See Art 19, Principle 6.
50 See Atlanta 5; Art 19, Principle 1.
51 See Atlanta 4(j).

ATTITUDES TO FOI

12.54   So it is reasonable to conclude that Scottish legislation stands up well to scrutiny by comparison with the statutory provision of our near neighbours and preferred international norms and principles. But what about attitudes to FOI? The obstacles identified in the UNESCO report mentioned earlier are not due just to deficiencies in legislation but to the attitude of those who are charged with implementing, enforcing and complying with the legislation. Commentators have no difficulty in finding evidence of bureaucratic coping mechanisms intended to circumvent the obligations of FOI, or even to defy them altogether. South Africa's Promotion of Access to Information Act 2000 affords some of the most extensive rights of any legislation, applying as it does to private as well as public bodies. Yet it has disappointed through a lack of use and compliance. Kate Allan, formerly of the South African History Archive, is of the view that "the culture of secrecy pervading public bodies is the primary limitation on the right of access to information".[52] This is manifest in "complete silence: a complete failure to actually acknowledge, process or respond to requests".[53] Even where authorities do consider requests, a broad interpretation of the exemptions is often taken to justify refusal and limited information is supplied regarding which records are held relating to the request, and the reasons for exemptions applying to that information. Professor Alasdair Roberts has extensively documented the measures taken by those in authority to avoid or limit the demands of statute. In Canada he found that the Government "honored the disclosure law in principle while limiting its disruptive potential in practice".[54] The Federal Government did so by recourse to litigation, by challenging investigations of alleged abuses of the right to information and by arguing for "expansive interpretation of key sections of the law, such as the provision protecting Cabinet decision making".[55] The obligation to respond to requests receded when many federal responsibilities – such as air traffic control and disposal of nuclear waste – were fulfilled by bodies not covered by the Access to Information Act. In Federal authorities the resources allocated to responding to requests were cut back, leading to delays and backlogs; complaints about these overwhelmed in turn the

52   K Allan (ed), *Paper Wars: Access to Information in South Africa* (Wits University Press, Johannesburg, 2009), p 199.

53   *Ibid.*

54   A Roberts, *Blacked Out – Government Secrecy in the Information Age* (Cambridge University Press, New York, 2006), p 88.

55   *Ibid.*

resources of the Information Commissioner. Behind the scenes the Government put in place a sophisticated system to monitor requests and identify those which might have a political sensitivity. Roberts argues that despite the progress made over the years the principle of governmental transparency has been limited by the "enclaves within government in which the 'right to know' has made little headway".[56] It is not difficult to find evidence of this in the utterances of those in the upper echelons of power closer to home.

In the UK, almost before the ink was dry on the Freedom of **12.55** Information Act 2000, the poltical reaction appears to have been one of "What have we done?". The express antipathy which FOI engendered in Downing Street, long suspected, is only now being revealed. Lobby correspondents have in the past authoritatively quoted unnamed sources that the Freedom of Information Act was "never loved"[57] and was regarded by Prime Minister Blair as "his worst mistake".[58] A slew of memoirs have confirmed this disenchantment. Jonathan Powell, Tony Blair's former Chief of Staff, said of the introduction of the Freedom of Information Act: "In retrospect, this was a mistake, not because secrecy is a virtue, but because policy making, like producing sausages, is not something that should be carried out in public."[59] Alastair Campbell feared FOI would be a disaster, regarding it as "an excuse for the media basically to clog up the whole government machine with ludicrous enquiries the whole time".[60] Tony Blair's verdict on his own legislation is one of incredulity: "Freedom of Information. Three harmless words. I look at those words as I write them, and feel like shaking my head till it drops off my shoulders. You idiot. You naive, foolish, irresponsible nincompoop."[61]

(I know from experience that politicians in successive Scottish **12.56** administrations have done more than shake their heads at the effects of FOI from time to time and certainly have vigorously challenged its interpretation – but it has to be said none has disowned it.)

What lies behind such dismissive exasperation? There are two **12.57** primary strands of complaint – one which is particular to central government and the other more widely shared by authorities – which are as commonly expressed in Scotland as in the rest of the UK. The

56 A Roberts, *Blacked Out – Government Secrecy in the Information Age* (Cambridge University Press, New York, 2006), p 18.
57 A Boulton, *Tony's Ten Years: Memories of the Blair Administration* (Pocket Books, London, 2009), p 10.
58 A Rawnsley, *The End of the Party* (Penguin, London, 2010), p 337.
59 J Powell, *The New Machiavelli* (Bodley Head, London, 2010), p 197.
60 A Campbell, *Diaries Vol II Power and the People* (Hutchinson, London, 2011), p 603.
61 T Blair, *A Journey* (Hutchinson, London, 2010).

first is that however desirable transparency may be, for those in government it does not outweigh the need for confidentiality when it comes to deliberation. The expectation seemed to exist that the legislation would be interpreted to reflect this view, but the decisions of Commissioners, tribunals and courts have let down Ministers and officials. Jonathan Powell has complained that "The real damage came when the Information Commissioner attempted to spread the net to capture advice to Ministers as well. This had been deliberately excluded from the initial rules".[62] This mistaken belief that advice to Ministers should be regarded as absolutely protected from disclosure as a class, contrary to the clear statutory provisions, is stubbornly persistent. In response to a request made under the previous voluntary Code of Practice on access to Government information, the UK Cabinet Office maintained that briefing notes prepared by officials in response to Parliamentary Questions could not be disclosed. At issue was a concern to protect not just the content of the notes but "the principle of whether or not officials were able to offer opinions and advice to Ministers in the knowledge that they were not likely routinely to be made public".[63] In his review of the case John Macdonald, QC said: "it is worrying that as recently as October 2002 the Cabinet Office was seeking to apply a crude test inappropriately and not considering the harm that disclosure of the actual information might cause".[64] Yet, as has been shown in Parts I and II, similar arguments using virtually the same words continue to be imported into refusals to disclose information under FOI in Scotland. So long as Ministers believe that the supposed intent of FOI is being subverted in this respect, the legislation is always vulnerable to proposals to change the law to match their preferred interpretation.

12.58   The second mindset is that FOI in practice has somehow not lived up to its aspirations. Robert Hazell et al have considered the claims made for FOI in UK Government papers prior to the legislation being passed, parliamentary debates and ministerial speeches. They conclude that FOI "has achieved greater transparency and stronger accountability. It has not achieved better government decision making, better public understanding or greater public participation".[65] They take the view that FOI "was oversold by its advocates and then by Ministers who adopted their arguments".[66]

---

62   J Powell, *The New Machiavelli*, p 196.
63   J Macdonald with R Crail and C Braham, *The Law of Freedom of Information (First Cumulative Supplement)* (Oxford University Press, Oxford, 2006), para 4.89AM.
64   *Ibid*, para 4.89AN.
65   Hazell *et al*, p 266.
66   *Ibid*.

They also conclude that FOI has failed to increase trust in govern- **12.59**
ment. This they ascribe not to a failing of FOI but to a failing of
the media which chooses to focus on "misuse of expenses, poor
performance, inefficiency and failures in government; stories whose
effect is to reduce, not increase, trust in government".[67]

There is no doubt that increased trust was expressed as an idealised **12.60**
outcome of FOI. On the last page of *The Secrets File*, the book which set
out the case for freedom of information in Britain back in 1984, the
belief is expressed that history would show that the introduction of FOI
had "engendered greater trust at all levels of society".[68] It is not clear,
however, that, on such a scale, this was anything other than a lofty
aspiration which, as Hazell *et al* point out, is unable to withstand the
witheringly sceptical examination of critics.[69] Even so, without seeking
to prolong discussion on an overblown claim, I would argue that, in
specific circumstances, FOI can contribute to greater trust. For instance,
however fairly or unfairly, polls regularly indicate a general lack of trust
in politicians by the public. Yet people in Scotland can reasonably trust
that MSPs are properly claiming expenses and that the parliamentary
authorities are rigorously monitoring claims, because at least on that
issue it has been demonstrated to be the case, because of disclosures
made under FOI. However, what if it is revealed that there has been a
systemic breach of trust through the exploitation of lax procedures,
which those in authority have sought to keep from public scrutiny? In
those circumstances we should not be surprised if FOI does not bolster
trust. Onora O'Neill has previously said in her BBC Reith Lectures that
"deception is the real enemy of trust"[70] and that furthermore, as she
acknowledges in her later work, "trust once squandered is hard to
restore".[71] The authority is hardly likely to be given credit for complying
with FOI, especially if it is obliged by a Commissioner or tribunal
to disclose such evidence; in fact, negative media coverage may be
"exacerbated by the appearance that it had to be dragged out of the
authority", as the former UK Commissioner has put it.[72]

---

67 Hazell et al, p 254.
68 D Wilson (ed), *The Secrets File: The case for freedom of information in Britain today* (Heinemann
    Educational Books, London, 1984), p 158.
69 Hazell *et al*, p 215.
70 O O'Neill, "Trust and transparency", BBC Reith Lecture, 2002: http://www.bbc.co.uk/
    radio4/reith2002/lecture4.shtml.
71 O O'Neill, "Transparency and the Ethics of Communication" in C Hood and D Heald (eds),
    Transparency –the Key to Better Governance? (Oxford University Press, Oxford, 2006), p 79.
72 Richard Thomas in oral evidence before the House of Commons Public Administration
    Select Committee, Tuesday 24 July 2007: http://www.publications.parliament.uk/pa/
    cm200607/cmselect/cmpubadm/984/7072401.htm.

12.61   The issue for those in authority is whether such reputational damage is always justified on a fair reading of the information disclosed. Authorities resent being obliged to feed the insatiable maw of the media with information unjustifiably destined, in their mind, to be turned into damning stories. Injury is added to insult by the cost of locating records in response to "fishing expeditions" the vast majority of which will be discarded in the trawl, in their view, for evidence of wrong-doing or controversy. Equally, journalists complain about FOI being used by authorities to suppress critical coverage by requiring particularly challenging press enquiries to be submitted in writing, causing them to become an FOI application, and allowing the authority to take 20 working days to respond – coincidentally neutering the news value of the information when it is released.

12.62   The even wider complaint by those in authority is that FOI rights are somehow being abused by those who were never the intended beneficiaries. These are held to include not only the aforementioned journalists looking for stories, but also elected representatives and their staff seeking to embarrass their political opponents, business people aiming to profit from information gathered at public expense and the persistent requesters demanding information only of interest to them and not to the wider public. This view prevails notwithstanding that the right of access was expressly said to be "open to individuals, companies or any other body" in the Scottish Government's consultation on the proposed legislation. There is nothing out of the ordinary in this. The profile of those in Scotland taking up the right to know appears relatively consistent with international experience. In Queensland, for instance, the Commissioner reports that 70 per cent of appeals to her in 2009/10 came from individuals; 11 per cent from companies; and 8 per cent from journalists.[73] The equivalent breakdown of appeals in Scotland in 2010 is comparable at 74 per cent from individuals; 8 per cent from companies; and 11 per cent from the media.

12.63   The preference for a worthy requester, such as a previously unknown citizen being helped to understand the deliberation of decision-makers, does not make requests from what are often termed "the usual suspects" any less legitimate. Nor does the conclusion that FOI has not (yet) made an appreciable contribution to the elevated

---

73   Office of the Information Commissioner Queensland, Annual Report 2009–2010, p 29. Taken from the profile of applicants making external review applications under the Freedom of Information Act 1992 and subsequent Right to Information Act 2009.

aspirations of a more trustful political discourse and participatory democracy devalue the worth of having achieved greater transparency and stronger accountability. As Hazell *et al* acknowledge, these two were the primary objectives of FOI.

For my part I tend to share a relatively pragmatic judgement of   **12.64** the merits of FOI laws.[74] As others have said, "surely what matters is whether the statutes work in practice", the test of which is: "Do citizens know more as a result of their enforcement?"[75]

Furthermore I gauge this not just by what information is put in the   **12.65** public domain in recognition of public interest, but what is put in the hands of individuals. Leaving aside headline-seeking media requests or commercially advantageous business applications, individuals tend to ask for information out of concern for something which directly affects that person, their family or their community. In this respect FOI has more to do with what has been described as "an increased sense of individual rights".[76] The real worth of freedom of information may lie in holding authorities to account for how they affect us personally, because "as individuals we expect not only that governments are fair, are socially just, but also that they are fair to us".[77]

This fine-grained accountability, used to benefit individuals   **12.66** and small groups, is evident in many of the Scottish case studies I have drawn on when determining "what information it is expedient to give the public"[78] concerning the operation of FOISA. Parents have used the information successfully to challenge the basis on which rural schools were being scheduled for closure; a father has questioned why his daughter had not been screened earlier by specialists for an eye condition after finding that other authorities did so; relatives of those who died or suffered from hospital-acquired infections have demanded data on the incidence of *C. difficile* in their local hospital. As well as being of direct value to the individuals and groups concerned the information has contributed to specific public policy. Legislation was subsequently passed[79] to safeguard rural schools by ensuring that a closure proposal would not be made until the local authority had explored all possible alternatives and fully assessed the likely implications of closure. NHS Highland changed

74 http://www.itspublicknowledge.info/inyourhands/about-applicants.html.
75 A McDonald, "What hope for freedom of information in the UK?" in Hood and Heald, p 131.
76 K G Robertson, *Secrecy and Open Government* (Macmillan, Basingstoke, 1999), p 159.
77 *Ibid.*
78 FOISA, s 43(2)(a).
79 Schools (Consultation) (Scotland) Act 2010.

its screening procedures for *amblyopia* (commonly known as lazy eye) to bring them into line with national guidelines. The Scottish Health Minister ordered an independent public inquiry into the occurrence of *C. difficile* infection at the Vale of Leven Hospital; several of the patients' relatives who used FOI to draw attention to the issue were named as core participants in the inquiry.

12.67   It is understandable that nationally significant outcomes are sought as evidence of the grand claims which sometimes burden FOI. But perhaps the real worth of freedom of information is to be found in the pages of local rather than national newspapers and by asking the people who requested the information what benefit FOI has been for them.

CONCLUSION

12.68   As Scotland considers how to take FOI forward there are still many challenges to be confronted. The interface between the public right to know and personal privacy remains a contested area. Judging the extent to which disclosure may result in the identification of any person is made more difficult by the ease of search for information about individuals using the internet. This reduces what a US Supreme Court judge once described as the "practical obscurity"[80] which existed when accessing personal information meant a physical search of paper records held in a variety of geographical locations. Trends in information disclosure and sharing through WikiLeaks and Twitter undermine the notion of considered release through the structured rules of FOI. The nature of official information has been changed by the informal and unguarded culture of e-mail. The retained volume of such unstructured information means that authorities may be unaware of what they hold. Cuts in public authority finances may generate pressure on government to relax the obligations of FOI or to deter requests through higher costs. The right to information is not keeping pace with changes to the delivery of public services through commercial and arm's-length bodies outside the scope of FOI laws.

12.69   These are challenges which Scotland faces in common with many other jurisdictions. However, in doing so we should acknowledge and protect the solid foundations laid down so far which have enhanced the reputation of FOI in Scotland, for, even on a cursory examination, the

---

80   US Supreme Court Justice Paul Stevens in *US Dept of Justice v Reporters Committee* 489 US 749 (1989) at 761, as quoted in Roberts, p 208.

strengths of the Scottish regime in law and practice are demonstrable. Public awareness of freedom of information is demonstrably high.[81] Citizens are making use of their rights – to request information and make appeals – the majority of which in Scotland are made by ordinary individuals rather than the press, politicians or commercial interests. A cadre of skilled FOI practitioners has emerged in public authorities, in private legal practice and in civil society. Authorities strive to meet their statutory obligations: timescales for complying with requests are generally adhered to and costs are very rarely imposed on the provision of information. Where assessments of practice have found performance failings there is a preparedness to implement improvements. The Commissioner's decisions are complied with and only rarely challenged in the courts. Above all, information which would not otherwise have seen the light of day is regularly being disclosed to the people who ask for it; that surely is the fundamental test of freedom of information in practice.

---

81 In 2009, 61% of respondents surveyed had definitely heard of FOISA and a further 14% thought they had; this compares with 49% and 20% respectively in a similar survey in April 2005, some 3 months after FOISA came into effect: Report of Public Awareness Research 2009 conducted by Progressive Scottish Opinion for the Scottish Information Commissioner.

APPENDIX 3

SCOTTISH MINISTERS' CODE OF PRACTICE

[NOTE: Footnotes to the Code of Practice are reproduced in the form shown in the original]

SCOTTISH MINISTERS' CODE OF PRACTICE   A3.01

ON THE DISCHARGE OF FUNCTIONS

BY SCOTTISH PUBLIC AUTHORITIES

UNDER THE FREEDOM OF INFORMATION (SCOTLAND) ACT 2002

AND THE

ENVIRONMENTAL INFORMATION (SCOTLAND) REGULATIONS 2004

December 2010
SG/2010/257

Prepared in consultation with the
Scottish Information Commissioner.

Laid before the Scottish Parliament by the Scottish Ministers on Wednesday 15 December 2010 under section 60(5) of the Freedom of Information (Scotland) Act 2002 and regulation 18(4) of the Environmental Information (Scotland) Regulations 2004.

CONTENTS

FOREWORD

The Freedom of Information (Scotland) Act 2002 ("FOISA") and the Environmental Information (Scotland) Regulations 2004 ("EIRs") enable the public to access information held by Scottish public authorities. These regimes require authorities to either make available the information requested by an applicant or to explain why the information is being withheld. Public authorities subject to FOISA must also have a Publication Scheme which sets out the information that they will routinely publish. The Scottish Information Commissioner is responsible for enforcing and promoting both regimes.

Under section 60 of FOISA and regulation 18 of the EIRs, Scottish Ministers may publish a Code of Practice which describes the practice which they consider would be desirable for Scottish public authorities to follow in connection with the discharge of their functions under FOISA and the EIRs. The Scottish Government has consulted the Scottish Information Commissioner about the content of this Code, and it has been laid before the Scottish Parliament. It supersedes two previous Codes of Practice issued by Scottish Ministers; one issued in 2004 under section 60 of FOISA and another issued in 2006 under regulation 18 of the EIRs (commonly known as the "section 62" Code of Practice). It also supersedes the Scottish Ministers' "Guidance for Scottish Public Authorities and Interested Parties on the implementation of the EIRs".

Since those earlier Codes and guidance were issued, a considerable body of guidance has been developed by the Scottish Information Commissioner, and this revised Code seeks to avoid duplication or overlap with this. It also avoids repetition of the statutory requirements contained in FOISA and the EIRs, but instead adds value to these where possible. It is therefore more concise than the first Codes, and is based around the particular provisions set out in section 60(2) of FOISA which prescribe its content. Where authorities require further information on the application of FOISA and the EIRs, they should refer to the guidance published by the Scottish Information Commissioner (see www. itspublicknowledge.info). Further guidance on records management is set out in the Code of Practice on Records Management, issued by the Scottish Ministers under section 61 of FOISA.

By setting out best practice as it has developed over the past 5 years, Scottish Ministers intend this revised Code to further support and encourage Scottish public authorities to act in both the letter and spirit of the law. It stresses in particular the best practice to be followed in providing advice and assistance to requesters, and promotes the importance of proactively publishing information. As such, the Code supports and promotes the improved openness and accountability of public authorities.

PART 1

INTRODUCTION

This Part explains the purpose of the Code; provides an overview of the main terms of the Freedom of Information (Scotland) Act 2002 (FOISA) and the Environmental Information (Scotland) Regulations 2004 (EIRs) (collectively referred to as "the regimes"); and explains the role of the Scottish Information Commissioner (further referred to as "the Commissioner") in enforcing the Code.

1. PURPOSE OF THE CODE.

This Code provides guidance to Scottish public authorities on the practice which Scottish Ministers consider it desirable for authorities to follow in connection with the discharge of their functions under the regimes.[1]

In particular it includes guidance on:–

- Providing advice and assistance to persons who propose to make, or have made, requests for information;
- The transfer of requests from one authority to another which holds or may hold the information requested;
- Consulting with persons to whom information requested relates, or with persons whose interests are likely to be affected by the disclosure of such information;
- The disclosure of contractual and procurement-related information;
- Dealing with complaints about the handling of requests for information; and
- The collection and recording of statistics about requests handling.

The Code sits between the regimes and OSIC's guidance. It contains good practice guidance to supplement the statutory provisions, but it is not intended to provide detailed, comprehensive guidance on the regimes. Such guidance is already available from the Commissioner.[2]

---

1 This fulfils the statutory obligation on the Scottish Ministers under section 60 of FOISA and regulation 18 of EIRs.

2 http://www.itspublicknowledge.info/Law/FOISA-EIRsGuidance/Briefings.asp.

The Code is not a substitute for the legislation and does not duplicate or conflict with the legislation. While the Code's guidance is not statutory, the Commissioner will promote observance of the Code and can serve a practice recommendation on any authority whose practice does not conform to the Code. Should an authority fail to comply with the Code it may be failing in its duties under the regimes. Authorities should, therefore, seek legal advice as appropriate to ensure that they comply with their statutory obligations.

2. MAIN TERMS OF THE REGIMES.

By way of an overview, it is helpful to outline the main terms of the regimes, both of which encourage a more open culture across the public sector by conferring on the public a statutory right of access to information of any age that is held by Scottish public authorities.

- Anyone may make a request for information. FOISA applies to all information[3] while the EIRs apply to environmental information only. Section 39(2)(a) of FOISA allows an authority to exempt environmental information which the authority is obliged to make available to the public under the EIRs (or would be so obliged if not for an exception in the EIRs). This allows the authority to respond under FOISA, and go on to consider the request under the EIRs alone. Authorities who do not claim this exemption for a request for environmental information are required to consider that request fully under both FOISA and the EIRs;

- The request may seek information which is held by another person on behalf of the public authority (e.g. information held by an outsourcing partner);

- The authority should reply to the request as soon as possible. Requests handled under FOISA must be answered within 20 working days. If the request is for environmental information and the information is complex and voluminous, the authority may extend this period to a maximum of 40 working days;

- A fee may be payable for receipt of the information requested. Regulations set out the basis on which fees may be charged for

---

3   A Court of Session Decision (Glasgow City Council and Dundee City Council *v* Scottish Information Commissioner [2009] CSIH 73, issued on 30 September 2009) clarified that FOISA provides a right to obtain "information" not copies of specific "documents". However, an authority can provide copies of documents if that is the easiest way to provide the information requested.

FOI requests, which are subject to an upper cost limit.[4] There are no comparable fees regulations for EIRs; when responding to EIRs authorities may charge "a reasonable amount".[5] Authorities should publish their scheme of charges for all requests for information.

- The right of access is not absolute. FOISA and the EIRs set out "exemptions" and "exceptions" respectively under which information may be withheld. Some information is completely excluded from an applicant's rights of access (e.g. information supplied in confidence by UK Government). If any information is withheld, the authority must explain why.

- In some cases the authority must also decide whether it is more in the public interest to withhold the information than to make it available. There is an inbuilt presumption in the regimes that it is in the public interest to disclose information unless the authority can show why there is a greater public interest in withholding the information. Where competing public interests are evenly balanced, the information should be disclosed.

- If the applicant does not receive a response or is dissatisfied with the response (e.g. because they have not received all of the information asked for), they may ask the authority to review their decision.

- If, after the internal review, the applicant is still dissatisfied they can appeal to the Commissioner for a decision on whether the authority has appropriately handled their request. Thereafter the applicant and the authority may have a right of appeal to the Court of Session on a point of law.

- Both regimes encourage the proactive publication of information Public authorities subject to FOISA must have a Publication Scheme which is approved by the Commissioner and specifies the information (including environmental information) that they will routinely publish. Under regulation 4 of the EIRs, authorities must ensure that the environmental information they hold is made progressively available to the public by electronic means, unless it was collected before 14th February 2003 and is not available in electronic form.

---

4 For FOISA, see the Freedom of Information (Fees for Required Disclosure) (Scotland) Regulations 2004 and the Freedom of Information (Fees for Required Disclosure under section 13) (Scotland) Regulations 2004. For EIRs see regulation 8.

5 Regulation 8(3) of the Environmental Information (Scotland) Regulations 2004.

3. BODIES WHICH ARE SUBJECT TO THE REGIMES.

The Scottish public authorities which are subject to the regimes are those which are listed in Schedule 1 of FOISA or designated in an order under section 5(1) of FOISA. These include the Scottish Government, local authorities, the NHS, schools, colleges and universities, and the police. Wholly publicly-owned companies (including those wholly owned by more than one authority) are also covered by the regimes.[6] Under the EIRs, additional bodies are subject to the regime if they fall under the control of a public authority covered by EIRs and they have public responsibilities, functions, or provide public services in relation to the environment.

Where a public authority is considering outsourcing any of its functions it should take steps to ensure that there is no resulting reduction in the public's rights to access information through requests and proactive publication. This may be by outsourcing to a wholly-owned company which will therefore be subject to the regimes. Where this is not possible, the authority must take steps to ensure public access to information relating to the functions which have been outsourced, as set out in part 2, section 4 of this Code (particularly information about performance and finances). This might be through the provisions of any contract in place.

4. ROLE OF THE SCOTTISH INFORMATION COMMISSIONER.

The Scottish Information Commissioner has duties and powers to promote the following of good practice by public authorities. This includes promoting observance of this Code.[7] While the Code's guidance is not statutory, Scottish public authorities are expected to adhere to the Code unless there are good reasons not to which are capable of being justified to the Commissioner. If the Commissioner considers that an authority is failing to take account of the guidance in this Code, he may issue a *practice recommendation* specifying the steps that the authority should, in his opinion, take to conform with the Code.[8]

The recommendation will set out in writing the particular provisions of the Code with which the authority is failing to comply. A practice recommendation is though simply that – a recommendation – designed to help the authority improve its compliance with the

---

6 Under section 6 of FOISA.
7 Under section 43 of FOISA and regulation 18 of EIRs.
8 Under section 44 of FOISA and regulation 17 of EIRs.

legislation. It cannot be directly enforced by the Commissioner. However, a failure to comply with a practice recommendation may lead to a failure to comply with the legislation which can result in an *enforcement notice* being issued by the Commissioner.[9] A failure may also be the subject of specific comment in a report by the Commissioner to Parliament.

If the Commissioner reasonably requires any information to determine whether an authority is complying with the Code (or with the provisions of the regimes), he may issue an *information notice* which requires an authority to provide the necessary information to him within a stipulated time.[10] The notice will explain why the Commissioner requires the information and give details of the authority's right to appeal to the Court of Session against the decision that resulted in the giving of an information notice.

The Commissioner may also refer to non-compliance with the Code in *decision notices* issued as a result of a request being appealed to him.[11] If a public authority fails to comply with an information notice, an enforcement notice, or a decision notice, the Commissioner may certify in writing to the Court that the public authority has failed to comply with the notice.[12] The Court may then inquire into the matter and may deal with the authority as if it were in contempt of court.

---

9   See section 51 of FOISA and regulation 17 of the EIRs.
10   Under section 50 of FOISA and regulation 17 of EIRs.
11   Under section 47 of FOISA and regulation 17 of the EIRs.
12   See section 53 of FOISA.

PART 2

RECOMMENDED BEST PRACTICE

1. PROVIDING ADVICE AND ASSISTANCE AND SEEKING CLARIFICATION.

The legal context

Section 15(1) of FOISA requires Scottish public authorities to provide advice and assistance to applicants and prospective applicants:

"A Scottish public authority must, so far as it is reasonable to expect it to do so, provide advice and assistance to a person who proposes to make, or has made, a request for information to it."

Regulation 9(1) of EIRs contains an equivalent provision.

Section 15(2) of FOISA and regulation 9(3) of the EIRs explain that authorities will be taken to have complied with this duty if they comply with this Code of Practice.

Authorities can also seek clarification from an applicant to enable them to identify and locate the information sought (section 1(3) of FOISA and regulation 9(2) of EIRS).

BEST PRACTICE

1.1 Authorities should provide training to ensure that their staff have sufficient knowledge of the regimes and establish responsibility at a senior level for overseeing compliance.

Authorities must ensure that staff in contact with the public can explain the procedures the authority has in place for complying with the regimes or, where an authority has dedicated FOI staff, that enquiries about the regimes are directed to them. Many applicants may be unaware of their rights or unfamiliar with the legislation and staff should be prepared to explain the key provisions of the regimes to potential applicants. Staff should also be able to explain the procedures which the authority has put in place for complying with the regimes, and to provide guidance on access to information for which the authority knows there is particular demand.

Meeting the requirements of the legislation and bringing about a culture of openness depends significantly on leadership from the top.

Authorities should ensure there is a clearly established responsibility at a senior level within the organisation for overseeing compliance with FOISA/EIRs and creating a culture supportive of the public's right to know.

1.2   Authorities should publish guidance for applicants which explains how to make an information request, the procedure the authority will follow in handling it, and when fees will be charged.

In particular, this should include an address (including an email address where possible) to which applicants may direct their requests for information or for assistance. Where possible the telephone number of a designated FOI officer who can provide assistance should also be provided. These procedures and information about the authority's charging regime should be referred to in an authority's Publication Scheme.

1.3   Authorities should be flexible in offering advice and assistance.

They should take into account the circumstances of each individual case; for example private individuals may be more likely to need assistance than large organisations or other public authorities.[13] Authorities should also have regard to their duties under equality legislation such as the Disability Discrimination Act in ensuring accessibility for all.

Advice and assistance can be given either before a request is made, or to clarify what information an applicant wants after a request has been made.

The obligation to provide advice and assistance continues at the point of providing information. For example, if directing the applicant to a website, the authority should take all reasonable steps to direct the applicant to the relevant section.

1.4   Authorities must provide appropriate advice and assistance to enable applicants to describe clearly the information they require.

This will be particularly important where an applicant has made a request which is invalid, for example by failing to clearly describe the information sought or, where they have requested documents and

---

13   This point was made clear in the Court of Session Decision, Glasgow City Council and Dundee City Council v Scottish Information Commissioner [2009] CSIH 73, issued on 30 September 2009.

it is still not reasonably clear what information they require.[14] The authority must provide appropriate advice and assistance to enable an applicant to make their request in a way which will describe the information they want reasonably clearly.

The extent to which an authority is required to provide such advice and assistance will depend on the particular circumstances of the case. For example, although there will be cases where the request is made by persons who can be expected to describe precisely what it is that they wish to receive, there will also be cases where requests are made by individuals who cannot be expected to express themselves with such precision and who need more support.

More generally, if an authority is unclear about what information the applicant wants and so whether the request is valid, it should obtain clarification by performing its duty to provide reasonable advice and assistance to the applicant. Where a request is not reasonably clear, advice and assistance could include:

- providing an outline of the different kind of information which might meet the terms of the request;
- providing access to detailed catalogues and indexes, where available, to help the applicant ascertain the nature and extent of the information held by the authority;
- providing a general response to the request setting out options for further information which could be provided on request;
- contacting the applicant to discuss what information the applicant wants.

The aim of providing advice and assistance is to give the applicant an opportunity to discuss their application with the authority, with the aim of helping the applicant describe the information being sought reasonably clearly, so that the authority is able to identify and locate it. The aim should not be to determine the applicant's aims or motivation. Applicants should not be given the impression that they are obliged to disclose the nature of their interest or that they will be treated differently if they do so.

This advice and assistance should be provided as soon as reasonably possible. The Commissioner will take a hard stance if any authority takes an unreasonable length of time to provide advice and assistance in order to delay the applicant submitting a valid request.

---

14   A Court of Session Decision (Glasgow City Council and Dundee City Council v Scottish Information Commissioner [2009] CSIH 73, issued on 30 September 2009) clarified that FOISA provides a right to obtain "information" and not a right to obtain copies of specific "documents".

1.5 Authorities should not delay in seeking clarification.

Where a public authority has received a valid request, but needs more information from the applicant to identify and locate the information, the authority should ask the applicant to clarify what information is sought as soon as reasonably possible. The statutory 20 working-day deadline for responding to a request will not start until clarification has then been received from the applicant.[15]

Authorities should note that clarification should only be sought from the applicant where it is reasonable to do so, and that the Commissioner would take a hard stance against any authority that uses clarification as a means of delaying dealing with an application.

1.6 When clarification is not received.

If, after seeking clarification and all reasonable assistance has been given, the applicant still cannot describe the information requested in a way which enables the authority to identify and locate it, then the authority is not required to proceed with the request.[16] In these circumstances, the authority should explain why it cannot take the request any further and provide details of its own review procedure and the applicant's rights to apply to the Commissioner for a decision. However, it is good practice to disclose any information the authority has been able to find which it considers may be relevant to the request and which can be disclosed under the provisions of the regimes (i.e. is not subject to any exemption/exceptions).

Where clarification is sought from the applicant but no response is received, the authority should remind the applicant after around 20 working days that it cannot proceed until the applicant responds. After 40 working days the applicant's right to review expires, at which point the authority should write to the applicant explaining that the case is now considered to be closed.

1.7 Seeking clarification of the name of the applicant.

Where an information request dealt with under FOISA is made by a person (such as a solicitor) acting on behalf of another person and that

---

15 As set out in sections 1(3) and 10(1)(b) of FOISA, and reg 9(2) & (4) of the EIRs.

16 Under section 1(3) of FOISA the authority is not obliged to give the requested information until it has received the clarification sought. Under regulation 10(4)(c) of the EIRs the request may be refused if it is formulated in too general a matter and the authority has complied with its duty to provide advice and assistance.

other person is unnamed, the application is not valid.[17] In line with the duty to advise and assist, an authority should explain to the person acting on behalf of the unnamed applicant why the application is invalid and how it can be made valid.

In practice, the identity of the actual applicant may not be a significant issue. For example, if the authority intends to provide the requested information in full it may do so while also explaining why the request was invalid.

In other cases, any doubt as regards the identity of the applicant may raise more significant issues.[18] For example, their identity will be relevant in determining whether the application is repeated[19] or if it is a "subject access" request under the Data Protection Act[20] or whether the information is reasonably accessible to the applicant.[21]

In such cases, if the authority has reason to believe that the request is being made on behalf of another person (e.g. through previous knowledge/experience of dealing with the requestor, or the subject matter of the request), it should seek clarification on this as soon as reasonably practicable.[22] It is important to note that if it transpires that the request is not being made on behalf of another person, it must be answered within the appropriate statutory period, calculated from the date the request was received (not from the date this clarification was provided).

1.8   Providing advice and assistance where a fee is payable.

Where a fee is payable the authority should notify the applicant as soon as possible within the 20 working day time limit. The statutory 20 working-day deadline for responding to a request pauses when the fee notice is issued and will resume once the applicant has paid the fee. If the applicant is unwilling to pay the fee, the authority should consider what information could be provided free of charge that may be of

---

17 This point was made clear in the Court of Session Decision, Glasgow City Council and Dundee City Council v Scottish Information Commissioner [2009] CSIH 73, issued on 30 September 2009.

18 This point was made clear in the Court of Session Decision, Glasgow City Council and Dundee City Council v Scottish Information Commissioner [2009] CSIH 73, issued on 30 September 2009.

19 Section 14(2) of FOISA.

20 Section 38(1)(a) of FOISA.

21 Section 25 of FOISA.

22 The Court of Session Decision, Glasgow City Council and Dundee City Council v Scottish Information Commissioner [2009] CSIH 73, issued on 30 September 2009, clarified that where an information request is made by a person acting on behalf of another person (such as a solicitor) and that other person is unnamed, the application is not valid.

relevance to the applicant's request and suggest how the applicant may wish to narrow the scope of their request accordingly.

It is good practice for the public authority to tell the applicant that they must pay the fee within three months of the date of the fees notice (60 working days under the EIRs) or the public authority is no longer any obligation to give the applicant the information. Where no response is received after the issuing of the fee notice, the authority should remind the applicant after around 20 working days that it cannot proceed until the applicant responds. After 40 working days the applicant's right to review expires, at which point the authority should write to the applicant explaining that the case is now considered to be closed.

1.9 Providing advice and assistance when the upper cost limit applies.

Where the cost of responding to a request made under FOISA will exceed the upper cost limit of £600 or the burden of responding a request under the EIRs would be manifestly unreasonable[23] (and so the authority is not obliged to comply), the authority may again consider what information could be provided below the cost limit, and suggest how the applicant may wish to narrow the scope of their request accordingly.

1.10 Providing additional information.

The duty to provide advice and assistance does not extend to providing additional information which falls outside the scope of the information request, or locating information held by other public authorities. However, in some situations it may be helpful to provide some form of clarification or context to their response to avoid the information disclosed being misunderstood or misinterpreted.

1.11 Authorities should communicate with the applicant about the progress of a request.

This should include providing an acknowledgement of receipt of the request, explaining who will be handling it and when a response will be provided. If there is likely to be any delay to responding to the request an apology should be provided to the applicant together with an estimated response date. The deadlines under both regimes are absolute and failure to comply is a breach of the legislation.

---

23 Section 12 of FOISA and regulation 10(4)(b) of the EIRs.

However authorities should note that if they apply the provision in the EIRs[24] to extend the response time up to 40 days, they must inform the applicant as soon as possible and within the original 20 working days.

2. TRANSFERRING REQUESTS TO OTHER AUTHORITIES.

> **The legal context**
>
> Where an authority does not hold the information requested but knows that another authority does:–
>
> *Under FOISA*, the request *cannot* be transferred without negating the applicant's rights to an internal review and then an appeal to the Scottish Information Commissioner. A notice under section 17 of FOISA should therefore be issued stating that the information is not held.
>
> (Special provisions apply to the National Archives of Scotland, who must transfer requests to the public authority who transferred the information to them[1].) [footnote *sic*]
>
> *Under the EIRs (regulation 14)* the authority must either:–
> (a) transfer the request (or relevant part of) to the other authority, or
> (b) supply the applicant with the name and address of that other authority to whom they may make a new request.
>
> (Under both FOISA and the EIRs an authority should bear in mind that where it possesses a copy of information produced by another person, body or authority, it "holds" it under the legislation and should deal with the request itself and not redirect the applicant, or transfer the request, to another authority. There are only two exceptions to this under FOISA:
> i. where the authority holds the information "on behalf of another person" (this includes another authority, body or any other third party); and
> ii. where the information is held in confidence by the Scottish Government, having been supplied by a UK Minister or a UK Government Department.

---

24   Regulation 7 of the EIRs.

BEST PRACTICE (RELEVANT TO FOISA ONLY)

2.1 When information may be held elsewhere.

If the authority is aware that the information requested is instead held by another public authority, the authority should provide the applicant with contact details of the authority holding the information and suggest that the applicant re-applies to that authority.

BEST PRACTICE (RELEVANT TO EIRS ONLY)

2.2 Authorities should contact the applicant about the options available.

In the first instance, the authority should contact the applicant as soon as possible within the statutory timescales to inform them that the information requested may be held by another public authority. It may be most helpful to suggest that the applicant re-applies to the other public authority and provide them with contact details. Alternatively the request may be transferred to the other authority if the applicant has consented to the request being transferred. In some instances where the two authorities are publicly perceived as linked, the differences between them should be explained.

2.3 The receiving authority should check that another authority holds the information.

If there is any doubt about whether another authority does hold the information, the receiving authority should consult the other authority to check the position. A request should not be transferred if there is any reason to doubt that the second authority holds the information. When consulting a second authority the identity of the person requesting the information should not be disclosed unless that person has agreed to this.

2.4 Public authorities should transfer requests promptly.

All transfers of requests should take place as soon as possible within the statutory 20 working days, and the applicant notified once this has been done by issuing a refusal letter under regulation 13 of the EIRs.

3. CONSULTING WITH THIRD PARTIES.

The legal context

Neither regime requires authorities to consult with a third party when considering how to respond to requests for information. (In this context, "third party" is a person or body whose interests may be affected by the disclosure of the information that is requested. They may, for example, have provided the information, or be the subject of it.) However in some cases good practice suggests that the views of third parties should be sought on the possible sensitivities of the information requested, such as potentially confidential information or personal data. This can inform the authority's application of exemptions/exceptions and (where appropriate) the public interest test.

In all cases though, it is for the Scottish public authority that received the request, not the third party (or representative of the third party), to determine whether or not information should be disclosed. A refusal by a third party to consent to disclosure does not, in itself, mean that information should be withheld.

NB: Information supplied by a Minister of the Crown or by a department of the UK Government and held in confidence is not "held" by a Scottish public authority for the purpose of the EIRs (regulation 2(2)) or FOISA (section 3(2)(a)(ii)) and hence is not subject to the regimes. When responding to an application for such information, the public authority should issue a notice advising that it does not hold the information for the purposes of FOISA or the EIRs, and explaining where the request should be redirected to (e.g. the relevant department of the UK Government).

The identity of the applicant will not usually be relevant to the consideration of the request and should not be revealed when consulting third parties unless requested. If the applicant is an individual their identity should remain withheld as this is personal data and its disclosure likely to be in breach of the Data Protection Principles.

BEST PRACTICE

3.1 Authorities should make third parties aware of authorities' duties.

Authorities should ensure that third parties which supply them with information are aware of authorities' duty to comply with the regimes and that information will have to be disclosed upon request unless an exemption under FOISA or an exception under the EIRs applies. Tenderers must be aware of authorities' duties under the regimes and the process of answering requests in advance of any requests being received.

3.2   Where consultation is recommended.

It is difficult to be definitive about the circumstances in which consultation would be appropriate, and much depends on the facts and circumstances of the particular case. Consultation is likely to be appropriate where a third party's interest in the handling of a request will be significant, for example because they are the primary focus of the information (e.g. as a business or an individual) or because disclosure would significantly affect them.

Consultation is recommended in all cases where:

- the views of the third party may help the authority to determine whether an exemption or exception applies to the information requested. For example, if disclosure would cause substantial prejudice to that third party's interests, or constitute a breach of confidentiality, the authority would need evidence to support that view;
- the views of the third party may help the authority determine where the public interest lies.

3.3   Where consultation is not necessary.

Consultation will be unnecessary where:

- the authority does not intend to disclose the information. For example, because it considers – based on reasonable evidence – an exemption/ exception to apply;
- the authority already has evidence from the third party that disclosure would, or would not, prejudice their interests; or
- the views of the third party can bear no influence on the authority's decision. For example where there is other legislation either preventing or requiring disclosure.

3.4   Where consultation may not be appropriate.

Consultation may not be appropriate where:

- in the authority's view there is no basis for withholding the information;
- the cost of consulting with third parties would be disproportionate. For example, because many third parties are involved; or
- where there has been earlier consultation on the status and sensitivity of the information.

In such cases, the authority should consider what is the most reasonable course of action for it to take in light of the requirements of the regimes, the potential effects of disclosure and the public interest. It will usually be appropriate to notify the third party about the release of information – see 3.8 below.

3.5   Consulting representative bodies.

Where a large number of third parties may be involved the authority may consider that it would be sufficient to consult a representative sample of them. If those parties have a representative organisation that can express views on their behalf, the authority may consider that it would be sufficient to consult that representative organisation.

3.6   When a response is not received.

Consultation with the third party should be undertaken as early as possible to allow time for the third party to respond and for the authority to subsequently consider the third party's views in responding to the request. The fact that the third party has not responded to consultation does not relieve the public authority of its duty to make information available, or its duty to reply within the statutory timescales.

3.7   Meeting statutory deadlines.

Meeting the statutory deadline for responding to a request must always take priority over consulting third parties. This will often mean that authorities can only allow third parties a short time to respond; this time should not be extended if that will prevent authorities responding on time. If the authority does not identify the need to consult third parties until near the deadline, instead of consulting, they should just notify third parties at the same time as they respond to the applicant.

3.8   Notifying third parties about the release of information.

When an authority has made a decision to release information it may, as a courtesy, notify any third parties who have a material interest that information relevant to them has been released in response to a request, regardless of whether they have been consulted. This ensures that the release does not come as a surprise. Notification is at the discretion of the authority and would depend on the individual circumstances of the information and what is judged to be a material interest.

4. THE DISCLOSURE OF INFORMATION RELATING TO CONTRACTS OR PROCUREMENT PROCESSES.

The context

This part of the Code provides guidance in dealing with and making available contractual and procurement-related information, whether proactively or in response to an information request. In particular, this section sets out:–

- "guiding principles" which authorities should consider in balancing the public's right to know with the need to protect legitimate commercial concerns; and
- best practice in dealing with contractual and procurement-related information.

It is not possible in this Code to provide definitive statements about whether specified types of contractual and procurement-related information should be made available. Each authority must make its own decision in light of the facts and circumstances of the particular case. However, in outlining the guiding principles and best practice, the Code seeks to promote a more consistent approach to the disclosure of procurement related information by authorities.

GUIDING PRINCIPLES

In making available contractual and procurement-related information, whether proactively or in response to an information request, the following guiding principles should be considered:–

Principle 1: Transparency in the use of public funds.

The public must be reassured that public bodies are spending taxpayers' money wisely. The type of contractual and/or procurement information produced may vary depending on the situation, but where held the public should be able to access :

- how much money is being spent;
- with whom that money is being spent;
- the nature of the services, goods or works that money is buying;
- what redress is available if those services, goods, or works are below an agreed standard;
- any cost benefit analysis that has been undertaken;
- any carbon footprint analysis that may have been undertaken;

- any equality assessment that may have been undertaken; and
- any sustainability assessment that may have been undertaken.
- any privacy impact assessment that may have been undertaken or justification as to why one has not been carried out.

In particular, the public has the right to know the full financial implications of long term and high value contracts, such as PFI/PPP contracts (subject to the exemptions/exceptions of the regimes).

Principle 2: Demonstrable diligence in managing contractors to ensure best value for money.

Information should also be made available which makes clear the extent to which the authority is actively managing its contractor.

For example, where it is appropriate to the individual contract, the public should be able to see whether:

- project management and procurement best practice principles are being applied;
- suitable checks and balances are in place to ensure proper monitoring of project performance;
- those checks and balances are being actioned effectively; and
- intervention on the part of the public authority is happening where necessary.

Principle 3: Respecting commercial interests.

The regimes and this Code are not intended to undermine a public authority's commercial relationships with the private sector. To protect the legitimate concerns of the private sector, authorities should consider appropriate use of the section 33 exemption in FOISA (commercial interests and the economy) or the exceptions under regulations 10(5)(e) and 10(5)(f) (commercial interests and breach of confidentiality) of the EIRS when considering disclosure of contractual and procurement related information. Otherwise, there could be a risk that:

- companies would be discouraged from dealing with the public sector, fearing disclosure of information that may damage them commercially, or
- companies would withhold information where possible, making the choice of the best contractor more uncertain as it would be based on limited and censored data.

BEST PRACTICE

4.1 When beginning any new procurement exercise, public authorities should ensure that bidders/suppliers understand the extent to which their information may be disclosed by the authority (either proactively or in response to an information request).

4.1.1 Including disclosure provisions in the procurement documentation.

Bidders should be made aware in Pre-Qualification Questionnaire and Invitation to Tender documentation that an authority is not able to hold information in confidence unless it is genuinely sensitive in nature and therefore is exempt from release (for example because commercial interests may be harmed,[25] or its disclosure would constitute an actionable breach of confidence).[26]

Withholding information under certain exemptions (e.g. commercial sensitivity) requires that substantial prejudice is demonstrated – the authority must be able to show that real, actual, significant harm would be caused by disclosure.

They should also be aware that the authority will not implicitly accept confidentiality terms, and that any confidentiality markings, whilst being noted, may have little weight if the information is requested (for example if it is apparent that the information is not sensitive).

However, an authority should recognise a bidder's legitimate commercial concerns. As such, best practice dictates that a bidder should be asked to identify information it provides to the authority that it believes to be truly sensitive, and to explain why and how long it is likely to remain so. The authority should make clear to the bidder that it cannot be bound by their views, but that they will help inform the authority in determining what information it can and cannot make available on request

The authority should undertake to consult with the bidder if it receives a request for any information highlighted as being sensitive, within the identified sensitivity period. The sensitivity of information will vary depending on the timing of the request. For example, information may be sensitive during the tender exercise, but may cease to be sensitive once the contract has been awarded.

The bidder should also be consulted if there is any doubt about the information's sensitivity, regardless of the specified period. If the

---

25 Exemption under section 33(1) of FOISA, or exception under regulation 10(5)(e) or (f), or regulation 10(5)(c) of the EIRs.
26 Exemption under section 36(2) of FOISA, or exception under regulation 10(d) of the EIRs.

authority considers that information is exempt from release because its release may prejudice the bidder's commercial interests, it must obtain evidence from the bidder to support this view. Of course, the final decision on the release or withholding of information rests with the authority.

This approach may not be appropriate for all tenders and contracts (for example it may be disproportionate or the volume of tenders/ contracts may make it impractical). If so, the criteria applied to contract review which is detailed below ("Reviewing older contracts which came into force before 1st January 2005 for confidentiality provisions") should be considered.

4.1.2 Inclusion of disclosure provisions in contracts.

The terms and conditions of a contract should contain disclosure provisions regarding information provided during the competition phase, but may also be expanded to include the disclosing of information by the contractor. Although not strictly a consideration under this Code (as it only applies to public authorities), it is sensible to tackle all these issues under a single "disclosure of information" (or similar) provision. Such provisions will be particularly relevant where the contractor is designated a "public authority" for the purposes of the particular contract by an order made under FOISA. Authorities should also notify contractors whose contracts involve environmental functions, responsibilities or services that they may themselves be directly subject to EIRs in relation to those contracts.

It is recommended that a provision is included in the contract to the effect that the authority will aim to consult with the contractor on any request for information which has been identified as being sensitive. (As described above in 4.1.1, where exemptions are being applied on the basis that release would harm a third party, the authority must have evidence from the third party that this is the case.)

As regards information identified by either party as sensitive, authorities may consider including that information in an annex which also sets out the reasons for sensitivity and the period of sensitivity. This will facilitate disclosure of the remainder of the contract should a request for information be received or if it is being published proactively.

As already indicated, there must be transparency in the use of public funds. In particular, contracts must reflect the fact that the public have the right to know the financial implications of PFI/PPP contracts (and other contracts entered into by the public sector at public expense), for example how much money is being spent, with whom, for what purpose and over what period.

4.2 Consultation with suppliers on disclosure requests.

As already indicated, consideration should be given to making express provision as to when consultation with bidders/suppliers will be appropriate where requests for information involve information provided by them. (Section 3 of this Code on "Consulting with third parties" provides general guidance on this issue.)

Where bidders/suppliers have been given the opportunity to identify sensitive material and have done so (and any declared period of sensitivity has not expired), then clearly consultation is needed if the request relates to that information. However, if it does not, then consultation is likely to be unnecessary. If the bidder/supplier has not identified any sensitive information, then consultation should likewise be unnecessary (unless the authority considers that an exemption/ exception may apply on the grounds that the information's release would nevertheless prejudice the bidder/supplier's interests). The authority will wish to consider, whether as a courtesy in such cases, bidders/suppliers are notified that a request has been made and are given the opportunity to comment as appropriate. The bidder/supplier then has a "do nothing" option if the request is of no concern to them. The authority still has a duty to respond within the relevant timescales.

As discussed in 4.4, information in respect of older contracts will have been provided prior to any understandings on information sensitivity being agreed. Therefore requests for older material that could have some commercial sensitivity should involve consultation with bidders/suppliers.

Even when a supplier or third party has indicated that information should be withheld and the public authority agree that exemptions or exceptions may apply, that does not mean that the public interest will necessarily weigh in favour of withholding information. The public interest test needs to be considered in each case, in light of the facts and circumstances prevailing at the time of the request.

4.3 Time limits for withholding information.

Most contractual and procurement-related information is only sensitive for a definable period of time. It is not, however, possible to be prescriptive about when the sensitivity will decrease; this time period will vary widely depending on the type of procurement information in question and the stage reached in the tender exercise.

The sensitivity of price information may decrease after a relatively short period, whereas "trade secret" information may be sensitive for much longer.

4.4   Reviewing older contracts which came into effect before 1st January 2005 for confidentiality provisions.

Some authorities will have existing contracts that pre-date the coming into force of the regimes in 2005, often by many years. These contracts may have wide reaching confidentiality provisions that are unsupportable under the regimes. Information covered by a confidentiality provision will only be exempt (for example under either sections 33(1) or 36(2) of FOISA) if the information is truly a trade secret or commercially sensitive, or disclosure would be an actionable breach of confidence. In these cases the authority should consult with the relevant suppliers to:

(a)   advise them that information covered by the contract may need to be disclosed under the regimes, irrespective of any confidentiality provision; and

(b)   agree procedures for consultation in the event that an information request is received.

It may be impractical or disproportionate to review every extant contract. Authorities may however wish to focus on contracts that are:

- large value;
- critical to the authority's function;
- controversial;
- longer term and still have a number of years to run; or
- otherwise likely to attract information requests.

4.5   Proactive publication.

Under public authorities' duty under section 23 of FOISA to have a Publication Scheme in place (see also section 7 of this Code) it is best practice for authorities to consider proactively publishing information relating to the procurement process and contracts, rather than wait until information requests are submitted to them.

Clearly, not all contracts will be of interest to the public, and authorities may wish to focus on publishing contracts in which there is a particular public interest (for example those which they consider to be of high value or long-term, or otherwise high profile). In particular, authorities should consider publishing information relating to the financial implications of long term and high value contracts, such as PFI and PPP contracts.

If an authority routinely publishes information under its publication scheme which is relevant to its contractual and procurement activities, it is easier for the public to access the information, and authorities can decide what information to publish as part of a systematic management process, instead of responding to individual requests with tight timescales. That said, this approach will inevitably have some financial implications (e.g. putting in place appropriate IT systems and staff training) and may not always be practicable.

5. HANDLING REVIEWS (COMPLAINTS).

The legal context

Under section 20 of FOISA and regulation 16 of the EIRs, any applicant who is dissatisfied with the way that an authority has dealt with a request for information may require the authority to review its actions and decision (unless the request was judged to be vexatious or a repeat of a previously answered application for information). A request for review must explain what issue the applicant is dissatisfied with (for example, the application of exemptions/exceptions, or the handling of the request).

Where an authority refuses to disclose information in whole or in part, or does not hold the information requested, it must, when responding to applicants, notify them both of their right to request a review and their subsequent right to appeal to the Commissioner.

A request for a review must be made no later than 40 working days following the expiry of the period for responding to a request for information or from the date on which the authority complied with the request, sent a fees or refusal notice or a notice that the information is not held. Under section 20(6) of FOISA, authorities have discretion to comply with a request for review after this period has elapsed if it considers it appropriate to do so.

BEST PRACTICE

5.1 Authorities should provide details of review procedures when responding to all requests.

This includes those where all information requested is being provided in response to a request, because the applicant may be dissatisfied in some way with the handling of the request or believe that further information might be held. However, it excludes responses to "business as usual" requests, where all of the information requested by the applicant is routinely provided and the authority has no grounds for suspecting there is any possibility that the applicant will be in any way dissatisfied with the response.

5.2   Applicants should direct their request for review to the appropriate person.

If, when notifying the applicant of their right to a review, the public authority has told them where they should direct a request for review, the public authority may reasonably expect those instructions to be followed. However, where an applicant fails to follow that procedure and sends the review request to the incorrect person and/or address, that does not invalidate the review request (provided the requirements of section 20(3) of FOISA are met). In such circumstances, the 20 working day period starts when the review request is first received by the authority so, if that person/address is in the correct public authority, they should forward the review request to the correct person/address as soon as possible.

5.3   Applicants do not need to expressly request a review.

If an applicant writes to the authority expressing dissatisfaction with the way in which the authority has dealt with their request, the authority should treat this as a formal request for review, provided it meets the requirements of section 20(3) of FOISA.

The applicant does not need to specifically ask for a review. They do however, need to specify why they are dissatisfied with the original decision in order for the review request to be valid. If this is not clear, or the request fails in any way to comply with s.20(3)(c) of FOISA or regulation 16 of the EIRs, whichever is appropriate, the authority has a duty to advise and assist the applicant in making a valid review request. The statutory 20 days timescale will not begin until a valid review request is made.

5.4   The review process.

It is important that authorities put in place appropriate and accessible procedures for handling reviews. The review procedure should be fair and impartial and it should enable different decisions to be taken if appropriate.

The procedure should be straightforward and capable of producing a determination of the review promptly (and in any event within 20 working days of receipt of the request for the review). The review should, where practicable, be handled by staff who were not involved in the original decision (however, see 5.5 below). It is important that the review procedure enables the matter to be considered afresh.

The reviewer should record the process undertaken when considering the review request, and produce a review report in order that the authority can learn from any good or bad practices identified. Where the review report highlights procedural errors, the authority should promptly take steps to prevent such errors reoccurring.

5.5 When an applicant complains that a response to their initial request has not been provided.

An applicant may submit a complaint to an authority if they have not received a response to their request within the statutory timescales. This is a request for review and should be handled accordingly by the authority. The authority's response:

- should deal with the procedural failure, apologising to the applicant and taking necessary steps to prevent a similar occurrence in the future; and
- must make a decision on the initial information request itself, i.e. either provide the information requested or withhold it if appropriate, explaining which exemptions apply; and
- Should inform the requester of their right, if dissatisfied with the response, to make an application to the Scottish Information Commissioner.

In such circumstances, the authority may consider it appropriate for the original casehandler to continue dealing with the request and issue the review response, rather than appointing a separate reviewer to start the case afresh.

If the applicant has misunderstood the deadline and complained before the 20 working day is complete, the authority should either respond to the applicant confirming the deadline or, if the authority's full response to the request is imminent and before the deadline, note in the full response that the request was completed within the statutory time limit. Following the guidance in 1.11 on acknowledging receipt of the initial request should ensure there is no confusion between applicant and authority about the deadline for the request.

6. COLLECTING AND RECORDING STATISTICS ABOUT HANDLING REQUESTS.

> **The legal context**
>
> Neither regime requires the collection or recording of statistics about handling information requests.

BEST PRACTICE

6.1   What should be monitored?

It is for each public authority to determine what information can most usefully be recorded under its administrative procedures, while satisfying itself that it is complying with the law (and is able to demonstrate this). Monitoring all requests, including routine queries which are handled regularly, may be disproportionate.

Monitoring activities should be proportionate to the volume of requests handled by an authority, but should include collecting information about:

- the number of requests received and whether they fall within FOISA or the EIRs;
- the proportion of requests answered within statutory timescales (there may also be value in monitoring the length of time it takes to respond to overdue requests);
- the number of requests that have been refused and the reasons for the refusal;
- the number of times a fee has been charged;
- the numbers of reviews that have been carried out and the outcome of such reviews; and
- the number of cases that are appealed to the Scottish Information Commissioner and the outcome of such appeals.

Authorities should proactively publish and update their FOI monitoring data online.

Authorities (particular those that are large, or geographically dispersed) should consider developing a tracking system to monitor the progress of current requests, ensure deadlines are met, and ensure consistent handling.

6.2   Establish and maintain a "disclosure log".

Authorities are encouraged to maintain a "disclosure log" of information requests, i.e. a publicly available description of some or all of the information which the authority has previously released under the regimes with, where feasible, direct online access to the information itself. Authorities may, for example, list all requests received or only those where the information is likely to be of interest to the wider public. Staff should be familiar with any such log and be able to provide guidance to potential applicants on how to make use of it. Maintaining a disclosure log may pre-empt information requests, by highlighting what information has already been made available.

6.3 Authorities should review their request-handling information.

It is good practice for authorities to regularly review their information and statistics on request-handling and performance, for example by reporting to senior committees or boards. This can help identify any issues with the handling of requests such as meeting the statutory timescales or identifying areas of work which are frequently the subject of requests.

7. PROACTIVELY PUBLISHING INFORMATION.

The legal context

Under section 23 of FOISA authorities must adopt and maintain a "publication scheme" which sets out what information they will routinely publish, how it will be made available and whether a charge is payable. The content of publication schemes must take account of the public interest in providing access to information about the provision of services, the standards attained and the costs of those services, and the facts or analyses which provide the basis for important decisions.

All schemes must have the approval of the Scottish Information Commissioner Authorities must keep their schemes under review to ensure they remain up to date.

Under regulation 4 of the EIRs authorities must take reasonable steps to organise information relevant to their functions with a view to its active and systematic dissemination, and to making it progressively available to the public by electronic means which are easily accessible (unless it was collected before 14th February 2003 and is not available in electronic form). Regulation 4(2) sets out the types of information to be made available.

Both regimes have an exemption for information which is otherwise accessible and reasonably obtainable (section 25 of FOISA and regulation 6(1)(b) of the EIRs). Authorities may apply this to information already published through their publication schemes (in other circumstances the test of whether information is "reasonably obtainable' is dependent on the circumstances of the applicant). The proactive publication of information can also reduce the volume of requests received.

BEST PRACTICE

7.1   Types of information that should be published.

In order to meet the requirements of section 23 of FOISA authorities should publish information about:

- their functions, how they operate (including their decision-making processes), and their performance; and
- their finances, including funding allocation, procurement and the awarding of contracts.

It is good practice for an authority to also consider regularly what other information is likely to be of interest to the public and could be published proactively, e.g.:

- Information which is regularly the subject of information requests;
- Information relating to forthcoming/recent decisions or announcements;
- Information about current issues which are attracting, or are likely to attract, significant public interest or media coverage.

7.2   Publication schemes should be kept up to date.

Authorities should ensure that the content of their publication scheme remains up to date, with new information being added as necessary. (Authorities should note that they must notify the Commissioner if they are considering removing information from their schemes, or making changes to their charging regime, as this may affect the Commissioner's approval of them.) It is good practice to monitor the types of information which are frequently requested and consider adding them to the scheme. Additionally, authorities must ensure that they are meeting the commitments made in their scheme.

7.3 Advising third parties about publishing information.

Where a third party is the subject of information which an authority intends to publish, it is good practice to alert them to the publication. For example, where authorities routinely publish information relating to procurement exercises, the contractors bidding in a tendering exercise should be made aware at the time of bidding that the information they provide may be made public.

7.4 Environmental information should feature in the content of publication schemes.

There is no requirement in the EIRs to produce a publication scheme or its equivalent. However, section 23 of FOISA makes no distinction between environmental and non-environmental information in publication schemes, and so environmental information should feature in the content of publication schemes.

7.5 Relevant private bodies should ensure that appropriate steps are taken to meet the requirements of regulation 4 of the EIRs.

The EIRs also apply to other bodies which are not designated under FOISA, including some private sector organisations (for example those under the control of a public authority and having public responsibilities, functions, or providing services in relation to the environment). As they are covered only by the EIRs, these other bodies are not under the FOISA duty to adopt and maintain publication schemes, but must comply with the requirements of regulation 4 of the EIRs to actively disseminate information.

7.6 Websites should be accessible to all and simple to use.

Information should be found readily on websites, for example by enabling search functions and having an alphabetical directory as well as tree structures. Information should not be "buried" on a site. Authorities should ensure that information is also accessible to people who cannot access the internet. This may be achieved by offering to print out information from the website on request.

INDEX

Note: **Bold** references denote paragraphs where the relevant legislation is reproduced.